THE
FUND

THE
FUND

RAY DALIO,
BRIDGEWATER ASSOCIATES,
AND THE UNRAVELING OF
A WALL STREET LEGEND

ROB
COPELAND

ST. MARTIN'S PRESS
NEW YORK

First published in the United States by St. Martin's Press,
an imprint of St. Martin's Publishing Group

www.stmartins.com

Design by Meryl Sussman Levavi

Library of Congress Cataloging-in-Publication Data

Names: Copeland, Rob, author.
Title: The fund : Ray Dalio, Bridgewater Associates, and the unraveling of a Wall Street
    legend / Rob Copeland.
Description: First edition. | New York : St. Martin's Press, 2023. | Includes index.
Identifiers: LCCN 2023032997 | ISBN 9781250276933 (hardcover) | ISBN 9781250276940
    (ebook)
Subjects: LCSH: Dalio, Ray, 1949- | Bridgewater Associates—History. | Bridgewater
    Associates—Employees. | Bridgewater Associates—Corrupt practices.
Classification: LCC HG4930 .C67 2023 | DDC 332.63/27—dc23/eng/20230804
LC record available at https://lccn.loc.gov/2023032997

Our books may be purchased in bulk for promotional, educational, or business
use. Please contact your local bookseller or the Macmillan Corporate and
Premium Sales Department at 1-800-221-7945, extension 5442, or by email at
MacmillanSpecialMarkets@macmillan.com.

First Edition: 2023

10 9 8 7 6 5 4 3 2 1

When you're rich, they think you really know.

—"If I Were a Rich Man," *Fiddler on the Roof*, 1964

CONTENTS

AUTHOR'S NOTE

Ray Dalio does not want you to read this book.

He told me as much. At the start of this project, I reached out to him by email to seek his perspective. He responded with skepticism about my intentions. After considerable back-and-forth, he elected not to be interviewed, as is his right.

I am endlessly grateful that hundreds of people in and around Bridgewater Associates trusted me with their time, and with their experiences. I also relied on contemporaneous notes, emails, recordings, court records, myriad other internal and external company documents, and published interviews and articles. All of the names that appear here are real, except for one pseudonym, used to conceal the identity of a former employee who alleged sexual misbehavior.

In some instances, the dialogue in this book comes directly from the subject; in others, it is from others in the room, or people briefed afterward, or those who listened to recordings of an event. It should not be assumed that the people quoted spoke to me. As the Pulitzer Prize–winning author James B. Stewart wrote, "Given the vagaries of human memory, remembered dialogue is rarely the same as actual recordings and transcripts. At the same time, it is no more nor less accurate than many other recollections."

As for Dalio's own recollections, the public lacks no opportunity to hear them. He wrote a bestselling autobiography-cum-self-help book, *Principles: Life and Work*. Over the past decade, he has given hundreds of media interviews on five continents, preaching the gospel of Ray. He's appeared on major broadcast and cable networks, popular podcasts, and magazine covers. He was interviewed by Gwyneth Paltrow. As of publication, nearly 2.5 million people follow him on LinkedIn. His TED Talks have been viewed nearly 7 million times and his most popular YouTube video more than 34 million times.

While Dalio is hardly the first financier to develop a taste for the spotlight, he might be the first to claim that he alone has discovered the solution to what he sees as two of mankind's greatest challenges: Our reluctance to disagree with one another, and our desire to pursue meaningful lives. Dalio has for years stuck to a narrative that all Bridgewater employees are judged on an equal playing field, and that any difference in rank or authority was due only to a rigorous system that susses out merit. The truth is rather more Orwellian. At Bridgewater, some are more equal than others.

This is the story of Ray Dalio, the most equal one of all.

—ROB COPELAND

THE
FUND

INTRODUCTION

A FEW MINUTES AFTER HANGING UP THE PHONE, PAUL MCDOWELL carefully smoothed his button-down shirt, knelt in the snow, and dry heaved.

McDowell wasn't so much upset as overwhelmed. The balding Canadian tended to shy away from big risks, yet he had just taken the biggest gamble of his life, negotiating with one of the world's wealthiest men—and winning, or so it seemed. Not for the last time, he wondered what the hell had just happened.

When his cell phone rang earlier that afternoon, McDowell was seated at his desk in the tiny office that counted as the Canadian headquarters for BearingPoint consulting, the sort of sad corporate advisory firm that picked up the projects that McKinsey & Company wouldn't touch. He picked up the phone and heard the low, gravelly voice of Ray Dalio.

"Paul," Dalio said, skipping any small talk, "it's so hard to find anyone like you."

McDowell felt his chest fill with heat. That anyone was calling at all—let alone laying on compliments—was its own feat. If McDowell was known at all to his colleagues elsewhere in the company, it was simply as the Canada man. Unlike many consultants, he loathed the slick presentations or client glad-handing endemic to the career. But divorced and in debt, he needed his well-paying job. He had made himself an expert in technology infrastructure, human resources, and compensation management—dull topics, but areas where hard work and a high tolerance for spreadsheets could whittle out a corporate life. Though McDowell often felt underappreciated, he also valued being something of an expert in how to find novel ways for BearingPoint's clients to make small changes that had big impacts on their operations.

It was confusing, and deeply flattering, that someone like Ray Dalio had sought him out. Dalio wasn't just any business titan; he was founder of one of the world's largest hedge funds, Bridgewater Associates, and a burgeoning celebrity in the financial world.

This was December 2008, and while most of Wall Street was being thrashed, Dalio was having the best year of his professional career. He had famously rung the alarm on the housing bubble, publicly warning a year earlier that mortgages seemed on the brink of collapse. He looked like an oracle, and so now Federal Reserve chief Ben Bernanke—the world's most important banker—consulted with Dalio on how to pull the country out of its tailspin. A week after McDowell's phone call, the New York Post would write, "Dalio has been so prescient about the state of the economy that reading his daily observations has been like reading the financial papers two weeks in advance."

The idea that Dalio needed McDowell made little sense. McDowell was one of a slew of consultants Bridgewater had brought in, and he helped not with the investments that made Dalio so much money, but the less sexy work of cleaning up back-office processes. But as Dalio described his situation, McDowell began to see how he could help. Bridgewater was growing at a punishing rate, Dalio explained, and he needed help to oversee the day-to-day management of the firm. He spent much of his time traveling the world, meeting with wealthy individuals and institutions and advising them on what to do with their money. McDowell, Dalio said, could be just the man to tend the store at the hedge fund's Connecticut headquarters.

BearingPoint had done some consulting work for Bridgewater and helped the hedge fund design a system to analyze talent, saving it money. McDowell figured his team had done a pretty good job because in 2008 alone Bridgewater added 211 new employees, ballooning the firm's ranks by more than a third in just one year. McDowell had not interacted much directly with Dalio, but when McDowell had, he had noticed immediately that Bridgewater's staff seemed in awe of the founder. There was scarcely a meeting where Dalio did not stop to share lessons from his experience, as those around him furiously scribbled down notes. His words were cited constantly by others, whether he was present or not.

One afternoon, while working out of a conference room at Bridgewater's headquarters during a torrential rainstorm, McDowell spotted the billionaire Bridgewater founder helping underlings dodge puddles as they carried in catered trays of lunch. McDowell made a mental note that such an important man would pitch in even when it seemed nobody was watching.

McDowell knew that Dalio had a reputation for hiring the best, regardless of résumé. Dalio would often say that he weighed values and character over specific skills. He instructed Bridgewater's recruiters to prize logical thinking and a tolerance for frank feedback from all employees, from the C-suite down to Bridgewater's janitorial staff. Don't just hire people to fit the job, Dalio would say, but people with whom you want to share your life. McDowell, Dalio now told him, was one of the few people the Bridgewater founder had met who met the mark.

"I think you would be fantastic," Dalio told McDowell. "You absolutely understand the way we are, and you can do anything here you want. You could even run the company."

McDowell was flabbergasted and momentarily speechless. That didn't matter much, because Dalio blazed ahead with his pitch, launching into an extensive explanation of McDowell's broad future responsibilities at Bridgewater. They included finding a way to reorganize staff across the company in accordance with Dalio's unique values. Dalio was on the hunt for a new chief executive to take over when the founder retired, and he told McDowell that he was one of a handful who could get the job.

"Paul, I am so thrilled about our partnership," Dalio said, finally wrapping up. "What do you say?"

"Ray, my only concern is that I've noticed that a lot of people seem to be intimidated by you. I don't want us to have that kind of relationship. I'd like us to be able to be very honest and straight with one another and not worry about that."

There was a long pause before Dalio responded. "I think the problem with those people, Paul, is that those people can't distinguish between 'goal' and task. You absolutely understand things at the 'goal' level." Finally, McDowell thought, here was someone who saw him as a leader.

McDowell asked about salary and was quoted a generous sum, more than a million dollars in the first full year alone including a bonus. "You'll make a ridiculous amount of money. Soon you'll be making *millions* of dollars," Dalio said.

Dalio then asked what McDowell was currently making, and in the spirit of the honesty the two men had just pledged, McDowell answered truthfully: Bridgewater's base salary alone was $100,000 higher than his current pay.

"Okay, actually, then that's what I'll pay. I only pay people what they're currently making," Dalio said airily.

McDowell's skin prickled. He had just been dangled, and had now apparently just as quickly lost, what seemed to him a small fortune. "Wait, you just said what I was worth. Why would I take less than what you believe me to be worth?"

"I can't believe a hundred thousand dollars a year is going to make a difference to you to join this place. Don't let that guide your choice."

The two men began to talk over each other, until it was clear Dalio's patience for this conversation had worn thin. "All right, Paul, I never, ever, ever do this, but okay, I'll pay what you ask. That's the deal."

The billionaire wished him a merry Christmas, and the line went dead.

THE DAYS and weeks that followed were a whirlwind for McDowell. He didn't for a moment take it for granted. He was forty-eight years old and reasoned he was long overdue to catch a break.

A descendant of coal miners in northern England on both sides for generations, McDowell came from what could charitably be called a modest background. The closest his family had ever come to glory was when his father briefly served as a guard clad in the traditional red dress uniform and bearskin hat outside Buckingham Palace during World War II. McDowell's parents moved to Canada three years before he was born, to a poor neighborhood on the outskirts of Toronto.

Though they were north of the U.S. border, the family in many ways exemplified a traditional American work ethic. McDowell's father rode a bicycle to work at an oil refinery and would return home after a long, dirty day only to head straight to the basement for a punishing sequence of pullups, push-ups, and sit-ups. He discouraged the household from watching a smash television hit of the era, *Hogan's Heroes,* because the sitcom mocked German soldiers. McDowell's father never quite lost his wariness of, and respect for, the other side, and he ingrained in his son a lingering vigilance against unsuspected dangers.

McDowell faced a lot of dangers growing up. He was perennially slight of build compared to his classmates, a distinction that became only more prominent when he skipped most of the fourth grade. He avoided attention from high school bullies by offering free tutoring in calculus. His voice hadn't changed by the time he went to college, where he spent much of his spare time in the library reading book after book on ham radios, the Soviet gulag, and the Watergate scandal.

In search of greater meaning to underpin a career, McDowell became fascinated by research into how to effectively manage a workplace through a controversial system called requisite organization. The theory posited that employees should be tested and ranked by their overall problem-solving ability—known as stratum—and that managers must always be more capable of complex, broad thinking than their subordinates. The downside, among others, was that requisite organization encouraged a highly structured corporate hierarchy that bordered on a caste system and justified extreme pay gaps between executives and the lower ranks. Lower-level workers, the theory held, were not merely performing different work from that of their superiors, but were intrinsically different from them; people were assigned work to which they were innately capable.

At Bridgewater, McDowell found the perfect petri dish for his interests. He started in March 2009 and was immediately thrust into weeks of emergency meetings. Everyone seemed in a panic to justify his or her position, in what McDowell would later learn was one of Dalio's regular reorganizations. The current reorg, McDowell was told, stemmed from Dalio's big-picture view of the economy. Convinced that the global financial recession was still in its early stages, Dalio had sought a series of what he called "beat-downs" inside Bridgewater. Most departments' budgets, no matter how small, had to be slashed by 25 percent.

Most interestingly to McDowell, Dalio was willing to take the same approach to personnel. On one of McDowell's first days, Dalio reminded him that just as the firm's hedge fund was, at its core, a machine, so was each person who worked there. The key was to figure out which people (Dalio called them "pieces of equipment") worked best together to produce the desired output, and to get rid of any unneeded parts.

Though McDowell found the approach a little impersonal, he saw its merits. Management as a machine, with its emphasis on the subordination of different roles at a company to one another, was just a rougher version of the philosophy of requisite organization. And one thing seemed certain: Dalio's approach—beatdowns and all—was wildly successful. A month after McDowell started, industry researcher *Alpha* magazine announced that

Bridgewater had leapfrogged no less than blue-chip firm JPMorgan & Co. to operate the world's largest hedge fund.

True to his word, Dalio immediately began relying on McDowell's advice. Dalio appointed the Canadian an adviser to the firm's management committee, which gave him an immediate seat at the table for decisions debated among the firm's top executives. Dalio often asked for McDowell's advice. By year-end, he had assigned McDowell to help figure out who at Bridgewater should be shifted into a different part of the machine or cut. McDowell suggested that evaluating employees on their stratum might prove helpful. Dalio loved the idea. *Let's do that immediately,* he said.

Eager to impress the boss, McDowell flew in a stratum expert. The three sat around a small table as their guest explained that stratum rankings were intended to help assign people into positions that fit them, roles that were neither too simple nor too complicated. Individuals underwent psychological interviews and were then ranked from stratum levels one through eight, based on their ability to independently process complex assignments. A factory worker might be a level one stratum, for instance, while the ideal chief executive would be ranked at least a level five.

Dalio pointed at McDowell. "What's he?"

The expert said that McDowell was roughly a six, stressing that this was a measure of cognitive judgment and temperament, one with the potential to evolve over time.

Dalio snorted and turned to McDowell. "If your stratum is so high, how come you're not a billionaire?"

McDowell swallowed hard before coming up with a response. Stratum, he told Dalio, was only one measure of a person. No single model could account for someone's age, accumulated wisdom, values, or background—to say nothing of just plain luck.

Even a high-stratum person, McDowell said, could wind up poor, and vice versa.

Shortly after, Dalio pulled McDowell aside and said that, while he liked the idea of stratum, he thought it could be improved and expanded. His idea was to rate and rank employees on different attributes that he had come up with over time. There were seventy-seven in total, such as determination and standing up for what is right. The ratings would be listed on what would eventually be called a baseball card, much as major league players had statistics listed for their win/loss records and so forth. The baseball cards would give everyone at Bridgewater a picture of everyone else's strengths and weaknesses. Everyone would rate one another, everyone would get a vote, and everyone would be judged in the same categories. Even better, every bit of information on every baseball card would be visible to all, so there would be instant accountability and no hiding the truth.

Dalio suggested to McDowell that perhaps he would like to take a leading role in the initiative.

McDowell was thrilled. This was exactly the sort of project he'd been studying for years—and one that could make his name at the hedge fund.

The assignment quickly turned into a headache. McDowell created one working prototype after another, only for Dalio to add and subtract new categories seemingly at whim. Many seemed less than scientific; one was called "practical" while another was "practical thinking." While it was easy to measure a professional athlete on balls or strikes, Dalio's metrics included nebulous areas such as "visualization." What was that, and could it, or similarly subjective areas such as creativity, even be numerically ranked?

One upside to the chaos was that McDowell had constant access to the boss. Dalio would often invite McDowell into his office, where the Bridgewater founder would lean back in his chair, chewing on Scotch tape, the dispenser refilled by an assistant, and review the cards' progress. The goal of all the ratings, Dalio would say, was to sort everyone at Bridgewater on a single scale. He often brought up new ideas; in one instance, he told a Bridgewater team to imagine training everyone to be a ninja, and then cloaking everyone in different colors, rather than sashes, to denote the best fighter. At Bridgewater the most important, overarching assessment would be called believability.

At one confab with McDowell several months into the project, Dalio took out an index card and jotted the word *believability* at the top, circling it several times, and drawing squiggly lines running down from it. Believability would be an amalgamation of all the ratings in each category and be listed in bold type at the top of the baseball cards. People at Bridgewater with high believability in certain categories would have their ratings of others counted more heavily than others. Dalio called this "believability weighting." What sense did it make to have the custodial worker's word ranked the same as the firm founder's?

McDowell understood the appeal of overarching ratings, but he thought

Dalio was missing a crucial complication. "You can't do that," McDowell told his boss. "You can't average the numbers there. . . . That's like taking your shoe size, adding it to your body temperature, and adding it to the time of day, and then dividing by three, and having it to the third decimal point, and thinking you have discovered something."

That analogy didn't seem to land, so McDowell tried another. "These ratings are not like a blood test that actually tells you what your white cell count is. They are approximations. They are just people's opinions of each other."

Dalio looked at McDowell, then gestured to the index card, the lines dribbling down from top to bottom. "Believability cascades. You should have done this. I just did your job for you."

Dalio walked out.

BY NOW McDowell had figured out that when Dalio said he had a solution to a problem, it was best not to argue. McDowell pledged to give believability a shot.

For months, he sketched and tested the idea. He asked top employees to rank one another on the notion of who was most trusted to make decisions in a given subject matter, starting from the top. The system began to work a bit dynamically. If a slew of Bridgewater executives gave an underling overall positive believability ratings, the subordinate's own opinion would begin to carry more weight. McDowell began to see how believability could be a way to identify talent across the hedge fund. Employees seemed to take to the idea, too, seeing it as a way to prove they were deserving of advancement. McDowell rolled out a prototype inside the firm in which staff could see one another's believability ratings on a one-to-ten scale.

Not long after that, McDowell's phone buzzed with Dalio on the line.

It was the first time the Bridgewater founder had called him one-on-one since his job offer in Canada. McDowell hoped for a compliment, but instead Dalio's voice snapped with anger:

"Why doesn't believability cascade?"

It does, McDowell explained. The baseball card prototypes crunched tens of thousands of data points.

Dalio didn't seem to see it that way. One of his subordinates had just flagged for him a suspicious finding: two people inside Bridgewater—one in investment research, the other a lowly information technology grunt—had higher believability scores than Dalio himself. People were beginning to whisper about it.

McDowell explained to Dalio that this was a sign the system was working, that Bridgewater was fishing out the pockets of talent in its ranks—exactly as Dalio had asked him to do.

Dalio's voice made no secret of his irritation. Why doesn't believability cascade *from me*?

McDowell thought back to Dalio's index card drawing. He realized that Dalio hadn't been sketching out the mere concept of believability on top. He had drawn himself quite literally at the head, bestowing believability to all beneath him.

The fix was obvious. McDowell assigned an underling to go into the software and program a new rule. Dalio himself would be the new baseline for believability in virtually all important categories. As the original, topmost believable person at Bridgewater, Dalio's rating was now numerically bulletproof to negative feedback. Regardless of how everyone else in the firm rated him, the system would work to keep him on top.

It would take more than two years to perfect the rigging of the believability system. The system was then rolled out for use on iPads, so that Bridgewater employees could input scores of one another in real time and see their scores dip or rise. Dalio's own ratings, hardwired into the system, remained sterling.

The man responsible for making Ray Dalio the paragon of believability would receive the promotion of his life. At year-end 2011, McDowell sat down with Dalio, and the Bridgewater founder handed over a sheet of paper on which he'd written McDowell's bonus for the year.

Dalio told McDowell that he would now be let into an inner ring at Bridgewater, the relatively small group of staffers who received what was known as phantom equity, or an ownership stake in the firm itself. Every quarter, McDowell would receive a check with a portion of the fees Bridgewater had earned from its clients.

Dalio grabbed the paper and scratched out the figure he'd handed over just a moment earlier. He replaced it with a new number $300,000 higher. McDowell was stunned at the amount of money so casually changing hands. Dalio handed the paper to McDowell and waved his hand toward the door, signaling him to leave with the new scribbles. "Just tell them that I gave you more."

As McDowell reached the door, Dalio spoke one more time.

"This means you're part of the family."

Part I

1

ONE GODDAMN PLACE

Nine months after Paul McDowell received the phone call that would change his life, another Bridgewater employee collapsed into tears. It wasn't ordinary crying, but a full-on meltdown, complete with chest heaving, gasping for breath, and animalistic sobbing.

Thirtysomething, with shoulder-length blond hair sagging limply, Katina Stefanova wasn't used to being in this position. She was, as widely viewed inside the firm, one of Ray Dalio's favorites—and she was usually the person who made other people cry. Her colleagues called her the Ice Queen.

Stefanova briefly looked around the table; a stoic clique of men and women stared back at her impassively. The late-summer sun streamed in through the windows, illuminating sterile white walls, fading carpeting, and industrial lighting that kept the whole scene punishingly in focus. If Stefanova craned her neck, she could catch a glimpse of a murky river—more a creek, really—winding aimlessly around the parking lot of the medieval-style stone building. The Middle Ages, she would later reflect, was an apt metaphor for the goings-on here.

This was 2009 in Westport, Connecticut, an immodest waterfront town on Connecticut's so-called Gold Coast about a ninety-minute drive northeast of New York City. A few miles north of downtown lay the backcountry, a thicket of massive Tudor-style mansions and matching guardhouses. Not far from a private school that instructed elementary schoolers in Latin and ancient Greek, a driveway shot off the main thoroughfare. A just-visible sign read, with no further details, ONE GLENDINNING PLACE.

Some would later coin another nickname: One Goddamn Place.

They didn't call her the Ice Queen for nothing. Stefanova had been through a lot, and she wasn't quick to crack. Pretty and tall, with long, straight blond hair and brown eyes, she had been forced to learn, early in life, to rely on herself. Stefanova grew up in Communist Bulgaria, the eldest daughter of a mechanical engineer father and chemist mom. In 1989, when she was twelve, the Berlin Wall fell and took her dad down with it. He lost his job, his hair, and briefly his mind. He started his own metallurgy company, became a multimillionaire, and lost it all again in 1997 to hyperinflation. He started over a third time.

By then, Stefanova was gone. She had met a group of Mormon missionaries in Bulgaria, who encouraged her to apply to Brigham Young University. Without telling her parents, she applied and convinced her grandfather to cover the one-way ticket. She wound up at one of BYU's junior college annexes, a two-year school in Idaho, with $200 in cash stuffed in her pocket and a thick accent that didn't help her make local friends. She worked every possible odd job. She helped keep the college grounds, worked in the library, and tutored. She was married not long after graduation.

A progression of rather staid corporate jobs later, she landed at Harvard Business School. There, she set her eyes on high finance. Though investment bankers and traders still ruled the roost in movies and television, in Cambridge in the spring in the mid-2000s, the most ambitious students aimed for hedge funds, a term that could mean just about anything. Some hedge funds purported to simply pick the best stocks, borrowing money to supersize their bets on or against companies they thought were due for greatness or for a crash. Other funds exploited kinks in the market, finding patterns in the ups and downs that their rivals were either too dumb or too lazy to discover. Still others hired scientists to write computer programs to decide automatically what and when to buy and sell.

One of the largest hedge funds on earth was Bridgewater Associates, and lucky for Stefanova, the fund was run by an HBS graduate, Ray Dalio. Founded more than two decades earlier, Bridgewater had stayed low profile even as it became enormous, investing more than $100 billion worldwide. Dalio was said to have prodigious skill at spotting, and making money from, big-picture global economic or political changes, such as when a country would raise its interest rate or cut taxes. This made both a lot of sense and none at all; what was it about Dalio and Bridgewater that made them so much better at predictions than everyone else in the world trying to do the exact same thing? There were rumors among competitors that it somehow involved ex-government agents whom Dalio had on the payroll.

Whatever was going on, Stefanova could see that it was working. Dalio was by 2005 a billionaire several times over, making him one of the wealthiest graduates in the history of Harvard Business School. That was enough to pique the interest of an immigrant who hoped never to return home.

THAT SPRING of 2005, Stefanova walked into a recruiting event on campus and headed toward a presentation hosted by Bridgewater. Dalio himself didn't make an appearance. He sent a top deputy, Greg Jensen, to make the pitch.

If the stereotypical hedge fund bro was constructed of hard angles—broad shoulders and a square jaw, often accompanied by endless talk about lacrosse—Jensen appeared to have misplaced the manual. He called himself Bridgewater's research director, a lofty title, but seemed barely out of college himself. He had moppish brown hair, dark circles under his eyes, unkempt eyebrows, a seemingly perpetual five-o'clock shadow, and, despite his youth, the unmistakable early signs of a potbelly.

It wasn't just Jensen's appearance that didn't fit the hedge fund mirage. As he spoke, his description of life at Bridgewater didn't sound to Stefanova like that of a high-flying investment firm. Jensen didn't have much to say about buying or selling stocks, bonds, or any other asset. Bridgewater, he said, prioritized meaningful lives and meaningful relationships, achieved by a path of reflection that led to self-discovery. It sounded more like getting high than high finance.

Jensen emphasized that Bridgewater employees worked through daily disagreements to arrive at radical truths and the answers to heretofore unsolvable problems. It was tough, and it wasn't for everyone, he said, puncturing the air with his index finger for emphasis.

The Ice Queen wasn't afraid of conflict, particularly if it came with a fat check. She submitted her résumé and it was swiftly rejected. Too many typos.

Then, she caught a break. Bridgewater had an unusual practice of drawing résumés randomly by lottery to schedule candidates for interviews, and Stefanova was a lucky loser that day. The hedge fund comprised only a few hundred souls, and Dalio was conducting interviews of most job candidates personally in Westport. Stefanova was told to take a Myers-Briggs personality test and invited to visit.

She arrived in Connecticut and was quickly ushered in to see the fifty-five-year-old Dalio. She noticed that he, too, didn't fit the typical hedge fund manager image. He parted his gray hair deeply and unflatteringly to the side, exposing a receding hairline that might have been covered up with a little more effort. His double chin and bulging cheeks suggested he wasn't one for organized fitness, and his clothing rotation might have been described as lumberjack chic—plaids, denim, and corduroy. He appeared not to own an iron. *The New Yorker* later summed him up fondly as resembling "an aging member of a British progressive-rock group."

Once the conversation started, Stefanova was immediately as transfixed as she was overdressed. Dalio queried Stefanova not on her background or acumen, but her psyche. He went over the answers to her Myers-Briggs test, drilling her on why, for instance, she had said she often let her head rule her heart. It seemed to Stefanova that he wanted to know if she was easily rattled. He said he was interested not in the decisions she had made that brought her here, but why she had made them.

"My weakness is I fall in love with intellectuals," she would later say. "I overvalue intellectual value over character, and Ray is just tremendously bright."

After a few minutes, without warning or explanation, Dalio ended the chat.

"Well, never mind. You're hired."

STEFANOVA STARTED at Bridgewater as a senior investment associate, and quickly found herself working with the firm's clients—including big pension funds and university endowments—helping to figure out which broad classes of investments fit their goals. Not yet thirty, she nonetheless felt old. Bridgewater typically hired fresh college graduates, almost all of them men, leading some staffers to joke that the cafeteria scene looked like a J.Crew catalog. An inordinate number came from Dartmouth, where Jensen had been president of his fraternity.

The work was tough, and her new coworkers were a strange, tight-knit bunch who seemed to spend much of their personal time with one another. Some even shared Dalio's personal doctor, who would come to the office, draw the curtains in an empty room, and see patients, including the Bridgewater founder. But Stefanova was used to not fitting in at new places and was happy to spend her days researching the markets. Early on, she sat in awe at a series of internal lectures from Dalio on conceptual macroeconomics, as he held forth for hours on the linkages between investment cycles in history. It was fascinating stuff. Dalio awarded her the highest grade in the course: an A-minus. Practically no one received an A, which Dalio told her was a score he could typically award only to himself.

The two became friendly. They enjoyed dinners together, where he would pepper her with questions about life growing up under communism, and she reciprocated by inviting him to her house. Stefanova, who hadn't quite shaken her Bulgarian accent, was amazed that this blue-blooded billionaire took her so seriously. Their conversations had a depth and breadth that she'd never before experienced in a work relationship—they would discuss philosophy, politics, business, and jazz, long into the night. He encouraged her to question her value system, and to question whether there were clear lines between right and wrong. He was a naturalist, of sorts, too, always talking about the sea. He donated heavily to the National Fish and Wildlife Foundation, and the organization named a new species of coral, *Eknomisis dalioi,* after him.

Stefanova found Dalio's dismissiveness toward societal rules particularly alluring. He would tell a fable about a ravenous pack of hyenas murdering a young wildebeest. The wildebeest may suffer, but its death is necessary to promote evolutionary improvement. Dalio saw himself as a hyena. "What is best is acting in your self-interest," he told her.

Dalio seemed to live his ideals. Stefanova and others around her regularly saw him blow up on underlings, over matters large and small; few people seemed to stay in his good graces for long. Behind his back, employees talked openly about who would be the chum in any given meeting, thrown out as a target for him to thrash at.

Stefanova, however, felt safe from this behavior—she was Dalio's mentee and friend. She worked on projects for him directly, putting in twelve-plus-hour days. He took to telling others, "Katina is one of my people," which nearly made her blush with happiness. She rose in the ranks at the firm. Her salary doubled every year, and others were assigned to report to her directly. Some at Bridgewater even began to whisper that she could someday be a candidate to succeed Dalio.

———————

THREE YEARS after Stefanova joined Bridgewater, Dalio approached her with a crucial task: to oversee the design of a new trading floor for the booming hedge fund. Stefanova figured he was giving her an opportunity to prove her worth.

Bridgewater was in a period of breakneck expansion. Between 2003 and 2004 alone, just before Stefanova joined, Bridgewater's coffers almost doubled from $54 billion to $101 billion assets under management. The tally would rise to a staggering $169 billion a few years later. Dozens of employees joined each month. Dalio's annual pay would soar past $1 billion, making him one of the wealthiest people in the world.

Stefanova took to her new duties with aplomb. With the excuse of having to learn how to design the ideal trading floor, she spent hours with Dalio and Jensen, querying them on what made Bridgewater tick. Though she wasn't permitted to see the details of the firm's live trading, she got a glimpse of the long reports the firm produced predicting whether financial markets were headed up, down, or sideways.

In her expanded role, Stefanova soon found herself with a dilemma over a technologist on her team. The man's wife also worked at Bridgewater—intimate relationships were common at the firm—and whether distracted at the office or otherwise, he was often slow to turn in his work. Stefanova suspected that she wasn't exactly being assigned the A team and sensed that Dalio might be testing her. The Bridgewater founder often spoke of the importance of holding everyone to high standards. "Don't tolerate badness," he said frequently.

If this was a test, an opportunity came soon enough to show that she had studied. Stefanova learned that the technologist had hired a new consultant to help but hadn't told her. When she confronted him, he admitted he'd been hiding it from her.

That was all Stefanova needed. "I hear you admitting you made a mistake, but now I'm wondering about your character, and about you personally." She tore into him for the better part of a half hour, then notified him that she intended to fire him.

Given the man's familial ties to Bridgewater, the matter made its way to Dalio and Jensen. They asked Stefanova to explain herself.

I am just doing what Ray would have done, she said.

Jensen leaped in to agree, saying pushing past badness was a core Bridgewater belief.

"What you need to do," Jensen said, "is look at how much it disgusts and appalls you. The disgust outweighs any sense of the person's feelings."

Dalio looked on with seeming approval. Lying, he often said, was one of the worst infractions imaginable at Bridgewater. He gave his okay for the firing. He typed out his assent in an email to the fired staffer, cc'ing most employees at Bridgewater.

The man's wife received the note, and the news, at the same time as everyone else. She stopped showing up to work not long after.

ON THE cusp of early fall 2009, on one of the days when the weather couldn't quite decide if summer was over yet, Dalio's mood, too, waxed and waned. The financial crisis had been a boon for Bridgewater, whose flagship fund was up headily during the worst of the 2008 crisis, while 70 percent of hedge funds lost money. As word got out, his fame grew. A few months earlier, he had sat for a glowing *Fortune* profile that described him as a "sturdy six-footer" who "works out of an unostentatious office brimming with photos of his wife and four children." A retired psychologist who was on the Bridgewater payroll part-time as a consultant was quoted saying, "If you took five organizational psychologists, locked them in a room, and told them to create the perfect blueprint for a corporate culture, this is about what they would come up with."

Dalio told the interviewer that he had discovered "the Holy Grail of investing," a series of trading formulas bound to make money, "by which I mean that if you find this thing you will be rich and successful in investing."

"If it were easy," the author posited, "everyone would do it."

The problem was, the Holy Grail had evidently run dry. Bridgewater was struggling to hit the mark again.

The reason had nothing to do with any trading formulas. Dalio was convinced that a second leg to the crisis was coming. He had even invented his own word for it, a *D-process,* a multipronged deleveraging, or winding off, of the markets. Dalio's desk had been sagging under the weight of twenty or so thick tomes on historical downturns, such as *Essays on the Great Depression* and *The Great Crash 1929.* The Bridgewater founder took furious notes on each of them, sticking Post-it notes throughout them and scribbling handwritten notes in the margins, noting abundant parallels to the present.

Evidently confident he was in line to make another killing by spotting another crisis, Dalio drove Bridgewater into full-on expansion. He didn't want help with investments—who needs a second Holy Grail?—but with management. He was now sixty years old, a reasonable retirement age, and although he had long told people he might not leave Bridgewater until his death, he was beginning to say he might need to hand off some of his operational responsibilities to underlings such as Jensen and Stefanova. He told staff that while no single person could be expected to replace him, in light of the growth of the firm, perhaps Bridgewater could design a system in which various responsibilities fell to teams of people.

It fell to Stefanova to bring in a new class of 2009 recruits. They would be called *management* associates (as opposed to *investment* ones) and would be guinea pigs for the next phase of Bridgewater's life. Such was the task of replacing the Bridgewater founder that he often said that hundreds more people would be required.

Stefanova tried to hire as Dalio might, with a great deal of personal involvement, but that couldn't possibly work on the scale now demanded. She couldn't keep up the pace. Dalio kept demanding more, and she kept falling short.

Finally, enough was enough. Dalio wanted to know why the management associates hadn't all been hired. He told Stefanova he wanted to get to the bottom of the problem—and he wanted to do it in front of a crowd.

STEFANOVA ENTERED the conference room where her performance would be interrogated, took a seat, and watched as the seats around her filled up with Bridgewater's top brass. Among the ten or so people present were Jensen, Paul McDowell, and a relatively new hire, Eileen Murray, a former Wall Street banker. Almost all outranked Stefanova.

Dalio sat across from her and began ranting, as by now she knew he was wont to do. Stefanova was months behind schedule on hiring, he said, and it was delaying no less than Dalio's own plans to step back from the firm. Something had to be done, he said.

It's finally happening to me, she thought to herself.

Dalio announced to the room that he would first "probe" and then deliver what he called a "diagnosis." In the probe he asked her to confirm that she had fallen short in his assignment. The diagnosis was that she was an idiot, a point he made over and over.

"You're a dumb shit!" Dalio spat. "You don't even know what you don't know."

No one else made a peep. Jensen sat next to Dalio, stone-faced, rearranging papers, occasionally looking out the window. McDowell tried mightily to fix his eyes on a speck in the ceiling. Few of the other people present—rivals, colleagues, and future chief executives of the firm among them—came to Stefanova's defense.

Stefanova thought of the Bridgewater internal handbook, written by Ray himself. "Bridgewater emphasizes rationality," it said. "Mistakes are not bad. They are opportunities to learn. If you don't face the mistake, you won't learn from it."

She decided to try that logic. The hiring pace wasn't news to Dalio, they had discussed it frequently, she told him. Stefanova thought she had been following his wishes to hold high standards.

"I was working really hard," she eked out. "I was doing my best. What would you have done?"

Dalio apparently wasn't in a teaching mood. If he had approved the pace of the hiring, he responded, then it was her fault for not telling him he was wrong. He repeated his diagnosis, calling her dumb, grabbing the table for emphasis. People in the room remember him screaming, waiting for her lip to quiver, then screaming at her again for failing to control her emotions while he screamed at her.

That was enough for Stefanova. She was just four years out of business school and facing off with the keeper of a multibillion-dollar fortune. This would be the first and last time she ever allowed herself to cry in front of him, and she made the most of it. It started slowly, then turned into a gusher. Mascara, mixed with hot tears, streamed down her face. Several others in the room forced themselves to look away, fearful that they, too, would crack.

Stefanova pushed her chair back from the table and, still crying, ran from the room. Meeting adjourned.

Stefanova's meltdown was downright operatic. Dalio must have known he'd crushed one of the firm's alpha dogs, one he'd helped build up. Now, he would make sure no one could forget it.

This was easier than it might have seemed.

In the center of the table that day sat a chunky black box, roughly the size of a VCR. A recording device, it captured every groan, grunt, and whimper as Dalio roared, and Stefanova crumbled. A handful of Dalio's lackeys would later listen to it over and over, marking up their favorite parts.

Shortly after Stefanova fled the room, Dalio told his leadership team that he was delighted at what he had wrought. This was the ideal exemplar of his pursuit of excellence at all costs, and of the radical truth seeking that Jensen had previewed for Stefanova earlier.

Dalio made clear that he wanted all to hear it. The tape was loaded into one of his most prized creations, Bridgewater's Transparency Library. This was an electronic repository of tens of thousands of hours of internal meetings, eventually encompassing both audio and video, ranging from raging debates among the management committee to dull economic chats between junior wonks.

There were so many tapes that some were never replayed, but this one surely would be. Dalio would make it a requirement. He ordered his team of editors to create a short version of the episode. In it he was cast as the hero. In his version of events, which focused largely on Stefanova's howling distress, Dalio was portrayed as a kind but firm questioner. The probe was cut down to just a few minutes, making Stefanova's reaction seem extreme and inappropriate.

Never one for subtlety, Dalio also wrote the title, "Pain + Reflection = Progress." After having it sent out to all thousand or so Bridgewater employees, he ordered that a version of the tape be played for job candidates, making it one of their first impressions of the firm.

Bridgewater presented Stefanova's grief to the job aspirants as the start to an open-ended conversation-cum-personality-quiz. Do you think she was dealt with fairly? Do you feel bad for her? There was a clear path to a high score. At the directive of Dalio and his top lieutenants, applicants too fast to express sympathy for Stefanova or, even worse, dismay at her treatment, were scored poorly and deemed bad fits. Those who admitted they found the display hard to digest saw their résumés swiftly meet the shredder.

There was another secret that Dalio would never divulge at any airing of the tape. The Bridgewater founder, who would later proclaim himself an expert on human behavior, was apparently unmoved by extenuating circumstances surrounding Stefanova's meltdown. She herself had told him about it before that awful day.

She wasn't only losing her composure because her billionaire boss was inches from her face, playing for the rafters in that day's performance. Her emotions weren't only off because she had made a mistake at work, and/or because of a confrontation with her boss. She wasn't just fearful for her job.

She was pregnant.

2

MISSY AND THE VIKING

THANKSGIVING 1970 IN THE PARK AVENUE DUPLEX OF GEORGE AND Isabel Leib was a grand multicourse affair. The day started with Bloody Marys under a century-old glass chandelier, then moved on to bourbon. By the time Anna, the Irish butler, got around to passing out candied ginger and mints, several generations of Leib men were happily drunk.

The Leibs were blue bloods even by the standards of their neighbors at 740 Park, the famed art deco luxury co-op later credited as home to more billionaires than any other in the United States. George, descendant of German immigrants and later Louisville meat-packers, was now chairman emeritus of the investment bank Blyth & Co., which he had steered through the Great Depression. Standing at six-five, with broad shoulders he'd maintained since his army days, George was called the Viking by his grandkids. His wife, Isabel, or Missy, was a foot shorter, with a sunny personality complemented by a pleasant Kentucky drawl. She was the granddaughter of a prominent Louisville publisher and had a chatty streak that could be disarming with neighbors, such as John D. Rockefeller, Jr., and guests such as the former King Edward VIII and Wallis Simpson, by then known as the Duke and Duchess of Windsor.

Only a handful of people in apartment 12A that Thanksgiving evening weren't related to Missy and the Viking, and most of them were staff. There was Anna running whirlwind duties in the dining room; the Finnish chef, Helen, tucking into her own dinner alone in the kitchen; and the Swedish housekeeper, Astrid, upstairs amid the six bedrooms. The only other nonfamily member was lanky twenty-one-year-old Ray Dallolio, clad in a coat and tie and seated at the table with the family as one of their own.

At first glance, Dallolio's presence made little sense. He was neither neighbor nor peer nor contemporary. He lived with his father, Marino, and his mother, Ann, in the New York suburb of Manhasset. The short twenty miles between the Dallolios' hamlet, in working-class Long Island, and the Upper East Side belied a cavernous gulf in circumstances. If the Leibs were on the final yard line of an all-American drive to success, Marino Dallolio was ambling a more circuitous route. He grew up on a farm near the southern tip of New Jersey and made his way to the big city not for wealth but for art. He studied clarinet, flute, piccolo, and saxophone at the Manhattan School of Music and then hit the road, playing solos in the big band era of the early twentieth century, on occasion under the name Mo Dale. Though Marino did offer his family brushes with celebrity—he played with legends including Benny Goodman and Frank Sinatra—he wasn't much of a presence at the Dallolios' three-bedroom home. Marino wasn't back until 3:00 A.M. many nights, thanks to gigs at such clubs as the Copacabana and the Waldorf-Astoria's Empire Room, and he would sleep until noon.

"We had a good relationship, but he was a very strong man," Ray Dalio would later recall. "And I was almost the opposite. I didn't take care of hardly anything; I didn't study in school, I would go out, play, and have a blast; all through my years I was disorganized. And so he was my yin to his yang."

Ray, an only child, would later say he wished he had grown up with brothers and sisters. Instead, he became close with his mother, who doted on him. On Saturday nights, she would bake chocolate chip cookies and they would watch horror movies. Besides her, his acquaintances were mostly adults. Lacking his father's patience to learn an instrument or four—and with middling grades that Ray blamed on a poor rote memory—he took mostly physical odd jobs, including delivering newspapers. He also shoveled snow, bused tables, and stocked shelves. At age twelve, he walked over to the Links Golf Club and offered himself as a caddy.

THE LINKS wasn't just any club. It had been a farm before being redeveloped into an eighteen-hole course by Charles B. Macdonald, considered the father of American golf course design. That level of history attracted a certain type of visitor—namely, Wall Street types out east for the day. They were movers and shakers, and whether or not Ray knew it at the time, he was learning how to act around—and appeal to—the rich and powerful.

For $6 a bag, handed out in the clubhouse parking lot, he hauled clubs for the financial elite of the era. They talked to him about markets, offered up stock tips, and gave him a view into a world very different from his own. One frequent golfer, Don Stott, was a second-generation broker on the New York Stock Exchange who collected rare French burgundies. Other members included the Leibs.

Ray on occasion caddied for George Leib, as competitive at golf as he was elsewhere, but it was Isabel who took a real shine to the youngster. Isabel could kindly be described as a recreational golfer. When playing with her husband, she came up with a special rule that she was allowed to tee up her ball at every stop along the fairway. George assented, reasoning the move could only speed up the game (most other caddies avoided the duo, wary of being stuck on the course for untold hours).

When Isabel had Ray with her at the Links, they talked about topics other than golf and finance. He impressed her with his knowledge of music—a conversational gift from his father. Though Ray had never been outside the country, he had picked up a cursory knowledge of European art and culture from other players, which he deployed with an easy fluidity. Isabel and George had met in Paris while she was traveling for a summer, and she remained enchanted by the Continent, and with this young man's ability to talk about it.

Isabel and George also took a shine to young Ray for other reasons. Two of their sons had recently been thrown out of boarding schools and forced into military academies. The eldest Leib boy made it as far as sophomore year at Princeton University before dropping out (he would eventually join the family brokerage). Now the bum streak threatened to extend into a new generation. Isabel's eldest grandson, named Gordon after his grandfather, had grown out long hair, was obsessed with the electric guitar, and was entering his third boarding school in three years, having been kicked out of the first two for underage drinking and smoking pot. Isabel was watching in real time as the namesake to her storied family went up in smoke.

Then there was Ray, three years older than Gordon. Their caddy was well-spoken, clean-cut, and had been working for the family for years. As she would later recount, it occurred to Isabel that he might be a positive influence on Gordon. She asked, Would Ray be willing to spend some time with her grandson?

As an incentive, she offered to send Ray with Gordon on an all-expenses-paid, six-week trip to London, Paris, and Rome. Ray would accompany the young man to museums, concerts, and restaurants and generally make sure he didn't end up in a ditch. It was an easy offer to accept, and Ray did.

"He understood what relationships were about way before anyone else did, and he used it to his advantage," recalled Rick Coltrera, a fellow caddy with Ray.

Whether through Ray's example, the contact high of the Continent, or simply the inevitable progression of time through a teenage phase, Gordon returned from that trip a changed young man. He cut his hair, replaced the guitar with classical music, and began making serious plans for college. His grandmother was thrilled. Ray had earned a permanent seat at her table for the holidays.

As RAY became close to the Leibs, his family life was suddenly overturned. One night, his mother had a heart attack. She lay on her bed as Ray attempted mouth-to-mouth resuscitation, to no avail. She died in front of him. Ray would later say that at the time he couldn't imagine being able to smile or laugh again.

Just nineteen at the time of his mother's death, Ray was still living at home. Though to the Leibs he'd become a paragon of good habits, his tendency to cut high school to surf left him with a C average and not many educational options. For his yearbook as a high school senior, he chose a quote from Henry David Thoreau: "If a man does not keep pace with his companions, perhaps it is because he hears a different drummer. Let him step to the music which he hears, however measured or far away." Ray wound up getting in, on probation, to a college a few miles from home, C.W. Post.

Post, as it was known to its largely blue-collar students, was described by one graduate of the era as "a very good community college" that awarded four-year degrees. If the reputation underpromised, the setting overdelivered. Post's manicured, approximately three-hundred-acre campus was named after the founder of the Post cereal company conglomerate and included his family's Tudor Revival mansion, often compared to Jay Gatsby's West Egg manse. Ray, a finance major, took up meditation his freshman year, and he would later credit it with helping him open his mind and improve his grades to straight A's.

Ray also began to use the knowledge he'd picked up caddying at the

Links. Encouraged by his golf contacts, he had begun trading a small sum across a variety of markets considered exotic for a casual investor of the era, let alone a college student. He made money in gold, corn, soybeans, hogs, and plain old stocks. Among his first investments: shares in Northeast Airlines, which he chose because it cost less than $5 and had a recognizable name. It quickly received a takeover offer and tripled in value. Trades like that, some spurred by advice from his players, soon added up to a stock portfolio worth several thousand dollars. It was "an easy game," as Ray later put it.

A few months into college, Ray gained something else: a new identity. He went to the Nassau County Clerk's office, like so many descendants of immigrants, and applied for an easier-to-pronounce last name.

Ray Dalio, first of his name, soon cashed in further on his association with the Leibs.

Isabel would have known from conversations on the golf course that her caddy had turned himself into a straight A college student deeply interested in financial markets. She saw a chance to make good on her debt to the young man for straightening out her grandson. She pestered her family to give him a shot, according to her grandson, Barclay. Her son, Gordon B. Leib, offered Dalio a summer job working for him as a junior clerk at Benton, Corcoran, Leib & Co., on the floor of the New York Stock Exchange (NYSE).

To prowl the floor at 18 Broad Street in the summer of 1971 was to be at the epicenter of the financial world. This was a prized ticket to a career that some considered not just a privilege, but what *The Wall Street Journal* called "a capitalistic higher calling." Dalio's work was grueling—in those days, stocks were traded manually, via ticket, and exhausted clerks spent their days running from one floor station to the next, passing trade tickets amid a cacophony of noise—but he was enthralled. When that August, President Richard Nixon pulled the U.S. dollar off the gold standard, suspending the exchange of dollars for gold at a fixed price, Dalio saw that as a bearish sign for stocks, as it nodded to the end of a heady era for U.S. hegemony. Instead, stocks rallied because the end of the gold standard gave new flexibility to policy makers to keep the economy humming. Dalio spent much of the rest of the summer enmeshed in deep thought about the difficulty of reconciling his intuition with reality.

Gordon, following after his son and mother, became the third generation of Leib to befriend Ray Dalio. An enthusiastic gambler who doubled as a casual sports bookie on the NYSE floor, Gordon would invite Dalio over for drinks, dinner, and backgammon. Gordon, so gifted at backgammon that he once won the European championship, would drill Dalio on the basics of strategy as they played ten or fifteen games in a row. Dalio picked it up fast.

Gordon later said that Dalio had received a mixed reception from co-workers at the stock exchange. "He was not very quick on his feet," Gordon told his son, Barclay. "He didn't have much of a sense of humor. He fit in with the team awkwardly, and at times he could rub people the wrong way with a mild air of arrogance."

Dalio was headed for a place where a mild air of arrogance was almost a prerequisite. Armed with strong college grades and an unusually stacked set of recommendations for the no-name son of a journeyman musician, he was headed to graduate school just outside of Boston.

To BE at Harvard Business School in the early 1970s was to experience an institution in a state of purposeful stasis amid the changing world around it. The school was rarely less than 90 percent male. Though difficult to get into—just one in four applicants made the cut—it would later become much more competitive. Most students were significantly older than Dalio, and many had already had meaningful careers or served in the military. (Dalio avoided being drafted and sent to Vietnam thanks to a doctor's note that flagged him as hypoglycemic.)

Dalio quickly stood out. HBS students typically modeled themselves on so-called value investors, who researched individual companies and looked for those with strong fundamentals or prospects to grow. Slow, steady, and sane. Dalio, hot off the NYSE floor, came in like a blitzkrieg, people who knew him then recalled. He styled himself a "technical analyst," as opposed to one who traded on hunches, and was on the cutting edge in his methods. From his single room with a shared bathroom in red-brick Gallatin Hall, named after a former treasury secretary, Dalio talked about patterns in stock charts, short selling, and ways to spot profitable inconsistencies between seemingly unrelated markets. He pinned up stock charts on his walls.

"In some ways, he was the most experienced of the inexperienced," recalled Joel Peterson, a classmate and friend. The two did a group presentation once, and Peterson was more than happy to let Dalio do most of the talking because Dalio said he had been studying the markets since he was a pre-teen.

"There was no jealousy—there's a lot of competition, and Harvard encourages it—but I never felt that with Ray," Peterson said.

Dalio took a risk between his two years at HBS. While other MBA students had their pick of prestigious summer offers in corporate management, Dalio headed back to trading, this time at Merrill Lynch. He chose the commodities team, of all places, then a snoozy Wall Street backwater because prices for assets such as gold and oil had been stagnant for decades. Dalio reasoned that their obscurity made the asset class an easy area to make money. He was wrong. After a summer working under the director of commodities—and sleeping on a cot in a studio apartment at night—Dalio had hardly made a dime.

He still considered his summer a success. Dalio learned that he loved working in commodities, which struck him as satisfyingly mechanical. The stock market was essentially a group of people furiously swapping pieces of paper, and there was sometimes not much reason why each piece cost more or less on a given day. Commodity prices were more easily defined. Beef cost what someone was willing to pay for a pound of it at the butcher counter.

Back at HBS for his second year, Dalio dove into the school's famous case method, which required reading ten-to-twenty-page real-world case studies, almost like puzzles, that dissected a complicated business or leadership issue that had no obvious answers. The cases were a mix of the fascinating and the tedious, and Dalio wasn't always a big fan. On one otherwise unmemorable evening in Dalio's second year, when most students were studying, Dalio marched without warning into his classmate Mike Kubin's room, just down the hall.

"I'm working," Kubin said, barely looking up.

Dalio picked up the case on Kubin's desk and threw it in the trash. "You don't want to be doing that. You want to be doing this."

Dalio walked Kubin back to Dalio's room. He had set up a table to play backgammon. The two HBS students played for hours.

EACH HBS class is divided into tranches, or sections, of around one hundred students who take core classes together. Many become so close that they consider their section their family.

For section H of the Harvard Business School class of 1973, the first six months after graduation were exciting. Bob Cook bought a BMW motorcycle for a trip across the country. Roy Barber and Marc Tumas went camping together around Montreal. Joel Peterson took a job in the south of France.

Dalio, as section H classmate Larry Schwoeri put it in a bulletin to classmates, blazed a different path:

"Ray Dalio had the most impressive title on his initial job—President of Dominick & Dominick Commodities. You may all check your *WSJ*'s now to see if (1) Dominick & Dominick are still in business, and (2) where the commodities market has gone in the last months. Good Luck, Ray."

Dominick & Dominick was still in business, if by a thread. The brokerage, founded in 1870, around the time Thomas Edison designed the first modern stock ticker, had plodded its way through its first hundred years. This included the commodities division. Dalio had a lofty title, a salary of $25,000 a year (the equivalent of a six-figure salary today), and not much else, because its business was in disarray.

As Dalio joined the brokerage, it made a move down market. It expanded into the retail space, the idea being that it could become a competitor to more well-known names. The stock market then cratered, and Dominick & Dominick's main retail fund blew up. To stay afloat, the firm was forced to hock four of its five seats on the New York Stock Exchange and one of its two on the American Stock Exchange. Many of Dalio's trades in the era were losers. They were "stupid to hire me, but they did," he later told a group of business school students.

No one could blame Dalio for the brokerage's troubles and he still boasted an HBS degree, so he next found his way to the powerhouse brokerage Shearson Hayden Stone. Dalio's Shearson job whisked him away from the mashing of the stock exchange floor into the wider world of wealth, where he was cast somewhere halfway between teacher and salesman. With the air of someone who had sat at the table with New York's financial royalty, he advised cattle ranchers, grain producers, and other commodities-dependent businesspeople on how to steady their businesses through complicated trades known as hedges, which paid off when the market was down and lost money when the market was up. Hedges didn't so much have to make money as not lose money. Shearson clients loved Dalio. One group of ranchers gave him the horns of a longhorn steer.

What happened next is a matter of some debate. Even the sequence of events is fuzzy. When Dalio later recounted versions of the stories, he would sometimes flip the order.

What is certain is that on New Year's Eve 1974, Dalio got into a heated argument with his boss. Dalio, angry and drunk, slugged his boss in the face over a momentary disagreement (one fellow financier later heard the confrontation described as a "sucker punch"). When Dalio returned to the office, he expected to be fired immediately. Instead he got a second chance.

A few months later, as a Shearson executive attending the annual convention of the California Grain & Feed Association, Dalio decided to spice things up. In one version of what happened, he brought a stripper to a private client presentation. Another version is more ribald: the stripper was paid to get naked in front of the crowd. Another narrative is a combination of the two: Dalio was giving an otherwise unremarkable flip-chart presentation at the conference and assigned the dancer to turn the pages.

No matter the exact details, the takeaway is consistent. Dalio had let his emotions, and taste for the dramatic, get the best of him. The consequence is not in dispute. He was unceremoniously fired by Shearson. Now almost twenty-six and out of work for the second time in less than two years, he needed help. It would come from his surrogate family.

GORDON B. Leib hadn't changed much since he had spent time with Dalio before his Harvard days. Leib was still at the NYSE, and still a popular bookie for his fellow brokers. Every day when the exchange closed, Leib would head to the New York Racquet Club for a steam and a swim, then play a few games of backgammon.

The Ray Dalio who asked to catch up over a drink struck Leib as having had a rough few years. Leib didn't know what had gone down at Shearson, but he knew that Dalio wasn't doing much besides living in a two-bedroom apartment in Manhattan with his Harvard classmate Bob Cook. The duo were egging each other on, drinking heavily, hosting parties, and taking wild trips. Their classmate Schwoeri captured the dynamic in the HBS alumni bulletin, noting that the two amigos had just returned from Rio de Janeiro, "where they had conducted an extensive market penetration study."

Leib soon learned the reason for this meeting. Dalio needed money. As was relayed to Barclay Leib, Gordon's son, Dalio pitched the elder Leib a sweeping plan to start a commodities import-export business, one that would ship physical commodities from the United States to buyers in other countries. It would be called Bridgewater, which had a nice consonance to it for a business that intended to move physical assets, such as soybean oil, across oceans.

"I need one hundred thousand dollars to make it one year," Dalio told Leib and other potential investors. Dalio was looking for 10 percent of that from each.

Leib, ever the gambler, weighed the odds that his mother's caddy would wind up founding a successful Wall Street firm, and concluded that the prospect was remote. While turning down his putative family member, he offered help: he introduced Dalio to other partners at Benton, Corcoran, Leib & Co., who invested in the new business. Dalio managed to get the venture off the ground.

About one year later, Dalio was back to ask for more. The earlier money was gone, he said. His new business had executed a total of two transactions. "It was more of an idea than a reality, and I had the name," Dalio later said.

Dalio had a new plan this go-around. It was more modest. Dalio planned to start a boutique consultancy offering the kind of advisory work he'd done at Shearson. The timing was shrewd, coming as commodities were rebounding and attracting the attention of ordinary investors. Dalio credibly pitched himself as one of the few on Wall Street who could comfortably talk his way through the state of play in the livestock, meat, grain, and oilseed markets.

Leib was intrigued, but he still figured it was folly to put money into a new business model from a young man who had a lot of growing up to do. Leib still didn't see the point of further entwining his comfortable life with that of Dalio. Others at Leib's brokerage also dropped out.

But Dalio didn't need them as much anymore. His roommate's girlfriend in 1975 set him up on a blind date with one of her friends, Barbara Gabaldoni. She worked at an art museum and spoke little English. No matter; as he later wrote in his autobiography, "We communicated in different ways."

Gabaldoni was complicated. She was brought up partly in Spain, where her Peruvian father served as a diplomat, and she once told a Bridgewater

employee that she had briefly been kidnapped as a child. This was potentially not just a consequence of her father's job, but of her maternal background. Though her last name was courtesy of her Peruvian lineage, her
first name came from her grandmother, Barbara Whitney, daughter of
Gertrude Vanderbilt and Harry Whitney.

Barbara Gabaldoni was a Vanderbilt Whitney, working at the storied
New York museum that bore her family name.

She would have no trouble helping out with Dalio's fledgling business.

3

ABSOLUTE CERTAINTY

FOR A GOOD LONG WHILE, DALIO FELT FREE.

Though he was running a new business, he felt little anxiety. Life was good. His commute was a short walk from his bedroom into the other bedroom, now set up as an at-home office. He had no trouble paying rent. Still in his twenties, Dalio was content to live moment to moment. He wasn't so convinced that this phase, or his enterprise overall, would last forever. If it didn't work out, he could just go out and get another job.

Matters moved quickly between Dalio and Barbara Gabaldoni. A private person, she let her beau take the lead in social settings. A few months after meeting, they had fully intermingled their respective lives, giving Dalio entrée into a new level of society. In 1977, the couple married and moved into a spacious Manhattan brownstone. The newlyweds lived on the top two floors, and Dalio worked on the bottom two. Not long after, Barbara gave birth to the first of four sons.

In part through exposure to his new in-laws, Dalio was beginning to undergo a valuable education about the strata and nuances of wealth, one that he would apply to his new business. The Leibs had been wealthy, but their money had come only recently. The Viking often told his grandkids about how in the 1920s he had sold his heaviest overcoat for the money to buy his first stake in the brokerage firm that later bore his name. Barbara Dalio came from older money.

The Vanderbilt fortune dated to 1810, when Cornelius "Commodore" Vanderbilt parlayed a $100 loan from his mother into a steamboat and railroad empire. When he died in 1877, his $100 million estate was worth more than the entire U.S. Treasury. By the time Dalio married into the family exactly one hundred years later, much of the fortune had been squandered on parties, sports cars, mansions, and horses. Dalio entered a family that was playing defense, trying to maintain what remained of one of America's great intergenerational bounties. Barbara let Dalio take charge of her part of what was left.

Dalio soon realized that families with generational wealth had different priorities. Traders on the stock exchange floor were always talking up their next bang-up idea, which inevitably boiled down to getting in front of a big market move that only they could see. Once wealthy, however, people were less consumed by the hunt for the next score. They were more focused on staying rich than getting richer, and their strategy focused on steady, long-term growth and the minimization of the risk of big losses. The same long-term outlook applied to businesses and institutions such as colleges and pension funds. These colossal pools of money wanted to grow their money steadily, at the lowest possible risk. Their biggest investment priority was to avoid the possibility of ruin. A person who could project understanding of that priority and the knowledge of how to achieve it could make a lot of money.

So, beginning in the late 1970s and stretching into the early 1980s, Bridgewater Associates was among the earlier companies to fine-tune ways to do just that.

Indicative of Bridgewater and Dalio's approach was its contract with McDonald's. The fast-food chain was secretly developing McNuggets, a major menu expansion. But the price of the main ingredient, chicken, was fluctuating like never before. McDonald's couldn't roll out a product to its three thousand restaurants worldwide and expect them to change the price every day. Dalio figured that the chicken market was volatile because of gyrations in the corn and soybean markets. Chickens eat corn and soybean, and when farmers had to pay more for the feed, they inevitably jacked up the price of poultry. Dalio advised McDonald's to fix its costs by using financial instruments known as futures. If corn and soybean became more expensive, McDonald's costs would remain the same. That gave the company a window to buy enough poultry at a stable price to roll out McNuggets.

Another client was the snack-food giant Nabisco. The conglomerate's problems overlapped with those of McDonald's: Nabisco's products used a dizzying variety of raw ingredients whose prices could swing wildly and hurt profits. Dalio helped Nabisco structure trades similar to what he did for McDonald's, though broader. He showed Nabisco executives how to invest money in a way that would not just fix the cost of commodities, but also reduce risk of earning less money in U.S. dollars than expected from a box of Oreo cookies sold in a country whose currency had depreciated. For such complex advice, Nabisco gave Dalio the formal authority to manage, without day-to-day oversight, a portion of its savings. This was a big step forward—it made him essentially one of the company's independent investment managers, as opposed to a mere consultant. And in what was a relatively novel arrangement for the time, Dalio received a percentage of the profits that Nabisco earned on the trades he directed. That gave him vast upside to earn a portion of what Nabisco earned—potentially far more than a simple flat fee on the amount of money he oversaw.

As he became a global trader, Dalio began to benefit from establishing himself as more than just an adviser of companies. He fashioned himself as an economist with a scientific approach to his work and as a global thinker who had insights on the history of business cycles. He wrote articles for obscure trade publications read by financiers and investors, such as a cattle magazine, allowing him to show off a deft understanding of esoteric markets. He started to write down in notebooks his reasons for placing a trade and tabulated the results afterward, creating a record of whether he had been right or wrong. He checked against history, too, to make sure his ideas were likely to work over and over. Dalio discovered that he was better off placing a large number of small bets, so if one went wrong, it wouldn't drag down the overall portfolio.

Further bolstering his big-thinker credentials, Dalio started to sell a daily market commentary letter, which contained his take on the pressing macroeconomic issues of the day. Coming as it did decades before such newsletters became commonplace over email, the letter, sent via fax and telex, was a hit. With the help of a small staff Dalio hired, Bridgewater distributed the letter widely to clients—who came to include Bunker Hunt, an oil magnate and then the richest man in the world—and the media. He held meetings at New York's Harvard Club. To some, Dalio charged for the newsletter, as part of a research package that went for $3,000 per month.

As Dalio's reputation and client list grew, he moved with Barbara and his growing family to suburban Connecticut, where he acquired a new title. Despite no formal training in the field, Dalio took to calling himself an economist of Bridgewater Associates. This economist had a slew of eyebrow-raising views about what was just around the corner.

ON WALL Street and in Washington a surefire way to get attention is to pull the alarm, and by 1981, Dalio saw nothing less than calamity ahead.

He crisscrossed the country, stoking anxiety as he warned clients and the media about troubling headwinds facing the world economy. Markets were turbulent, gold was spiking, unemployment was on the rise, and oil prices had more than doubled in only one year. Fearful of inflation, the U.S. central bank hiked interest rates as high as 21 percent in 1981, hoping to encourage saving rather than spending. The economy ground into recession. While the Reagan administration stubbornly insisted it was on the right track, Dalio saw it differently. The United States was headed for a historic economic collapse, the worst since World War II, and Dalio said as much to anyone who would listen. "You could lose half the housing industry, Pan Am, Chrysler, maybe Ford and many other companies," he warned in a March 1982 interview with *The New York Times*. "There is no hope. It is a hard reality," he said a few months later.

Dalio's Chicken Little tour produced significant returns, though not immediately for his bottom line. The organizers of the Contrary Opinion Forum, a group of self-described professional pessimists, invited Dalio to speak at their annual confab on the banks of Lake Champlain in Vermont. Dalio's talk was dark even for that crowd. "Why can't doom be gradual?" one attendee asked.

An even bigger opportunity arrived a few months later in the nation's capital, when Dalio was invited to speak to a joint committee of Congress focused on rising unemployment. Full of swagger, he marched into the hulking Rayburn House Office Building, dressed in a black suit and gray striped tie, with the whispers of a receding hairline almost entirely concealed by the sweep of his dark brown hair. Now thirty-three, he looked younger.

This was a big moment for Dalio, and he would have known he would have to work to stand out amid the roster of heavyweights testifying. He was clearly on the undercard; Paul Volcker, chairman of the board of the Federal Reserve, wasn't due to speak for another month. As Dalio reached for the microphone, Parren J. Mitchell, representative from the state of Maryland, fiddled distractedly with the lit cigarette in his mouth. Dalio soon attracted the attention of all in the room.

"Following the economy of the last few years has been rather like watching a mystery thriller in which you can see the dangers lurking around the corner and want to yell a warning but know it won't be heard," Dalio began. "The danger in this case is depression.

"Although it's been a long time since the economy has suffered from one, there is such a disease as depression, which we as economists should know how to diagnose. Today's economists are about as familiar with depressions as today's physicians are with long-dormant plagues."

Since 1800, Dalio said, the United States had experienced fourteen major depressions, all following the same historical patterns. The fifteenth was plainly imminent. "This is what we call the depression process," he said.

One congressman at the hearing called Dalio's demeanor "more grim than the ghost of Hamlet's father."

That's because if recession was one thing, depression was another. Not many analysts were bold enough to make that call. Armed with one of the scariest predictions an investor can make, Dalio landed a spot on *Wall $treet Week,* the nation's premier business television program. In the three weeks since his congressional testimony, Dalio had become only more self-assured. He sat relaxed in front of the cameras, arms wide at his sides. He didn't blink as he spoke.

"I can say with absolute certainty that if you look at the liquidity base in the corporations and the world as a whole, that there's such a reduced level of liquidity that you can't return to an era of stagflation."

Translation: there wasn't enough money left in the world to save us.

All the confidence in the world couldn't save Dalio from the facts. The same month as his television appearance, the recession ended. The stock market had bottomed in August, a few weeks before his speech to the Contrary Opinion Forum.

The depression that never happened cost Dalio dearly. He lost clients and his own money. He laid off his small staff, reducing the firm to just one employee, himself. To recover, he would need to develop more than a Cassandra act.

He was clearly good at helping companies think through complicated global economic dynamics, so he threw himself headlong into research. The economic newsletter he had been writing became his primary focus. He ramped up distribution of what were now called *Daily Observations.* He sent them to old clients, to people he had never met, and to journalists looking for story ideas. He told few people what the topics would be in advance, so when the notes showed up by fax, it was a bit like unwrapping a surprise gift. One of the livelier pieces was titled "What Is a Jeweler?" The article posited that jewelers, with their collections of pricey products waiting to be sold, were not substantially different from Wall Street traders "long," or betting on, gold and precious stones.

Dalio had presented similar theses to McDonald's and Nabisco, which also hoped to avoid losing money in unexpected market shocks. If the market price of gold went up, all the better for jewelers, who would be sitting on rings and necklaces suddenly worth more. But the opposite was true, too—even an otherwise successful jeweler could go bankrupt if the market turned down. Dalio's solution was futures instruments. He recommended that jewelers trade gold futures, essentially contracts that allowed them the right to buy gold later. These contracts were designed to rise in value when the price of gold fell. Profits from the futures would cushion whatever losses the jewelers sustained from being "long" via the gold-laden items in their display cases. If Dalio had proven a less than stellar predictor of an economic crash, this type of targeted hedging strategy was firmly in his wheelhouse.

The plainspoken research steadily begot business for Bridgewater outside the usual corridors in Manhattan. A top executive at Banks of Mid-America in Tulsa, Oklahoma, began sharing it with subordinates. He called it the best thing he'd ever read on how the economy worked. The bank hired Bridgewater at $18,000 a year, in part to have Dalio on retainer to chat through the bigger issues when needed. As clients such as Banks of MidAmerica started to ask for more elaborate advice, Dalio added a matrix to the newsletter with instructions on what investments to buy or sell on any given day depending on the direction of various markets.

One newsletter landed on an important desk just a few miles away from Dalio in Stamford, Connecticut. Paul Tudor Jones, five years Dalio's junior, was also a Wall Street outsider—Jones hailed from Tennessee—and like Dalio got his start as a commodities broker. While Dalio had been struggling, however, his friend Jones was riding a hot streak. He turned down Harvard Business School to start an eponymous investment firm that was a near-instant success.

Jones knew Dalio had been knocked around by his depression call, but the Southerner saw Dalio as a potentially undervalued asset. Jones saw an opportunity and invited his friend in for a chat.

"Have you thought about trading the stuff you're writing about?" Jones asked.

Jones laid out the plan. Dalio would have full access to the resources of Tudor Investment Corporation, and they would work together to develop what could become an investment fund. The goal wasn't to make the most money possible in the shortest time, but to design a system that produced steady and sustainable gains, at the lowest possible risk. The ultimate barometer would be the program's Sharpe ratio, a decades-old calculation of a portfolio's returns in relation to volatility, or how much it swung. The higher the better. A strong Sharpe ratio was 2.0, though a ratio of 3.0 or even higher wasn't out of the question for top investors.

Dalio agglomerated his findings from years of writing newsletters. He distilled them all into what was essentially an "if this, then that" trading method. *If* interest rates went up in one country, for example, *then* Dalio would automatically sell bonds in another to compensate. The approach seemed genuinely systematized, in that it all but removed Dalio's day-to-day decision-making from the investment portfolio. He could only make changes by conducting deep research and changing the rules themselves based on historical data, as opposed to reacting one-off to any momentary market move.

After several months of tweaking the blueprint, Dalio was satisfied. He brought it back to Jones, who handed it off to his team to analyze. The verdict: Dalio's approach produced a Sharpe ratio of less than 1.0.

Jones's Southern accent did little to mask his palpable frustration: "What the hell am I supposed to do with this?" he asked Dalio.

Jones had given a friend a fair shot and been rewarded with a design that failed the most important criterion. Jones would later tell an associate that he had judged Dalio to be unquestionably intelligent, but not much of an investment manager—certainly not up to the levels of Tudor Investment Corporation.

What about the trading system? Dalio asked on his way out.

Jones snorted, "Take it with you."

DALIO PRESSED on, apparently convinced he was onto something. He headed for someone who would take almost any meeting.

Hilda Ochoa-Brillembourg had a lofty title that didn't quite match the reality: chief investment officer for the World Bank pension investment division. Her job was to protect the retirement savings of thousands of employees of the austere financial institution. This can't-win job was in the backwater of an organization whose every employee thought he or she could do better. The premises, too, reminded her that she wasn't exactly doing the company's most exciting, globe-trotting work. The main World Bank offices boasted finely finished floors and wood desks. Ochoa-Brillembourg sat at a metal desk on linoleum flooring, reading Dalio's daily research notes.

Ochoa-Brillembourg considered herself a precise judge of talent. She liked to put the World Bank's money with young investors hungry to make their mark. You couldn't get smaller than Bridgewater Associates; it didn't then have a cent under management, according to internal firm documents from the era.

Yet when Dalio came to ask for an investment, he was far from a stranger. Ochoa-Brillembourg had gone to Harvard for graduate school, so they had an easy start to the conversation. The more he talked, the more he struck her as having a brilliant mind. He recalled granular economic details from countries and industries that seemed otherwise unrelated, combining, for instance, the latest currency prices with nineteenth-century railroad bond prices. He could see connections and seemed to be able to predict which domino in a far-flung place would knock off another elsewhere. To Ochoa-Brillembourg, her visitor seemed quick to determine which data points were important, and which were just noise. She hadn't heard of Dalio's busted depression call from a few years earlier. His newsletters never mentioned it, and Dalio didn't bring it up.

Ochoa-Brillembourg figured Bridgewater Associates was worth a moon shot, with some precautions. The World Bank pension fund would fork over $5 million of its savings, only to be invested in the relatively tame area of domestic fixed income. Ochoa-Brillembourg allowed Dalio to make international bets, but maintained that Bridgewater would be judged only on its relative performance to the U.S. bond market. If Dalio lost his shirt going afield, there would be no excuses.

When talk came to fees, Ochoa-Brillembourg held all the cards. Dalio agreed to manage the portfolio for a flat 0.20 percent annual fee, or $10,000 a year. That was less than he charged for the newsletter alone. But it was a new start.

4

PURE ALPHA

THE FROZEN GRASS CRINKLED UNDER DALIO'S BOOTS AS HE STRUG-gled to sit comfortably on the wood bench. The choice of setting—outdoors, at night, in the dead of a Connecticut winter—wasn't his. But the subject of this article wasn't in a position to negotiate. The editors of *Forbes* wanted a visual that befit the theme of the piece, so Dalio donned blue jeans and a madras jacket and perched on the bench, following the photographer's instructions. In the final photo as printed, his face would be half obscured by shadows. This wasn't to be a subtle message.

"Does a depression lie ahead? Ahead, hell, it's already here, says Raymond Dalio," *Forbes* began.

It was February 1987 and Dalio was back to the blues. This time around, his gloomy view had been tipped off by nothing less than the American way of life. The U.S. consumer was borrowing too much, saving too little, and blowing money on new television sets, Dalio said. Though the stock market had doubled in the preceding two years, the country was in denial and the bill was coming due. "When you feel rich, you begin to consume your wealth," he said. "People need to go broke and feel economic pain to understand the benefits of saving and hard work."

If the dreary tune was a Dalio standard, the instrument was something else entirely. Since paring the company back to three employees in 1985, he had grown Bridgewater into what the magazine described as a respectable, midsize firm. Dalio now led what *Forbes* identified as a staff of forty-four in offices in New York, Los Angeles, London, and Hong Kong.* The firm managed some $20 million, four times its sum from two years earlier. Global clients such as Citibank and the Soviet press agency TASS were

---

* This wasn't accurate—Bridgewater didn't have close to that staff, or those offices—though Dalio evidently did not press for a correction.

among those who had received Dalio's recent research report, titled "The Decline of the American Empire."

How long do we have left until the crash? *Forbes* asked.

"Another year or so," Dalio answered.

Eight months later, on October 19, 1987, what would be known as Black Monday, the thirty-eight-year-old Dalio could say he had predicted what was the largest one-day drop ever in the U.S. stock market. Stocks dropped nearly 23 percent in a single day, leaving investors large and small shell-shocked. *The Wall Street Journal* described the sidewalks of Manhattan's Upper West Side brimming with young traders wandering about, dead in the eyes, looking as if they had just fled some sort of natural disaster.

Fifty miles to the northeast, Dalio was counting his winnings. For the first time in a decade, bearishness had paid off—for him, and for Bridgewater. He had followed his own advice and was short, or betting against, stocks headed into Black Monday. Bridgewater also held U.S. Treasury bonds, traditionally a safe-haven asset that performed well in times of stress. At year-end, Bridgewater's accounts were up 27 percent, many multiples the return for the stock market.

Though the raw performance figure was impressive, Dalio's take-home would have been relatively modest. With $20 million of client funds, Bridgewater simply didn't have enough in its coffers to produce a windfall. Plenty of clients were happy to read Dalio's research reports, but few had entrusted him with their money. Bridgewater's investment advice was apparently seen as nice to have, not need to have. After Black Monday, Dalio watched as Paul Tudor Jones became world-famous after making roughly the same pessimistic call on the markets. The difference was that Jones had $250 million in assets as the market crashed. Jones personally made an estimated $100 million that year off his cut of the trading gains. Dalio saw clips of his friend starring in a PBS documentary, *Trader,* which followed Jones to his eighteen-bedroom weekend estate.

To have a shot at that kind of life, Dalio didn't just have to be right more often. He had to be right on a far-larger scale.

THE FIRST stop was a return to television. Dalio got booked on the air as a guest on a panel hosted by a charismatic, up-and-coming Chicago talk-show host, who introduced him:

"My next guest warns that we better get used to being completely dependent upon Japan or else take a complete cut on our standard of living. He is Ray Dalio, economist, money manager, and CEO of the Bridgewater Group."

The episode was titled "Foreigners Taking Over America." The studio audience, which included laid-off steelworkers and the like, was in a huff about a flood of Japanese money bidding up prices for U.S. real estate. The crowd didn't quite know what to make of Dalio, in a trim blue pinstripe suit. He laid out his view that American economic power was on its last days.

"You become in the stage where you're beginning to get poorer and you still think of yourself as rich—"

"That's real bad," Oprah Winfrey cut in.

"That's real bad. And that's where the United States is. You'll judge your living standards based on how you drive around in expensive cars, say, 'If I can consume like this, I must be rich, it doesn't matter how much I've borrowed in order to do that.' It's attitude, is what I'm saying."

"Do y'all agree with this? Do you agree with this theory?" Winfrey asked the audience.

Several cried out, "No."

Dalio was undeterred: "What we are seeing we have seen through hundreds of years. We have seen the ascendancy and descendancy of civilizations. It's due to the fact that we are overconsuming. We are trading our freedom for VCRs."

Winfrey took a caller who suggested that racism might be at play. The Japanese were the first people of color to be permitted to invest in the United States in size. Winfrey punted to Dalio: "What about, Ray, the caller's point about addressing the Japanese because they are the first people of color to buy up so much land?"

Dalio, who until this point had been a mostly forgettable presence in the episode, seized on the opportunity to grab attention. "To clarify that, the Japanese are racists. There's no doubt about the fact that the Japanese are racists," he told Winfrey.

This earned him a smattering of applause.

Winfrey shot it right back to him. "That sounds like a racist statement."

"No, I just think it's a fact of life. I have a lot of Japanese clients. I go out and I eat and drink and I know these people, and I am telling you that they are racist. That's a fact of life. That's a reality."

He raised his arms up to near his head, the universal sign for surrender, as if to say, *Don't shoot the messenger.*

Dalio had again grabbed the spotlight by saying what few others would.

OFF AIR, Dalio didn't have to try quite so hard because Black Monday had done him an immediate and lasting favor. It scared the heck out of a generation of deep-pocketed investors.

Dalio seized the moment. About two years earlier he had hired, as one of Bridgewater's first employees, a full-time marketer, Chris Streit, an older man who had been managing director at Merrill Lynch, which had considered putting money into Dalio's firm. Streit was well-known enough to merit a public announcement, which Bridgewater put out with more than a little overstatement: a notice in a trade publication to mark the new employee's hiring identified Bridgewater as having $700 million under management. Streit knew that eye-popping sum wasn't even close to correct. He assumed that Dalio had counted the assets of everyone who received a copy of Bridgewater's newsletter—even though most had no money with the firm. "There was a lot of stretching in those early days," Streit later recalled.

Streit quickly learned that to his new boss, appearances mattered. Dalio both lived and worked out of a sprawling converted barn in Wilton, Connecticut, and while decades later he would speak wistfully about the pastoral setting, in the moment it didn't fully match the impression he was trying to project. He already had in his sights highly status-conscious clients: the Chinese.

Less than a decade before, Deng Xiaoping had begun to liberalize China's economy, and now for many summers Dalio had taken his wife with him to China, where he would meet with businesses still far off the radar of the financial mainstream. One of his earliest clients was the China International Trust and Investment Corporation, or CITIC, a state-run conglomerate with close ties to the ruling Communist Party. When a CITIC executive asked Dalio to host his daughter during a weeklong trip to America, Dalio assented—then asked the gray-templed Streit to put her up instead in Streit's Greenwich manse and drive her in his Mercedes, Streit recalled. It was critical that she go home and tell her parents that Dalio and his seemingly experienced colleagues exuded success.

The largest targets for Dalio and his new marketer were so-called institutional investors. Unlike retail investors, or individuals who buy and sell for themselves, these large investors are run by professional money managers who make decisions for a larger group of beneficiaries, such as pension funds. By the early 1990s, institutional investors controlled close to 40 percent of the stock of America's large businesses, and much of the debt, too. They were the whales of Wall Street, large in size but tricky to approach. The men and women in charge of these investments could be finicky, conservative, and even provincial, concerned as much about losing face as they were about losing money.

Dalio recognized the state of play. His risk-averse attitude was an easy fit for the era, and though it might be easy to dismiss his approach as a marketing gimmick, plenty of big-name competitors were making similar efforts, without commensurate results. Dalio courted pension funds in particular, armed with a playbook designed to appeal to anyone worried about another market crash.

Rusty Olson was one of them. The chief of the Eastman Kodak employee pension fund was in desperate need of a new plan. More than half of the pension plan's money was invested in annuities, leaving the solvency of thousands of Rochester, New York, retirees hanging precariously on the performance of a complicated Wall Street product—an issue top of mind after Black Monday. Olson was taking an average of one meeting every three days with salespeople who claimed to have the answers. On the recommendation of his friend Ochoa-Brillembourg of the World Bank, Olson agreed to see Dalio.

Though the markets were recovering steadily since Black Monday, no one would have known it from listening to the Bridgewater founder. Dalio brought dread to every meeting, seeing worse days around the corner ("He devoutly believes in the corruption of the economic soul," wrote one interviewer). Dalio talked up a coming depression in 1988; a three-year recession starting in 1989; back to depression in 1990; was still beating the drum of depression in 1991; and had tweaked his call to "a modern-day version of a depression . . . like a hangover after one of those great parties but one that never goes away" in 1992. "The U.S. economy is behaving essentially as it did in the thirties," Dalio said. "This is not a recession, it is a depression."

It wasn't. But Dalio didn't sell Olson solely on the accuracy of Dalio's public forecasts. He came in armed with counterintuitive research. Dalio said that Kodak could reduce the risk of its heavy tilt toward the stock market not by betting less but by betting more, using leverage, or borrowed money. What Dalio was recommending was both counterintuitive and innovative for the time, because leverage was typically seen as a risky move. But he told Olson that Kodak could safely "lever up" in a range of relatively sturdy markets outside stocks, such as U.S. and international bonds. Individually, these bets might not match the return of stocks, but by magnifying the wagers with leverage, the cumulative bets would add up. Importantly, the overall effect remained low-risk, because the markets in which Dalio deployed leverage were placid enough that they rarely swung much. So went the refrain Dalio delivered to Olson and others several times a week, trying to drum up business.

"If you can do this thing successfully, you will make a fortune. You'll get the pot of gold at the end of the rainbow," Dalio would say.

Olson was sold. He put the pension's money into Dalio's firm. "A new way of thinking," Olson later called it.

SOMEONE ELSE was with Dalio on that trip to Rochester. Bob Prince, the treasurer of the Tulsa bank whose boss had taken a shine to Bridgewater's research, had accepted an offer to move to the Northeast and work for the growing firm. Nearly ten years younger than Dalio, Prince was quickly becoming the founder's professional other half.

A handsome, blue-eyed Midwest native, Prince played collegiate golf at the University of Tulsa and stuck around for his MBA and CPA. Easygoing, Prince made friends easily, including with the members of his favorite band, the Ushers, the sort of new-wave, alternative-rock group that didn't make it out of the 1980s. Prince struck friends as the sort of young striver who would eventually be honored for a lifetime of service to his community church, not necessarily someone who would fund one.

Prince was not quite the big-city type when he moved to New York with his girlfriend to commute to his job at Bridgewater. Living in a typically undersize Manhattan apartment, Prince marveled that his local bodega boasted such a wide variety of fruits and other goods. When a friend from Oklahoma came to visit and check out the new digs, Prince crowed about Dalio, saying his new boss had high expectations for everyone who worked for him and asked them to treat him the same. Mistakes weren't allowed to linger—they were identified and addressed head-on in real time. Coming from a snoozy Midwestern bank, Prince found this a bracing and exciting change. "I'm learning so much," Prince told his friend. "It's a fresh, unique management style."

Physically, Dalio and Prince made a complementary pair. While Dalio steadily put on weight and dressed like a high school teacher with two pairs of khakis in rotation, Prince was known for showing up to meetings in a clean white polo shirt that showed off his biceps. Temperamentally, they played off each other, too. Dalio was prone to rambling, while Prince had a focused, even tone.

At Tulsa, Prince studied under Professor Richard Burgess, a finance professor with unusually sharp takes on what was known as modern portfolio theory. MPT, invented in the 1950s, was a technique to build an investment portfolio by examining the past returns and volatility of disparate asset classes. The trick was to split money among investments that don't necessarily correlate, or move together, to avoid the chance that any one market event could cause calamity. Burgess shared with his students his model to let them mix and match investments—an experiment in how to produce the highest possible performance at any given level of risk. He could never have imagined his lessons would mint a billionaire among his students, and it was a credit to Prince and Dalio that they alone would figure out its potential.

In the months after Prince joined Bridgewater, the firm moved out of Dalio's barn to an office in a strip mall a few miles south. There, Prince, Dalio, and a small team tended to what was becoming an increasingly impressive client list and several hundred million dollars in assets under management. Kodak was joined by such blue-chip U.S. companies as General Electric, Mobil, and DuPont, as well as state-employee retirement plans including those of Connecticut and Wisconsin. Dalio was a master at wooing old-line firms that were more worried about holding on to their money than to making gobs more of it.

Dalio was attuned not just to the advice he was offering, but to the manner of delivery. Before Kodak executives showed up for one meeting, Dalio asked his staff to ensure the visitors' itinerary included a stop by Bridgewater's back office, so that they might observe Bridgewater's newly purchased colossal and expensive Kodak printer.

Dalio could be intense, yet disarmingly oblivious of his actions. Employees liked to retell a story that took place a few years after Prince joined, when the firm had fewer than two dozen staff. Dalio came into the office sick, with a meeting scheduled on his calendar. Halfway through the meeting, he reached over for the garbage can, dragged it next to his chair, and vomited. "Then he pushed it aside and we continued the meeting like nothing happened," a former employee told *Maxim*.

Far from its being a turnoff, Bridgewater and Dalio found that his intensity was a selling point. It was an early version of the hustle-porn mentality that would decades later take over Silicon Valley and make celebrities of entrepreneurs who worked, ate, and slept at their desks.

Bridgewater's trading was also ahead of its time. In those days, before ever more sophisticated algorithms would become de rigueur across Wall Street, Bridgewater's investing relied on a heavily manual sequence. Dalio and his staff would study the history of how governments reacted to market moves and divine whether any connections might apply to the current markets, often using an early version of the graphing program Microsoft Excel. Tables were stacked with yellow legal pads with handwritten rules—essentially just a record of whether a given trade made money—and handheld calculators.

Dalio was the group's free spirit. He could spend hours alone in his office, hair mussed, flannel shirt askew, shoes off, feet on the desk, smoking a pipe. The relaxed pose belied that he was anything but casual. On one occasion, Prince had to run in and interrupt his solitude.

"Uh, Ray," Prince said, "I forgot to do the trades."

Dalio turned red. "How could you possibly do that?"

To an interviewer Prince later described Dalio's reaction as that of "a fire-breathing dragon."

For Dalio, a mistake was never just a mistake. It was an opportunity to dive into the individualistic human psychology that led to errors—particularly ones that Dalio himself might have avoided. He often said that he had made a string of them early in his career—allowing his emotions to rule in his blowup with his boss, for one, and being too categorical in predicting calamity ahead in his testimony to Congress. He believed he had successfully identified the causes of these mistakes and corrected for them, and he was determined to impart this wisdom to his charges, to prevent such errors from repeating in the future. In one meeting with Prince,

Dalio delivered blunt feedback. Prince would need to open himself up to more criticism, both internal and external: "You trust yourself too much. You don't work through it well. If you had less confidence . . . you would have been much more successful."

No doubt helped by the fact that the feedback was delivered privately, and from one man to another who was close to a peer, Prince took it as helpful coaching from the boss.

BY SHEER assets, or the sum of money that Bridgewater invested for clients, the hedge fund continued to grow rapidly in the late eighties and early nineties. The firm's assets under management doubled in a single year to $1.2 billion in 1992 and would nearly double again the year after. But behind that success, Bridgewater's business had a fundamental problem. When the firm did its job well, its success was nigh invisible.

This was as much a feature as a bug, and it dated back to the type of work Dalio had been doing since his first job out of business school. What he then called "managing risk" had morphed over the subsequent decade or so into what Bridgewater now described as a "hedge portfolio." If a client owned a portfolio of European stocks, for instance, Bridgewater might put on a series of trades to minimize the impact of European-currency price changes. Assignments such as these were valuable, but only to a point. It was tough to be seen as superlative when the result of a job well done was a steady return rather than a big hit. So in addition to the hedges, Bridgewater began pitching clients on what it called overlays, or extra trades, such as buying up currencies that Dalio and Bridgewater thought were due to appreciate, or shorting, or betting against, others. Though this took Bridgewater out of the realm of strict risk reduction, Dalio would point out that he was well incentivized to be careful. Bridgewater would only be paid for these additional trades if they did well, or at least helped avoid losses, as a percentage of the overall money made or saved.

This was, in all but name, a hedge fund.

Hedge funds dated to 1949 when a middle-aged ex-communist spy and sociologist, Alfred Winslow Jones, started the first such fund with $100,000. Jones borrowed money to make additional bets, using some of the additional capital to short stocks he thought would underperform. The result was "magic," as one biographer put it; in a rising market, the longs would rise more than the shorts because the shorts were weaker companies.

The opposite was also true. When the market fell, these weaker companies would fall faster than Jones's relatively sturdy longs, so the fund's profits from its shorts would outweigh its losses from the longs. The whole ballet relied on Jones's accurately identifying the effectiveness of his stock picking, so he closely tracked in a leather notebook the performance of his picks against the overall market. If the market was up 10 percent and in the same period his longs were up 15 percent, Jones attributed the five-percentage-point difference to his skill.

This worked until it didn't, when disastrous stock picks sent Jones's fund crashing 35 percent in 1970. As he faded from prominence, so did the industry he inspired. Investment bankers and junk bond financiers took the place of hedge fund managers in the popular imagination. The industry emerged from its two-decade hibernation with a bang largely thanks to the Hungarian-born trader George Soros. In what became front-page news in 1992, Soros was credited with breaking the Bank of England with billion-dollar bets against sterling. When Soros was hauled in front of the U.S. Congress to answer for himself, the most frequently asked question he heard was "Just what is a hedge fund?"

Soros answered, "The only thing they have in common is that the managers are compensated on the basis of performance and not as a fixed percentage of assets under management."

Soros added, "Frankly, I don't think hedge funds are a matter of concern to you or the regulators."

Dalio must have known the danger of being lumped in with that sort of bravado. After his highly public busted 1982 call, the last thing he needed was a reputation as a showman. Dalio's clients were some of the most staid institutions in the corporate world. He would have to slow play the move.

As he had for going on two decades, Dalio came at it with reams of research. He announced to clients that he had gone through his thousands of investing insights and thrown out roughly nineteen out of every twenty. If he wasn't totally confident in a rule's ability to predict market moves, it wasn't worth keeping around. Dalio rebranded the resulting assemblage of finance principles his "top 5 percent" and put out an open call for investors interested in putting money with this cream of the crop.

The product flopped. "It sounded good, but after a while, I realized most of it was fluff," said Chris Streit, who was tasked with marketing it.

After all, what investment firm would advertise access to the *bottom* 5 percent of its discoveries?

Dalio tried a wonkier tack. He began talking up the concepts of alpha and beta. Beta was the return that any investor would expect to get simply from exposure to the markets. If the average bond appreciated 8 percent, then the first 8 percent earned from holding a vanilla portfolio of bonds would be considered beta. Beta was neither inherently good nor bad—it was just nothing special. Alpha, on the other hand, was the extra juice. Alpha was what a talented investment manager could earn on top of the beta return. If, in the aforementioned scenario, Bridgewater's bond portfolios rose 10 percent, then it had added an additional alpha of 2 percentage points.

Cleaving out investment performance in this manner was hardly a new revelation. It was exactly what Alfred Winslow Jones had done four decades earlier with the notebook that tracked his stock picking. But Dalio didn't just help exhume the topic, he brought it back wrapped in a shiny label, *alpha*.*

Dalio took the idea of alpha, or as he called it, "alpha overlay," to his first client, the World Bank. If he could produce genuine alpha, would the pension fund be willing to pay him a performance fee on it? Ochoa-Brillembourg turned him down. Dalio was a smart man, but from her seat, the oldest cliché on Wall Street was an investment manager who came up with exciting new products that carried a higher fee. She had seen time and again the pattern of young firms growing ever larger and then focusing on lining their own pockets. And she had noticed that for all of Dalio's grandiloquence, the trades that Bridgewater had recommended for the World Bank were essentially just bets on whether interest rates would rise or fall. Every trader on Wall Street had an opinion on that. No longer convinced that Dalio had any special edge, she pulled the bank's money from Bridgewater.

Ochoa-Brillembourg was surprised to learn that her fellow institutional investors were less skeptical. To them, paying top dollar for alpha made a lot of sense, so long as they believed that their investment manager was the best and brightest. Dalio had a head start on making that impression— after all, he had for years been sending out a daily newsletter in which he prognosticated on a dizzying variety of markets worldwide. A handful of

---

* While it is unlikely that Dalio *invented* the use of *alpha* in this context, he was unquestionably among the earliest to market it at scale.

major investors, including Kodak, staked Dalio's new idea with a cumulative $11 million—no small sum, and an endorsement of Dalio's approach.

What they put money into was a new Dalio invention, a stand-alone fund called Pure Alpha. The name had a double meaning: it clearly communicated that Bridgewater was focusing on its best ideas, or alpha, while also positioning the growing firm as the alpha, or top dog, of its peers.

Dalio insisted that unlike returns from rivals such as Soros, his alpha was not derived from one man's decision-making. It stemmed from an investment system that took precedence over all else.

PURE ALPHA was hot stuff. It produced positive investment performance from its first year, 1991. In 1993, when the stock market was up 7 percent, Pure Alpha shot up 32 percent, before fees; in 1996, it was up 34 percent, while the market gained 20 percent. Importantly, while some years Pure Alpha beat a standard mix of stocks, bonds, and other assets and some years it didn't, what it almost never did was lose money outright. It was remarkably reliable, making it attractive to investors who didn't want to risk losing their shirts.

New funds poured in, doubling Pure Alpha's coffers roughly every year for nearly a decade to almost $3 billion by 1999. Some of the new investors were intermediaries, wealth managers tasked with finding the best money managers for their clients. Bridgewater was so in demand that Dalio instructed staff to turn away money from so-called funds of funds, or organizations that pooled money from small investors to farm out as a group. Too down-market, he told others at Bridgewater. Instead, Bridgewater took in money from the big institutional investors like the ones Dalio had long courted, including entities from as far away as Australia and Japan. The chief investment officer of Singapore's biggest sovereign wealth fund became an acolyte. "Making money on a constant basis is the Holy Grail, and Ray and Bridgewater have done that," he later said.

That language wasn't an overstatement, inasmuch as Dalio did often say he had discovered what he termed the "Holy Grail of investing." The grail was a twist on an old Wall Street maxim: the importance of diversification. Whereas Soros made his name—and a fortune—taking a big swing against the Bank of England, Dalio saw Bridgewater as a singles hitter. In its first decade, Pure Alpha performed better than the Standard & Poor's 500, a broad basket of U.S. stocks, only half the time. But Dalio was able to say, with considerable truth, that his fund's performance came at lower risk because it so infrequently lost money. Whatever the annual performance, investors could be assured that the trading was due to Bridgewater's systematized sets of rules, rather than any singular trade or prediction from the founder.

"Compared to a lot of other hedge fund managers, he took a very disciplined approach," said the famed contrarian investor Marc Faber, who met with Dalio frequently during the era.

Dalio highlighted the firm's emphasis on sussing out diverse bets. "A lot of people think the most important thing you could do is find the best investments. That's important, but there is no great one best investment that can compete with something like this," Dalio would say, referring to the grail. "The magic is, you only need to do this simple thing. The simple thing is to find fifteen or twenty good, uncorrelated return streams, things that are probably going to make money—you don't know, but they have a good probability of making money—that are uncorrelated."

Another advantage of this spread-the-seed approach was that it rendered Dalio's view-from-the-top macroeconomic pronouncements somewhat beside the point.

Amid Pure Alpha's extraordinary growth, the Bridgewater founder continued to give frequent media interviews in which he identified imminent market crashes that rarely happened. Dalio predicted a bear market coming in 1994; a "blow-off phase of the U.S. stock market" in 1995; "bombs away" for the Dow Jones Industrial Average in 1997; and a "deflationary implosion" for 1998. Each time, he explained away the misfires as a learning opportunity—Bridgewater was a place where mistakes were encouraged because they allowed the firm to add more data points to its outlook and further refine its investing rules. As long as the wrong calls didn't dribble down into Bridgewater's client accounts—and by and large they didn't—they attracted important attention to a growing firm. Fifteen years after his off-base testimony before Congress, Dalio was again on call for policy makers. Economic advisers to President Clinton asked to be added to Bridgewater's research-distribution list. Clinton administration treasury secretary Larry Summers called Dalio for private advice.

If the specifics of Dalio's big-picture calls weren't making money for Bridgewater, what was it? The answer was a bit of good management, and a bit of good fortune. True to his word, Dalio wasn't the end-all decision maker on Bridgewater investments. He relied on rigorous research into what he termed "signals," or quantitative indicators that a market was due to rise or fall. If the signals pointed to trouble ahead, or even to uncertainty, Bridgewater would buy or sell assets accordingly—even if Dalio's own gut might have told him otherwise. Thus while what Dalio pronounced publicly may have been true of his feelings in the moment, those views didn't necessarily translate to Bridgewater's portfolio. To employ such an automated, systematic approach was, for the era, genuinely original.*

Another moneymaker for Bridgewater was Bob Prince. Dalio had delegated the lion's share of research on bonds, or fixed income, to his longtime colleague. Prince made bonds, particularly U.S. Treasuries, considered the safest of all, a mainstay of Bridgewater's client accounts. The move proved prescient and profitable. Treasuries went on a long streak of strong performance, up double digits some years, including in 2000, when the stock market dragged badly and busted currency bets weighed on the rest of the Bridgewater portfolio.

For his work on bonds, Prince became first among equals among the Bridgewater investment staff. Little by little, Prince told friends and colleagues, Dalio began lending Prince money to buy equity in Bridgewater itself, making Prince a minority owner. (Bridgewater said these loans were arranged by the firm, rather than Dalio personally, though given his overwhelming ownership stake and management control of the firm, the distinction was somewhat without a difference.) The gift turned out to be particularly valuable in the aftermath of the dot-com bubble burst, when Dalio earned media acclaim for predicting it (few reporters noted that he had made the same call virtually every year). To Bridgewater's credit, Pure Alpha lost just 1 percent in 2000 (when U.S. stocks were down double digits on average) and gained 9 percent in 2001, another ugly, down year for stocks overall. His well-deserved recognition grew. Money continued to pour into Bridgewater from clients new and old, and the firm swelled from roughly one hundred employees in 2001 to almost double that two years later.

Hence, Dalio became ever more wealthy just as many of the nouveaux riches of the first internet era were losing their shirts.

As he mulled over what to do with the abundance, he asked those around him to help come up with another new product that involved only

---

* A lawyer for Dalio said, "Over time, Mr. Dalio has said many things that were consistent with how Bridgewater systems were positioning the firm."

the deepest, most easily tradable markets and could handle the huge paychecks now coming his way. The team came up with what Dalio called a "postmodernist approach to portfolio theory." It was designed to stay steady, without active intervention, through various periods of growth and inflation—essentially through all possible economic conditions. Dalio branded it the All-Weather portfolio because it could steer an investor through rough seas.*

Unlike Pure Alpha, which could bet in virtually any market worldwide, All-Weather was basically a whole lot of bonds. The asset mix was 13 percent equities and 87 percent fixed income. It also used generous leverage. All-Weather juiced its returns on relatively low-yielding fixed income by borrowing money to boost the bets. This move was straight out of Dalio's Holy Grail, as well as the work of Prince's former Tulsa professor Richard Burgess. The leverage was theoretically safe so long as it was only used in low-risk investments.

All-Weather contained a great deal of something else that Dalio had long talked about avoiding: beta. The fund's returns came from whether the markets in which it invested went up or down, not from any specialized trading talent of Bridgewater's. Bridgewater bought or sold investments only to keep the proportion of various assets roughly in line (for instance, if bonds appreciated, the firm would sell some, to prevent them from becoming a disproportionately large part of the portfolio). Clients, having been drilled for years by Dalio himself on the importance of seeking alpha, were nearly universally uninterested; it fell to Prince to convince Britt Harris, a friend who ran the Verizon Investment Management pension fund, to stake the new fund with $200 million.

Dalio went considerably bigger. He said he put virtually his entire life savings into the All-Weather fund.

JUST HOW much that might be wasn't well-known outside some of those in his tight circle in Westport. Unlike mutual funds and other widely held investment vehicles, hedge funds such as Bridgewater weren't required to publicly report their size or performance—and few hedge funds volunteered the information.

The mystery added to the industry's allure, and a cottage industry of

---

* A lawyer for Dalio said, "All-Weather was not built with the goal of attracting client money."

trade publications sprang up to attempt to figure out just how rich these traders had become. In 2003, Dalio made his public debut on *Institutional Investor's* Rich List, a ranking of the wealthiest hedge fund managers. He came in at number fifteen with an estimated $110 million in personal earnings that year, largely thanks to the performance fees he earned from Pure Alpha. The next year was even better; Dalio made $225 million, just two spots down from his friend Paul Tudor Jones, who had been so dismissive of Dalio's investment system.

Yet, Dalio made a point of emphasizing that he wasn't in it for the money. He was fascinated by the beauty and sophistication of nature. For fun, he traveled to Canada on fishing expeditions and bowhunted two-thousand-pound Cape buffalo and wild boars. He snowboarded in Vermont. Bridgewater had moved into a new headquarters, an unmarked, custom-built campus made up of glass and midcentury fieldstone buildings and tucked into the woods next to the Saugatuck River in Westport, Connecticut. It didn't look like much, and that's how Dalio said he liked it. He said he hated flashy cars and mansions, such as the thirty-thousand-square-foot homes built over onetime country cottages in his new hometown of Greenwich.

"Yuck," he once told an interviewer. "Why not flash diamonds, too?"

Publicly, Dalio professed to seek a higher ground above the brute accumulation of wealth. The money was simply the proof for what would become a crucial logic chain: Bridgewater's investment rules had helped produce Dalio's wealth, thus following those rules could be said to lead to wealth. Those investment rules were culled from Bridgewater's economic research, which Dalio credited to his tendency to back-test, challenge, and amend as needed. Thus the money proved to Dalio that his philosophical approach worked. One could not exist without the other.

Like technology titans who clothed themselves in a higher purpose than merely slinging online goods or apps, Dalio's life work began to seem more important than the running of an investment firm. He poured himself anew into Bridgewater's economic research papers, but now seemed less interested in the puzzle of the markets than in the patterns of thinking they exposed. He was consumed by the idea of boiling down complex problems into singular answers. "Maturity is the ability to reject good alternatives," he would often tell Prince. "If you chase them all, you never have enough critical mass to really wrestle any one of them to the ground."

When the editor of the Bridgewater newsletter brought him the daily drafts to peruse, Dalio would ask him to set aside the papers as he dictated new notes. "What is our philosophy? What are our core values?" Dalio would ask. After a few talks with Dalio, the newsletter editor eventually came up with five or so pages of Dalio's philosophy that boiled down to prizing the ability to argue with one another without fear of offense. The document ran five or so pages—plenty, the editor figured, to make that overarching point.

Dalio spoke frequently about stepping back from day-to-day management of Bridgewater as soon as possible. By year-end 2005, he announced, he hoped to end virtually all of his management roles and to resign as president of the firm.

Prince considered himself more a peer than a successor—he wasn't interested in taking over—but he, too, was a believer in Dalio's approach. "At first, I figured he was the way he was because he is Italian, and that all of this open and direct stuff was just a rationalization of his personality," Prince told colleagues. "But over time I understood the merit of the argument and I believe it to be essential to success."

In training documents handed out to incoming Bridgewater hires, both men compared working at the firm to serving in the military. Dalio would tell new hires, "Imagine, in the midst of war, that there is a general who seeks the opinions of his lieutenants about the battle ahead, but also has to discuss whether his delivery style is 'appropriate.' Now it is the same general who wants opinions about his leadership in past battles from his lieutenants. Imagine how discouraging it would be to the lieutenants if, rather than responding to the content of their criticism, the general complained about their delivery styles."

Prince delivered a similar rejoinder to Bridgewater recruits: "In war, the enemy, the ally, and the consequences are clear. Imagine if you asked a fellow soldier to cover you while you charged the enemy, but then he forgot. Bullets are whistling past your head as you dive back into the foxhole. Do you craft a carefully worded inquiry as to why he didn't cover you? . . . Of course not. You tell them straight and direct. And that is what they would want from you. We really can't be any different if we are going to achieve what we are capable of and survive in this battle where everyone else fails."

There would be many battles to come.

5

ROOT CAUSE

TAP. TWITCH. TAP. TWITCH. TAP. TWITCH.

As the distant taps grew closer, Britt Harris struggled to keep himself from breaking. Each sound seemed to cause an involuntary reaction. Harris's pulse quickened, his face flushed, and beads of sweat began to drop from his forehead onto the mess of papers assembled in front of him.

Stout, bald and forty-six years old, Harris was supposed to be at the top of his career. The son of a Baptist preacher and a religious man himself, with a well-worn Bible in his office, he thought he'd arrived. He was supposed to be running this place. Instead he was a puddle.

After what felt like an eternity, the taps reached the door. The hinge creaked open and Ray Dalio awkwardly sidled into the room, his lower body clanking in a loud cast, courtesy of a hip injury he told underlings was incurred crossing a river a few weeks earlier on vacation in Mexico. Dalio slid out a chair, crashed into it, and gestured to Harris.

"I'm just here to watch," Dalio said.

Hiring Harris as CEO had been Dalio's idea. Bridgewater was officially a behemoth: $55 billion in assets under management in 2003 had nearly doubled to $101 billion just one year later. Dalio could no longer run the firm by himself while staying on top of the markets. He didn't look far for help. Harris was a close friend of Bob Prince's, and a major client, running Verizon Investment Management, the second-largest corporate pension fund in the United States. He had been the only one willing to put retirees' money in Bridgewater's fledgling All-Weather when so many others had passed. What better sign of wisdom could there be? "We at Bridgewater Associates have worked with Britt for many years and developed an enormous amount of respect for his abilities," Dalio said publicly as he announced the hire.

A different message awaited Harris when he showed up for work at Bridgewater in late 2004. Dalio told him on one of his first days, "You're not the CEO."

Not functionally, at least. Dalio remained president, chief investment officer, and head of the firm's powerful management committee—with veto-proof control over major decisions at the hedge fund. Harris could be part of meetings, but he'd have to work his way toward the levers of power—to "find his box," as Dalio put it. Dalio started Harris close to the bottom in client services, overseeing the marketing department. This wasn't much of a gig. The firm had a rule forbidding anyone besides Dalio from talking to the press. Bridgewater had neither need nor want for extensive advertising.

For clients, perhaps the most effective point of contact was Dalio himself. He was proving masterful with the world's wealthy. He told one Bridgewater executive that he'd recently cozied up to the head of Abu Dhabi's sovereign wealth fund, taking him on hunting trips to New England and helping him pick out suits on London's Savile Row. Billions of dollars in investments flowed in. This was part of Dalio's near-constant crisscrossing of the globe, from California, where the largest public-employee retirement system in the United States became a Bridgewater client, to Norway, Sweden, and the Netherlands, with their giant government-affiliated funds. The average account size swelled to nearly $400 million. Pure Alpha, the flagship fund, became a scarce good. Dalio continued to periodically open and then close it to new investment, saying the fund couldn't possibly handle more money, a sales strategy that also made it seem like a more attractive scarce good. Clients who wanted to put more money with the firm were told Pure Alpha was closed but All-Weather was open.

Harris gave the marketing gig an honest try. As he started around the New Year, he tried a fairly vanilla idea he'd employed at Verizon. He asked everyone in client services to contribute to a strategic report on what needed to be improved in the months to come. Two weeks later, the report was completed, and Harris ordered a celebratory barbecue meal for the team as they went over the findings. Everything seemed to be going smoothly.

So Harris was shocked when he opened his BlackBerry to an email from a junior employee, Charles Korchinski, someone Harris wasn't even sure he had ever formally met. The email copied in Bridgewater's entire management team, including Dalio. "Some feedback," Korchinski began.

It was great that they got ribs for lunch, he said, but the entire exercise had been rudderless. The team was hardly into the New Year and half of them were already burned-out. Some had pulled all-nighters to rush out the report and to reformat the pages to suit Harris. None of them knew the point of this exercise—and anyway, shouldn't they spend time asking clients for their thoughts, not each other? The floodgates opened. Others on the team chimed in, too, with their own complaints. Dalio went to see Harris.

"What do you have to say about that, Britt?"

What Britt had to say, he confided to a colleague, voice rising, was "Who the hell is Charles Korchinski?"

Harris had no way of knowing it, but he was starring in the origin story of what some at Bridgewater would call the "MC cycle." A newcomer would be hired with fanfare into the firm's management committee (MC) to what seemed to be a lofty role. Within the first few days, the person would usually be asked to complete a basic assignment outside their usual expertise. After a suitable period of failure, Dalio would publicly question the person on their shortcomings (this step might repeat several times). Sooner or later, the new hire would likely depart, and the next new member of the management committee would be introduced. Inside the hedge fund, Dalio described this process as natural—and a way to weed out the unworthy from Bridgewater. He was applying his approach to investing rules—testing what worked, and throwing out what didn't—to human resources.

The MC cycle did not take long to run its course with Britt Harris. Just a few weeks after starting at Bridgewater, he fell ill and began a series of extended absences from the office. For several weeks, he did not sleep for a single night, a period that he later described as "hell on Earth." On the days he did show up, he was pallid, often nonverbal, broken, mirroring the plant in his office, which was slowly turning brown from lack of attention. Bridgewater staff began taking bets on who would survive longer, the plant or the boss.

Similar thoughts crossed Harris's mind. His father had died at fifty-three, and Harris told colleagues he feared he might be on an even faster path. Less than half a year after his start, the CEO of Bridgewater Associates quit. "In classic total transparency," Harris recalled, "Ray asked me to address the entire population of Bridgewater before I departed . . . a few minutes that I will never forget. Nothing could have been more difficult for a man in that condition." Years later, Harris would say that his breakdown was connected to factors other than his work. He said that apart from his wife, no one was more supportive than Dalio, concluding that the Bridgewater founder's final order to him was "an act of ignorance combined with a devotion to transparency which went too far."

Publicly, Dalio released a statement that read: "After six months of reflection, Britt decided it wasn't for him."

Harris went directly from Westport into intensive treatment for depression.

HAVING MASTERED, in his view, how to build a set of investment rules, Dalio set out to do the same for management.

As Dalio told those around him, he had learned two quick lessons from the Britt Harris experiment. One was that the Bridgewater management system largely worked. The hedge fund had ingested, and spat out, an unsuitable hire. The second lesson was that Bridgewater needed to do a better job bringing in the right people and getting them up to speed quickly. For the latter task, he assigned the up-and-coming executive Katina Stefanova to devise a training program for the hundreds of new hires.

Beginning in 2006, Stefanova drilled each incoming class to model their behavior after the firm founder's. Just as Dalio had painstakingly culled his hundreds of investment rules into the top 5 percent, so, too, should Bridgewater employees take a critical eye to how the firm was run. She summed up the Bridgewater mentality with one of Dalio's oft-used phrases: "Taste the soup." All employees ought to imagine themselves as a chef responsible for the food coming out of the kitchen. "A good manager needs to do the same," Dalio would say. When employees identified imperfections, they were directed to memorialize the moment in the "issue log," an internal registry visible to all that tracked all complaints large and small.

Though people entering their quibbles into the issue log were asked to grade them on a one-to-five scale of severity, the practical effect was that any issue was a problem, and all problems needed solving. "No one has the right to hold back a critical opinion without speaking up about it," Stefanova told newcomers, borrowing another of Dalio's phrases. "Don't tolerate badness."

So as Bridgewater got bigger, the firm began to focus on problems that were ever smaller.

Employees would check the issue log constantly, eager to see who and what in the organization were being exposed. Each entry in the log identified the complainant as well as the offender or, as Dalio called it, "the responsible party" (RP). The best way to get the attention of peers was to pile on new complaints about an existing RP.

Once the RP was identified, the next step was to investigate the "root cause." Dalio often cited the hypothetical example of a person who missed a train departure. The proximate reason for the error might have been that the person didn't check the train timetables; the root cause was that the person was forgetful. Dalio had little patience for the idea that mistakes by Bridgewater staff could simply be momentary misjudgments. Each mistake was nothing less than a referendum on the person who made it.

The issue logs flourished. Dalio added a requirement that each person at the firm log a minimum number of issues per week (ten or twenty at various points) or have his or her bonus docked. If something went wrong and hadn't previously been exposed in the issues log, all those aware of the incident who should have filed about it earlier would be punished with low review scores.

An employee was said to have left the office bathroom to discover that he had been logged by a bystander for failing to wash his hands. He had to answer for the root cause of his decision.

Another new Bridgewater associate, not long out of Harvard College, logged about wilted peas at the cafeteria salad bar. Dalio saw the post and pressed the hedge fund's new chief operating officer on what she was doing about the matter. She responded, "This is ridiculous. I shouldn't be spending my time on this." Dalio disagreed, saying there was no such thing as a small problem at Bridgewater.

It escaped few at Bridgewater that shortly thereafter the peas were pristine.

Not just junior staff were raising complaints. Prince logged complaints and sometimes went beyond that. One early evening, past the popular hours for caffeine consumption, he fired off an all-staff email:

From: Bob Prince
Sent: Wednesday, June 07, 2006 5:23 PM
To: Bridgewater

Subject: The coffee pot

About 1 in 4 times that I get a cup of coffee the pot is empty. When that happens, I take a minute and fill the pot. Given that a coffee pot holds about 36 cups, I should only confront an empty coffee pot about 1 time in 36. If I am a light coffee drinker (I am) my odds should be even lower. What must be happening is that many other people are confronting the same empty pot before me and leaving it empty for someone else to fill. . . .

It is just a matter of doing the right thing with no associated punishment or reward. The same principle applies to many things inside and outside of work, of course.

There weren't many complaints about the coffee after that.

PRINCE'S PRINCIPLE didn't stand alone for long.

As word spread that Dalio was regularly checking the issue log, a problem of scarcity emerged. Beyond that there were only so many complaints to be made about the cafeteria, the firm's most important, heavily attended meetings began to raise the risk of multiple individuals logging the same issue. This diluted the potential that any one complainant might earn the credit for the flag. The remedy was to inspect one's closest coworkers at times when nobody else was. A newly promoted Bridgewater manager took this approach to the extreme. Her job included supervising the secretaries, and she began listening in on their calls and taking notes on their absences from their desks. One by one, the secretaries began to quit. As their desks grew empty, the issue log filled up with cries to find the RP. Several layers of managers began investigating their subordinates to determine who was responsible for the turmoil belowdecks.

Dalio saw the logs and interviewed the new manager, writing out notes as the woman spoke. By the end, Dalio had diagnosed the apparent problem. It was himself. He hadn't been clear enough about his framework. What it came down to, he said, were principles. His investing principles were plainly working. Those related to management and office culture needed work. He sent an email to the firm with some initial ideas.

The email was, charitably, a mess. Dalio had copied various emails from subordinates complaining about one another and pasted them into a Microsoft Word document. Various lines were enlarged or shrunken, all in different formatting and colors. Dalio interspersed his own commentary throughout, mostly in incomplete sentences. Most at Bridgewater ignored Dalio's email. Prince told a colleague these were "Ray's principles"—one man's opinion, not much else.

Dalio didn't let up. Now in his late fifties, he reflected on his life to that point and wrote to the firm, "So what is success? It's nothing more than getting what you want."

Dalio sought something that must have seemed so proximate, yet was exasperatingly hard to achieve. If only everyone around him would act as he would act. But, as he often told underlings, it irked him that every time he looked in one direction, a bug seemed to buzz by the other ear. People just couldn't be trusted to do the right thing.

The issue log was useful, but it wasn't the complete answer. It inherently looked backward, reporting what had already become problems. Bridgewater needed a rule book for how to behave in the moment, to prevent suboptimal behavior. Dalio began circulating drafts of ideas.

"So, I believe there is an incredible beauty in mistakes because embedded in each mistake is a puzzle and treasures to be had if you solve the puzzle. If you recognize that each mistake is probably a reflection of something you or others don't understand about how to interact with the world as it is, and you figure out what that is, you will gain one or more gems, or what I call principles," Dalio wrote to the firm's staff.

These principles became The Principles, two words that over the next decade would become synonymous with Dalio and Bridgewater worldwide. The work on this new list animated Dalio. He came up with some slowly, and others all at once. He took time out of his day to come up with new ones, and new Bridgewater hires worked with him on them. The Principles grew from roughly ten to dozens, then more than two hundred, some a paragraph or longer apiece. They promised nothing less than self-improvement, achieved through a rigorous course of fighting one's suboptimal instincts.

MANY AT Bridgewater loved The Principles, which to some seemed like the natural extension of Dalio's rules-based investment system, now applied outside of mere money management. Everyone would now have a chance to absorb some of Dalio's successes, and to model themselves after the luminary in their midst. It bothered few that an animating doctrine of The Principles was that conflict was the key to achievement. It made a certain natural sense, especially at an investment firm where a wrong investment idea could cost money, that some of life's maladies could be avoided by hashing out disagreements, to reach the best possible answers. As Dalio put it in an early version of The Principles, "Bridgewater people have to value getting at truth so badly that they are willing to humiliate themselves to get it."

Dalio said, "I know I'm pretty extreme in these beliefs. For example, as a hyperrealist, I have a non-traditional sense of good and bad. I believe that being good means operating consistently with natural laws."

The theme of nature's order ran throughout The Principles. Dalio included in a draft version a quote erroneously attributed to Darwin: "It is not the strongest of the species that survives, nor the most intelligent that survives. It is the one that is the most adaptable to change." Dalio went on:

> For example, when a pack of hyenas takes down a young wildebeest, is that good or evil? At face value, that might not be "good" because it seems cruel, and the poor wildebeest suffers and dies. Some people might even say that the hyenas are evil. Yet this type of apparently "cruel" behavior exists throughout the animal kingdom. Like death itself it is integral to the enormously complex and efficient system that has worked for as long as there has been life. . . .
>
> Supposedly, if you throw a frog into a pot of boiling water it will immediately jump out. But if you put a frog in room temperature water and gradually bring it to a boil, the frog will stay in the pot and boil to death, reflecting the principle that gradual changes are much less likely to be perceived than abrupt changes.
>
> Never say anything about a person you wouldn't say to him directly. If you do, you're a slimy weasel.

And then a footnote:

> Pain can be just as rewarding as pleasure, though by definition it is less enjoyable.

The Principles contained their own lexicon. Dalio called them "our common language." To the outsider, they would appear nearly impenetrable. There was "tasting the soup," or breaking down an assignment into its component parts. To "double-do" was to have two people perform the same task. If problems arose, a manager was expected to "diagnose" the likely reason and then "probe" subordinates to find the root cause. After the probing, those unsuited for their roles were said to "lose their box" and enter a period of limbo in which they were expected to find a new job inside the organization. If successful, the journey ended in "getting through to the other side." If not, the employee would be "sorted," or fired.

Much of The Principles imposed doctrine for how to decide whom to sort and into which boxes.

> We definitely do not want people who value making money above all else to work at Bridgewater because we believe that doing so is inconsistent with the total enrichment (i.e., including all forms of rewards) of the people who work at Bridgewater, Bridgewater as a company, our clients, and our industry. . . .
>
> Not all opinions are equally valuable so don't treat them as such. Almost everyone has an opinion, but they're not all equally valuable. Many are worthless or even harmful. So it is not logical to treat them as equally valuable. For example, the views of people without any track records or experience are not equal to the views of people with great track records and experience.
>
> A drilldown is the process by which you and your group gain a deep enough understanding of the problems in an area. . . . Drilling down is a form of probing, though it is broader and deeper. Done well, it should get you almost all of the information needed in about five hours of effort. . . .
>
> The most important qualities for successfully diagnosing problems are logic and the willingness to overcome ego barriers (in oneself and others) to get at truth.

Some more, including footnotes:

> Having truth on your side is so extremely powerful in so many ways that I believe it is better to have blind faith in it rather than being expedient about when to use it.
>
> Constantly get in sync: getting in sync is the process of fighting for truth. . . . Don't believe it when someone caught being dishonest says they have seen the light and will never do that sort of thing again. Chances are they will.
>
> With their increased usage, not only will they be understood, but they will evolve from "Ray's principles" to "our principles," and Ray will fade out of the picture.

Throughout 2006 and 2007, Dalio solicited feedback from others at Bridgewater on his findings and came back satisfied. "There has been virtually no disagreement on the validity of these principles by people who have probed them," he later announced. "It should go without saying that you should feel free to challenge everything I say."

Few did, not in any substantive way, according to generations of Bridgewater staff. To question The Principles was not just to question Dalio ideas, but the very case for his success. Dalio credited the guidelines as the building blocks to Bridgewater's investing machine, and who was to say they weren't? Although even some of his closest colleagues would privately say that individual Principles seemed a bit wacky, in total they seemed sensible when viewed as part of an overall path to personal growth. And The Principles spored so slowly that no one could identify a singular moment when they turned extreme.

Before long, Bridgewater roughly split into those who viewed The Principles as an interesting philosophical discourse, and those who considered them canon. Among the former were most of the firm's investment staff, for whom the new rule book had little impact on their day-to-day lives. The Principles didn't tell them which world economies would outperform others, or how to trade currencies. It might have encouraged them to debate one another, but an unprofitable investment couldn't be made otherwise through The Principles.

For others at Bridgewater, particularly those without clear responsibility for the firm's day-to-day trading gains or losses, The Principles were gospel. They memorized The Principles and quoted from specific lines without notes. They codified the language, constantly talking about the need to "get in sync" with one another. They came to be known by others by a name: The Principalians.

Everyone at Bridgewater could name the Chief Principalian, for he seemed to carry a spiral notebook of The Principles everywhere he went.

6

THE BIG ONE

GREG JENSEN WAS DALIO'S GOLDEN BOY. BY MID-2007, HE WAS WIDELY seen as the Bridgewater founder's next-in-line.

Befitting his station, Jensen's background was as inauspicious as his mentor's. He grew up in upstate New York in Niskayuna, an unabashedly middle-class suburb of Schenectady, near the state capital of Albany. Even as a youngster, Jensen had heavy, dark eyebrows that prematurely aged his square face. He was the sort of reserved high school student who didn't leave much of an impression—neither a loner nor a varsity star. He had a girlfriend and an awkward tendency to crack inside jokes that fell flat outside his modest circle of friends. In his senior yearbook, he was listed under "Pictures Not Available."

Niskayuna High School was hardly a feeder for the Ivy League, but Jensen scored high in a slew of advanced-placement classes and was accepted to Dartmouth. He excelled in a rigorous major of economics and applied mathematics. He also bloomed socially.

Jensen joined a fraternity, Zeta Psi, and lived in its redbrick, white-columned house on Dartmouth's fraternity row. Zete, as it was known, was a place that took in the nice guys, though that wasn't where its reputation ended. During Jensen's sophomore year, during the rush season when new undergraduates try out various Greek organizations, an anonymous group of student crusaders spread across campus to pin up posters with each fraternity's reputation. One poster read, "Rush Zete, where we don't let our drunken womanizing interfere with our sensitive guy image, or vice versa."

Jensen was elected fraternity president. Most evenings he could be found in Zete's basement, where a Ping-Pong table—sometimes two—perched on plastic garbage cans for legs. A drain in the floor let out the dregs of Budweiser and Milwaukee's Best, the fraternity's preferred brews. In addition to formal duties such as fixing the front door and replacing the kegerator, he acted as an unofficial social captain. Not infrequently, a brother would file downstairs to the basement to find Jensen holding forth with a small group. If the newcomer begged off an invitation to join, Jensen would offer to chug a beer with him to catch him up.

Unlike some of his Zete brothers, Jensen limited his friendships to the fraternity, and people who knew him then recalled that he could be short with members who developed interests outside the fraternity. During his senior year, he became close with the newer pledges, several years his junior. This us-versus-them mentality would later serve him well at Bridgewater.

Jensen faced an early leadership test when one Zete announced he was gay and that he planned to hang a rainbow flag out his window. About half the fraternity thought the flag should fly, reasoning that they ought to prioritize their brother's wishes. Jensen disagreed. The rainbow flag was damaging to their institution, he told his brothers. He had no objections to inducting a gay fraternity brother, but he didn't want to be seen as a member of a gay frat. The flag never went up.

Several of Jensen's fraternity brothers went to work for Bridgewater after graduating, so his following them there as an intern was no surprise. He started in the frenetic trading division, which had only marginally matured since Prince's time there in the company's early days. It could be a struggle just to complete the trades, as there were more and more client accounts to service. Before the end of the summer, the intern was upbraiding his senior colleagues. "You have to be like McDonald's—be prepared at any time for any order to come in," he once said. Jensen's willingness to speak up impressed Dalio, and he was hired full-time.

Dalio took to the young Jensen, and perhaps he filled a void in Dalio's life. Though Ray and Barbara had four sons, none showed signs of sharing their father's interest in finance. Dalio's eldest, Devon, was a natural athlete and accomplished amateur Ping-Pong player in his youth. In a story he later told to a Bridgewater employee that was widely retold inside the firm, Dalio once invited the teenage Devon to play Ping-Pong at a party with his father and his friends. The youngest person there by a generation, Devon made easy work of the competition. Then Dalio offered him a bet: play another game for $5 stakes. When Devon won that one, Dalio challenged him to double or nothing, $10 for the next game. This was followed by a $20 challenge, then a $40 one, and so forth. After dozens of games, an apparently exhausted Devon finally lost. Devon cried, in front of his father and his friends, but, as the story went, Dalio would not let his son play another game to make it up. It was a lesson on the value of money, Dalio said.

The other Dalio sons were an eclectic bunch. One, Matt, was sent to live with a family friend in China for a year at age eleven. Another, Mark, was more interested in environmental science than investing. Another son, Paul, was bipolar, manic-depressive, and spent years in treatment. The Dalio family later helped fund a movie, written and directed by Paul and starring Katie Holmes, based on his experience. While speaking to an audience before a screening in Connecticut, Paul Dalio offered an anecdote from his childhood: On Christmas mornings, when the Dalio sons gave their father a gift, the Bridgewater founder would tell them immediately whether it was a good or bad choice. If bad, Dalio would detail why it was off base.

Greg Jensen would essentially become Dalio's fifth son, in addition to his formal role as the hedge fund's head of research, the top investment deputy to the Bridgewater founder.

Jensen soon took responsibility for smoothing out the boss's rough edges. After meetings, he would translate for newer employees what Dalio meant when he gave instructions and coach them on how to use Dalio's favorite phrases. In 2006, Dalio took Jensen along on an important business trip to Beijing, to introduce him to some of Bridgewater's most valued clients. Dalio gave Jensen a copy of one of Dalio's favorite books, *The Hero with a Thousand Faces,* by the late American professor Joseph Campbell. Dalio told Jensen that they were both on journeys similar to those of the heroes studied by Campbell—ones filled with trials, battles, temptations, success, and failure.

The younger man was soon promoted to Bridgewater's management committee.

Jensen was one of the first at Bridgewater to apply the strict instructions of The Principles to his work. As head of research, he'd noticed a steady decline in the quality of the hedge fund's daily economics note—the same one that had helped Dalio impress clients and the media so many years earlier. The insights were stale, and drafts often arrived late from the research analysts tasked with compiling them. The solution, Jensen announced, was found in The Principles. Borrowing a phrase from Dalio's manifesto, he conducted loud "drill down" interviews of everyone in the trading department. He came up with ideas such as a button at every desk, meant to be pressed by staff when they detected a mistake, to better track when errors were made in trading or in the writing of the *Daily Observations*. At any other firm, this might have been viewed as the ordinary work of a manager helping smooth out problems on his team. Jensen, however, would not hear of accepting credit personally. He told colleagues that credit belonged to Dalio and The Principles.

It wasn't just Jensen's department that needed help. After its monster start to the new millennium, Pure Alpha was barely bobbing in the green in 2005 and 2006. Dalio was, as ever, somber on what lay ahead. He told clients that the firm's internal crisis indicator, a measure of threats to the economy, was near a record high. Americans were taking on too much debt, particularly to buy homes. He recommended shifting money out of stocks and stockpiling gold. He saw established Western economies, particularly in Europe, on the decline, and thus he pressed shorts against the euro in 2005 and 2006.

One area he did like was emerging markets, where he saw China and India on the rise. Those growing economies would create new demand for oil—Dalio compared the situation to sucking strongly on a straw that had no more room to give—and he predicted oil prices would shoot up to over $100 a barrel by late 2006. In fact, the euro was up 11 percent in 2006, and its performance was exceeded by that of the Dow Jones Industrial Average. Oil was flat that year, and so was Pure Alpha. It seemed that Bridgewater's investment machine was not infallible.

The Bridgewater founder's persistent pessimism became a source of ribbing among the Bridgewater ranks. Parag Shah, the firm's head of marketing, opened one meeting with a too-close-for-comfort joke. "He's called fifteen of the last zero recessions," Shah said of his boss.

Dalio didn't laugh.

The dry run was somewhat awkwardly timed, coming as it did after Bridgewater had raised so much new money. The firm grew from $33 billion under management in 2001 to $167 billion in 2005. Yet because Bridgewater collected a roughly 2 percent annual fee on the assets it managed, regardless of investment performance, the firm's top brass received progressively higher paydays as the fund's coffers expanded.

In 2006 alone, Dalio personally earned $350 million. This was noteworthy enough that in May of the following year, Bridgewater's office line rang with a call from *New York Times* reporter David Leonhardt. The reporter had never before spoken to Dalio, but now had some questions for the man who was making so much for himself, if not quite so much percentagewise for his clients. The call was passed through various intermediaries until it eventually reached Dalio.

As Shah listened in close by, Dalio explained to Leonhardt that he must be misunderstanding the firm's investment strategy. Bridgewater wasn't about shooting the lights out year after year: "When we have a bad year, we're essentially flat. And when we have a good year, we have a great year."

Makes sense, the reporter replied. He asked with whom was he speaking.

Dalio paused a beat. "My name is Parag Shah."

Another pause, as Dalio listened to the follow-up question.

"Oh. What is my title?"

Shah's heart rate spiked. He knew that Dalio had no clue of the answer. At Bridgewater, roles and titles changed often. Shah fumbled for a pad and scribbled down the answer: head of marketing. He passed the note to Dalio.

Dalio quickly shook his head. Too puny. "A Bridgewater executive," Dalio told the reporter.

The article, published the following day under the headline "Worth a Lot, but Are Hedge Funds Worth It?," was a broad overview of the hedge fund industry. Bridgewater wasn't a focus, but halfway down, Leonhardt did include the following quote:

"'When we have a bad year, we're essentially flat,' Parag Shah, a Bridgewater executive, told me. 'And when we have a good year, we have a great year.'"

AFTER NOT speaking to *The New York Times*, Shah found himself under fire for speaking to *The New York Times*. Almost immediately after the article went live, Shah noticed that a colleague had added a new entry to the Bridgewater issue log, flagging Shah for breaking company policy on not speaking to the media. Shah didn't know whether to tell the truth. If he admitted it was Dalio who gave a false name to the reporter, Shah would implicitly be accusing the Bridgewater founder of violating The Principles' rules on lying. Shah reasoned it was better to take his lumps.

There were plenty of other distractions. It was May 2007, and home prices were in a tumble. Real estate agents in formerly hot property markets were reporting that they suddenly couldn't close deals. Some market watchers were predicting calamity ahead.

Amid the gathering economic clouds, just five days after the *Times* interview, Dalio spoke to another reporter, from the financial periodical *Barron's*. This time, he used his own name.

The interviewer asked if the public should be worried about the weakness in real estate.

"I don't think of them as warning signs," Dalio said. He called it "a little hiccup related to the subprime-lending problems." He still believed investors, particularly from China, would continue to bid asset prices up and keep the market humming. He was riffing on a Wall Street adage, that there were greater fools out there, ever willing to buy someone out at a higher price.

The interviewer asked, "Do you see any risk of a U.S. recession?"

"No, not now. There is plenty of money washing around." Dalio continued, "Everybody is flush with liquidity and it would be shocking to me if this little subprime problem essentially spread and sank the economy."

The subprime problem would soon spread and sink the economy.

Two types of hedge fund moguls made a fortune during the housing crash. There were the true gunslingers, such as John Paulson, whose eponymous hedge fund earned $20 billion gambling straight-up on a housing market crash. The mentality of Paulson and his brethren was the natural successor to that of Soros of a generation earlier. They viewed speculation as no different from any other form of investing—simply an efficient way to separate a group of people bound to lose money from a group bound to make it. Inasmuch as the former category included individuals and small investors who lost everything they owned, including their homes, the Paulson types were not exactly celebrated in the popular imagination. They mostly kept quiet.

Dalio was not one for reticence. He would brag for years that he had called the financial crisis. And he had, in a way. In the months after Dalio's *Barron's* interview, he called it every which way.

"This is the big one," he wrote in Bridgewater's *Daily Observations* note in August 2007. Yet he allowed himself some wiggle room: "This is not an economic crisis; it's a big financial market adjustment."* Bridgewater forecast the damage as minor compared to past events, characterizing it as "a self-reinforcing panic move away from high-risk investments to low-risk investments in which badly positioned leveraged players get squeezed." The pain, Dalio wrote, would be mostly isolated to specialized investors who had loaded up on mortgages. Any fallout was bound to run its course quickly over the next four to six months.

As it had been since Dalio's first prediction of an economic collapse in 1982, what was bad for the economy was good for his business. A few weeks after his "big one" prediction, Dalio made his first appearance on the Forbes 400 list of the richest Americans, at number 82. The magazine pegged his net worth at $4 billion—more even than that of Paul Tudor Jones. And for all Dalio's professions of disdain for showy displays of wealth, he appeared to be enjoying his own. In December 2007, as the world economy teetered, Dalio organized an event at which the British rock-and-roll singer Eric Clapton was paid $1.5 million to perform a private, roughly hour-long concert at a Connecticut country club. Another $1 million donation was reportedly thrown into the charity of Clapton's choice.

As the housing crisis spread, Dalio discarded many of his earlier caveats on the uncertainty ahead, settling back into the dark storyline he'd spent three decades polishing. In January 2008 he wrote to Bridgewater clients, "If the economy goes down, it will not be a typical recession." He predicted a disaster in which "the financial deleveraging causes a financial crisis that causes an economic crisis." This earned him not just another slew of media interviews, but for the first time serious attention from Washington, D.C.

He sought an audience with Ramsen Betfarhad, a deputy assistant to Vice President Dick Cheney, in an effort to raise the alarm. Dalio showed up at the meeting with a stack of papers that indicated U.S. banks were sitting on trillions of dollars in potential losses, leaving Betfarhad spooked. Dalio also encouraged central bankers to print more money to buoy the economy. He launched into dire appeals to Treasury Department undersecretary David McCormick and at the New York Federal Reserve Bank, startling bank president Timothy Geithner. Two days after the Geithner meeting, the blue-chip investment bank Bear Stearns collapsed. Dalio's

---

* Dalio would later only partially quote this note in a book he authored titled *Principles for Navigating Big Debt Crises*, in a chapter that argues he predicted the financial crisis. Dalio left in the phrase "the big one," but omitted "this is not an economic crisis."

well-timed warning sealed a relationship between the Bridgewater founder and the future treasury secretary.

In these meetings and others, Dalio portrayed himself as a kindly supplicant offering a public good. There was merit to this; in sharing Bridgewater's research with those in a position to make policy decisions, he was offering for free the type of insight for which clients around the world paid Bridgewater top dollar. Of course, Bridgewater also stood to benefit.

While Bridgewater's automated trading systems were positioned relatively conservatively, in 2007 and 2008 Dalio himself ordered a number of manual adjustments so the fund would profit more heavily from an overall decline, investment staffers there then recall. Throughout this period, he had placed a series of bets that would pay off if central bankers printed money to revive the economy—the exact move he had predicted. Bridgewater bought up Treasury bonds, gold, and commodities and shorted the U.S. dollar. The moves paid off. When central bankers pumped money into the economy, the result was that while the average hedge fund lost 18 percent in 2008, Pure Alpha ended the year up roughly 9 percent. Thanks both to the flagship fund's strong performance and the flat fee that Bridgewater collected on the assets it managed overall, Dalio personally ended up making $780 million that year.

The market would hit its nadir in March 2009. The following month, Bridgewater leapfrogged its rivals to become the world's largest hedge fund.

As the world hit rock bottom, Ray Dalio was on top.

Part II

7

LOOK OUT

When Paul McDowell moved from Canada in March 2009 to advise the management committee of the world's biggest hedge fund, the mild-mannered former consultant found it hard to reconcile the misery of the wider world with what was going on in Westport.

McDowell considered himself lucky. The unemployment rate was charging above 8 percent—a level unseen in three decades—yet here he was at a job that paid more than he'd ever made. Life at Bridgewater didn't just seem to be pressing forward as normal, it was thriving. The hedge fund had grown so much that he now had nearly a thousand coworkers, and many of them seemed to be friends inside and outside of work. Helped by a shared sense that they were among the fortunate few to work for a booming company in an era of global distress, they seemed to be growing closer every week. McDowell learned that the firm had bought its own forty-five-foot coach bus and spent in the range of $1 million on a full renovation into a limousine, rechristening it the "Rockstar Bus." The bus would pull up to the hedge fund's headquarters at the end of the day to take employees to bars, restaurants, casinos, or even one of Dalio's homes.

The Bridgewater founder kept a town house in Manhattan and would sometimes invite staffers over. Many were flattered; others found it a bit of a sad offer to watch Dalio ramble after hours in New York about The Principles to people who worked for him, sometimes instead of his spending time in Connecticut with his wife or children. He would regale visitors with a story about how he was once chided by the police as he smoked pot on the front stoop. Some chuckled at the image, filing it away as a reminder that Dalio had human foibles of his own.

Perhaps Dalio's favorite venue was a Connecticut colonial estate that Bridgewater had purchased a few years earlier, hidden from street view, up a long, curving driveway that led to a bluff with sweeping views, around the corner from the fund's main headquarters. Bridgewater poured millions into renovating it, maximizing the number of bedrooms at the end of a winding staircase so that staffers could stay overnight rather than commute late back to their homes. Dalio lined the place with photos of Bridgewater's early days, many featuring himself, and hired a chef to cook meals. There was a pool, a Jacuzzi, and ample alcohol. The mansion was rechristened the Lookout, though many Bridgewater employees were encouraged to keep that name a secret from family and friends. Dalio often stopped by, even when he wasn't explicitly invited. The master bedroom was nearly always left empty for him, except when the other beds were at capacity.

The Lookout was for adults only. Exotic entertainment was so commonplace that Bridgewater decided to put rules in writing. "Stripper Policy at The Lookout," read the official document. "All guests are to be informed when making their reservation that there will be 'Special Entertainment that night.'"

The farther off-site, the further the fun. Dalio owned what he sometimes called a "cottage" in rural Vermont, which he opened up to clients and staff alike. He brought one of Bridgewater's major investors from Japan there on a hunting trip, and together they shot what Dalio's personal assistant described as "a very large and unique looking bird." Dalio had it stuffed and mounted. The taxidermy was in good company. Under vaulted ceilings in the log cabin–style home's main room were stuffed animals of all sizes from Dalio's hunting trips around the globe.

Not long after he started, McDowell was invited to a retreat at the Vermont house. He was flattered at first, telling friends he imagined late-night strategic chats, mano a mano with the Bridgewater founder. McDowell's excitement tempered when he received instructions to bring a sleeping bag. Around seventy or so mostly junior staffers would be there, most half his age. He took solace in that Dalio would be there, too, along with a new senior executive, David McCormick, recently hired at Bridgewater after meeting Dalio at the Treasury Department. It certainly didn't make sense to turn down a chance for face time, however brief, with his new boss—especially not if a potential rival was there.

The floors were crammed with air mattresses by the time McDowell showed up carrying a Bertrand Russell book as a backup plan. Dalio perched himself in front of the fireplace, enthralling the assembled group seated at his feet. He was relaxed and self-assured, beaming as he offered a new explanation for his success, which hinged on the idea that he was hardly different from anyone else. All I am is a poker player, he said—a poker player with a lot of chips. Everyone laughed.

The hours went by and the alcohol came out. McDowell grabbed his book and his sleeping bag and went searching for a quiet spot. The adjoining carriage house was full, as were the bedrooms in the main house. McDowell peeked around doors until he found a small gym, blissfully empty. He unfurled his sleeping bag, took out a flashlight, and read his book to the sounds of distant, jubilant screams. Eventually he fell asleep.

Around 4:00 A.M. McDowell was awakened by what he later described to coworkers as "the sound of human replication" next to him on the floor of the gym.

McDowell weighed his options. He was in a new country in a new job in the middle of a global financial crisis. Was it worth speaking up, not knowing who was inches away, and whom he might embarrass? He took a deep breath, stuck his hands over his ears, and waited for it all to end.

MCDOWELL LEARNED to sit out most of the future festivities to which he was invited. He had a handy excuse: he was in a relationship with the woman soon to be his wife. An unofficial spousal support group, organized by some long-term Bridgewater staffers, could teach her the company's ways and how they might affect her home life, but McDowell had never brought his professional afflictions home.

Katina Stefanova was trying, and failing, to remain so stoic. She knew McDowell—he was at the table during her infamous taped interrogation by Dalio—but didn't think much of the new hire besides having made a mental note that he was one of the men who'd sat silently as she sobbed. Still pregnant, she had more proximate concerns. In the days and weeks in 2009 after her probing, she did not return to work. She repeatedly replayed the episode in her mind; it was keeping her up at night and jolting her in the darkness with sweats.

Dalio called her a number of times and left voicemails, asking her to confirm that she saw the incident as part of her natural evolution, and saying that he was only trying to help her break through her weaknesses. It often felt as if there were no escape.

From home, Stefanova began to realize that though it felt to her that Dalio had cornered the market on pain, she briefly had something equal: power. She was flattered that a billionaire was blowing up her cell phone. She knew that Dalio had been hinting for months prior that he might step back from running the firm in favor of someone else. Stefanova thought, *If I play this right, that might be me.* So she returned to her old job, working under Dalio as if nothing had happened. But something had changed. She had to answer constant queries from colleagues about her broadcast interrogation, which the Ice Queen answered with a frozen smile. She had a new, if unwelcome, type of celebrity.

Stefanova needed a new ally, and she found one in Eileen Murray.

Murray, fifty-one years old, was, like McDowell, a new Bridgewater hire with hopes of running the firm herself. She was the prototypical Bridgewater senior hire, seeming to many a shade desperate at that point in her career, with good reason to put up with humiliation. She had spent most of her career at the giant investment bank Morgan Stanley, rising through the firm's back office, the unsexy, blue-collar area for paper-pushing kids with big work ethics and light intellects. Murray had an accounting degree from Manhattan College and was mostly known for wearing cowboy boots and no makeup to meetings. The middle one in a gaggle of Irish American children, Murray never married, though she took frequent trips to Walt Disney World and was prone to quoting from the Harry Potter series.

Murray left Morgan Stanley in 2007, at exactly the wrong time. She had accrued millions in stock options that dropped precipitously during the financial crisis. Her next job, as chief executive of a start-up hedge fund, was similarly ill-timed. The fund, which was trying to raise money as the world was losing it, closed after less than a year.

Murray and Stefanova were already acquainted. During her first day of interviews at Bridgewater, Murray was invited to watch Stefanova probe another employee. As Murray walked into the room, Stefanova paused for a few seconds, warmly introduced herself, then slid the smile off her face and turned back to interrogation mode. Murray was immediately freaked-out; she reflexively looked toward the doors, fearing they were locked. Murray would reflect on the moment for years afterward, wondering what would have happened if she had trusted her instinct and headed for the door.

A few weeks after her return to Bridgewater, Stefanova reasoned she might hitch a ride on the new hire. Stefanova asked to speak with Dalio one-on-one. He was only half paying attention as she walked into his office.

"I think it's best for me if I next work for Eileen," she said slowly.

He was still barely with her. "Why?"

"Because I admire her."

This got his attention. Dalio snapped up from his chair and leaned on his desk, hands straddling either side, peering over at Stefanova. His brown eyes flashed with a seeming mix of anger and hurt. Stefanova could swear she detected a hint of confusion, too.

"You don't admire me?" he asked, stuttering a little.

Stefanova felt a mix of confusion and derision. How could Dalio not realize that she was still hurt from her humiliating probing? But she knew he was still the boss—and if one thing seemed to get Dalio bothered, it was a compliment to someone other than him.

"Of course I do," Stefanova told Dalio, with a soothing tone.

With Dalio's ego at least temporarily assuaged, Stefanova was permitted to report directly to Murray.

NOT LONG after Stefanova's reunion with Dalio, he invited her and Murray to celebrate with him and a group at the Lookout. Also in attendance were a cluster of management associates—the people whose slow hiring had led to Stefanova's taped interrogation. She could not escape the suspicion that the invitation was for Dalio to demonstrate in front of a crowd that she had been forgiven and brought back into the fold.

Stefanova was by then visibly pregnant, and one of the only people not drinking. She felt safe, though. The group was mostly women she had hired herself, having reasoned that the rest of Bridgewater was male-heavy enough to take the balance. Having Murray there helped, too. The group sipped on cocktails around a fire in the living room.

As the event was winding down, Dalio broke the silence. "Croon for me."

There was silence, and some polite laughter. Dalio had turned sixty that year, and he was surrounded by mostly young women, some around the age of his own children. They worked for him. This was something less than a choice.

The ladies started politely. Murray forced a smile. They all took turns singing holiday songs, one by one, going around the circle, a carol or two. Dalio was clearly delighted. He rarely smiled, but he was enjoying this.

Stefanova could feel her face getting hot. Her turn was coming around. She couldn't do it. She wouldn't do it. She excused herself to use the restroom.

Sure enough, as soon as she closed the door, she heard Dalio's voice float in from a distance. "Where's Katina? I want Katina to sing."

Stefanova was not religious, but she swore a silent prayer. Before she could make an excuse, she heard Murray's voice. "She's not feeling well," adding a comparison to how pregnant women are.

Someone suggested it was now Ray's turn to sing. He said he had just the verse in mind, an old maritime song, one that he said was one of his favorites, performed by a folk singer under the pen name Salty Dick. Dalio didn't need notes to recall it. He chanted from memory:

A matlow told me before he died
And I've no reason to think he lied.
He knew a whore with a cunt so wide
That she could never be satisfied.

So he built a bloody great wheel
Two balls of brass and a prick of steel.
The balls of brass were filled with cream
And the whole fucking issue was driven by steam.

Round and round went the bloody great wheel
In and out went the prick of steel
Until at last this whore she cried,
"Enough, enough, I'm satisfied!"

Now we come to the sorry bit
For there was no way of stopping it
She was split from cunt to tit,
And the whole fucking issue was covered in shit.

Seated on the toilet, Stefanova couldn't see Dalio's delivery, but she could hear the satisfaction in his voice, and the small laugh he added to certain lines. As the song continued, Stefanova realized a new advantage of her hiding place. Though Stefanova couldn't see Dalio, he couldn't see her either, or he would have seen that she was cringing, no longer nause-ated just from the pregnancy.

Crouched in the bathroom for a long while after the singing was done, Stefanova swore two things to herself:

I'm not one of his anymore.
I'm getting out.

8

A DIFFERENT KIND OF COMPANY

While the global economy enjoyed a bounce back in the second half of 2009, inside the Bridgewater offices Dalio seemed in a perpetually dark mood.

Paul McDowell and his colleagues assumed the firm's investments had something to do with it. The same month McDowell joined, Bridgewater threw its All-Weather fund into what was called depression mode by reducing borrowed money to a minimum in an attempt to stave off potential losses. Dalio believed the stock market wouldn't bottom out until the next year; when it instead climbed sharply throughout most of 2009, Bridgewater's funds weren't positioned to profit as they had been the prior year.

The markets, however, couldn't completely explain Dalio's dour attitude. He seemed in perennial disappointment with those around him, for reasons that had nothing to do with stocks or bonds. McDowell was assured by his new colleagues that this was a by-product of Dalio's grueling ongoing effort to codify the Bridgewater culture for future cohorts. All new hires were handed a ninety-page printout, stapled in the top-left corner and labeled "The Principles." Follow these, they were told, and you'll go far here.

Though The Principles were going on five years old, all at Bridgewater could notice that Dalio continued to add to and subtract from them at whim. McDowell noticed, too, that the most successful Bridgewater employees appeared to live the rules as they were written. An obvious favorite for Dalio was a young woman named Jen Healy. He would sometimes refer to her as "my daughter." Hired directly out of Princeton University, Healy took to The Principles with fervor. On one occasion, she was vexed for hours after noticing a colleague wearing an unflattering new sweater. Didn't The Principles require her to share her critical feedback so as to help the woman improve? Healy decided to do so but was talked out of it at the last moment by another colleague.

To abide by The Principles didn't just require vigilance of thought, but of language. One word awry could set off Dalio. Roughly three months after starting, McDowell sat in on a meeting between Dalio and a Yale-educated lawyer recently hired to help oversee the firm's management. There was a decent crowd; in addition to the invited staff, each executive had brought his or her chief of staff (in Bridgewater parlance, their *leveragers*). Held in Dalio's private conference room, overlooking a river where Canada geese honked happily, the meeting skidded off track when the lawyer told the Bridgewater founder that he was still waiting for feedback from the hedge fund's various executives on his proposed changes. The newbie employee apparently wasn't on the top of their call sheets.

"I've tried," the lawyer said.

"People who only try are useless to me," Dalio responded.

The new hire took the weekend to think and apparently decided there were certain limits to what he would tolerate for a paycheck. He was raised to be a gentleman, and this was no way to act. He sent his resignation to Dalio, who accepted.

When Healy found out, she decided to say something. After all, The Principles indicated that even the lowest-level employees ought to speak up if they witnessed something wrong. She asked Dalio why he had spoken so coarsely to a new member of the Bridgewater family, in front of a crowd no less.

I believe in the value of giving feedback, Dalio said.

Healy suggested that there might be a way to deliver such feedback in a more collegial manner.

"I'm tired of sugarcoating things," Dalio responded. "I don't believe in it."

Healy would evidently have an impact, but not in the way she might have intended. All soon noticed that Dalio had added a new line to The Principles: sugarcoating creates sugar addiction.

THE DUALITY that McDowell noticed in Dalio—seemingly eager to teach, yet so frequently punishing to those trying to learn—deepened as the weeks went on. The Bridgewater founder's temper seemed to flare most acutely when he wandered too far from investing. In the world of financial figures, Dalio was undeniably in his element. Dalio could cite, from memory, the specifics of an esoteric economic event from years earlier. He hauled home briefcases of research on weekends and would arrive on Monday ready to debate them with whomever he encountered first. Watching Dalio on top of his game, drawing out connections that no one else could see between seemingly unrelated events, was electrifying.

Whether on his Manhattan stoop, in front of the fire at the Lookout, or in the office, Dalio thrived in front of a crowd, and as Bridgewater grew, it provided him ample audiences. Staffers would note that in any meeting Dalio could be counted on to leap on his feet with little notice and take to the whiteboard. His go-to move was to grab a marker and draw a squiggly doodle with a positive slope headed from the bottom left to the top right of the board. The x-axis was time, and the y-axis was level of improvement. This was Dalio's manifestation of the ideal thought process. The loops represented feedback—often criticism—that accompanied the identification of mistakes. Though these loops seemed to take progress temporarily backward, in time the doodle rose steadily up the axis, indicating that the loops ultimately led to improvement. Dalio would pair the drawing with a flat line, which represented death. A lack of loops (The Principles called them "bad quality feedback loops," as a euphemism) led to death.

Since feedback was necessary for progress, Dalio decided that everyone at the firm should offer it. Vigilant to the danger of too much sugar, he made a rule that all those at Bridgewater, regardless of position, should split their feedback between the positive and the negative. Those who leaned too heavily toward the former would see their bonuses cut.

Dalio recognized the heterodoxy of his instructions. Humans by nature wanted to avoid conflict, or, as he put it, to avoid "touching the nerve." He said that mankind was prewired for a fight between two sections of the brain: the amygdala, which produces anxiety, and the prefrontal cortex, which is capable of reflection. The prefrontal cortex was the "upper level you" and the amygdala was the "lower level you." To hear Dalio tell it, these two parts of the brain were normally in conflict—and the amygdala fights dirty. It "hijacks" the brain, flooding the mind with emotion and creating a "fight or flight" instinct that distorts rational decision-making. "That damned amygdala," Dalio once called it publicly.

He had apparently been able to overcome his own such reflex. Through meditation, Dalio said he was able to all but separate the amygdala and prefrontal cortex, thus freeing himself from being controlled by emotion.

He credited this ability for his understanding of the psychological factors that lead to successful trading and company management. Dalio offered to subsidize meditation classes for anyone at Bridgewater who wanted to follow in his path. Many took him up on the offer.

Dalio began to present himself as a model for exemplary behavior. He compared himself to the Dalai Lama. Like his holiness, Dalio knew he wasn't going to be around forever, and from what he witnessed at Bridgewater, merely handing out copies of The Principles did not ensure that they were followed. He needed a way to make the manifesto come alive, not just for those who had in-person exposure to him, but to all. The most obvious step was to record virtually everything that Dalio did or said at the hedge fund. That, too, wasn't enough. It wasn't realistic to expect everyone, in addition to their daily responsibilities, to follow along on Dalio's day. So Dalio began making notes throughout the day of the various lessons he found himself teaching. Bridgewater used a team of videographers and editors to turn the film into daily quizlets, called Management Principles Training.

The MPTs were mandatory for all and accompanied with questions based on that day's film. One MPT referenced a video of someone describing his experience at the firm. The accompanying question read:

> Later, the person describes how it felt for him when he received a piece of harsh feedback from Ray. True or false: This person is allowing pain to stand in the way of his progress; if he doesn't change his approach to be able to manage pain to produce progress, he will probably have a life that will underlive its potential.

Soon there were enough videos to create a far-larger assessment. Dalio had a team comb through the MPTs to produce what was called a Principles Test. The exam had five sections and took hours to complete. The test was billed as "closed book": staffers couldn't consult their written copies of The Principles while answering. The test was required for everyone at Bridgewater.

Question:	*Which of the following definitions of* arrogant *is what we mean when we use it at Bridgewater?*
Correct Answer:	*A person who has an unjustified and exaggerated confidence that his/her opinion is correct.*

There was a yes-or-no portion.

Should we have truth at all costs so that if a person lies they should always be fired?

Some of the questions nested into one another, turning inward:

Q: *About what percentage of the Bridgewater population would steal if they could get away with it?*

Q: *Are you one of them?*

Q: *Did you answer the last question honestly?*

Q: *Looking around you, what percent of the people you have contact with do you think will need to be sorted for Bridgewater to remain excellent?*

Q: *Do you think that maybe you should be one of those people?*

The tests were graded largely on alignment with Dalio's answers and the written Principles. Scores were kept. Now, Dalio needed a way to track, and use the accumulating data. For that, he turned to one of his newer hires.

THE SO-CALLED baseball card project assigned to McDowell was going nowhere fast. Soon after Dalio tasked his new executive with creating an easy-to-read snapshot of employees' personal statistics, McDowell told colleagues he realized the assignment was a double-edged sword. As Dalio wanted constant updates, it kept McDowell closer to the Bridgewater founder than most others at the firm. It also meant McDowell had more opportunities to screw up than anyone else.

McDowell was not the first to help in this effort, but rather followed the work of a psychologist, Bob Eichinger. Nine years older than Dalio, Eichinger was in the twilight of his career. Decades earlier, he helped come up with a human resources aid called success profiling, in which employers were asked to sort a deck of sixty-seven cards, each labeled with bromides such as "decision quality," in the order of importance for a given job. Though the approach didn't catch on, it earned Eichinger a national reputation as someone interested in the challenge of applying scientific methods to career development. Dalio, a year or so before hiring Mc-Dowell, brought on Eichinger as a consultant to help build Bridgewater's own system. Dalio began flying job candidates out to see the psychologist at his office in Minnesota for screenings.

"Start with the words 'I was born,'" Eichinger would say, "and keep talking until you get to the moment of us two sitting here."

Eichinger and McDowell clicked immediately; Eichinger began referring to McDowell as "one of the chosen ones." They shared an interest in astronomy, and both believed that one could chart human behavior just as one could chart the stars. That isn't to say they saw the task as easy. Without a clear rubric, it would be as if staring into the sky without a telescope—just a mesh of dim, distant dots. Both men were confident that they were uniquely suited to building the right equipment. According to Eichinger's evaluations, McDowell was a highly conceptual thinker, capable of seeing the big picture in ways that most people couldn't. When Eichinger asked McDowell, in one of their first chats, if he had any self-doubts, McDowell responded that his main concern was that he wouldn't have a sufficient remit at Bridgewater to do what was needed.

"I just want to make sure that I report to Ray," McDowell said.

Eichinger looked across at him curiously. "Paul, everyone reports to Ray."

As McDowell dove into the baseball cards, Eichinger sought more data for Dalio. Eichinger helped convince the Bridgewater founder to put every employee through a barrage of personality testing. The most famous, Myers-Briggs, had to be administered by a psychologist, such as Eichinger, and bucketed people in sixteen different personality types. Dalio sat for the test and was graded an ENTP: extroverted, intuitive, thinking, and perceiving. He spread the good news throughout Bridgewater—it fit him exactly. After the rest of the staff took the test, Dalio was less excited, people at Bridgewater at the time recall. The data showed that Bridgewater seemed to have accumulated as many as six times more ENTP personalities than would have been predicted by a normal distribution. There were two possible explanations: either Bridgewater's hiring approach attracted a certain type of personality—or more than a few people at Bridgewater had given answers to the test with an eye toward landing in the same category as the boss.

Eichinger got to work on a more bespoke solution. In a presentation for Dalio, he called it a "people qualities model," and its slogan was "Bridgewater: A different kind of company; a different kind of person." The qualities were arranged as a triangle, with the most important, and rare, attributes at top. The pyramidion—the area where junk foods, sweets, and other rarities might be listed on a nutritional triangle—held five agilities: mental, change, people, results, and cultural. Cultural agility was described as "being a hyperrealist: deeply understanding, accepting and working with reality."

The next level down on the triangle held eleven "elements," such as bright, smart, adaptable, and so forth. Next came fifty-two "competencies" to search for in current and future employees.

Building off his old deck of sixty-seven playing cards, Eichinger gave Dalio a list of proposed competencies.

They included:

- Intellectual Horsepower
- Patience
- Perseverance

- Managing Diversity
- Confronting Direct Reports
- Conflict Management

- Time Management
- Approachability
- Humor

Dalio went through the list and crossed off those that weren't needed.

- Intellectual Horsepower
- ~~Patience~~
- Perseverance

- ~~Managing Diversity~~
- Confronting Direct Reports
- ~~Conflict Management~~

- Time Management
- ~~Approachability~~
- ~~Humor~~

This competencies list passed from Eichinger to McDowell, who immediately folded it into the Bridgewater baseball cards.

To call them cards was a bit of a misnomer. These were vertical, multiple-page printouts, with more statistics than Eichinger could ever have imagined. True to his suggestion, they listed the five agilities, then quickly went broader, subdividing into more than a hundred categories such as "learning on the fly," "directing others," and "personal disclosure." Each category was accompanied by a box for a 1 to 10 rating. While a handful of Eichinger's suggestions made the cut ("confronting direct reports"), the categories were more often ones lifted from The Principles. The first section of an early baseball card held an employee rating for "living in truth," closely followed by one for "probing—not letting people off the hook."

The baseball cards grew and grew. Dalio asked for the results on Eichinger's original personality tests to be on there, so on they went, Myers-Briggs rating and the rest. Then came a section for the weekly MPT videos, to memorialize both how reliable each employee was at completing them, and how accurately their answers matched Dalio's. New categories proliferated, adding on like scaffolds to a rising building that never seemed to reach its apex. New ratings were tacked on—from supervisors, subordinates, members of the management committee. A prominent box was added for Dalio's own diagnoses.

Though they were still manual printouts for the moment, Bridgewater would hire the design firm IDEO, famed for its work on Apple's first mouse, to come up with a digital solution. IDEO's prototype was for a spell described inside Bridgewater under a new code name, the Vassal, a medieval term to describe a person under the protection of a feudal lord. The cost would quickly run into the millions of dollars.

In mid-2009, McDowell showed Eichinger a working model with the psychologist's work incorporated into the hedge fund ratings system. Eichinger was more than satisfied. "This is as good as this shit gets," he told a colleague. McDowell sent off some results to Dalio for approval, making sure to choose samples from employees with whom the Bridgewater founder was close.

Dalio was summering at his villa in Spain when he sent word that he'd reviewed the ratings and wanted to chat. Eichinger called in from Minneapolis, while McDowell and a crew from headquarters dialed in from Westport.

"This is no good." Dalio rifled through a few results, including one from Jen Healy. "I know Jen. This isn't what she's like."

Redo it, he said.

Eichinger, seventy years old, appeared crestfallen. This was years of elaborate, technical work, and now it was being thrown out by one man's gut impulse. Eichinger told McDowell and others that he quit, though he would later describe it as an amicable parting.

Mortality was on Dalio's mind. As he neared his sixties, he renewed his chat of retirement. Though he told some people at the firm he expected to be carried out only in his coffin, he also said he wasn't hoping to carry all his titles to that end. Ever since the Britt Harris saga, Dalio had held both CEO and cochief-investment-officer roles. The pace was punishing, particularly as neither ends of the firm were performing up to his expectations.

On the investment side, Dalio's sustained belief in a prolonged depressive period during 2009 was coming back to bite. Bridgewater had put All-Weather into depression mode at what turned out to be the market nadir, guaranteeing that the fund missed out on the lion's share of what was a roaring return for the global market. Pure Alpha was also positioning too cautiously and performing unimpressively compared to peers. Bridgewater told clients not to trust what they saw in the markets. A few months into the boom, Dalio wrote to warn against a "misleading impression that the economy and markets have returned to normalcy."

Bridgewater's day-to-day management was, if anything, worse. Dalio's disappointment in the baseball card project mirrored larger frustrations with the crew he'd assembled at the firm. As the number of Principles bloomed, reaching 277 in total, so, too, did the number of potential CEO candidates.

First there were Murray and David McCormick, an Army Ranger before he served in George W. Bush's administration. There was also Tom Adams, who joined Bridgewater from Rosetta Stone, the maker of foreign-language-learning software. Julian Mack moved east to Westport from Chicago, where he was running McKinsey & Company's Midwest operations. Niko Canner came from another consultancy, Booz & Company. The new hires were often assured that they had a shot at the CEO role—they'd just have to prove themselves first. Most started as advisers to the management committee, and would essentially sit around patiently for new assignments from the Bridgewater founder.

The hires would have a shot to prove themselves because life at Bridgewater was a constant churn. Though the official company line was that one-third of employees left in eighteen months—the remainder, as Dalio would say, made it through to "the other side"—many at Bridgewater suspected the true figure was more complicated. Some staffers started as consultants, then never pursued full-time roles. Others left before their official end dates; Bridgewater paired generous severance with strict nondisclosure agreements, which staffers were happy to sign on their way out. As a result, people stayed on the payroll long after they had physically left Westport. So constant was the swirl of incoming and exiting employees that even Dalio was sometimes unsure who was in and who was out.

He wasn't entirely blind, however, to the bodies disappearing around him. Near year-end 2009, he asked Stefanova and others for a report summarizing the reasons behind the elevated level of terminations and resignations over the preceding eighteen months. The task was delegated to Bridgewater's head of employee relations, Tara Arnold, who produced a report for the firm's management committee. "In the five years I've been at Bridgewater, this is the most important email I have sent to date," Arnold began.

From: Tara Arnold
Sent: Tuesday, October 06, 2009
To: Management Committee

Subject: Important—Smoke at Bwater

... The "problems" I'm highlighting below should be considered "smoke." ...

1. Major players in the company are experiencing burnout. . . . . .
2. Our reputation in the marketplace is suffering.
   - 19 percent of our offers in 2009 have been rejected. This compares to 15 percent in 2008 and also comes at a time when market conditions are rough and we know people *need* jobs. If we look at the last three months in particular, our rejection rate is nearing 25 percent. . . .
   - Per Cigna, our total cost of antidepressant medication and overall mental health prescriptions per member have increased in the past year. In addition, the Benefits Department and ER Team are seeing an increase in employees asking about mental health physicians. . . .
   - Our exit interviews state that outside of Principles training, there is a huge void in core job training/career development. . . .
   - A few newer employees have been speaking to me directly about being insecure in their jobs and about a fear that any day they could be fired. . . . I've also heard more recently from a few employees (who have been here 3+ years) that they feel the principles that Ray outlines are being taken literally. . . .
   - In some places the culture we have here is so misunderstood that some candidates believe we are a cult and "crazy."

Arnold closed by pointing out that not all of the issues she raised were reflected on companywide quantitative surveys. The lack of hard data, she explained, seemed to be due to fear. To get to the root cause, Arnold and Stefanova jointly proposed an anonymous survey of employees. The survey would be "in line with our philosophy of getting to the truth at all costs," as Arnold put it.

Dalio wrote back that same evening, "Your description is not a balanced version of reality."

From: Ray Dalio

Sent: Tuesday, October 06, 2009

To: Tara Arnold; Management Committee

Subject: RE: Important—Smoke at Bwater

Tara—Thanks for that note I'm sure that all of what you said is true to at least some significant number of people here. . . .

I recognize that working here is very hard—harder than I'd like. I am not removed from that reality as it probably is as hard on me as it is on most others. . . .

I believe that Bridgewater will be great only if the people in their jobs either 1) do great work or 2) have insights and speak openly about how it can be great. . . .

Personally, while there are serious bad outcomes of the sort that you mentioned, I believe that they can be successfully dealt with if we deal with them intelligently and openly. . . .

Before Arnold could respond, Dalio emailed a two-sentence follow-up:

From: Ray Dalio

Sent: Tuesday, October 06, 2009

To: Tara Arnold; Management Committee

Subject: RE: Important—Smoke at Bwater

Tara—To the extent that you can tell me who I should speak to that is having these problems, or that you can encourage them to speak to me, that would be good. Open communication about reality is essential.

For those who remained, at the end of this trail lay a bounty. That reminder of just how lucrative life at Bridgewater could be was embodied by Bob Prince.

Prince, a decade younger than Dalio, on the surface seemed the natural successor to the firm founder. The onetime wide-eyed Midwestern transplant had long since become one of Bridgewater's more well-liked executives. Prince rarely cited The Principles, and especially seldom once out of earshot from the Bridgewater founder. Prince was quick with a kind word and had an open-door policy for those upset by Dalio. Prince would often soothe employees by telling them that Dalio had been rough on him, too. Prince would tell a story about how Dalio was apparently so convinced that his longtime partner was a dreadful manager that Prince was for years forbidden from even hiring his own chief of staff. When one job applicant asked Prince during an interview what the most important things were to him Prince answered, "Family, God, and Bridgewater, in that order."

The categories blended on his fiftieth birthday party, to which he invited many at Bridgewater. Midway through the evening, he rose to give remarks, though not of the sort typically associated with birthday fetes. For the last twenty-five years, he told the assembled crowd, he had been deeply in hock—to Ray Dalio. The Bridgewater founder had generously given his partner the annual chance to buy a stake in the company, but the price of this opportunity rose every year as the firm grew in value. So Prince went to the only person he knew who could arrange that type of loan: Dalio. Prince had amassed a debt that he described to be in the range of hundreds of millions of dollars, to be earned back through his employment at Bridgewater. Not until this milestone birthday, Prince said, had Dalio told him the debt had finally been worked off. Prince said he marked the occasion by driving to a local beach, lighting a bonfire, and burning the loan documents, an act that he mimed in front of the crowd.

His friends, family, and coworkers erupted in whoops and cheers.

After that day Prince seemed palpably different. His wife bought him a Bentley. He took helicopter lessons and began holding forth in some detail about the life of a chopper pilot. He and his wife started building a megachurch on some of the most expensive land in the country, spending $120 million on real estate alone.

More than a few Bridgewater staffers looked at Prince's path and became determined to emulate it. They could put up with a few years, or decades, of misery if it ended with such a reward.

For Prince, though, the path stopped there. He found a way to keep himself away from Bridgewater's management maelstrom and to flatter Dalio all at once. Whenever his name came up for a broader role, Prince would remind all who would listen about his limitations. He pointed to training videos that Dalio had commissioned of his partner's shortcomings. "I can't manage," Prince would say. It was better for everyone if he kept to his own corner.

Though Prince would remain at Bridgewater, he would from then on be all but out of the loop from Dalio's management of the firm. Prince remained cochief investment officer—which had the effect of allowing Dalio to boast publicly of their stable partnership—but spent much of his time on economic research that seemed to go nowhere, or on the low-cost All-Weather product that his former Tulsa professor had unwittingly helped design. Prince essentially took ownership of the B side of the investments. He neither challenged Dalio nor regularly stuck up for anyone who did. Many at Bridgewater would privately confess jealousy that Prince seemed to be able to collect a paycheck and go home.

If Prince eschewed a leadership role, his cochief investment officer took a different tack. Greg Jensen charged into a leadership void. The Chief Principalian was the only person at Bridgewater besides Dalio himself with a hand in all facets of the firm. Dalio made no secret of his fondness for the younger man, and in 2010, the Bridgewater founder came the closest yet to handing over the keys. As part of his latest plan to step back, Dalio announced that he would take on the role of "minister/mentor." Jensen would not just be cochief investment officer, but also cochief executive—a pair of roles that had only ever previously been held by Dalio himself.

As for who would join Jensen in the C-suite, Bridgewater now had plenty of candidates, visibly eager to diagnose and probe their rivals. What it didn't have was someone to referee the tournament. If The Principles were about anything, they were about tearing into the firm's troublesome corners and flushing out every detail. They called for videotaped, public internal "trials," or investigations of even the smallest problems at the firm. For $7 million per year, Dalio brought in a lawyer who just so happened to be a famed former prosecutor, telling staff that the new hire would be a "godfather" at the firm.

His name was James B. Comey.

9

COMEY AND THE CASES

THE LIFE OF A HEDGE FUND LAWYER CAN BE A SOGGY AFFAIR. CLIENT agreements must be drawn up, tax documents figured out, and trade confirmations triple-checked. A good portion of each year is spent pouring over the hundreds of pages of mandated compliance filings, to be produced for regulators who will neither read nor understand any of it.

The Bridgewater legal department under its new general counsel, on the other hand, was turning into a hive of activity.

Jim Comey was far from a household name when he joined Bridgewater as general counsel in 2010. He existed somewhere on the scale of pseudo-politico-muckety-mucks as someone whose name might make a difficult, but fair, Final Jeopardy question. Comey was best known for his two-year stint as U.S. attorney for the Southern District of New York, where he prosecuted Martha Stewart for insider trading. He later became deputy attorney general in the Bush administration and landed in the headlines for taking a stand against domestic spying. Comey made no secret to friends of his financial motive for jumping into the private sector. He had five children and one was headed for Harvard Law.

In his first days at Bridgewater, Comey would find that his new gig came with certain costs, the first of which was his pride. He was told he had been assigned the thirty-one-year-old Bridgewater cohead of research, Matthew Granade, as his "ski partner," as the hedge fund called it. The idea was to have someone a few feet away at all times to assess the new hire's strengths and weaknesses and help him adjust to life at the hedge fund.

Comey quickly headed down the wrong slope. He often acted as if the rules did not apply to him. At six foot, eight inches, he would sometimes reach toward the ceiling to deactivate any hidden recording devices in the light fixtures.

Comey tended to speak in meetings from his experience, so Dalio and Jensen would quickly correct him that he should apply the firm's principles rather than his own. Comey once pointedly asked about Dalio's prized squiggle, meant to represent the constant loop of improvement. If time was on the bottom axis and the squiggle was sometimes moving leftward, then wouldn't that suggest that Dalio had invented time travel? Dalio's daily assigned coursework also left Comey wanting. In recorded remarks shared widely, if furtively, inside Bridgewater, Comey described the training videos as mindless and repetitive. At the end of each video, as Comey saw it, there were only three answers: (a) My mother wears combat boots, (b) I put kittens in blenders, (c) Ray is always right.

Yet, Comey stayed. With a new Democratic administration in Washington, D.C., a Republican lawyer had few immediate prospects to land a high-profile government job. Comey was smart enough to course correct—he was soon citing Principles with such frequency that Dalio told the whole firm that his new general counsel was a "chirper," one of the worst criticisms the Bridgewater founder could dole out. Chirpers repeat stale ideas rather than coming up with their own. Never one to blame himself for making a poor hire, Dalio instead began probing Granade on whether the researcher was skiing close enough to his partner.

Perhaps aware of his disfavor, and evidently eager to finally prove his worth, Comey made himself available to Dalio on matters large and small. Soon enough Comey had an opportunity to earn some points.

A relatively new lawyer on staff, Leah Guggenheimer, had taken to The Principles with gusto. A Harvard Law grad, she was ostensibly a leverager, or chief of staff, in the operational side of the organization, but had earned a reputation for spending much of her time on energetic use of the issues log, including writing up a colleague for failing to bring in bagels on the agreed-upon day. (A third colleague, on hearing of this complaint, told Guggenheimer to "grow the fuck up.") Eileen Murray didn't have much patience for her, and after the two clashed a few more times, Murray held a trial and a vote of Guggenheimer's colleagues ("Don't you agree this isn't someone you want working here?" Murray asked). All but one voted to let her go. Her salary was cut off.

A few weeks later, Dalio caught wind and didn't like the idea of penalizing an employee—even a tedious one—for sticking to The Principles and speaking her mind. He called in Comey for a second opinion.

Comey seemed to sense an opening to impress his new boss. "Do you want it done like case law?"

Dalio energetically confirmed that he did.

"Well, Ray, the trial has happened. It's gone through due process. It looks like it followed The Principles. So reopening it doesn't make any sense, unless we hear it de novo."

"What's that?"

"You assume that the other trial never happened and you look at everything fresh."

Dalio was fine with that.

Comey threw himself into the investigation. He relistened to all the tapes, including the one of Guggenheimer being told to grow up ("That was magical," Comey remarked). Dalio then assembled a new, larger hearing and invited Jensen, Murray, and everyone else involved to sit in. A recording device sat at the center of a large table as Dalio invited Comey to give opening remarks.

The general counsel wasted little time in saying that his review indicated the firing was justified: "I listened to the tapes. Even nice, polite Paul McDowell tells Leah to 'grow the fuck up.'"

McDowell, seated in the back, froze. Time seemed to stand still for him. He didn't want anything to do with this.

Jensen piped up, "Paul, that sounds like you were discouraging people from pointing out problems, and we don't tolerate that here. We want people to point out problems."

McDowell choked out a response on the fly: "It was the level of the problems. It didn't make sense."

Lucky for him, the trial moved on.

Dalio concluded that beyond adjudicating the blow by blow of the bagels, Comey had performed a poor diagnosis: "You didn't get to the root cause." Dalio ordered a third investigation.

This time around, Comey applied brute force. He searched the records of Guggenheimer's company-issued cell phone and found that she'd turned it on at home after her first trial. When she protested that she needed to save personal contact information, Comey said she should have asked for permission. He also began searching through the files on Guggenheimer's office computer. Amid the usual mundanity, Comey came upon what he thought was quite the kompromat. Guggenheimer, a single woman, was using the computer to send messages on dating websites. Some of the messages bordered on blue—"near pornographic," Comey told some at Bridgewater.

Dalio saw it differently. "What is pornography?" he mused. People have their private business, and the messages weren't nearly a fireable offense, he concluded.

"Weak case, Jim," Dalio said.

Dalio offered to keep Guggenheimer on, and she considered it. First, though, she wrote to him asking to be paid her back salary from her time away.

"Are you kidding?" he responded. He couldn't be seen to be doling out money to people who had been put on trial.

"Do you want to look good, or be good?" Guggenheimer asked.

He chose the former.

Embarrassed in more ways than one, Guggenheimer decided not to return.

COMEY'S RESPONSIBILITIES included oversight of Bridgewater security. This vast role gave him an excuse to poke and prod in virtually all corners of the firm. The Principles prescribed nothing less. As one Principle laid out, "You should have such good controls that you are not exposed to the dishonesty of others."

The taping of meetings represented just the tip of the surveillance ecosystem at Bridgewater. A former FBI official was head of security, and he hired a slew of ex-agency colleagues to work under him. Not only did cameras cover seemingly every inch of the property, but they seemed to be watched in real time. Staffers who left their desks even briefly would return to sticky notes left on their computer monitors admonishing them for failing to put up a screen saver. Keystrokes and printouts were tracked. Custom hardware allowed the copiers to keep a record of every photocopy. Even including an attachment on an email had to be approved one by one. The obsession with secrecy and security extended beyond the work of the firm. New employees were often warned to be careful about their use of the company gym, which lent out clothes. One staffer, exhausted after a particularly tough workout, absentmindedly walked out wearing a pair of Bridgewater loaner socks. The employee was let go not long after.

The investment staff was forbidden by diktat from socializing outside work with anyone employed at a major Wall Street competitor, as reported by the hedge fund trade magazine *Absolute Return* (Bridgewater would later deny the existence of such a rule).

As Comey's search for office bugs indicated, most Bridgewater employees had a quite reasonable fear of being listened in on, whether at Bridgewater's offices or beyond it. Some employees took out the batteries on their company-issued cell phones when they were with family or friends, so convinced were they that any device connected to Bridgewater was recording at all times. The security department all but encouraged the idea by declining to answer directly when asked by employees whether phone microphones could be turned on without notice. Investment employees were made to turn in their personal phones each morning and place them in signal-proof lockers for the day. For everyone else, when personal calls had to be placed during company time, many trudged out of the office and into the surrounding woods. That lasted roughly until a rumor circulated inside the fund that Comey's team was studying how to install devices in the trees that could intercept phone calls before they reached surrounding cell phone towers.

As head of security, Comey reported to Jensen, who seemed eager to prove that he took the protection of Bridgewater's secrets as seriously as Dalio. But with little evidence of actual offending behavior to snuff out, they created their own. Comey helped come up with a plan to leave a binder, clearly labeled as Jensen's, unattended in the Bridgewater offices. It worked like a charm. Comey watched as a low-ranked Bridgewater employee stumbled upon the binder and began to peruse it. Jensen and Comey put the employee on trial, found him guilty, and fired him, with Dalio's approval.

The tight surveillance inevitably kept people on edge, always sneaking glimpses at the ceilings, as if to remind themselves of the cameras above. The tension grew tighter the closer one got to the Bridgewater founder. A former employee recalled that on one otherwise unremarkable day, Dalio's secretary checked on his office and discovered it empty, door ajar. She was immediately alarmed; Dalio of all people would never leave his sanctum unprotected. She ran into an adjoining conference room and informed the assembled group that Dalio had been kidnapped—and asked what The

Principles indicated should be done next. Roughly thirty seconds later, Dalio appeared in the doorway. He had been in the restroom and now had sharp questions about why his secretary was up from her desk.

DURING SOME days, weeks, and months at Bridgewater the whole firm seemed to be consumed by whom to hire and whom to fire.

In Comey's era, in 2010, a mild-mannered Brit, Michael Partington, whose wife was friends with Jensen's, was in charge of recruitment. Partington had come to Bridgewater after a twenty-year career leading recruiting at McKinsey & Company, the blue-chip consulting firm. This made him an expert on the topic. McKinsey was famously said to receive more than 1 million job applications per year, from which it selected less than 1 percent to hire. To perform a fraction of that work—the hedge fund only needed hundreds of new hires each year—Bridgewater started Partington at more than $2 million per year.

Dalio introduced Partington to the firm as the man who would bring Bridgewater "to the promised land."

The firm was still considerably far from that goal. Onboarding required a torrent of data, both qualitative and quantitative. Job applicants were herded into a room and asked to debate hot-button issues such as abortion while a Bridgewater staffer looked on and took notes. A financial publication reported that those who made it to the next phase would be directed, on top of the personality tests already required, to hand over five years of income tax filings to prove that they weren't exaggerating their prior salaries. The hedge fund also reportedly asked, without explanation, for applicants' dental records, including their history of requesting painkillers.

Once they started, newcomers were immediately thrown into the Bridgewater ratings system, reflected on their baseball cards. Hundreds of Bridgewater employees were now rating one another in real time, a process called dotting. The cards were filled with dots, or numbers, on a 1-to-10 scale, representing each individual instance that a person was rated by his or her peers. Dots could be added twenty-four hours per day because, thanks to the company's elaborate taping system, employees who weren't in the same room as one another were able to dot one another ex post facto.

An early, common problem for incoming employees was that a generally blank baseball card devoid of ratings was an invitation to be branded with negative dots by one's colleagues.* There was little incentive to stick out, and every incentive to pile on. It took only a few days for newcomers to figure out that the best way to earn high ratings was to agree with others already ranked highly. This inevitably meant hewing closely to the views of the hedge fund's top brass. Dalio or Jensen would not uncommonly stop a meeting in its tracks and poll the room on whether some subordinate was doing a good job. How Dalio felt on the topic was rarely a mystery.

Though the baseball card system was supposed to make it easier to re-assign staff into the right roles, it mostly gave everyone a platform to opine on every topic. The Principles seemed to mandate nothing less—they said it was the responsibility of every person to identify badness as it happened. Each day brought new hires to be probed on new problems cropping up, creating new cases for Bridgewater's archive of taped transgressions. The cases veered frequently into the personal. When Dalio heard rumors that a thirtysomething on Partington's team was in debt, the Bridgewater founder assembled a group of roughly fifty people to witness Dalio question the junior employee on the reasons why. The diagnosis was filmed and sent out to the firm afterward as an example of how The Principles could be applied to both professional and personal matters.

The case did not reflect well on Partington. Roughly a year into the recruiter's Bridgewater career, Dalio sent out a companywide poll: "Does Michael Partington add value?" The nays piled up.

"You haven't taken us to the promised land," Dalio told him.

Dalio cut his salary in half.

THERE'S PISS *on the floor.*

So read the email from Dalio to a group that included McCormick, the former Army Ranger brought in to help run the Bridgewater machine.

Everyone at the hedge fund would soon learn the backstory. Dalio had excused himself from a meeting and walked to the nearest shared bath-room. After relieving himself at the urinal, he glanced down. There was piss on the floor.

This couldn't be allowed to go on, Dalio said. Whose was it? And who

---

* Lawyers for Bridgewater said, "Through the onboarding process and using the results from person-ality assessments as a starting point, new hires were encouraged to reflect on their own strengths and weaknesses."

had permitted it to happen? "If people can't aim their fucking pee, they can't work here," Dalio proclaimed.

Dalio's interest in the men's room set off an investigation, wrapped around a series of probings, all to come up with the right diagnoses. It was a true circus. Dalio himself hauled the head of facilities in for questioning. Dozens of staff were assigned to a rotating guard, standing outside the restroom to take notes on all who entered—and whether they left clean floors. After each visitor, a member of the cleaning staff would rush in to mop up the tile. New urinals were brought in for testing. Stickers were frantically applied to the porcelain to give men a more effective target. Then the exact placement of the stickers themselves was probed.

Such was the unmistakable badness of it all that everything was filmed and a case was made for all to learn from.

THE PISS case, as it became known, reflected an increasing pattern of Dalio's. He was seemingly constantly agitated. Even his eldest son, Devon, hired at Bridgewater to a relatively unimportant operational role, wasn't immune, several people who worked with him recalled. One former Bridgewater executive recalled several instances of Devon's standing just outside a door on the Bridgewater campus, upset and near tears.

Dalio was perhaps most unforgiving about the lowest-level tasks of the firm. He exhibited a short fuse when he became aware of what seemed like rudimentary problems that could easily be fixed through the careful application of The Principles.*

Thus the blue-collar men and women in charge of custodial, secretarial, and other such tasks at the hedge fund were in a danger zone. They had inarguably the most limited prospects for a lucrative future outside of the hedge fund; their day-to-day responsibilities were not obviously different from those at any other business, there being only so many ways to stack paper next to the printers, or to patrol a parking lot. But Bridgewater paid lavishly—more than $200,000 a year for secretaries, one recalled. In exchange, they were expected to hew to—and be graded under—The Principles like everyone else. Their professional lives were consumed with tumult. The bus drivers were often under investigation for keeping their vehicles too hot or too cold (sometimes both at the same time, per competing com-

---

* A lawyer for Dalio said he "treated all employees equally, giving people at all levels the same respect and extending them the same perks."

plaints). Few at Bridgewater would take note if the snack bar refrigerators were filled each morning, but a supernova of furious dot ratings would land on the lowest-level employee if supplies of a soft drink ever ran out.

Assistants would be down-dotted if their bosses arrived late to a meeting, even if it wasn't their fault, on the logic that it was their responsibility to keep the schedule.

Though some at the hedge fund held misgivings about applying full force against the firm's lowest-paid members, Dalio evinced no such unease. Others eventually followed.

One didn't even have to be inside the Bridgewater offices to run afoul of expectations. A security guard found himself in the hot seat after switching up the parking passes that attached to the employees' cars' rear windows, to make it easier to spot potential impostors. One employee wrote an email complaining that the new passes were so big that they blocked his windshield view. He cc'd Dalio and Jensen. Dalio decided to make an example. There was a probing, a diagnosis, and two men lost their *boxes,* or their jobs, in Bridgewater parlance.

Bridgewater wound up using the new parking passes anyway.

Even more memorable bedlam came during what became known as the whiteboard case. During a meeting, Dalio rose from his seat and picked up a dry-erase marker to draw on the room's whiteboard. Midway through sketching a flow chart, he went to write over some of the work, grabbing an eraser attached to the board. For a few seconds he rubbed the eraser on the board, then froze. He turned to the group, gesturing behind him.

The eraser hadn't fully eliminated the marking; instead it had smeared, almost imperceptibly; light ink remnants across the board.

This is badness, Dalio announced. Who was responsible?

Whoever it was, wasn't in the room. One of Dalio's leveragers rushed out to find the responsible party. That, too, didn't produce a fast answer. There was no record of who had chosen the whiteboards.

No responsible party meant the whole facilities department was responsible. For roughly the next six weeks, Dalio devoted himself with fervor to a drill down of the team. With cameras rolling, he called them in for a demonstration at the whiteboard. He kept drawing on the board and erasing it, over and over. How could he have been the first to notice?

The facilities staff reacted as if their jobs were at risk, which was true. First they brought in giant pieces of cardboard as mock-ups and asked

Dalio to show them exactly how and where he planned to use the equipment. Then, said one person involved, "We ordered every single whiteboard on the market." As each board came in, the staff paraded it past Dalio and took notes on his requests. They even tried electronic whiteboards, which didn't have to be manually erased. Those were quickly thrown out because, according to a little-known state disability rule, such boards had to be set relatively low to the ground for wheelchair access and Dalio didn't like the height. And he didn't like that the problem was taking so many man-hours to be solved.

"You're all bumping into one another!" he said.

The whiteboard case created two lasting legacies (three, if one counts that the whiteboards were eventually replaced). The videos of the investigation were edited together under a particularly memorable title: "How many facilities people does it take to put up a whiteboard?" This offended many members of the department, who felt that they were being mocked for following the boss's orders.

The second effect was that a new phrase entered Bridgewater's vocabulary. For years to come, whenever Bridgewater's professional staff were frustrated with the services of the firm's facilities staff, someone could be counted on to jump in with the quick diagnosis: you're all bumping into one another.

THE INTENSE focus with which Dalio attacked even the most mundane problems earned him a nickname among some of the rank and file. He was Ray-man, after Dustin Hoffman's Oscar-winning portrayal of an autistic man.

It was, however, far from a majority view at the hedge fund that Dalio was off the reservation.

If the Management Principles Training did one thing effectively, it memorialized the organization's shortcomings. It was impossible to view the cases and not internalize Dalio's genuine disturbance that the whiteboards weren't up to code, that someone might worry about parking passes that block the driver's view, that food in the cafeteria needed improvement, and so forth. While the cases portrayed the Bridgewater founder as singularly capable of remedying the issues, Dalio often made a show of seeming resigned to carrying out this undignified work in the trenches. If a theme linked all the cases, it was that the Bridgewater founder was being failed by those around him. In one video Dalio distributed of himself diagnosing why a subordinate had failed, Dalio stood in front of the man and wrote on a whiteboard, *Needs a shrink.*

Curiously, despite all of these lessons, and the reflection they spurred, circumstances never seemed to improve—for several reasons.

The first was that Dalio had amassed a team of leveragers, assistants, and analysts whose roles included listening to recordings made firmwide, fast-forwarding to the spots that might bother the Bridgewater founder, and pitching them as a case. For each case that made the cut for firmwide airing, a slew more didn't. There was always another crisis to be found. The livelihoods of many depended on it.

In some ways, Dalio's livelihood depended on it, too. The knowledge that any careless moment might turn into a monthslong case was a powerful way to keep everyone hewing close to The Principles. The last thing any employee wanted was Dalio peering in post hoc, asking why one person or another didn't "taste the soup," in the words of The Principles. Each staffer covered his or her own back, probing, rating, and dotting as if somebody was watching. Invariably, somebody was.

With so many cases producing so much data, the baseball card team, despite a full-time squad of assigned software engineers and myriad high-priced consultants, couldn't make heads or tails of it all. So Dalio decided to go back to basics. He asked Bridgewater's nearly three hundred managers to redo their own cards, rating themselves all over again in more than a hundred categories. He gave a deadline of a week. The instructions were to now use an "absolute scale." Dalio helpfully laid out examples for what merited a 1, 2, 3, and on. Those who missed the deadline were reminded via email that a demerit would be "recorded on your reliability gauge."

Roughly 1 percent of the group, or nearly a dozen employees, missed a second deadline. Some were out of the office; others were just busy helping run the world's biggest hedge fund. A few assumed they had been incorrectly included in the assignment, as they weren't managers of anyone. Regardless of the reason, they all opened their emails to a frantic reminder from Dalio's leverager, copying in the Bridgewater founder: "Get these done ASAP."

Before anyone could, an email arrived from Dalio himself: "Those who didn't get them in and didn't communicate with you after being nagged twice are fired."

Before anyone could respond, he emailed again: "Who disagrees with my view that people who can't do what they are asked or have a quality communication when asked to do something twice are not the sort of people that you want to rely on?

"Anyway, there [sic] not the sort of people who I want to work here."

10

THE OFFENSIVE

For the first half decade of their life, The Principles were confined to Bridgewater. They metastasized and metamorphosed outside the public eye. Most company newcomers hadn't even heard of them when they were handed a Principles printout during orientation by what Bridgewater called its "culture carriers." Paul McDowell was one of the carriers. Roughly once a month, he would stand in front of a group of new hires and deliver the same speech: "Newton had his *Principia*. Ray has his Principles. The only difference is that Newton's were limited to physics."

The rules were presented to the newbies as a secret menu filled with acquired tastes that would not only seem more palatable over time, but also improve their lives inside and outside work. This was a winning pitch—being let in on a secret was alluring.

The doors blew open in May 2010, when the finance blog *Dealbreaker* got its hands on The Principles. The blog introduced the document, which it called "The Tao of Dalio," with a healthy hit of snark ("WTF is this shit?" read the introduction). The blog quoted an anonymous employee who said, "The Principles are pretty cultish, as is the culture of the whole company. At one of our town halls [Dalio] handed out personally signed copies of them to everyone."

Dealbreaker oscillated between quoting directly from The Principles, which it called "Ray's Rules," and mocking them:

Be the Hyena. Attack that wildebeest.

CAN YOU HANDLE THE TRUTH?

Make sure to look people in the eye and tell them they suck.

When telling them they suck, don't beat around the "you suck" bush.
 Really lay into their ass.

Dalio read the entry with horror, feeling it mischaracterized his life's work. That the post was published by a finance blog with three writers and an unknown audience did not seem to ameliorate his feelings. If nothing else, *Dealbreaker* was widely read in the world of finance. He sat for an interview with *The Wall Street Journal* to provide a response. It would be the first time he discussed The Principles publicly, in depth.

He told the reporter that the overarching philosophy amounted to "hyperrealism," or the notion that brutal honesty leads to the best results. Bridgewater, he said, banned talking critically about people outside their presence—and if the rule was broken three times, the employee could be fired. "Most people actually love this rule," he said. If it seemed strange to outsiders, that wasn't Dalio's concern. He wasn't interested in discussing The Principles, as he put it, "in front of the world."

What he didn't say was that the smallest of rebellions was brewing inside the firm. And it was directly related to The Principles themselves.

THE INSURGENCE, if it could even be called that, was led by Julian Mack. He joined Bridgewater around the same time as Comey, after the financial crisis. Like the general counsel, Mack was a confident, tall man with a side part who fit in easily with Bridgewater's new crew of alpha males. Mack quickly became friends and lunchtime running partners with David McCormick, a broad-shouldered, former four-time letterman on the army wrestling team who rarely turned down the chance to remind visitors of that (he tore his ACL senior year, though he competed in the national championships despite the injury). McCormick later received the Bronze Star for leadership helping clear minefields during Operation Desert Storm. Like Mack, he was a McKinsey alum.

Both men were hired into similar roles and told they were serving on the Bridgewater management committee as a means of auditioning to be CEO.

Mack's day-to-day responsibilities included oversight of Paul Mc-Dowell, the baseball cards, and other tools meant to rate employees on various Principles-based attributes. This assignment, in practice and perhaps also on purpose, opened him up to criticism. Dalio's continuous additions and revisions to the Principles meant that whoever was in charge of building Principles-related tools was bound to land in his crosshairs.

Mack wasn't six months into his term at Bridgewater when others began speculating when Dalio would decide that Mack was a "responsible party" for another delay in the refinement of the baseball cards and ratings operation. This could not, by Dalio's way of thinking, be his own fault; it had to be someone else's, and this time it was Mack's. Dalio called a group of the top executives, including McCormick, together to discuss whether the problem was that Mack's work was slow because he wasn't fully embracing The Principles. This wasn't a full-on trial, but what Dalio called a diagnosis—essentially a chance to criticize an executive at length on tape, with the recording sent out under the guise of a "learning opportunity."

In Dalio's diagnoses, the Bridgewater founder did much of the talking. Mack's problem, Dalio said, was that he wasn't a big-picture thinker. He got stuck on what Dalio saw as small issues, such as asking underlings whether a given Principle made sense, and never had enough time to tackle larger tasks. Mack allowed himself to be ruled by emotion. These being common criticisms of Dalio's of most everyone around him, some in the room had to fight to stay interested.

"You're shooting in the wrong direction," Dalio told Mack, borrowing a line from The Principles.

McCormick chimed in, "Yeah, I would agree."

During diagnoses people commonly agreed with Dalio to distance themselves from the person under fire. In this instance, though, McCormick was turning on a friend. The room suddenly shifted. Mack seemed to weigh his options: Would he take the slight in stride or swing back?

First Mack addressed Dalio calmly, "I can see why you think what you're saying could be true."

Then Mack turned to McCormick. "But I don't think David is being truthful."

Mack told the group that on their runs, outside of earshot of anyone else, McCormick complained about Dalio and Bridgewater. The message was clear. Dalio was surrounded by sycophants and he didn't even know it.

This was a bombshell. Not only had Mack accused his friend of being a slimy weasel, Mack had struck hard at the core of the Bridgewater management system. What did it say about Dalio if he didn't even realize that some people in his inner circle hadn't bought in?

Dalio decided to expand the diagnosis to include McCormick. True leadership is an attempt to get at the truth at any cost, Dalio said. He pulled together a team to listen to all the recorded tapes of Mack and McCormick in meetings at Bridgewater, and to report on which of them was honest. Dalio said the investigation would continue at the next week's management committee meeting.

News of the coming showdown spread through the firm. Some people privately went to Mack and confessed their own misgivings. Others backed McCormick, pointing out that he had done what virtually everyone else at Bridgewater did at every opportune moment. To them, to take Dalio at his word about "brutal honesty" was nothing but brutal stupidity. All Mc-Cormick was guilty of was agreeing reflexively with Dalio—which made him savvy, if nothing else.

Mack and McCormick could scarcely make eye contact at the next management committee meeting, several people present recall; it seemed likely that their time as running partners was over.

Dalio opened the proceedings. "I'd like to understand what's true—"

McCormick cut in, "I have something I'd like to say first. I've been in combat. I've had men under me, when we were going into a life-and-death situation. The only way we could do that as soldiers is to know that we had each other's loyalty. I don't feel like I could go into combat here because you're giving Julian the time of day on what he said."

"It's not about loyalty," Dalio responded. "It's about truth."

Dalio turned to Mack. "What is the truth?"

The truth, Mack told Dalio, is Mack had spent the past week hearing from Bridgewater employees that they were scared of telling the truth.

"You've hardwired a system of thought that is believed to be inherently superior to other logic. When questions are asked about the system, you get them answered through the system," Mack told Dalio. "Preserving a theology through its theology ends up with theology squared."

Dalio quickly shifted from the investigation of McCormick to a defense of The Principles. Here he was, inviting criticism in front of all. This very conversation, Dalio said, proved the merit of the system.

"How much more open-minded could I be?" he asked.

He now turned the argument on Mack. Dalio had invited a careful presentation of the evidence, supported by any data that could be found. Instead, Mack had come back with furtive whispers from unnamed supporters. It didn't say much for these putative supporters that they hadn't been forthright in the first place.

Transforming what had started as a simple diagnosis into a full-fledged, highly produced inquisition, Dalio next called a town hall for hundreds of employees. The walls were retracted between several training rooms and the cafeteria, to fit in the most attendees possible. The proceedings were recorded for later relistening by all.

Dalio and Mack sat on chairs in front of the crowd, passing a microphone back and forth.

"So Julian feels that things are wrong here," Dalio said.

Mack, posture straight and voice steady, made his pitch. "I think the culture here is suppressing people's true feelings."

Dalio threw up his hands and handed over the mic to Mack. "Ask them."

Mack stood, facing the horde. "Who here feels repressed?"

No one raised their hand.

"You see—" Dalio said.

"Nobody?!" Mack yelped. "Nobody is going to stand up? Some of you have been in my office telling me about this."

Silence again.

Dalio took back the mic. "I don't know what you're complaining about, Julian. It's you that has the problem."

Mack was let go at the next management committee meeting. He packed up his desk the same day. He would never speak publicly about his experience at the firm.

MACK MAY have misjudged his base of support, but he was well-liked nonetheless. His departure before year-end 2010, after such a high-profile internal clash with Dalio, threatened to cast a pall on what had been a spectacularly profitable year.

The Bridgewater investing machine was on a powerful streak. This was less due to any singular new idea than a conflux of old ones. The global economic recovery that began in 2009 was slowing down, and Bridgewater had per usual been betting on market woes. The hedge fund's holdings of so-called safe-haven assets, such as bonds and gold, tended to outperform in times of caution, and they were in renewed demand in 2010. A leveraged version of Pure Alpha, using borrowed money to juice returns, soared 45 percent in that year alone. All-Weather gained double digits. In 2010, Dalio made just over $3 billion personally, nearly doubling his net worth.

Thus 2011 presented as the perfect time to go on the offensive.

Dalio still seemed to smart from his experience with *Dealbreaker* and the increased media exposure it wrought, and seemed eager to show the world that he wasn't just another rich dilettante. He hired a public relations firm and told them that his goal was to establish a public persona on the level of that of Berkshire Hathaway founder Warren Buffett. In addition to his legendary record as an investor, the Oracle of Omaha was seen as a friend of the common investor—a man who spoke plainly, lived frugally, and wasn't afraid to take on Wall Street orthodoxy. Tens of thousands of Berkshire faithfuls flocked to Nebraska each spring to hear Buffett speak. Dalio hungered for such a platform. His new advisers told him that Buffett's reputation hadn't emerged by accident—that he had carefully cultivated a circle of journalists who could be counted on to carry his views to the world. Dalio pledged to colleagues that he would do the same.

Dalio's other model, as he often said, was Steve Jobs. Dalio's obsession with Jobs—and it could fairly be called that—had begun a few years earlier with Apple's release of the iPod touch. It was essentially the iPhone without the phone, with a large multicolored touch screen to display media. Dalio immediately wanted everyone at Bridgewater to have one. One idea was to load a copy of the rapidly expanding Principles onto each and require everyone at Bridgewater to carry their iPod from meeting to meeting, thus ensuring that a copy of The Principles was never more than an arm's length away. To acquire that many iPods, Dalio moved dozens of Bridgewater's technology contractors—temp workers who made hundreds of dollars per hour—off their posts and ordered them to wait in lines at Apple stores across the New York region. They were told to wait as long as it took, while billing Bridgewater their normal rates for their time, to buy as many iPods as allowed and bring them back to Westport.

Jobs may have started as an engineer, but he built an empire encompassing films, smartphones, retailing, and music. Even casual users of Apple products knew the company founder's name. Though by 2011 Jobs's health was failing, his renown was still growing, thanks to the author and journalist Walter Isaacson, in the throes of a publicity tour for what would be a bestselling, seminal biography of the hard-charging Apple executive. Isaacson didn't shy from anecdotes that showed Jobs behaving rudely to subordinates; if anything, Jobs's brusque behavior was connected to his success. The book, later made into a film, featured a black-and-white cover headshot of Jobs staring directly into the camera, pinching his chin. It would have been a powerful image for Dalio, so clearly impelled as he was to be seen as a historic figure.

Fortunately for the Bridgewater founder, that image of Jobs stuck in the mind of Kip McDaniel, a journalist crammed in coach on a long, against-the-headwind flight from New York to Los Angeles.

McDaniel's work was not at risk of being adapted into Hollywood movies. He was the founding editor in chief of *Chief Investment Officer* magazine, a quarterly that published specialized pieces for what could charitably be described as a limited audience. He was familiar with Bridgewater, in part because the hedge fund had helped get the magazine off the ground by paying it to publish some stories ("Risk Parity Consultant Views Survey, Sponsored by Bridgewater"). Using in-flight Wi-Fi, McDaniel shot off an email to a Bridgewater staffer. Would Dalio be interested in chatting for a piece that compared him to Steve Jobs?

Before the plane was wheels down, McDaniel confirmed a three-hour, one-on-one interview with the founder of the world's biggest hedge fund at his Manhattan town house.

The next issue featured Dalio on the cover in a facsimile of Jobs's book pose, complete with Dalio pinching his chin. The piece noted Jobs's infamously short temper and observed, "As at Apple, working at Ray Dalio's Bridgewater can be an experience in humility." Still, McDaniel took pains to point out some meaningful differences: "But where Dalio uses cold logic, Jobs seemed to rely on instinct. Ray Dalio is Steve Jobs with a business school degree." The headline for the profile on the cover asked, "Is Ray Dalio the Steve Jobs of Investing?," a question that McDaniel intentionally left unanswered in the piece.

Over time, the question mark faded. The next publication to compare the two men was *Wired,* which in an article about Apple acolytes included Dalio as an example and said he "has been called 'the Steve Jobs of investing,'" a reference to McDaniel's piece. That was enough to get Dalio's official biography on Bridgewater's website changed to read, "Ray has been called the 'Steve Jobs of Investing' by *aiCIO* Magazine and *Wired* Magazine."

ON OCTOBER 5, 2011, Jobs succumbed to pancreatic cancer. Dalio noted in his usual daily economic commentary to clients, "This is no ordinary day, this is the day Steve Jobs died."

Dalio began to talk about Jobs ad nauseum, and some at Bridgewater concluded that he was less interested in Jobs's accomplishments at Apple than in his outsize public persona. In Jobs, Dalio could see a model for his own hero's journey. Both men were, charitably, viewed as jerks. Both had multiple legs to their careers. The difference was that while Jobs in his second stint had built Apple into a universally envied model for the technology world, Bridgewater was mostly known just in finance.

Dalio concluded that the difference wasn't in their work, but in their messaging. The solution was to have Walter Isaacson write Dalio's biography. Those around him didn't pursue it the first few times it came up, but Dalio persisted in asking if it was possible, so Bridgewater staffers put out the request. Word came back from Isaacson's camp: it was a pass.

Dalio's disappointment showed, and an opportunity presented itself for David McCormick. What few would have known was that Dalio and Isaacson were more intertwined than it might have seemed. Dalio was a donor to the Aspen Institute, a white-shoe networking group for millionaires and billionaires to rub shoulders with former politicians and well-known intellectuals. McCormick was on the Aspen Institute board of trustees. Isaacson, who earlier in his career was the head of CNN, was now the Aspen Institute president.

McCormick rang him up. Perhaps, as a favor to a patron, Isaacson would be willing to travel to Connecticut and speak with Ray?

The visit was soon upgraded. Bridgewater went all out for Isaacson, treating him as a visiting dignitary. Rather than cram everyone into a conference room, the firm rented out the Inn at Longshore, a luxe spot on the Long Island Sound that typically hosts weddings. The venue put out hundreds of white chairs in front of a waterfront stage erected for Dalio and Isaacson to speak in what was billed as a fireside chat.

Isaacson didn't think much of the event in advance. He figured he would dust off a version of the remarks on Jobs's leadership that he'd been giving to corporations worldwide since the book's release. These usually included a few stories about Jobs mixed in with behind-the-scenes anecdotes from Isaacson's interviews for the book. Afterward, maybe he'd sign some copies and hold forth on some leadership lessons he'd learned.

He soon figured out that wasn't going to work. As he sat awkwardly across from Dalio, Isaacson had to wonder why he was there at all. Dalio was doing most of the talking, launching into a long soliloquy on his views on leadership. The topic du jour was *shapers*—a term that did not appear in Isaacson's book, but one that most everyone in the audience had heard multiple times. Dalio usually employed the term to make a contrast to a disappointing subordinate, as he did with Jim Comey, to upbraid the employee as a chirper, not a shaper. A shaper was a visionary leader, and to hear Dalio tell it, he had found precious few inside Bridgewater, save for himself. The qualifications to be a shaper outside Bridgewater were fairly nebulous. A shaper was curious, independent, and determined to achieve goals, Dalio said. He tended to proclaim people shapers after they had spent a long time speaking with him. Bill Gates, Elon Musk, and Reed Hastings all met with Dalio and were pronounced to be shapers.

In the midst of his soliloquy, Dalio stopped, suddenly seeming to remember that he was there with a guest. He gestured to Isaacson and asked, *Wouldn't you agree that both Steve Jobs and I are shapers?*

Isaacson's eyes darted side to side and he let out a nervous cough. He might have been a corporate guest, but he was a journalist, too, and he had demanded—and received—complete independence from Jobs in writing the book. Isaacson certainly wasn't about to aggrandize Dalio just for picking up his guest's travel costs. Isaacson dodged the question a few times, then launched into his pat talk.

Once it became clear that Isaacson wasn't interested in shapers, Dalio slumped in his chair and was more subdued for the remainder of the talk.

IF DALIO's Isaacson gambit failed, his overall effort to raise his public stature did not. A dribble of media interviews in summer and fall 2011 turned into a flood. Dalio soaked up the spotlight, on all platforms. Some weeks it seemed as if anyone who asked for an interview got one. As part of the blitz, Dalio made a triumphant return to television. In addition to the usual appearances on the business networks, he scored a coveted slot with television host Charlie Rose. This put Dalio in the same chair once occupied by

Jobs himself, to say nothing of U.S. presidents and the world elite, and across from an interviewer with a healthy respect for the rich and powerful. As Rose told Dalio on air:

"The two reasons that people are enormously curious about you: Number one is simply the objective success of what Bridgewater has done and become. And secondly, there are interesting questions as to how you think about the world.

"You always make the point that you know what you know and that's equally valuable."

Dalio said, "I want people to criticize my point of view. If you can attack what I'm saying—in other words, stress test what I'm saying—I'll learn."

"So therefore people will be free to tell you what they think, because you know that it will not be held against you, and you can benefit from it."

"That's right."

The two men came close to finishing each other's sentences.

"So anybody in a meeting at your company can stand up and say, 'Ray—'"

"Absolutely."

"'—you're absolutely wrong.'"

"Of course."

"'And you have not been precise and your assumptions are flawed.'"

"The number one principle at our place is that if something doesn't make sense to you, you have the right to explore it, to see if it makes sense."

Off set, Dalio and Rose became fast friends. During one catch-up, Dalio raised the idea of starring in his own television program, based on the time-tested TV-courtroom model—with Dalio as judge. Guests would come on air with big-picture questions, such as "Is there a God?," and Dalio would help answer them, using The Principles. Rose would be present to help guide the conversation. Dalio returned to Bridgewater from that chat excited; he told scores of underlings about it, and many assumed it was formally in development. To Rose, however, the idea represented no more than faint, casual musings. "I was enormously busy," he said. The idea never got off the ground.

Dalio had better luck dictating his terms with print publications, where writers champed at the bit to include the famous financier in their projects. When the author Maneet Ahuja requested an interview for her upcoming book, Dalio agreed on the condition that he could review the copy. Ahuja accepted his demand. She devoted the first chapter in her book, *The Alpha Masters: Unlocking the Genius of the World's Top Hedge Funds*, to Dalio. As the book title suggests, the chapter depicts Dalio as a noble, nearly Solomonic leader. It included her description of her walk through the halls of Bridgewater with its founder, observing, "Once a natural reserve filled with large lakes, there is a serene ambience to Dalio's inner sanctum." She evidently wasn't invited to one of the trials that took place therein.

Dalio also allowed generous access to academic psychologists, adding an imprimatur of scholarship to The Principles. Harvard's Robert Kegan and the Wharton School's Adam Grant were separately granted audiences with Dalio and chaperoned into Bridgewater meetings. The access earned Dalio near-fawning sections in books by each man. Kegan, in *An Everyone Culture: Becoming a Deliberately Developmental Organization*, concluded that Bridgewater was a "deliberately developmental organization" with an "inquiry-based culture." Kegan and his cowriter described Dalio as "a well-read aficionado of brain science" and suggested that through that study the Bridgewater founder had mastered self-analysis. "Bridgewater is an object lesson in the error the rest of us make when we settle for less in defining human nature," Kegan concluded.

For his book *Originals: How Non-Conformists Move the World*, Grant all but republished, under his own name, Bridgewater's talking points. "Although he has been called the Steve Jobs of investing, employees don't communicate with him as if he's anyone special," Grant wrote.

Grant noted, "Bridgewater's secret is promoting the expression of original ideas."

After observing several Bridgewater meetings and watching edited clips from others, the Wharton professor interviewed Dalio, who told him, "I'm unoffendable." Asked by Grant to rank The Principles by importance, Dalio demurred. Grant wrote that Dalio seemed particularly interested in "independent thinkers: curious, non-conforming, and rebellious. They practice brutal, nonhierarchical honesty. And they act in the face of risk, because their fear of not succeeding exceeds their fear of failing.

"Dalio himself fits this description."

It was Bridgewater through the looking glass.

The pièce de résistance of the media tour, or at least so Dalio hoped, was to be an extensive profile by *The New Yorker*, the talisman of the journalistic elite establishment. Dalio invited the reporter, John Cassidy, in to witness the firm's operations and promised unprecedented access. Here was a chance for Dalio to earn a seal of approval from a renowned magazine and to once and for all erase any lingering haze around his approach. First, he allowed Cassidy to sit in on the "What's Going On in the World?" meeting, in which fifty or so members of the Bridgewater investment staff debated economic trends to start each week. Afterward, Dalio probed an employee for the reporter's benefit. Dalio also sat for an interview and instructed a top-to-bottom contingent of Bridgewater staff to do the same (each interview was taped by Bridgewater, and each employee sat with the reporter only in the presence of a Bridgewater public relations representative). Bob Elliott, a twenty-nine-year-old investment team member, told the magazine, "Once you understand how the machine works, you have the ability to take that and study and apply it across markets." Michael Partington, the recruiter, addressed the firm's turnover, explaining that people "self-select" out on their own. Comey, too, made an appearance, remarking on Dalio, "He's tough and he's demanding and sometimes he talks too much, but, God, is he a smart bastard."

Cassidy appeared to have observed Bridgewater more carefully than some of his journalistic and academic peers. The piece hardly endorsed Dalio's approach to life and work. The article went to great lengths to point out the firm's oddities, calling it "the world's richest and strangest hedge fund." The reporter didn't just describe the culture he had observed, but what he hadn't: "In the time I spent at the firm I saw senior people criticizing subordinates—but not the reverse."

The piece had another small but meaningful incongruity by publication, one that Bridgewater's representatives didn't seek to clarify. Partington was actually already gone. It wasn't self-selection, either. Just before the article was published, Dalio fired him.

11

TRUTH FACTORY

Inside Bridgewater, there was no great mystery as to why the recruiter had to be replaced. Despite the hedge fund's expanding collection of efforts used to find staff, attrition was still a major issue.

To those outside Bridgewater, it might seem inconceivable that the firm could succeed in replenishing the ranks, given the seemingly endless cycle of people departing. But an advantage of the turnover was that for every new trial, diagnosis, or plain old indignity, there was a new hire for whom the experience was fresh and new. For many, all they knew of Bridgewater at first were the laudatory media interviews of Dalio and the comparisons to Steve Jobs. To show up and be presented with an atmosphere so radically different from the public narrative was to many not just a shock, but an incongruity that could not immediately be explained. If some left quickly, many others, rather than give up, turned inward, questioning themselves on why they couldn't seem to fit in with the Bridgewater "family," as Dalio so often called it.

Though Dalio nearly always talked of Bridgewater and its Principles as a wholesale invention, his emphasis on family and on the journey of self-improvement had many forefathers. The modern self-help era is traditionally traced to the 1960s—the cusp of Dalio's formative years—when the "human potential movement" grew out of the counterculture of the era. Proponents believed in a so-called hierarchy of needs, in which self-actualization, or achieving one's full potential, was more important than food, water, or even love. By the late 1980s, self-help icon Tony Robbins had released his first infomercial; he would soon advertise that he had "identified the fundamental principles of success conditioning," which he would reveal in a series of books.

While Robbins pitched workshops that could cost thousands of dollars, what Bridgewater and Dalio dangled was potentially even more enticing: the promise of self-improvement *and* a hefty payday. In 2011, Dalio made headlines for earning nearly $4 billion personally. His heir apparent, Jensen, was reported to have made $425 million. Though Dalio would often talk about the lure of Bridgewater as a beacon of self-improvement, a pot of gold at the end of the rainbow was perhaps the greatest recruitment tool. To those already at the hedge fund, the higher pay was known as "the Bridgewater tax," the premium of 20 percent or more that the company paid staff compared with what they could earn at competitors. "For as many times as dot quotas and issue logs were a thing, after a while you just start to realize you can ride it out because it's ever changing," said one sixteen-year Bridgewater veteran.

Many were eager to talk about why they left on their way out the door. Matt Granade, Comey's ski partner, had no choice but to leave. After seven years in investments culminating in his ascension to cohead of research, Granade was paradoxically doing less meaningful work than ever. His day was largely consumed by listening to tapes of probings of his team—when he wasn't being probed himself. He told his boss, Jensen, as much: "I like to work at businesses that do things. This place is like a kibbutz with a hedge fund attached."

True to the Bridgewater MO, staffers were encouraged to sit for an exit interview, and to write down the explanation for their departure. These notes were disseminated fairly widely, and occasionally one stuck so close to the nerve that it went viral inside the firm. One such reflection came from a relatively junior analyst, Kent Kuran.

Kuran came from a recruitment archetype whose supply was nearly endless: the new college graduate, with little to no work experience. Bridgewater recruiters consistently filled the pipeline with young men, with a heavy tilt toward alumni of Dartmouth, Harvard, and Princeton. Kuran joined Bridgewater after graduating from Princeton with a history degree. He was part of the cohort of management associates hired by Katina Stefanova.

Nineteen months later, he was out, burned out by the company culture that Dalio spent so much time promoting publicly.

"Through long stints at my time here, I would barely manage a few bites of lunch and on four occasions I actually vomited in the bathroom. I don't think I'm at all exceptional in this sense of fear. In what is supposed to be a hyper-open culture, meetings with senior management seem unbelievably neutered," Kuran told Bridgewater human resources. "I suspect Ray is out of touch with this dynamic given the fact that he recently asked people to raise their hands if they feel discussions are less than open."

From: EmpRelations_Help
To: HR_ExitInterviews

Subject: Exit Interview: Kent Kuran

Reason for Leaving: Career Change/Performance
Comments:
The immediate reason for leaving was losing my MA box due to Ray and David's data points on me. . . .

Somewhere between watching the fourth and fifth manager in my neighborhood be deemed inadequately conceptual, unable to synthesize, etc., while performing what would be considered modest responsibilities at another firm, the principles lost some of their initial magic for me. . . .

Knowing that any hour of the day Ray might respond unpredictably to a daily update or that any casual comment in a meeting might lead to a seminar about how one's "thinking is poor" generates tension and fear. It probably doesn't help that 50+ percent of "management training" consists of watching the "sorting" (could you find a more Orwellian word?) of one once respected colleague or another. . . .

There's an unhealthy drive to the negative that's often debilitating. Just a few weeks ago I literally couldn't think of any significant strength other than the charitable "hardworking." People seemed to be on the prowl to discover my weaknesses but strengths were underappreciated. . . .

BW was sold to me as an empowering place, where relatively young people can challenge the status quo and make a big impact. Fast-forward and it was drilled into me that it's bad to have opinions to the point that I felt like a Catholic schoolboy looking at porn whenever a nonconventional thought came into my head. . . .

On the perks and social end, the place beat expectations.

Several of Kuran's now-former coworkers printed out copies of his missive, expecting that it would disappear from Bridgewater servers at any moment.

PLENTY OF new souls lined up to take Kuran's place. Jesse Horwitz was one of the next to arrive. Horwitz was hunting for a new job after dropping out of his first year of Harvard Law School, and friends encouraged him to apply to Bridgewater. He got an internship offer. He was familiar with the firm's reputation as a tough place to work, but he considered it an intellectual challenge.

Horwitz's slim shoulders and pale skin fit in well with the rest of the intern class of 2011. He sat wide-eyed on his first days as Jensen addressed the incoming horde.

"Bridgewater is a truth factory. It just so happens that we produce investment truth. If we wanted to, we could cure cancer," Jensen told the group.

Horwitz was enthralled with the idea of being at a place where only the toughest survive. After his internship, he stayed on full-time as an investment associate, reasoning that Bridgewater was as good a place as any for a twenty-three-year-old to explore a career in finance.

He was quickly disappointed to learn that, despite his title, he wasn't involved in any actual investing. He was assigned to be mentored under a Princeton-educated Bridgewater research executive, Karen Karniol-Tambour, and though she had been at the hedge fund already for five years, she didn't seem to be much closer to investing than he was. There they were, mere feet from what Bridgewater called "the investment engine," yet neither of them had much of a clue about what was going on.

That is not to say there wasn't work. On top of what could be hours of daily training videos, Horwitz received what he considered to be respectable exposure to Dalio's priorities. Horwitz was assigned to a team of senior analysts producing a project assigned by the Bridgewater founder. With an eye toward broadening Bridgewater's public reputation for thought leadership, Dalio wanted to put out a research project on how to predict gross domestic product, or GDP, for any country for the upcoming decade. This sort of wide-ranging topic might consume a ballroom of economics Ph.D.s—and produce no agreement—but Dalio said that he had already cracked the equation. He had researched the topic in the early 1990s and determined that the level of indebtedness in a country could predict future GDP. Dalio told the team that, unfortunately, he'd misplaced the file that contained the spreadsheet. But he said it shouldn't be hard for the staff to re-create the equation, given that he had already given them the answer.

In three to five hours Horwitz's team had their own answer. The one metric highly correlated with how much a country would grow was the number of hours per week its citizens worked. That had a correlation of about 0.6 (0 being no correlation and 1 being perfect), making it a respectable indicator. This made intuitive sense: a lazy populace was unlikely to fuel a nation's growth. The group also determined that Dalio's answer made less sense. Actually it didn't make any sense at all. They couldn't find any debt statistic that correlated substantively with GDP, and no amount of mathematical torture could make it so. The group tried telling Dalio as much, but he wouldn't hear it. He kept sending them back to redo their analysis. Horwitz later told friends he was reminded of Joseph Smith, the founder of the Church of Jesus Christ of Latter-day Saints, who said he had uncovered golden plates containing sacred texts, yet couldn't produce the plates for examination.

Finally, after several months, Horwitz's group found a complicated series of equations that in a roundabout way connected public debt with GDP. Horwitz's boss set up a time to present it to Dalio and brought the team. Before he looked at the research, Dalio pointed at the group.

"What are those?" he said.

It took a moment for Horwitz to realize that Dalio was referring to him and the other assembled underlings. Horwitz's supervisor piped in, introducing Horwitz as an analyst. Dalio responded by wondering aloud why his analysts needed analysts of their own.

Horwitz's supervisor pivoted. These are just typists, he said, shooing Horwitz from the room. Horwitz was certain he was about to be fired. He learned afterward that Dalio had asked for an investigation on why there were so many analysts.

Horwitz was told he would keep his job, but the experience left him shaken. He took a week's vacation in San Francisco. Some three thousand miles of distance cleared his head and he realized that while law school may not have been his calling, this certainly wasn't either. He gave his notice on his return, with a note to Karniol-Tambour.

I understand you've had a positive experience, he told her. The difference, as he saw it, was that she had joined the company before a period of rapid growth. "I don't think it diminishes your experience or the organization to say that it's a bigger company now. There aren't the same opportunities now."

She replied quickly, in short, "You are wrong."

Horwitz didn't want to leave on a bad note. He thought of The Principles, which reminded time and again that sometimes two people just don't see things the same way.

I guess we will have to agree to disagree, Horwitz told Karniol-Tambour. She wrote back again, "You are wrong."

HORWITZ DIDN'T quite receive the clean break he hoped for. After Bridgewater, the twenty-four-year old decided to start his own investment firm, hardly an extraordinary move, as many of the biggest hedge funds in the world—to say nothing of many failures—had been started by traders who first worked at other firms. Horwitz's operation might technically have been a hedge fund, but with no sizable money to trade and no real prospects for raising any, it was more like an elaborate personal brokerage account. Still, Horwitz and a fellow former Bridgewater employee decided to give it a go. They knew they weren't allowed to use any proprietary investment information from their time at the firm, but that didn't seem like a problem, since they didn't have any.

This did not deter their former employer. In a letter to the two Bridgewater emigres, the Bridgewater legal department under Comey accused the fledgling firm of stealing the hedge fund's secrets. *What secrets?* Horwitz had to wonder. The closest he had gotten to Dalio was being asked to leave the room.

The situation got stranger one weekend morning when Horwitz received a phone call from a friend still at Harvard Law.

"You won't believe it. Jim Comey's daughter is talking about you."

"Maurene Comey?" Horwitz nearly spat back. She had overlapped with him at law school. The two were far from close, though they knew each other's names. She was on track to be a federal prosecutor like her dad.

"I was just with her at a party," Horwitz's friend told him. "She's saying her father is going to crush you for trampling the noncompete. He's really excited to come after you hard."

This news from Cambridge struck Horwitz as a mix of scary and absurd. Horwitz was a law school dropout hoping to trade stocks on his laptop. Jim Comey was Jim Comey—and he apparently had nothing better to do than gossip with his daughter about a piddling former employee. Still, the legal letters kept coming, and Horwitz realized Bridgewater expected him to surrender. What Bridgewater didn't count on was that while Horwitz might not have much money, he did have access to free advice. He asked his mom, an attorney, to help him write back to Bridgewater, asking them to specify their accusations, and to go to arbitration. The specifics never seemed to materialize. Bridgewater gave up.

Horwitz's fledgling hedge fund flopped. It neither made a cent in the markets nor raised any money from investors. Comey needn't have bothered to try to bury the start-up, and by then he was onto bigger targets.

12

SEX AND LIES, VIDEOTAPED

THERE ARE PRECIOUS FEW PERKS THAT A MAJOR DONOR TO HARVARD University cannot acquire. Fork over a seven-figure donation for a red-carpet tour of campus; closer to eight figures garners special help with undergraduate admissions; at $150 million there may well be erected the [Ken] Griffin Financial Aid Office; for $400 million step right up to the Harvard John A. Paulson School of Engineering and Applied Sciences.

Though some have no doubt tried, one prize not up for auction is a case study from Harvard Business School. First conceived in the 1920s, HBS case studies are written on tough business decisions and told from the perspective of the person in charge. The cases are distributed widely, both to students and the public. Executives of all stripes covet a chance to star in an HBS case because they seemingly convey the imprimatur of Harvard. Dalio had read his share of cases at HBS, and starring in one would further burnish the narrative about him and The Principles that Charlie Rose and other journalists had been so helpful in spreading.

Professors Jeffrey Polzer and Heidi K. Gardner were accustomed to being pitched by ambitious business leaders, so when Dalio in mid-2011 was given an audience to discuss the possibility of an HBS case about Bridgewater, they were prepared to turn him down. Their expertise was organizational behavior, not finance. As Dalio went on and on about radical truth and transparency, it struck the professors as a whole lot of theatrics.

Both sat up straight, however, when they later learned of the possibility of telling something more than the tale of Dalio's success. Bridgewater had a new sheriff, Jim Comey. Had there ever been an HBS case about a tough prosecutor, known for taking on terrorists, becoming a hedge fund executive? How about the challenge of absorbing him into a place as strong-willed as Bridgewater? Dalio proposed that the Harvard professors not just take his word for it. He was willing to hand over the video evidence and open up Bridgewater's Transparency Library. It would be a truly multimedia HBS case that showed Comey's struggles and successes at Bridgewater.

The professors were sold. Another rich hedge fund manager talking about himself was one thing; Comey, on tape, was another. They got to work, watching hundreds of hours of footage sent over from Westport.

LORDY, THERE was plenty to watch.

Comey had become intensely close to Jensen, the relationship being fruitful for both sides. Jensen needed to prove that he was a managerial talent as well as a gifted investor if he was to be separated in Dalio's eyes from the rest of the executive horde. Comey, meanwhile, would need more help with The Principles if he was to shake his chirper label. No one was more conversant in Dalio's philosophy than Jensen.

The two were united in their dislike of Jensen's co-CEO, Eileen Murray. Jensen made little secret of his view that she was wholly undeserving of sharing his title. To hear him him say it, Murray stuck out like a pimple in Bridgewater's blue-blooded executive suite. She'd grown up in a housing project in Queens, where she woke up early to beat her five siblings to the single bathroom they shared. Her older sister ruled the television remote and hated to give in to her siblings' wishes, so Murray learned to ask to switch the channel away from her favorite shows, knowing that her sister would refuse and keep the station put. "At a very young age, I learned a little bit about the psyche of a bully," Murray once said.

Murray came home one evening to discover her neighbor lying in the hall, spread-eagle, his pockets turned out, shot in the head. The incident hardened her. She had little patience when, early in her career before join-ing Bridgewater, a male colleague ribbed that her skirt might get dirty on the job. She replied, "You would look awfully good in a skirt. And I have a sense that you want to wear one." She rarely wore skirts. She never married, never had children, and talked frequently about her dogs.

Dalio, always looking for undiscovered gems, was visibly taken by Mur-ray's spunk. She had that natural fight in her that The Principles espoused. And like him, she possessed a charming lack of artifice. She sent emails off the cuff, all lowercase, with typos, suggesting she was too busy to give anything her full attention. Murray was able to return the Bridgewater founder's volleys as quickly as he served them, and the two developed a rapport. When Dalio announced to his deputies that he had instructed a team to develop a software tool known as the pain button, for staffers to use in distress, Murray led out an audible snort.

"Where's the pleasure button?" she asked Dalio.

"You want a pleasure button? You invent the goddamn pleasure button. I invented the pain button," Dalio replied.

"You actually already have a pleasure button if you check," Murray retorted.

Dalio seemed to enjoy the breaks in the tension that so often surrounded him. Though Murray flunked almost every one of Bridgewater's behavioral metrics—her stratum rating was a one—Dalio kept promoting her. She was made co-CEO within a year of starting.

Murray's role left her in charge of the unsexy half of the firm, operations, where she oversaw the interlocking agreements between Bridgewater and its clients and counterparties around the world. She hired a slew of fellow former Morgan Stanley colleagues, all loyal to her. Some stayed with her on weeknights at her Westport home. It visibly frustrated Jensen, for whom Bridgewater was the center of his identity, to be put on the same level as a newcomer who had no hand in the firm's investments and who seemed to be building her own, off-grid center of power. It was like handing over the kitchen of a five-star restaurant to the junior waitstaff.

In Murray's fast ascent, she overlooked one complicating factor: The Principles. She was a career woman, and she dismissed the whole manifesto as yet another altar to the ego of an older man. She bragged to her ex–Morgan Stanley crew that she never bothered reading The Principles.

Comey and Jensen would make her pay for that.

The proximate cause of Murray's lesson in the application of The Principles was innocuous enough. A job candidate mentioned to a Bridgewater executive that he was familiar with the hedge fund's head of accounting, Perry Poulos, one of Murray's new hires. The job candidate evinced surprise—didn't they know Poulos had been fired after twenty-seven years at Morgan Stanley? Surely Murray would have told the firm all about it.

The tip was quickly passed to Comey, who gave Jensen a heads-up. Comey grabbed a former FBI agent on the Bridgewater staff and went to intercept the unsuspecting Poulos. The duo pulled him into a conference room without warning.

"Hi, guys," Poulos said.

"We just want to know, is there anything in your background we should know about?" Comey responded.

"I had some things there, but it's all cleared up now."

"You wouldn't mind if we ask a few questions and look a little more?"

There's really nothing to find, Poulos said. Go ahead.

He exited the room, heart racing, and soon found Murray. She knew, as he did, that he had been let go from Morgan Stanley after questions were raised about his expenses. While this wasn't exactly the ideal background for an accounting executive at the world's largest hedge fund, Murray sensed a larger target at play.

"It's not you," she told Poulos. "It's me. They are trying to get to me."

Comey called in Poulos for another interview.

"Did you talk to anyone about this?" Comey asked.

"No."

"Are you sure?"

"No, I haven't talked to anyone."

"You live with Eileen, don't you?"

Knowing Bridgewater's reputation for intimate relationships, Poulos assumed Comey was sniffing for a romantic angle. During the week, Poulos said, he sometimes spent the evening at her place, as other new employees had also done. There were plenty of bedrooms, they spent nights separately and he even paid her rent.

"Even that evening, after we spoke, you didn't talk to her?" Comey asked.

"I don't remember saying anything in particular."

The answer evidently didn't strike Comey as credible, so the same question was asked of Eileen. Did she speak to Poulos? She answered no. Murray was instructed to write a memo with everything she knew about Poulos's background.

The email that landed in Comey's inbox, labeled as sent from Murray's BlackBerry, was pristine. The grammar was clean and every word was properly capitalized. Comey showed it to Jensen. Both agreed it could not possibly have been written by her. Comey, as head of security, had access to security cameras. He pulled the footage and showed it to Jensen. Murray, sitting at her desk, was on camera, clearly in conversation with a subordinate in the minutes leading up to the email's being sent. One could even pinpoint the moment she asked her subordinate to hit send.

Comey and Jensen pulled Murray into another meeting.

Are you sure you didn't talk to anyone about this? they asked.

"Of course not."

Even as the words left her mouth, Murray must have known she had made a mistake. The email was obviously not hers alone. She had worked on it with an assistant, dictating phrases and going back and forth until they had come up with clean answers. She had been visibly nervous that she was walking into a trap and wanted to get it all exactly right. But now she was in a deeper hole of her own making. She had now been dishonest twice—once about speaking to Poulos, and now about typing the email. Worst of all for Murray, she knew that Jensen would be only too happy to call her out on it.

Before Jensen had a chance, Murray fled to Dalio and confessed her sins. She had lied only out of panic. She hadn't been feeling herself, she said. She had just been trying to stay out of Comey's crosshairs, and to keep Poulos away from the dragnet, too. "It was a white lie," she said.

Dalio paused to confirm that the tape recorder was on and then said that Bridgewater was a place where liars were punished. There would have to be a trial.

It wasn't just a trial, it was *the* trial. The investigation of Murray and Poulos went on for nine months. Cameras rolled all the while as Comey and Jensen probed Murray and Poulos on their transgressions. Everyone at the firm saw footage of Murray sitting at her desk, dictating the infamous email. The inquest didn't stop at Murray's pair of confessed lies. Comey seemed to act as if he had gotten Al Capone on tax evasion—once Comey had her in court, he had an excuse to investigate her whole life's story. Murray walked past Comey's office one day to see the walls covered in newspaper clippings, and sticky notes, all about her, with lines drawn all over like a police sketch board on a procedural television series. She felt sick to her stomach.

It seemed to Murray and those sympathetic to her as if Dalio couldn't get enough. He sat in as judge and turned the investigation into a real-time case, called *Eileen Lies*. Videos were released weekly, as serialized viewing for all Bridgewater staff. The updates were a combination of reality television, soap opera, and cinema verité. Comey played bad cop; in one video, he told Poulos, "Just tell the truth, it might make you feel good." Jensen cast himself as the victim. "You lied to me," he told Murray. "I want to trust you, but it's going to take time."

New episodes of *Eileen Lies* continued to air even after Poulos was fired, and after Murray's assistant—called to testify against her boss—decided to resign instead.

OUTSIDE BOSTON, Professor Heidi Gardner sat in her office, gobsmacked. She had been looking forward to doing an HBS case study about Bridgewater's idiosyncratic culture. For a long while now, however, Bridgewater had been sending over videos straight out of the theater of the absurd. Much of the entire business of Bridgewater, as Gardner could see it, seemed to be consumed by Jim Comey—*Jim Comey!* Gardner marveled—employing enhanced interrogation techniques on a middle-aged woman. Gardner and her HBS partner couldn't figure out why the former prosecutor cared so much. But they also couldn't get enough of it. Maybe Dalio was right; maybe the hedge fund's culture was doing its job, rubbing off on Comey, turning him into a true believer in Dalio's ways. Either way, this case was going to be hot stuff.

What the professors didn't know was that the series finale was already in production. After the better part of a year, even Comey and Jensen could wring no more juice out of the incident. Jensen presented his final argument: Eileen was an inveterate liar, and an avowed violator of the most sacred of The Principles. She had to be fired, for the good of the firm. Comey backed him up. Comey couldn't, he told Dalio, imagine sitting on the same management committee as a person who didn't live up to Bridgewater's values.

Dalio punted. Murray had lied, he ruled, but she hadn't been proven to be a liar. The whole incident, Dalio told the firm, was a learning experience. It inspired him to write two new Principles. One dealt with white lies—they were acceptable, in small quantities. The other new Principle: "Everything looks bigger up close." With the perspective of time, he had realized that Murray's offenses were forgivable. Of course, she would have to pay penance. He stripped her of her co-CEO title, bouncing her down to firm president.

Everyone was unsatisfied. Murray had lost her role and her dignity. Comey and Jensen were even more apoplectic—they had proven their case and lost anyway. Even those sympathetic to Murray felt that she'd skipped mostly free on behavior that would have gotten anyone else fired. What was the point of The Principles if they could be modified to overlook past infractions?

Bridgewater employees weren't the only ones disappointed. As Murray's trial concluded, the Harvard Business School professors received an urgent message from Bridgewater. Comey now refused to be a part of their case. Bridgewater immediately yanked the professors' access to videos of him. They no longer had permission to make an HBS case about Comey whatsoever—even if they left *Eileen Lies* out of it. There was no window for negotiations.

The solution was to start from scratch. Out went Comey and the overarching idea that Bridgewater was successfully working to bring in the next generation of leaders. HBS needed an easier task. The case instead wound up including a fairly straightforward history of the world's biggest hedge fund. Though the professors requested certain footage, Bridgewater selected and edited each of the nineteen video clips that made it in. Dalio, apparently still smarting from Comey's refusal to participate in the case study, took an acute personal interest. When the Harvard professors sent Bridgewater's team a copy of the final text for approval as agreed, Gardner was forced to spend hours on the phone with Dalio himself, going line by line as the Bridgewater founder argued about semicolons, sentence structure, and whether there were any dangling participles (there were not, in her opinion).

Doesn't this guy have anything else to do? she thought to herself more than once.

The videos attached to the HBS case began with Dalio speaking to the camera: "For me, Bridgewater is a dream come true. I mean, you have to understand that when I formed it, I didn't know anything. I was two years out of school, I didn't have any money. The only thing I had is what I cared a lot about, and for me that was—"

Here, midsentence, the video suddenly cuts, to Dalio facing the opposite direction. It's another take entirely.

"—meaningful work. In other words I wanted to be in a mission to beat the markets, to be the best . . . and meaningful relationships."

A few seconds later, a graphic appears on-screen, a triangle, inscribed inside with the words TRUTH AT ALL COST.

Much of the case was about giving and receiving feedback in the Bridgewater way. A video was included from a management committee meeting. Dalio, Jensen, McCormick, and others sat around a messy rectangular conference table, in front of a whiteboard with WHERE'S THE VISION? scribbled on it in red ink and circled several times. Niko Canner, a gray-haired member of the management committee who didn't look much younger than Dalio, was among the group seated. Dalio sat across from Canner, staring back, not breaking his gaze and frozen from the waist up. Canner delivered his feedback with considerable caution:

"So how does Ray mentor? I would separate out some different elements. There's part of mentoring that is about help [sic] people see themselves more clearly and accurately, and I would say that you are the best that I've ever seen on that dimension—"

The video cuts to black and picks up at an indeterminate point later. Canner:

"Then there's another dimension of mentoring, um, that is about, um, pull [sic] out the best performance that human beings are capable of. And I'm still learning how good you are at that. My sense is, only okay, sort of in the middle of the pack of high-achieving people—people who are at sort of your general level of achievement—"

A third cut.

"And then there's a third piece that's about, um, more the sizing people up, knowing what people are capable of, knowing who to bet on, and how. My sense of that is evolving—"

Cut.

"I look at those attributes in relation to mentoring and then say, over the past six months, my sense is not dramatically different from what I'd expect, but maybe a little bit less well specifically relating to mentoring than I would have expected with that sense of attributes."

When the HBS case was released, Gardner was careful to neither endorse nor condemn the Bridgewater style. The professors had intentionally not attempted to determine whether the firm culture had any measurable impact on its historical investment performance. Gardner wasn't even sure if such an analysis was possible. She would introduce the case to her students by saying, "We are not holding this up as an exemplar and saying, 'If you were smart, you'd do what Ray does.' We are saying, 'Take a look.'" As a scientist, she felt she had done the best with data that was available to her.

Dalio was delighted with the HBS case. He made sure Bridgewater's marketing team sent copies of it to Bridgewater's clients around the world.

As TIME passed after *Eileen Lies,* Jensen seemed to turn sanguine. He was CEO of the world's largest hedge fund, on his way to becoming a billionaire. As important, his onetime rival, Murray, was damaged and demoted. This was most obvious in the formation of Bridgewater's new Ethics Committee, as Dalio called it. On account of her trial, Dalio left Murray off.

Jensen worked long hours, many of them closely with Dalio (said one former Bridgewater investment staffer, "Greg spoke Ray"). Each could boast a savant-like memory of historical economic minutiae, and the pair would volley ideas at length, while subordinates gathered around in awe. Since Jensen spent so much time around Dalio, Jensen often received ratings from Dalio—and since Dalio was so highly rated, Jensen's ratings soared each time Dalio rated him positively. Jensen parroted Principles so often around the Bridgewater founder that many around Jensen could only guess whether he was serious or on a yearslong quest to remain teacher's pet.

Yet those around Jensen also saw the toll that Bridgewater exacted on him. He came in some days hungover and didn't hide it; when asked if he had been out late drinking, he would simply say yes. He was an enthusiastic host and attendee of Bridgewater company retreats, where he demonstrated an oddball sense of humor. At one Bridgewater confab, he hired an actress to dress up as a stripper and pretend to be the same one that Dalio had hired decades earlier to present at a conference—the incident that helped get the Bridgewater founder fired from his early job. No one else at Bridgewater dared attempt a joke at the expense of the company founder, earning Jensen respect even from those who thought the stunt was in poor taste.

Jensen was essentially the hedge fund's social chair. Every time a new crew of postcollege recruits started, he seemed to make friends with them all. People wanted to be around Jensen, and to be Jensen. He attended parties with junior staff, though he was often the oldest person by far. He would frequently fly to Las Vegas with other Bridgewater employees; during one trip, his wife, who had stayed home to nurse their infant twins, complained to friends that she had fielded a fraud-alert phone call from his credit card company concerning the amount charged at a strip club. That wasn't the only example of his behavior seeming to be stuck in his fraternity era. At one party for Bridgewater staff, Jensen dared his direct reports to puke on his head in exchange for $500.

Jensen struck a particularly memorable presence at the annual summer retreat the hedge fund hosted at the Mohonk Mountain House, a Victorian era resort perched on a New York lake less than two hours' drive from Bridgewater headquarters.

The summer 2012 management associate retreat was billed as a team-building event for Bridgewater managers in training, sans family. It quickly turned into the Greg Jensen experience. He was both the most senior employee present and the person who seemed to sleep the least. Daytime was tame, filled with off-the-rack team-building activities and hikes. Jensen really got going when the sun went down. One evening, what was billed as a fireside chat, or a chance to ask burning questions of the Bridgewater CEO, turned into more of a comedy roast. With a Bridgewater recruiting executive acting as emcee, Jensen cracked jokes about his travels with Dalio. When Jensen was asked to describe what it was like to sit next to Dalio in a sauna in Japan, he cracked a joke about whether Dalio's high stratum rating had any relationship to his personal anatomy.

This was followed by skinny-dipping and a campfire event. Jensen challenged the attendees—men and women alike—to take off their shirts and throw them into the flames to prove their bond with him and one another. Dozens took him up on the offer. Replacement shirts were handed out for the walk back to the hotel.

Jensen seemed to have his eye on one attendee in particular, Samantha Holland, only a few years his junior. Bridgewater's rating system had identified Holland as an up-and-comer who spoke her mind. A public school graduate who worked for a spell in the Bridgewater facilities department, she had an adventurous grit that Jensen's usual underlings in the investing department did not. Jensen had noticed her rise and had been advising her on how to take her career to the next level. She told friends that she'd begun to believe that Bridgewater was a place where she could go far.

After the crowd had dispersed from around the fire, Jensen invited Holland out alone. It was just the two of them, both married, around the dimming embers.

Take your shirt off, he said.

She did.

They moved to the hot tub.

The other Bridgewater employees at the retreat might have been drunk, but they weren't blind. They saw Holland return to the Mohonk Mountain House alone with Jensen. Whether genuinely outraged or merely cognizant of a chance to make their own name by calling out Dalio's top deputy, some in attendance complained to the Bridgewater founder afterward that the weekend had made them uncomfortable.

Dalio once again put Comey in charge of uncovering the truth.

With his tape recorder running, Comey interviewed many of those who'd attended the retreat. Jensen told him that everyone, including Holland, had voluntarily gone topless. When Comey sat down with Holland alone, he asked her a pointed question: Did you feel you had a choice? She took a pause before answering. She hadn't been physically forced, she explained, but Jensen far outranked her. She told Comey she didn't feel that she had a choice.

Comey presented his findings to Dalio, who moved to sweep the episode aside. Dalio announced to everyone at Bridgewater that he had investigated the party, and that there need be no further questions.

As for Comey's interviews with Holland and Jensen, it was as if they never happened. Those recordings, and others from Comey's investigation, were kept out of Bridgewater's Transparency Library. Dalio assured Jensen that the tapes would be pulled from circulation.

IF COMEY felt discomfort about the investigation of the Mohonk retreat, he did not make a known issue of it. But by this time he'd come to see that a job at the world's biggest hedge fund was not the slam dunk it had once seemed.

What had started as a chance to cash in on his reputation had turned into a potential reputational risk. Comey's name was being whispered about for high-level government jobs, and what was happening at Bridgewater had the potential to burn, rather than burnish, his résumé. How could he justify his investigation of Murray, especially since he had failed to nail her? Or that Jensen received no meaningful sanction for his late-night behavior.

One more inquest was left on the agenda. Almost alone among media, Dalio's old antagonist *Dealbreaker* had continued to report on Bridgewater with a skeptical air. Every so often the blog was rewarded for its skepticism with a leak from Bridgewater. In spring 2012, *Dealbreaker* hit a new mother lode. A fax came in on the website's anonymous tip line with the instructions for The Principles Test, given to all employees to evaluate their memorization of the Dalio manifesto. The instructions, written by one of Dalio's leveragers, or chiefs of staff, were characteristically stern. The Principles Training Team, the leverager wrote, would "audit for cheating, and cheating will be dealt with severely." The same team would "keep track of lateness or unexpected absence," and employees were instructed to "think twice about calling in 'sick'!" *Dealbreaker* quickly posted a piece on it.

It took Comey less than twenty-four hours to find the leaker. Comey pulled surveillance footage from the company's fax machines and saw that an employee had printed the instructions, searched the Web for *Dealbreaker*'s and Charlie Rose's fax numbers, and faxed off the document. Reviewing the footage, Comey came to an embarrassing revelation. The culprit was a five-year Bridgewater veteran who was a West Point graduate and a member of Comey's security team. The investigation was handed off to Jensen.

The Bridgewater CEO got to work probing. Though the security officer first denied sending the fax, he quickly admitted that he was frustrated by the upcoming Principles Test. He specifically cited Dalio's earlier interview with Charlie Rose: How could Dalio claim The Principles were open to criticism, then prescribe a test on adherence to them? Jensen asked why the employee hadn't spoken out internally first, and the officer said he had. Jensen made a note to probe the officer's bosses next.

Even those who sympathized with the officer's argument weren't surprised to learn that he'd been fired. Many were shocked, however, when they opened their Principles Tests and discovered that Jensen had decided to make an example of the officer. A new entry on the test named the leaker to all, laid out the whole investigation in gory detail, and asked employees to agree that he had been dealt with appropriately. In addition to detailing the preceding events, the entry contained Jensen's own conclusions on the officer's failings: "It appears now [the officer] has harbored ill-will and for whatever set of reasons failed to address it (based on my conversation seemed to be lack of logic and high confidence that he knew what it 'should' be)."

Considerably more secrecy surrounded Comey's own resignation in October 2012, which came without an immediate explanation from Dalio.

Questions piled up, and when employees were asked to vote at a Bridgewater town hall on queries to be answered, the top-voted topic was Comey's imminent departure. Comey laid out his thinking in an email:

From: Jim Comey
Sent: Wednesday, October 03, 2012
To: Bridgewater

Subject: Why is Jim leaving?

. . . I like Bridgewater very much. I love the idea of our culture of transparency and truth and find both addictive. . . .

Like all of you, I have strengths and weaknesses. Among my strengths are some leadership abilities that are not critical here, but that are both needed and highly effective in the rest of the world. I smiled (and winced) when I saw the list of leadership competencies that had been omitted from the baseball cards because they are some of the things that have made me effective elsewhere: humor, communication, team-building, adaptability, dealing with paradox, etc. . . .

But those competencies are also what makes work and life fun for me. I derive great joy from interacting with people, with all their (and my) foibles. I delight at a clever turn of phrase. I enjoy satire, the occasional sarcasm, the puncturing of pomposities and human vanity. . . . . . .

There is something in the logic-based, relentless pursuit of excellence that is inconsistent with the kind of joy that animates me. In particular, it may be something about the utterly unforgiving nature of the search for alpha that creates an institutional personality. I'm not saying Bridgewater's personality should be different; only that it is different. Bridgewater reflects Ray's personality, which is a cool thing. But he and I are very different people. . . . . . I will be better as a public sector leader and teacher for having been here. . . .

Nothing is final, of course, and all of life is a squiggle (with conceptual time on the X-axis), but that is my thinking today and I wanted to be transparent about it.

Jim

Part III

13

THE MACHINE

I F J IM C OMEY'S FLAMING OUT BOTHERED D ALIO A WHIT, HE DIDN'T
show it. He had plenty of public praise to fall back on. For the first time,
in 2012, *Time* named the Bridgewater founder to their list of the World's
100 Most Influential People. The article that accompanied his ascension to
the list was by no less than former Federal Reserve chairman Paul Volcker,
who wrote:

> For many hedge funds, success is elusive; the larger the fund, the more dif-
> ficult it is to maintain outstanding performance. Bridgewater's Ray Dalio,
> who manages $120 billion in investor money, has defied the odds over a
> quarter-century. That in itself may not qualify Ray, 62, to sit among the
> influential. What matters more is that he has strong and a bit unorthodox
> convictions about the workings of the economic machine. The judgments
> that have emerged have been prescient. Ray was, for example, one of the
> first to recognize the risks of the excessive indebtedness and leveraging
> of the U.S. and some European economies. . . . [H]is curious and active
> mind is reflected in the fact that, while he does have an oceangoing ship,
> his "yacht" is equipped for deep-sea exploration.

In summer 2012, an urgent message from that yacht, sent from the
Ogasawara Islands, south of Japan, shot across the globe in an instant,
pinging satellites until it landed some seven thousand miles away with Ray
Dalio. *M/V Alucia* was trawling the deep waters surrounding the "Galapa-
gos of the Orient" for a rare find.

Come quickly, the message read. *You won't believe what we've found.*

Dalio had bought *Alucia* on a whim a year earlier after learning that
it had helped plumb the depths of the sea to find the remains of an aircraft

that had seemingly disappeared. The hulking, gray, fifty-six-meter ship looked as much like a destroyer as a billionaire's plaything. The ship carried submarines with bubble-like hulls of clear plastic, capable of carrying the Bridgewater founder—an amateur scuba diver—thousands of feet beneath the sea. When Dalio wasn't on the boat, he lent it out to researchers worldwide. This latest expedition was a hunt for the giant squid, a terrifying and mysterious creature with eight long tentacles, two arms, blue blood, and eyeballs the size of a human head. The squid, which famously (and fictitiously) attacked Captain Nemo's crew in *Twenty Thousand Leagues Under the Sea,* had never been viewed alive—until now.

One perk of being the head of a hedge fund with a constantly expanding collection of new executives eager to prove their worth was that Dalio could come and go as he pleased. His attendance didn't always seem to matter much because the firm was pumping out cash. A few months before *Alucia* set sail, news broke of Dalio's latest payday. He had earned $3.9 billion in 2011, again mostly from Bridgewater's investments in U.S. government bonds, and the associated fees paid by clients. What worked before was working again.

No one else at Bridgewater enjoyed quite the same flexible work schedule as Dalio, so when the call came in from *Alucia,* Dalio called up his old Harvard friend Michael Kubin. How would Kubin like to be one of the first people on earth to see the mythical giant squid? They would fly first to Tokyo, then take a twenty-five-hour ferry ride to an island close to the vessel. The ferry's air-conditioning was on full blast, and Kubin recalled sitting up all night, teeth chattering, unable to get a wink of sleep. He marveled at Dalio, a few inches away, snoozing blissfully. Kubin figured it must have been Dalio's famed meditative practices.

The next morning, a bleary-eyed Kubin asked how his friend managed to achieve such impressive shut-eye.

"I didn't tell you? I took an Ambien," Dalio said.

The friends were supposed to be on board *Alucia* for a week, going underwater frequently to try to spot the squid. On their second day, they emerged from an unsuccessful submarine attempt to an unlucky greeting from the ship's captain. Two typhoons were bearing down on their position. Dalio and Kubin were forced to retrace their steps back to Connecticut. A few weeks later, scientists on board captured extensive footage of the squid.

DALIO RETURNED to Westport visibly disappointed. He had been galvanized by the hope to achieve a maritime discovery unknown to all others, but for all his resources, the long journey had been for naught.

Back at headquarters, he was on a parallel quest of sorts, a hunt for a unifying, singular scientific discovery to explain his success. The Principles didn't quite do it. Though Dalio often said they were the backbone for everything that worked well at Bridgewater, The Principles contained almost nothing substantive on investing. Without a unifying explanation of its investment process, Bridgewater risked two unacceptable consequences. The firm could be dismissed as just lucky, the inevitable single hedge fund out of thousands that flipped a coin to the same side twenty times in a row. Perhaps equally dreadful, Bridgewater might fade in time; Wall Street was littered with the corpses of once-hot funds that were unable to explain their periods of poor performance.

So Dalio derived a sibling to The Principles, but for investing. It was a metaphor of sorts. He called it "How the Economic Machine Works." Like The Principles, the economic machine was purported to be deterministic, wide-ranging, and capable of prediction. The machine, as Dalio drew it on whiteboards in countless client meetings and media interviews, amounted to a series of straight and squiggly lines, representing such categories as worker productivity and national debt, which could be measured in countries throughout the world. Put together, the cause-and-effect relationships between these factors constituted a formula that Dalio said could model whether a given country would succeed or fail (for instance, countries with low worker productivity tended to accumulate high debts, making it advantageous to bet against them). The machine told Dalio that countries such as China, brimming with hard workers and high savings rates, were bound to eclipse nations such as the United States and the United Kingdom.

"As with human bodies, I believe that the economies of different countries have worked in essentially the same ways for as far back as you can see so that the most important cause-effect relationships are timeless and universal," Dalio would say. The machine was a mirror into the future, based on the past.

A few weeks after Dalio's return from his search for the giant squid, he resolved to put the idea of the economic machine through its paces. He invited the British historian Niall Ferguson to a sit-down in Westport. Ferguson was a safe bet to understand the importance of Dalio's discovery. He was a Harvard professor (many of his former students worked for Bridgewater), prolific author, and like the Bridgewater founder a bit of an iconoclast. One of Ferguson's animating philosophies was that Western civilization was more fragile than it appeared. Ferguson was also on retainer as a paid consultant for a number of financial firms, and when he got the invitation from Bridgewater, his first thought was that, if he played his cards right, he might have a chance to make some spare change.

Ferguson's hope burst when he read the more than one-hundred-page document sent over from Bridgewater laying out the economic machine. He noticed almost immediately what he considered to be fundamental flaws. The paper ignored that one nation's culture might lead to better or worse economic outcomes. It also discounted what Ferguson called "the caprices of decision makers," including the role of human agency and ingenuity that could, for instance, lead one country to declare war on another, or to choose peace.

If this work had been done by one of his graduate students, Ferguson would have flunked the person. He couldn't believe that he was reading, as he put it, the "holy texts" of Bridgewater.

Never one to shy from a good argument, Ferguson traveled down to Bridgewater. What he found reminded him of a university lecture hall. Rows upon rows of chairs were set up, filled with young Bridgewater staffers, assembled to hear his take on the master's work. Dalio introduced his guest, then sat down on a chair to the side. Ferguson stood at the front, took a deep breath, and glanced down at the notes he'd jotted down a few days earlier. *Der liebe Gott steckt im Detail,* he read. (Literally, "The good God is in the details.") He began genially.

"You're the guy who has made billions. I'm just a professor. But as a professor, here are my thoughts. There isn't a way of modeling the historical process, and there's definitely not a way of modeling the choices that highly indebted countries make."

Ferguson stole a glance over at his host. Dalio was still sitting, but Ferguson and others present could tell he was on his way to steaming, shaking his head slowly, legs beginning to tap with antsiness. The professor pressed on. While it was possible to cherry-pick historical examples of nations that had collapsed under their debts, plenty of countries had grown fast enough to render the debts moot. Also: wars, coups, cultural changes, competing legal systems, effective and ineffective political leaders, and all sorts of other factors, including human consciousness, couldn't ever be quantitatively measured, let alone cleanly placed into a formula.

"There is no cycle of history. It's a fantasy," Ferguson said.

Dalio jumped to his feet, shaking. The professor was claiming the secret of Dalio's success couldn't possibly be so.

"Where's your fucking model, Niall?" he bellowed at his guest.

The room stood still. There was no model—that was the whole point. The world, and its people, were endlessly complicated. There was no cracking that nut. Before Ferguson could get that full thought out, Dalio repeated himself.

"Where's your fucking model?"

It was about this time that Ferguson realized he wasn't going to be hired at Bridgewater anytime soon. Employing a stiff British clapback, Ferguson turned to Dalio with a sniff and chose his words carefully. "I always feel that when someone uses the f-word, they're losing the argument."

The professor wrapped up his talk and headed for the door. Not long after he got home, he heard from one of his former students who had been among the rows of Bridgewater employees in the room. After Ferguson departed—and with everyone still present—Dalio had called for an instant poll. Who won the debate: the Bridgewater founder or the guest?

Dalio won, of course.

FERGUSON'S REACTION appeared to be an anomaly. Dalio had little trouble convincing outsiders of the worth of his system.

It was a good time to be Ray Dalio, and a good time to be selling Ray Dalio. The firm was as big as ever—managing more than $141 billion at year-end 2012—and continued to expand. New money flowed in from teachers' retirement systems, the U.S. heartland, and even the Transport for London, an agency of London's local government responsible for retired train workers' pensions. That Bridgewater's flagship fund had narrowly avoided its first losing year in more than a decade seemed to bother neither its investors nor Dalio. Pure Alpha rose just 0.6 percent in 2012, but Dalio was paid $1.7 billion anyway. He blamed a lack of conviction in himself for the muted year. The problem, he told clients, was "relatively small position sizing." In other words, the firm believed it was right, but was too cautious.

Another factor competed to draw Dalio's attention from the firm's investments. Money was on the agenda—his own money. As Dalio raised more funds for Bridgewater's coffers, he was fervently working on a parallel track to withdraw his own.

Dalio faced, in Wall Street parlance, a liquidity problem. Untold billions of dollars of his fortune were locked up in his ownership of Bridgewater. Unlike stocks, bonds, and the other relatively easily sellable assets that the hedge fund bought and sold for clients, Dalio had no easy way to turn his paper ownership of the firm into real profits. While Bridgewater was surely worth something—if 2012 proved anything, it was that Dalio's enterprise could continue to hoover up billions of dollars in annual fees without making clients much money that year—just how valuable wasn't clear. There was no obvious way to calculate its worth, or to guarantee that the firm Dalio built would endure past his exit. Hedge funds were not unlike pricey restaurants founded by celebrity chefs: without the name above the door, customers might not keep showing up. Dalio was keenly aware that hedge funds more commonly withered than flourished with the handoff to the next generation.

Dalio got around that huckleberry by announcing that he didn't intend to leave. Bridgewater was merely undergoing what he called a "planful transition" from its original set of managers (namely, Dalio) to the next, including Jensen. Though the Bridgewater founder said he was sticking around out of love of investing, there was another equally good reason. Bridgewater was likely only worth top dollar with him at the helm. To be paid the most possible for his ownership of the firm, he would need to stay on a while longer.

To find a buyer, Dalio opened his Rolodex. Bridgewater rang up Wichita, Kansas, asking the billionaire brothers Charles and David Koch for money to buy him out. The hedge fund dispatched Jensen and Prince to remote Lubbock, Texas, where they implored the board of the Teacher Retirement System of Texas to buy in. Dalio himself handled the farthest entreaties: China, the Middle East, and Singapore. He flew to Singapore in person, bringing with him a small team for a private meeting with the prime minister's wife, head of one of the nation's giant sovereign wealth funds, Temasek Holdings. There, with a piece of noodle hanging awkwardly from his tie, he spoke a bit about the investment world and then held forth at length on the hedge fund's employee ratings systems.

The latest and greatest of his inventions, he told the group, was a software application called the Dot Collector. The software was preinstalled on iPads given to every Bridgewater employee and was omnipresent at all moments in the firm. The Dot Collector was a supercharged, real-time version of the baseball cards—it aggregated every piece of feedback, or dots, given by everyone at the firm to one another and assigned an overall numerical value in seventy-seven categories of human qualities, such as "living in truth" and "probes deeply to know how the machine is working." The most exciting breakthrough of the Dot Collector, Dalio said in Singapore, was that he had finally figured out how to balance all the data properly. A team of Bridgewater engineers had nailed a proprietary X factor, known as believability. With believability added to the equation, dots from certain individuals at the firm could influence employee ratings disproportionately. It guaranteed that the most believable people at Bridgewater were heard above the fray. Believability was the key to maintaining a meritocracy.

On the same trip, Dalio sat for an interview with a local Singaporean paper and spoke of his ambivalence about wealth and its accoutrements: "Status is unhealthy. I don't like luxuries." He pointed to a $150 Orvis watch on his wrist. "Money is not a goal in itself."

The targets of Dalio's pitch had a commonality besides controlling some of the most vast wealth on earth. They were Bridgewater clients, having already in some cases invested billions of dollars in the firm's funds. But this was a different opportunity. Dalio wasn't offering to help spread their money across markets throughout the globe. He was suggesting they hand it to him directly. In return, Dalio promised these longtime clients a piece of the scarcest of all goods: his hedge fund firm. He told them that Bridgewater was an enduring institution, one whose investment process was systematic, repeatable, and based on rules that no one else could match. The argument was so powerful that for large investors, Bridgewater began to be seen not just as another investment manager, but as the default, safest choice. Among those tasked with investing money for deep-pocketed entities, there began to circulate a telling phrase: "No one ever got fired for hiring Bridgewater Associates." In other words, even if the fund didn't perform well, no one could be blamed for choosing a name as reliable as Bridgewater to manage money.

Importantly, in this line of thought, it mattered little that the firm founder would inevitably leave. Dalio was leaving behind The Principles, which guaranteed that future leaders of Bridgewater would always have the benefit of the founder's instructions.

The world tour paid off. Singapore's government-run funds agreed to purchase a sliver of Dalio's ownership of Bridgewater. Texas Teacher Retirement got in, too: the public employees' retiree fund paid Dalio $250 million for a 2.5 percent private-equity stake in Bridgewater. The math meant that 100 percent of Bridgewater would be valued at $10 billion. Dalio still owned more than half of the firm. Just like that, his paper ownership of the firm was worth something very real indeed.

DALIO VISIBLY celebrated his largesse by shopping for a new house. The man with the $150 watch bought the most expensive single-family home ever sold in America. Called Copper Beech Farm, suggesting something rather rustic, it was actually a fifty-one-acre compound, boasting a French Renaissance–style estate overlooking a mile of private frontage on the Greenwich, Connecticut, waterfront. An eighteen-hundred-foot-long driveway kept the property hidden from view, though from certain angles a clock tower could be seen peeking above the trees. The home sale included a couple of private islands just off the coast, for a total of $120 million.

In interviews, however, Dalio continued to profess his lack of interest in the trappings of success. He commissioned and narrated himself a thirty-minute YouTube video on his theory of the economic machine, complete with cartoon figures and a wacky Western-infused soundtrack. "The economy works like a simple machine, but many people don't understand it," Dalio intoned in a voice-over. "This has led to a lot of needless economic suffering. I feel a deep sense of responsibility."

As free advice from a billionaire hedge fund manager, the video was an instant hit. As it approached a million views, Charlie Rose called Dalio to offer him an interview on *CBS This Morning*, a national show with an audience in the American heartland. Dalio accepted. It was his broadest platform yet and a chance for him to be cast for the masses as a benevolent billionaire. Seated across from Rose, both men clad in dark suits, Dalio leaned in, unblinking, and launched into his usual spiel about Bridgewater as CBS splashed a chyron across the screen, RAY'S RULES.

"We get to basically the fundamentals of how people think differently— what people are good or bad at, what they're like," Dalio said. "It's like getting into the intellectual Navy SEALs, that's what the experience is like. The key question is, Can you get over your ego barrier? It's painful. There's a mental pain, like a physical pain in the Navy SEALs. Can you get over the ego barrier? Can you just find out what's true?"

Rose moved quickly to a larger question, one that seemed to suggest he had begun to notice the irony of Dalio's claiming to have conquered his ego while he sat for an interview viewed by millions.

"You said you have to leave your ego outside, yet is there not within you this huge ego—"

Dalio cut Rose off, "Noooo," he responded, drawing out the word and shaking his head.

"Wait, let me hear you. Ego, because you want to be the biggest and the best hedge fund—"

"Noooo."

Rose gave his evidence: "You don't want to be the biggest and the best hedge fund. You want to say, 'I have defined the economic machine which is the way the economies of the world work. I'm laying it out for you. This is the way it works. Not that way.'"

"Is that ego?" Dalio responded.

"I'm asking. Why isn't that ego?"

"Well, I think it could be motivated, people could think of it as motivated by ego."

"Is it altruism?"

"It's altruistic."

"Is it really?"

Dalio's voice suddenly whined higher with audible impatience. "Listen, yes." He paused for a moment. "I'm sixty-four years old. I don't want to have fears. Fears of being open."

"With the enormous success that you've had, what do you want?"

"I just want to evolve. Everything is just personal evolution. What happens is, I think the natural order of things is that you have these different challenges, and then you accomplish those challenges and then evolve."

THE CBS interview helped Dalio's "How the Economic Machine Works" video rack up even more views. (Rose's cohost, Gayle King, even said on air after the interview, "Now I want to go see his YouTube video.") It crossed the 1 million mark, then 5 million, then 10 million, and past 25 million. Dalio amassed a deep following across the globe. From students to professional investors to housewives, all were intrigued by the billionaire hedge fund manager giving away the secrets to his success. Strangers would approach him in public and thank him for his insights or ask for his autograph or a photograph. Emails poured in. The caddie from Long Island had become a celebrity.

Dalio's former HBS classmate Kubin watched the transformation with amazement. Kubin, a serial founder of start-ups, had gone to school with plenty of successful men and women, but Dalio was attaining a whole new level of fame. The two men's vacations (usually accompanied by their wives) became more elaborate, as in some foreign lands Dalio now amounted to a visiting dignitary. On a trip to Israel, the Kubins and Dalios were ushered in to meet Shimon Peres, the country's former prime minister. Kubin could only otherwise imagine this entry into a thrilling world.

Yet a bit of the argumentative Dalio always seemed to stick around, even on a vacation. On the group's travels during a characteristically scorching Israeli summer, it was particularly hot at the Western Wall, the ancient historic artifact and active religious site in the heart of Jerusalem. A punishing midday sun bore down on the group as the men separated from women, per Jewish custom, to approach the wall. Kubin expected to quickly jot down a note, as was tradition, and slip it into a groove of the wall. However, Dalio fell into an animated conversation with a stranger—one of the many Orthodox Jews congregating at the wall for prayer. Kubin could overhear snips of the conversation.

"Why do you pray?" Dalio asked. "What is it you get out of it?"

Kubin allowed himself a private laugh. Here they were, at the most famous attraction in Israel, on a sweltering-hot day, and Dalio was taking the time to question a stranger.

More often than not, though, it was just the two friends, and a crew. They sailed islands across the globe, going anywhere Dalio heard had great diving. Having narrowly missed the giant squid, they made sure to get the timing right to see spinner dolphins off the remote archipelago of Fernando de Noronha, off the coast of Brazil.

Though Dalio's yacht boasted a stellar wine collection, Kubin said his friend more often sought new experiences, rather than a chance to blow off steam or simply relax: "He doesn't use his boat for recreation. There's always a purpose."

Kubin noticed that his friend tended to stick to an independent streak. On one sail, near Costa Rica, the pair traveled with a set of expert divers. Their help was needed because Dalio was dead set on diving with the whitetip reef sharks. The sleek, roughly five-foot-long creatures liked to hang out close to the ocean's floor, near coral reefs, and rarely came near the surface. During the day, the sharks rested in caves, so the best time to catch a glimpse was at night, when they were out hunting. The instructors gave Dalio and Kubin clear instructions: Hover above the sharks, but don't go below them. If you do, the sharks will mistake you for prey and attack.

"You don't have to tell me that twice," Kubin said.

Dalio and Kubin suited up, hooked up their tanks, and dove into the water with their guides to the serene waters under the surfaces. The instructors had chosen the location well; there were plenty of sharks. Kubin glided a bit, admiring the view. Then he noticed Dalio, moving quickly to position himself below the sharks for a closer view—exactly what they'd been warned against.

Dalio's guide yanked him toward the surface—"literally grabbed him," Kubin said—and pulled him, dripping wet, toward the boat. After giving Dalio a once-over, the expert diver, shaking his head, walked over to Kubin's guide.

"I've seen that happen before," one guide said to the other. "There was nothing left but the tank."

The other instructor responded, "I've seen them eat the tank, too."

14

PRINCE

Dᴀʟɪᴏ's ᴛʀɪᴘs ᴀᴡᴀʏ ꜰʀᴏᴍ Bʀɪᴅɢᴇᴡᴀᴛᴇʀ ᴘʀᴏᴠɪᴅᴇᴅ ᴀɴ ᴏᴘᴘᴏʀᴛᴜɴɪᴛʏ for Greg Jensen. Perhaps with an eye toward proving that he could stand in for Dalio in the founder's absence, Jensen did his best impression of the boss.

The first visible step was to build his own base of power. His house parties helped with that, as did flying a group of his internal loyalists to the Super Bowl one year in a private jet. Everyone wanted to stay in Jensen's graces, and to be invited into his crew—some women at Bridgewater even called themselves "Greg's Angels." But the social clout wasn't quite enough. Dalio held the purse strings, and it was well-known that the Bridgewater founder was prone to doling out raises or pay cuts on a whim. Jensen apparently decided that he, too, could be a rainmaker. He began paying out million-dollar bonuses to members of the investment team from his own pocket, an unusual move that made some staffers less likely than ever to cross him.

He also found a way to get Dalio to pay the investment staff more. Even by the standards of hedge funds, Bridgewater had a particularly strict policy forbidding its staffers from trading in personal accounts, lest they use knowledge from the world's biggest hedge fund for personal profits. Jensen, though, knew that even the firm's most junior analysts were desperate to trade on the side using their own ideas, and he helped convince Dalio of a work-around, called the trading game. Bridgewater investment staffers could put on dummy trades (betting that a certain stock would go up, for instance), and Dalio would take the other side. Dalio was essentially acting as the market. If the stock went up, Dalio would pay the difference; if it went down, the Bridgewater employee would owe Dalio. The proposal appealed to Dalio's competitive edge, and he assented.

With the investment staff sated, Jensen turned to the rest of Bridgewater. Given how much weight Dalio put in The Principles rating systems, it was no surprise that Jensen moved Paul McDowell over to report to him directly. Then Jensen began filling the ranks with more people of his own. In early 2013, he brought in J. Michael Cline, a journeyman entrepreneur and private-equity executive, to serve as Bridgewater's vice-chairman. Cline had cofounded movie-ticket vendor Fandango before another of his ventures, a credit card services conglomerate, landed in legal trouble over aggressive debt-collection tactics in emergency rooms, cancer wards, and hospital delivery rooms. Cline, broad shouldered and with a full head of dark hair in his fifties, had a confident air and was prone to quick decisions. He seemed unlikely to wilt in the Bridgewater fray. In his interviews at the hedge fund, Cline mentioned that he was fan of "negative 360s," a practice of calling around to find the most unflattering feedback possible on new hires or business partners. It was the only way, Cline said, to really know whom one was dealing with. Jensen ate it up, saying, "We're soulmates. We think the same way."

To pair with Cline, Jensen needed an enforcer to replace his departed ally Comey. Cline came up with a name: Kevin Campbell, a longtime management consultant. Campbell demanded attention when he ambled into a room. He was, as one Bridgewater staffer approvingly put it, "four hundred pounds, but with the energy of a bear." Campbell was swiftly hired.

Campbell was assigned work to clear the chairs around him. Eileen Murray had been demoted in the wake of her trial, *Eileen Lies,* but was sticking around and agitating for her co-CEO title back. She had in her corner Katina Stefanova, who reported to her, and who to Jensen's visibly unending annoyance still seemed to occupy a soft spot in Dalio's heart. David McCormick, still in the executive ranks after the clash with his former friend Julian Mack, was another clear threat.

Jensen had the upper hand on them all. He knew The Principles better than anyone else, and everyone knew how important it was to Dalio that they be followed strictly. Jensen was also the primary exemplar of demonstrating that while it was admirable to follow The Principles in private, the real reward came from brandishing them as loudly as possible, ideally with Dalio in the room. When the Bridgewater founder returned from one of his trips, Jensen made his move.

The occasion was an ordinary check-in meeting—to update Dalio on what had gone on while he'd been away—and the crowd wasn't small. There were no such things as small crowds when it came to Dalio. The only hint that the meeting would be unusual was a poll sent out to employees a few minutes before: Is your time-off accounting correct? It was oddly specific.

Jensen and Murray filed into the room separately, each with their own coterie, like boxers approaching the ring surrounded by a dozen or so in their crews. Seated across from Jensen, Murray steeled herself for the usual drill down. Instead, Jensen addressed a man to her side—one of her direct reports, a five-year Bridgewater veteran. Jensen began pleasantly enough.

"How are you? Taking any time off? Getting any relaxation?"

"Just golfing, here and there."

"How much time would you say you've been taking?"

"Nothing out of the ordinary."

A gleam crossed Jensen's eyes, people there recall. Jensen stole a look at Dalio, then at Murray, then quickly glanced at the cameras in the corners recording the whole thing. Seeming to milk the moment for all it was worth, Jensen slowly picked up a binder in front of him and dropped it back on the table. It landed with a thump, the only sound in the room. As he spoke, his voice lost any trace of friendliness, taking on an acid tone.

"You're entitled to three and a half weeks' vacation, and you've been out of the office for six weeks." Jensen pointed to the binder. The evidence was in there. He'd had his team check the security footage.

"I don't know if this is the right forum to talk about this," the employee protested. "Maybe we could move it off-line—"

Dalio stood up, cutting off the conversation. "This doesn't look good. What is it, were you here or not?"

"I think we should get on with the meeting," the man said.

"We should do it now," Jensen said.

He called up Kevin Campbell, Jensen's hulking, deep-voiced prized hire. Campbell shifted the topic to Murray. This was a problem of management, he said gravely—or lack thereof. Murray had the wrong people in the wrong jobs, and she didn't even notice if they were around. It was a violation of a crucial Principle: "Understand the differences between managing, micromanaging and not managing."

Dalio turned to Murray inquisitively. She was nearly speechless. This is an ambush, she said. Jensen hadn't even given her a moment to review his vaunted binder of evidence. Dalio agreed to allow her the evening to review it and instructed her and the employee to appear in front of the management committee the following day for a full trial. Jensen began to prepare for the cross-examination.

He never got the chance. Before the sun had risen, the employee had hired a lawyer, who negotiated a paid exit. The employee went to Dalio and said the whole endeavor was a farce: "Your questioner is the executioner. It's rigged."

Without a warm body to probe, Dalio's interest in the topic evidently evaporated. He'd already done a trial of Murray; it would have been too soon, and probably no fun, to conduct another so soon. Jensen showed up the next day jacked full of energy, ready to deal the body blow, but no one was left to flay. A chance to add a notch to his belt had slipped through his fingers.

MANY AT Bridgewater, both friend and foe to Jensen, thought it obvious why he stuck around. It had been four years since Dalio's 2009 announcement of an imminent retirement, and many—Jensen included—still spoke as if it might happen any day. Jensen just needed to bide his time until Dalio, by choice or divine intervention, made the inevitable exit. Into the void, Jensen would step in.

For a few moments, it seemed that might come relatively quickly. In June 2013, Dalio received a scary medical diagnosis of Barrett's esophagus, a tissue condition that frequently leads to deadly cancer. He was given as few as three years left to live. In a journal entry Dalio jotted down for himself the next day, he wrote, "this news has focused my attention on the end more clearly."

Dalio shared the news widely inside Bridgewater, where it earned him a well-deserved period of sympathy. To many, the vulnerability he shared made the Bridgewater founder seem relatable, and underscored what he often said about the hedge fund being a place for the formation of meaningful relationships. They were being looped into some of the most intimate decisions a person could face.

Dalio gathered his top deputies, including Jensen, and told them he felt a renewed impulse to step back. In an edited recording Dalio later released publicly, the conversation went as follows:

"I want to do it with a real sense of responsibility. I really do care about Bridgewater—I care about you all."

His words received audible "yeahs" in the room.

"Everybody has got to get used to me not being around, and work ourselves through that. The reason you're in this room is I consider you to be like family, like I can have conversations with you, I can trust you, we're in it for, in a sense, committed for, you know . . ."

Here Dalio either trailed off or the tape was edited to remove the time frame of the commitment.

"Reality," he added, "is beautiful."

Within five weeks, Dalio had a new diagnosis. He spoke to a number of other doctors and eventually underwent a relatively minor procedure that revealed his prognosis wasn't dire at all. He was at no particular risk of a deadly cancer—and his impulse to leave Bridgewater seemed to evaporate once more.

THOUGH HIS promised ascension seemed in permanent stasis, Jensen was collecting a consistent consolation prize. Over just three years, 2011, 2012, and 2013, industry researcher Alpha reported that he made $815 million in total. While just a fraction of Dalio's compensation, it was also enough to vault Jensen onto the industry lists of the highest-paid hedge fund managers—he made more than most of those who ran their own firms.

Only a handful of people knew, however, another reason for him to stay. The Bridgewater founder had concocted a complicated arrangement in which the more money that Jensen seemed to make, the more he actually owed. Dalio had challenged Jensen, as a condition of the younger man's employment, to slowly buy out the Bridgewater founder's ownership. Jensen didn't have nearly enough money, so Bridgewater lent it to him—essentially transferring slivers of his ownership each year, building up a gigantic IOU to the hedge fund's majority shareholder, who just so happened to be Dalio. Jensen's debt skyrocketed as the value of Bridgewater rose. When Dalio sold a piece of the firm to the Texas teachers' pension fund, not only his own stake was impacted. Since Bridgewater was now worth more, it made Jensen's own tithe that year even more expensive as well.

The result of the arrangement was that the hefty paychecks that seemed, to outsiders, to be hitting Jensen's bank account were actually repaying the loans. Much that seemed to be Jensen's went to paying off his debt to Dalio, vis a vis

Bridgewater (some of the rest went to paying out the bonuses that Jensen gave to his staff). The situation added enormous pressure on Jensen to keep Bridgewater's investments in the green. He accomplished that, but only by a hair. Pure Alpha made just 5 percent in 2013 and 4 percent in 2014, while All-Weather alternated between up and down years. For Jensen, it was the exact wrong time for Bridgewater's vaunted investment system to hit a cold patch.

Midway through the rocky stretch, Dalio's personal financial advisers arranged a meeting with Jensen. The team had noticed that Jensen's debts were piling up, and they were worried that the two men's fates were becoming uncomfortably intertwined. If Jensen couldn't pay up, it could blow a hole in Dalio's fortune. Their job, the advisers explained, was to stop that from happening.

They asked Jensen to put up collateral to guarantee the loans.

He stared back blankly.

"I don't have anything," Jensen said. "Just my house."

The group agreed to punt the issue for another day.

JENSEN HAD no choice but to dig in deeper at Bridgewater, hoping for Dalio to keep his word and retire. Jensen's house parties became longer and more frequent, with bacchanalia nearly every Friday night. He reconnected with Samantha Holland, his former paramour, who still worked at Bridgewater, where her six-figure annual pay helped make up for some of the indignity of her earlier investigation. Jensen began confiding in her his frustrations with his station at the firm, people who know them recall. The two of them laughed about the colliding versions of Dalio—the sympathetic, kindhearted character he played in his media interviews and in the period after his medical diagnosis, and the hard-edged one they saw so often at Bridgewater. That they had both survived their earlier dalliance made the second go-around even more exciting.

In Holland, it seemed as if Jensen had someone fully in his corner whom he could trust. While he had a front-row seat to the Ray Dalio experience, Holland let him in on the view from the nosebleeds. She told him the lower-level employees were terrified of crossing Dalio and saw Jensen as their best hope for saner times ahead. All were biding their time for him to rise up. Jensen seemed to swell with the confidence of a man on a mission greater than himself. Bridgewater needed him just as much as he needed Bridgewater.

So many years into Dalio's retirement transition, there was little chance of forcing the matter—especially not with the hedge fund's investments skidding sideways. Dalio would need to see for himself that the protégé was ready to run the firm. Jensen cast his eye across the firm and landed on the area most important to Dalio's heart: The Principles. If Jensen could find some way to show Dalio that The Principles were in stable hands, that might just be enough.

The Principles had continued to grow. What was an 83-page treatise in 2010 had swelled to 110 pages by the next year and was 208 pages in one printed version given to staff. An entire team was responsible for helping Dalio make updates. The "pain button," now live after extensive development, had transformed into a dynamic version of Pain + Reflection = Progress. It contained a dial for staffers to twist in a 360-degree motion to input their level of unhappiness at any given moment while being probed, diagnosed, or just plain criticized. "It's like a psychologist," Dalio said. There was also the Dispute Resolver, which asked employees to input their two sides of an argument and theoretically came up with who was in the right according to The Principles. Most ubiquitous of all was the Dot Collector, the ratings tool that Paul McDowell had helped develop and that Dalio had demonstrated for clients in Singapore. Dotting was turning into a near addiction for Bridgewater staff. The hedge fund's engineers ran an analysis and determined that, on average, employees were opening the app every twenty minutes throughout the workday, either to rate one another or to check on their own metrics.

Dalio seemed thrilled with the expanding assemblage of Principles tools on the company iPads that every employee toted around. The collection of apps, once called the Vassal, was given a new name: the Book of the Future. Though the apps were still a secret to the public, the promise of the Book of the Future was talked up constantly inside the firm. Once the book was completed, Dalio often said, he would no longer be needed to manage Bridgewater.

To call it a book was confusing because its centerpiece was yet another piece of software still under development. Dalio called it Prince, short for "Principles." Prince was to be the equivalent of Siri, the voice-activated assistant on Apple products. Just as billions of consumers around the world spoke to Siri to get the answers to their queries, so, too, would Prince be the singular source for answers according to The Principles. The product was first intended for use inside Bridgewater, and then, Dalio hoped, by the world. As he told one group at Bridgewater, the Book of the Future was to be as historic as the invention of Apple's first iPhone. If it sounded far-fetched, Dalio often pointed out that Steve Jobs, too, had cast off naysayers on his way to changing the world.

In laying out the assignment to Bridgewater's technology staff, who included Paul McDowell, Dalio summed it up as "You're having an argument with your wife, you pick up the iPad, and you say, 'Prince, what do I do?'"

McDowell responded, "Ray, if I pulled out my iPad and used that line in the middle of an argument with my wife, seconds later my face would be shaped like an iPad."

Dalio didn't laugh.

To DALIO, once the Book of the Future was live, it would solve the most pressing problems left at Bridgewater. Finally, there would be no excuses for deviating from The Principles. Prince would be Dalio's voice in every meeting. The new technology seemed set to solve Jensen's quagmire, too. With Prince in the room, maybe Dalio would see that he didn't always have to be.

Thus the two men were in pursuit of the same goal, for different reasons.

The world's biggest hedge fund opened up its purse strings for the Book of the Future. Millions of dollars, and then tens of millions, were earmarked for engineers, designers, technical writers, and any equipment needed. Seemingly no idea could not be taken seriously and not be given funding. One employee mentioned that capsules could be swallowed that would transmit, electronically, one's blood pressure, stomach acid levels, and other health metrics. That data might be useful, for instance, during a staff diagnosis of someone to see if the person was truly comfortable with the Bridgewater approach. There would be no way to hide the pain, or other physical reactions. Another staffer said he had read about headbands and skullcaps that detected real-time brain wave activity and tension in the scalp. Dalio responded enthusiastically to both ideas—he hoped they would show whether the amygdala, as he often discussed, was being incorrectly stimulated!—and Jensen dutifully allowed the ideas to be explored.

For his star creation, Dalio hunted for star power. The Book of the Future was the most important project he'd ever worked on, he told some underlings, and he said he wanted it to launch with a bang. One morning after Christmas 2013 he burst into Bridgewater headquarters full of excitement. The night before he had seen a new movie, the Oscar-nominated *Her*, about a forlorn single man, played by Joaquin Phoenix, who falls in love with his Siri-like virtual assistant, voiced by Scarlett Johansson. Dalio, too, had apparently been taken by Johansson's sultry work. "Let's get her," Dalio said. "We'll pay her to be the voice of Prince."

Bridgewater's staff couldn't get Johansson's representatives to return their calls.

Jensen was more successful with another big-name recruit. It had taken more than twenty years and nearly fifty different iterations to get Siri off the ground, and Jensen didn't intend to wait nearly that long for Prince. He helped bring in the famed computer scientist David Ferrucci for the project. Ferrucci was as close to a celebrity as there could be in artificial intelligence. He had worked at IBM and led the team that created Watson, a question-answering computer system that successfully competed on the quiz show *Jeopardy!*

Ferrucci said publicly that he was enthuasiastic to join Bridgewater to help on macroeconomic modeling, i.e., to help predict the direction of markets. This made perfect sense; any other hedge fund would gladly have put Ferrucci to work on investments, deploying his talents to making money for the firm's clients. Jensen went in another direction. Jensen put Ferrucci in charge of a new team that operated behind locked doors and went by a strange name, the Systematized Intelligence Lab. Its main task was to add artificial intelligence to Prince and the iPad apps that made up the Book of the Future. Ferrucci, for all his stated enthusiasm, remained many steps removed from the meat of Bridgewater's investment engine.

While Ferrucci got to work, Jensen laid out the path for his own endgame. He planned to cleaver off half the firm's operation. There would be the hedge fund firm, led by Jensen. The other part, called NewCo., would contain The Principles and associated software, including the Book of the Future. With Dalio's permission, Jensen put dozens of people at Bridgewater to work on figuring out the proper ratio of staff and resources to split between the two companies. He hired consultants and drew out detailed plans. As Jensen told others at the firm, NewCo. was more than a place for The Principles. It was a place for Dalio. Jensen's hope was that the Bridgewater founder would be so hopped-up on the Book of the Future that he would be happy to move on from his hedge fund work, leaving the mother ship to the younger man. Finally, Jensen would have his throne.

WHAT SEEMED like a mutually beneficial plan unraveled in classic Bridgewater fashion: over a pebble that sparked an avalanche.

The issue in early 2014 was internet access at the Lookout, the local mansion owned by the hedge fund. Dalio experienced trouble connecting his phone there, and he asked for a plan to fix it. The request dribbled down the line to a pair of low-level employees who reported to the firm's head of real estate. The two men and their boss, with Dalio's assent, planned to upgrade the house's wiring. They looked into the cost, then went to Dalio's office to deliver the estimate: $4,500.

Dalio leaped out of his chair. "Where's Greg?"

Dalio made his way toward Jensen's office, with the underlings trudging reluctantly behind. Without knocking, Dalio pushed open the door. The group shuffled in behind him, heads sunk.

Dalio pointed to his head of real estate. "This guy is out of control. He can't manage."

Jensen, startled, looked up quizzically.

Dalio ranted that it couldn't possibly cost $4,500 for a simple internet upgrade. To him, it was clearly an issue for The Principles. If this was Jensen's doing, the problem hadn't been properly managed or diagnosed.

"Greg, what are you doing about managing this?"

What Jensen had been doing was running a $150 billion hedge fund, including a burgeoning technology operation, with a staff of fifteen hundred and counting. Dalio's pay in 2014 was $1.1 billion. He made thousands of dollars every minute. The quoted sum for internet was not far off from the bar bill at Jensen's frequent parties. Even to Jensen, who knew the importance that The Principles placed on small errors, this must have felt like something unworthy of his and Dalio's focus—and as if the elder man was looking for an excuse to find something wrong.

That answer wouldn't do. Instead, Jensen choked out that he hadn't been closely following the matter, but that he sure would from then on.

He needn't have bothered. Like a dog with a bone, Dalio began gnawing on the job that Jensen had been doing as CEO. Not long after giving it the okay, Dalio shelved the plan for NewCo. Jensen steamed quietly—it felt to him as if Dalio was protecting his own status as the firm's sole overseer.

Indeed, at the midpoint of 2014, it seemed that everywhere Dalio looked he saw badness. By all available evidence, he placed the blame on

Jensen. To a degree, he was right. Jensen's results on investments were an obvious sore spot. Dalio had bequeathed him the hedge fund's vaunted investment system—the equivalent of a thoroughbred—and it was running like a mare. Pure Alpha's low-single-digit returns were not just failing to keep pace with the booming global economy, but were even coming in short of those of the average hedge fund. Dalio betrayed little worry publicly, but in Bridgewater's investment meetings, he lashed out at the team, regularly grouching that he had left the firm to "idiots." He ordered a new set of beatdowns to wring costs out of the company.

Thanks to the issue log, Dalio could find plenty of evidence of the firm going haywire. One issue was the caller identification display on the Bridgewater's hundreds of desk-line phones. When external calls were placed from inside the firm, the hedge fund's name would appear truncated on the receiver's display as BRIDGEWATER ASS. When no one was quick to take responsibility for this, an investigation was launched, accompanied by a series of drill downs. All the while, the display sat unchanged.

Food was, again, a persistent headache. To assuage Dalio's concerns about costs, the firm switched to a cheaper catering company. Almost immediately, the issue log was filled with complaints about how the beautifully sliced avocados on the salad bar had been replaced by a mushy, premade guacamole-like product in perpetual shades of brown. Matters didn't get better for dinner service, generally provided by delivery to staffers who stayed late. One staffer ordered brown rice with his dinner and was dismayed to find plain old white rice when he opened the carryout container. Into the issue log it went. So convinced were many at Bridgewater that the food was an affront to the senses that one junior staffer boxed up a selection of one day's cafeteria spread and sent it through interoffice mail to Dalio himself. This rather literal interpretation of The Principles' "Taste the soup" worked. Dalio seemed to interpret the delivery as a cry for help. He said he would personally oversee the diagnosis of what was going on with food service.

The result of Dalio's intervention was twofold. First, Dalio directed another new caterer be hired—with a higher budget. Food got a lot better, and Dalio could credit himself as having solved the matter.

One unintended consequence, for those who knew about it, happened to the man in charge of facilities, including the cafeteria. He was subject to near-daily attention from Dalio and his direct reports about the failures in facilities. A few weeks into the usual probings, the facilities executive collapsed at his desk, gasping for air and grasping at his chest, according to two people who were there that day. An ambulance came to the office to carry him away. The man survived the apparent heart attack, but didn't stay at Bridgewater afterward for long.

PLENTY OF people, even The Principalians, were disturbed by the scene of a colleague being carried out. Yet few openly vocalized it. At best, such complaints tended to elicit a premade metaphor that had been cited dozens if not hundreds of times in speeches to staff, and in Dalio's interview with Charlie Rose. Working at Bridgewater, Dalio said, was like enlisting as a Navy SEAL. Only the toughest could survive. The reward for those who endured was to be surrounded by "meaningful work and meaningful relationships," Dalio said. He called that end goal "the other side." To get there required crossing the gauntlet of Principles trainings, probings, dottings, and the rest. "If you get to the other side and you get through it and you have these relationships," Dalio would tell self-help proponent Tony Robbins, "then it's powerful."

If anyone should have been far onto the other side, it was Jensen, who had been hired as an intern and never left. His still-new hire Vice-Chairman Michael Cline saw it the other way. The people that he'd encountered at the world's biggest hedge fund did not seem to be motivated by the goal of reaching the nirvana that Dalio so often described. Beyond the obvious incentive for employees working at any for-profit enterprise—money—Cline concluded that staffers at Bridgewater were spurred by another factor: fear. It was not only the fear of being embarrassed or called out under one Principle or another. An ever-present fear also was that a job at Bridgewater was a once-in-a-lifetime shot at self-improvement, and that to fall short was to tacitly admit that one was not capable of making the cut. Bridgewater had no middle ground—only that those who were in were in, and those who weren't were out. Dalio's SEALs did not socialize with the grunts.

"It's the feeling of being excommunicated. No one wants to be excommunicated from this special place. That's the fear that drives so many people here," Cline told a colleague. "And it's a wood chipper. You've got to keep your sleeve out of the wood chipper because the moment your sleeve gets caught, you're in it."

Cline, to those around him, seemed to see himself as above such insecurities. He had been handpicked by Jensen to help run the firm, and it was obvious that Jensen valued him as an ally. Cline tended to gesticulate every which way as he lectured longtime Bridgewater staffers on the right way to get things done. He was well on his way to the other side.

But Cline would get caught in his own wood chipper. The beginning of his end came in a meeting attended by Jen Healy, the young Bridgewater associate who was close with Dalio. Cline was in the process of telling Healy how to do her job better when he leaned over and put his hand on her bare knee. As he continued to talk, Healy sat frozen, seemingly waiting for the moment to end.

Healy left the meeting and went to tell Dalio what had happened. He sat and listened, then responded, "You should be flattered."

Word got around about the incident with Bridgewater's latest rising star, and Healy found herself visited by a string of women at the firm. They encouraged her to press the matter and to speak out internally. They were certain that Healy was one of Dalio's favorites—surely he would have her back. But Healy responded with ambivalence. It had been just a few moments for Healy, but if she pursued the complaint, she was sure to find herself reliving it over and over. If Dalio adjudicated it via his previous methods, it could mean months of videotapes, testimony, and cross-examination.

The idea made Healy's head spin.

Healy decided not to pursue the complaint. Cline escaped a trial, but with a new reputation as having gone too far with one of Dalio's chosen people, he was damaged nonetheless. He departed before his first anniversary at the firm.

FOR JENSEN, Cline's departure created a dual headache. Part of that was obvious. The man whom Jensen had introduced as his soulmate and partner at the hedge fund had left under untoward circumstances. That gave Dalio fresh excuses to come down harder and harder on the younger man.

Jensen's other problem—that he was spending alone time again with Samantha Holland—was a secret to all but a few at the firm. While Holland had been promoted, Jensen still handily outranked her, and he was ultimately everyone's boss as CEO. This time around, a person with knowledge of their interactions recalled, the pair were significantly more careful. They exchanged little more than knowing looks when they passed each other in the corridors of Bridgewater. Instead of rendezvousing at official retreats, they were careful while around other employees. Once a safe distance from the mother ship, Jensen would let his guard down. He would drink heavily and complain to Holland that getting Dalio out of the firm seemed like a Sisyphean task.

The weeks slipped by, and with them so did the pair's vigilance. On a 2014 evening, Holland and Jensen went out in New York City with a group of fellow employees. The drinks flowed and the hours ticked by. Finally it was time to leave and the group split up to fit into cabs. Jensen and Holland shared their cab with others, though that didn't stop them from some rather obvious displays of affection. To cap it off, they asked to be dropped off at a hotel.

Word soon got back to Dalio that Jensen was backsliding. The Bridgewater founder pulled his longtime deputy aside, man-to-man. Was it true? Jensen denied it. He told Dalio that while he and Holland had a strong connection, they had never had sex or come close to it. The relationship was purely collegial, nothing more.

Dalio also called Holland in for questioning. Entering his office, she was visibly nervous, unaccustomed to close attention from the Bridgewater founder. She must have known that it was potentially her word against that of the heir apparent, but she could assume that Jensen, who had often held himself up as a paradigm of The Principles, would be honest.

Dalio asked Holland if anything of an adult nature was going on between her and Jensen. "Trust in truth," she later told friends she thought to herself, citing the operative Principle. So she answered yes, the two had a budding relationship. They were spending a lot of time together, and they had gotten a hotel room with obvious intention. They would have had sex but Jensen had been too drunk to perform.

Holland assumed that would be the end of it. She had answered honestly and had nothing left to share. But Dalio clearly remained bothered—seemingly not by a superior having a romantic relationship with a junior employee, but by the difference between their two versions of events. The Principles read, "If there are important disagreements, they must be resolved." Dalio put the Bridgewater Ethics Committee on the case and charged them with coming to a conclusion.

The committee consisted of three senior Bridgewater men, Dalio included (Murray was left off, on account of *Eileen Lies*). Under the guise of transparency, Jensen and Holland were questioned together. Holland sat, gobsmacked, as Jensen described the pair as only friends. She produced the hotel receipt, showing that they had been together in a single room. Jensen said that was evidence of nothing. She was starting to get angry, and worried. Dalio seemed unable to accept that Jensen, whom Dalio had elevated above all others and even vacationed with, was being dishonest. As Dalio told some afterward, Jensen was, thanks to Dalio's own cascaded ratings, judged by Bridgewater software to be one of the company's believable employees. If Jensen was lying, what did that signify for the soundness of the system as a whole—or for Dalio's own judgment?

Holland emerged from the Ethics Committee meeting expecting to be fired. Instead, Dalio asked to see her again. Trudging in alone, she prepared herself to recap the events once more. Instead, he told her that he was declaring the equivalent of a mistrial. He seemingly couldn't decide whose story to believe, but the status quo could not continue. He suggested that Holland accept several months' salary in severance and voluntarily leave.

She responded that she was hiring an attorney instead.

"Why would you need that?" he responded.

HOLLAND CALLED the most famous attorney she had likely heard of: Gloria Allred, known for representing victims of sexual harassment. Allred took her as a client almost immediately. A lawyer from Allred's firm spoke to Dalio on the phone at length, taking him through his and Bridgewater's potential liability. Not only had Dalio ignored all standards of procedure for investigating such workplace misconduct by investigating it himself, outside of human resources, he was told, but he'd potentially impugned Holland's reputation. The Ethics Committee might have a catchy name, but it was a legal nightmare. In no universe, Holland's attorney said, was it appropriate for three older men untrained in such matters to question a woman about her relationship with the CEO. Allred's firm assured Dalio that they wouldn't hesitate to go public with a lawsuit.

When the call ended, Holland's phone buzzed from Allred's firm's line. The lawyer told her that Bridgewater was offering roughly three years' salary for her to leave quietly. In exchange, Holland would drop any potential claims and agree never to speak publicly about her experience. If she did, the lawyer reminded her, Bridgewater would be sure to go after her.

Holland took the deal. That afternoon, Bridgewater security guards stood at her desk and watched as she packed up her things. The guards escorted her past silent coworkers, into the parking lot to her car. After the better part of a decade at Bridgewater, Holland never went back. She bought a Land Rover with some of the settlement money.

Bridgewater, however, followed her. Though she couldn't tell her former coworkers why she'd left, they seemed to hear some version of what happened. Every few months, she would receive a flurry of notifications from LinkedIn, the professional social network where she kept a profile, telling her that a bunch of strangers at Bridgewater had suddenly clicked on her account. She resigned herself to some level of private infamy among those in the know.

Restricted from telling potential employers the real reason she left her last job, Holland found herself launching into such generalities during job interviews that she gave the impression of just another flunk-out who couldn't cut it at the world's biggest hedge fund. The woman who'd early on been recognized by Bridgewater as an up-and-coming talent couldn't get another job for years. When she finally did, it was at a fraction of her former salary.

Holland left Bridgewater in mid-2014 with a settlement worth $1 million and change. That year, Greg Jensen was paid $400 million. The two never spoke again. Jensen kept his job, but Dalio had helped bury a problem that Jensen would be desperate to keep secret—and Jensen had to know there would be a price to pay.

15

SHOOT THE ONES YOU LOVE

Holland's departure didn't get much attention. Bridgewater employees not uncommonly left suddenly—by choice or not—without explanation.

At Bridgewater you were in until you were out. Dalio sometimes referred to former employees as ex-spouses and said that asking their opinions on the firm was akin to asking a divorcée what his or her former partner was like.

Departing staffers were nearly universally pressured to sign two-year noncompetition agreements, swearing not to work for any firm that could be considered a competitor, a category that included not just other hedge funds but many companies in financial services. The contracts barred former employees from telling future employers anything beyond anodyne reasons for their departure from Bridgewater. The contracts may have been so broad as to be unenforceable, but in any case, staffers signed them anyway, often reasoning that landing on Bridgewater's bad side had no upside. One junior employee, let go in 2014, noticed that the wall of silence seemed to run in only one direction. While interviewing at a New York financial firm for her next job, she told the hiring manager that she had worked at Bridgewater and said the hedge fund would surely confirm at least her dates of employment. The manager called her later and said that the reference check had instead resulted in a tongue-lashing from the world's biggest hedge fund. "Why the fuck would you want to hire her?" she was told a Bridgewater employee said to her new prospective employer. "Do you realize you're messing with Bridgewater?"

Katina Stefanova, who had herself mostly cut Bridgewater castoffs out of her life, knew firsthand how openly derisive the hedge fund could be to former staffers. So she found the silence over Holland's exit to be particularly odd. Stefanova was friendly, if not close friends, with Holland and knew her to be unusually close with Jensen. It made no sense for someone like her to disappear for no good reason. Stefanova suspected that Jensen had to be involved somehow. This was more than an educated guess. Stefanova had her own history with Dalio's right-hand man.

EVER SINCE Jensen's promotion to CEO, Stefanova had been searching for her own path forward at Bridgewater. Though she could still call herself an adviser to the firm's management committee, Jensen had the bigger job, the bigger paycheck, and the bigger personality. Stefanova was still the Ice Queen. Everyone knew she was friendly with Dalio, but that was about it. She hosted no parties, and if she had, few would have attended.

Stefanova also now had two children, and she rarely showed up for Bridgewater's frequent celebrations. One Friday evening, however, the hedge fund invited the staff to stick around the office to celebrate a firm milestone. Stefanova nursed a drink and watched the mayhem slowly build around her. A few hours in, Stefanova was exhausted from having done more mingling than she had in years. She began to make excuses to leave.

Suddenly, she felt a hand grab her ass. She whipped around raring for a fight, to discover Jensen, slurring, a crooked smile on his face. He was drunk, she surmised. Seeing no point in arguing with a man who could barely string his words together, Stefanova walked away.

Out of a mix of genuine disgust and what even she would concede to friends was a bit of opportunism to land a blow against an old rival who had long since eclipsed her, Stefanova told Bridgewater about Jensen's wandering hands. Perhaps banking on her closeness with Dalio, she expected the firm to take it seriously—to call for a full trial, as Dalio had so many times before on far smaller infractions.

Dalio would eventually tell Stefanova that he asked Bridgewater's video team to pull any available footage from the party. He reported back that he'd come up empty. What video could be found showed no contact between Jensen and Stefanova. There was no evidence to back her up, Dalio told her.

Stefanova dropped it.

But she couldn't shake the feeling that something had gone awry with Holland. In the wake of her colleague's exit, Stefanova continued to poke around for the backstory. She pulled aside her boss, Eileen Murray, who had no answers, either. The women were apparently out of the loop.

That was a familiar feeling for Stefanova. Since hiding in the bathroom as Dalio sang the filthy poem, she had steered clear of the Bridgewater founder's inner sanctum. Her work consisted increasingly of overlapping projects assigned by Murray, investigating the management of one part of the firm or another. No sooner would Stefanova finish than another reshuffling would commence. Though this mostly kept her a safe distance from Dalio, it also left her restless and frustrated. The Harvard MBA had come to Bridgewater to become a billionaire, and while she lived a comfortable suburban life in a Connecticut town about twenty minutes from Bridgewater's headquarters, she was nowhere near the level of Dalio or Jensen. With each passing day, the clock was running out on her chance to advance, and to make a fortune.

Stefanova began to ramp up her trading in her personal account, with her own money. This was permissible and unremarkable at Bridgewater, which like most hedge funds had rules governing how to do so. In addition to requiring employees to give the firm access to their personal brokerage records, the policy had two main components. The first was that staffers had to pledge not to use their knowledge of Bridgewater's investments to make their own trades. The goal was to prevent an employee from, for instance, buying up a particular currency just before Bridgewater's hedge funds did the same, thus benefiting from the price rise as the firm's billions flowed in. This instruction was easy for Stefanova because she had no specific knowledge of Bridgewater's investments. The second part of the policy required employees to notify the firm's compliance department in writing of each personal trade before it was executed, and to wait to get permission back. This portion of the policy was frequently ignored. There was a long backlog of trades to be approved, and the wait for approval could stretch for days—an eternity to a Wall Street trader looking to buy or sell at the right price. Stefanova and others frequently received at least one warning post hoc for pulling the trigger on trades too quickly, before compliance had its say.

Two of Stefanova's investments, in the government-backed mortgage giants Fannie Mae and Freddie Mac, were particularly volatile. Shares in these were a common bet among hedge funds, though Bridgewater had no public positions in them. Fannie and Freddie had been in flux since the aftermath of the 2008 financial crisis, when government officials seized the firms' profits for the U.S. Treasury. Lawsuits ensued that could reverse the move and send share prices soaring. Stefanova thought there was a good chance of that and bought some shares for herself.

Thus Stefanova reacted with some horror when she looked down at her phone one day to see a breaking news article flash across her inbox: Congress had reached a bipartisan agreement to get rid of Fannie and Freddie. She immediately thought of her portfolio. If the deal went through, her shares could be worthless. She needed to sell. She wrote to Bridgewater compliance, asking for approval.

No response.

So she tried again the next day.

Still no response.

Stefanova tried to stop herself from stealing glances at her portfolio, but she couldn't help herself. She kept checking and watched it shrink and shrink as the prices of Fannie and Freddie stock cratered. With every passing moment it seemed that more of her money disappeared. She sent another request. Silence.

Finally she couldn't wait any longer. She sold the shares without permission. She waited for the inevitable note back, slapping her on the wrist for the infraction.

Instead she was called into a meeting with Dalio, Jensen, and a host of others. Dalio opened the meeting by confirming that it was being recorded. The topic, as Dalio put it, was "Do you trust Katina?"

The Bridgewater founder started by offering that he, for one, had lost his faith. Then he went around the room. The group quickly coalesced around that view. Jensen said that he had investigated and found Stefanova to be a repeat offender of Bridgewater's trading policy. He showed evidence that Stefanova had received repeated warnings about her trading. Stefanova saw the ending coming from a mile away. She had broken the rules, and under The Principles, that made her a slimy weasel, unworthy of trust. She was let go, with no severance, and allowed a few days to wrap up her work.

After the better part of a decade at Bridgewater, Stefanova had just one card left to play: her relationship with Dalio. Bluffing more than a little, she told him that she knew all about what had gone on between Holland and Jensen. She listed off years of other gripes, including that Dalio had continued to distribute the recording of her sobbing during interrogation, even after it was unquestioningly known she was pregnant at the time; that parties with strippers had occurred at the Lookout; that women had been pressured to take off their tops at a retreat; that Jensen himself had his own history.

The latter in particular stung her, she said. Why is it, she recalls asking Dalio, that everyone seemed replaceable except his surrogate son?

Dalio told her to stop changing the subject. This was about her behavior, he said, not anyone else's.*

Stefanova shot back a dark look. "If you keep this up, no woman will ever want to work here."

Dalio had no answer for that. He agreed she should be fired, and the conversation marked Stefanova's last day at Bridgewater. She left with a legacy of two seminal internal cases to her name. The original one, "Pain + Reflection = Progress," showed her under verbal assault from Dalio. That one, still available for consumption by all, was now joined by a second case, which amounted to her public hanging for the trading violation. The recording contained none of her complaints about the firm's culture, and all of Dalio's complaints about her. This case, titled "Do You Trust Katina?," was accompanied by a questionnaire asking viewers if they agreed that she should be fired.

Nearly everyone answered no to trusting Stefanova and yes to her firing.

IF TO Stefanova it must have seemed that Jensen had once again gotten away scot-free, to Jensen, as he told friends, it didn't feel that way. Dalio came and left Bridgewater as he pleased. He had been bailed out not once but twice by Dalio and now he remained in the older man's debt as much as ever. Control of Bridgewater seemed to be slipping further and further from Jensen's grasp.

Leaving was not a viable option. Jensen's personal finances were so intertwined with the firm's—and with Dalio's, that thanks to Jensen's loans from Bridgewater that were all but loans from the founder himself—that leaving could mean financial calamity. Jensen redoubled his focus on the hedge fund's investments. He often missed meetings at which Dalio was likely to be present, with the stated excuse that he was needed on the investment team.

The result was that by summer 2014, nearly a half decade after his purported retirement from the firm, Dalio had returned to running the show in

---

* Lawyers for Dalio and Bridgewater said that "Stefanova did not raise the complaint about Mr. Jensen until after Bridgewater had decided to fire her. Bridgewater investigated Ms. Stefanova's complaint at the time and determined it was false."

force. As was the pattern, he took a buzz saw to what had gone on in his absence from formal management. A new round of beatdowns were ordered to fix departments that Jensen still theoretically oversaw. Each day seemed to take on the same pattern. Dalio would open the issue log, focus on an offending incident, and call in the responsible parties to be probed in front of cameras. As Jensen was still ostensibly in charge, he would often be summoned as well. He would trudge into the room, shoulders sagging, to testify to his ostensible failure of management oversight. No problem appeared too small for Dalio's attention. Even a stray piece of paper left at the shared printers could be cause for investigation, under an official policy that read, "In all cases, abandoned print jobs must be issue logged."

After a few weeks of this, enough was enough. Bridgewater had sixteen hundred full-time employees, and just as many issues seemed to be cropping up every day. Dalio called for a town hall. The company's facilities staff crammed as many chairs as they could into the largest room that could be found. Space was carved out for a video team in the corner to record Dalio's words for anyone who couldn't fit in person. One by one, people filed in, chattering nervously, waiting to hear from the firm founder. Jensen sat at the front, head occasionally hanging low, expressionless, as Dalio emerged.

Bridgewater, Dalio said, was failing its founder and as importantly it was failing its Principles. A shake-up was needed—and everyone, from top to bottom, would participate. There would be more investigations, more diagnoses, and a new crop of public hangings, all as prescribed by The Principles. It would go on as long as was needed to get the firm back on its feet.

Dalio paused a moment and motioned to the cameraman. "Get the camera on me right now."

With a shuffle of activity, the videographer moved in closer.

Dalio looked straight into the lens. He spoke flatly, matter-of-fact, without affect. "Two-thirds of you should be fired."

There was a brief murmur in the room. One person present remembered being torn between whether to laugh or cry. But it soon became clear this was no joke. Dalio talked about the pain that he felt to have to take such a step. He said he knew that the pain would be worth it, to achieve what needed to be done.

He gestured fleetingly to those around him. "Sometimes, you have to be willing to shoot the ones you love."

This line would immediately be added to The Principles.

"And we need to love the ones we shoot."

Dalio left the stage. Those present filed out much more quietly than they had entered. Jensen couldn't have helped but wonder if Dalio's latest Principle was aimed squarely at him.

16

ARTIFICIAL INTELLIGENCE

THOUGH THE NEWEST PRINCIPLE REFERRED TO SHOOTINGS, ITS APPLI-cation was fortunately less than literal. A round of firings started almost immediately, many conducted for the first time with the help of the nascent Book of the Future. Managers took out their iPads, sorted their employees by ratings in the Dot Collector, and laid off those whose numbers were below average. The process had a depersonalized, numerical coolness that underlined the importance of taking The Principles seriously, and of protecting one's ratings at all costs.

Paul McDowell watched with a mix of amazement and fear. As much as anyone besides Dalio, the Bridgewater ratings system was McDowell's creation. He had taken the baseball cards from mere idea to reality, and tweaked the weighting in the ratings to make Dalio's opinion carry more heft than anyone else's. Now McDowell was in charge of the rapidly expanding Principles-fueled software applications. By any reasonable standard, this was the culmination of the grand promise that McDowell had been offered when he started at Bridgewater six years earlier. Management was operating as a machine, and McDowell had assembled the factory line.

A pit formed in McDowell's stomach as he watched his creation lurch into action. Dalio and the rest of the Principalians fanned out across the firm, wielding McDowell's tools, shooting the ones they loved. Anyone who walked into a meeting and saw his or her supervisor sitting plaintively, iPad open to the Dot Collector, ready to read out stats within, knew the end was likely near. McDowell's work had become judge, jury, and executioner.

What bothered McDowell more than anything else, he told friends, was that the tool, which amalgamated individual data points to come up with omnibus ratings, hadn't been subject to independent testing. The little real-time analysis that McDowell had been able to perform showed a sad state of affairs, scientifically. When rating one another, employees tended to stick closely to the existing marks. If a person, for instance, had an average score of 7 in a category such as "Fighting to Get in Sync," most of his or her new ratings would come in between 6 and 8. Instead of incentivizing the telling of tough truths, the system supported their hiding, or at least a degree of inertia. "Down-dotting" (Bridgewater-speak for giving a poor rating) a coworker resulted in an outsize risk the recipient would return the favor, producing a downward spiral for both. Thus, stasis largely ruled. Among those who regularly gave out fresh critical ratings to employees was Dalio. Staff lived in fear of a critical Dalio dot because it would disproportionately push the employee's average down immediately and be followed by a cascade of similar negative ratings from others who saw the new, depressed baseline. There was no escaping the pile-on. It was death by dots.

McDowell saw, with no particular dread, a meeting invitation land in his inbox. Jensen was gathering an audience to chat with Kevin Campbell, the big-boned former management consultant brought in as co-COO. Campbell's purview included technology, so it made sense for McDowell to be in the room (under The Principles, nothing could be said about someone's work behind his or her back). McDowell and others had heard that Campbell was fed up with the Bridgewater system. Even small decisions seemed to require an extended examination of the various dots involved, and Campbell, an experienced professional, was not shy about expressing his eagerness to cut through it all. Though McDowell privately agreed with much of that perspective, the Canadian didn't dare say anything of the sort aloud, let alone act on it. And he was about to be reminded of the merits of staying quiet.

Campbell lumbered into the room to find Jensen at the head of the table. McDowell and a few others sat along the sides. Jensen reached for the intercom and conferenced in Dalio. Once the Bridgewater founder was on the line, Jensen turned his attention to Campbell. Jensen asked for an update on the executive's work.

Campbell said he was continuing to slim down the hedge fund's processes.

Jensen waited, then dangled a dangerous thread into the conversation.

He said that he had heard that Campbell had been complaining to others about how long it took to get even the simplest tasks done at Bridgewater.

"Why didn't you escalate to me and Ray?" Jensen asked. "Why are you talking about decisions that others have made without getting them in the room?"

Campbell stuttered nervously. He said he wanted to cast a wide net for opinions first. He cited a colleague who had told him he shared Campbell's views.

Jensen cut Campbell off. Jensen said he had already listened to the tape of the conversation Campbell was referencing. It was a disgrace, Jensen said, to hear two underlings talking as if they knew how to run the firm better than Dalio and the other top Bridgewater executives. Jensen suggested that Campbell might have been ratted on by the very man Campbell had confided in.

"How do you know that he knows what he's talking about?" Jensen asked. "You can't trust him."

Campbell began to shift his body uncomfortably in his seat. His pace of speech quickened, and his voice began to crack. He tried to explain what he had said on the tape. "I didn't know you were going to listen to it." He appeared to be holding back tears.

"It doesn't matter if you expected it or not," Jensen said.

Campbell looked around the table, as if hoping for a lifeline. None would be found. He started sobbing. It was an awful sight. The room was quiet for a spell, save for the sound of perhaps the largest man in the building crying into his hands.

Suddenly Dalio's voice crackled in, partially clouded in static through the speaker, as if a visit from a ghost everyone had forgotten was haunting the house. "Is Kevin having an emotional reaction?"

"Very," Jensen deadpanned.

Campbell excused himself for the restroom.

A few moments later, McDowell followed Campbell there. McDowell opened the door to find the executive looming over the sink, splashing cold water on his face, struggling to regulate his breathing. Water dribbling down his chin, Campbell looked up at McDowell.

"There's just . . . so . . . much," Campbell said, pausing for breaths. "It keeps . . . coming at me . . . from . . . every direction."

Campbell returned to the room and said as much to the group. But it was too late. While he was gone, he had already been down-dotted for failing to take tough feedback. The damage was done. A case was made based on the incident, broadcasting his crying to everyone at the firm. A new Principle emerged, seemingly in his honor, barring anyone at Bridgewater from claiming to have too much on his or her plate. Campbell didn't wait around for the final shooting squad. He was one of hundreds of staffers to quit or be all but forced out before year-end 2014.

Others of Bridgewater's heralded new squad of executives, as well as the hundreds of employees under them, stuck around. They were being paid millions of dollars to walk from room to room parroting the firm's philosophies, and they appeared happy to take the paychecks until The Principles were turned on them.

One such executive was Niko Canner, the onetime CEO candidate who costarred in the HBS case study about Bridgewater and was held up in it as a paradigm of speaking truth to the Bridgewater founder. Canner was habitually obsequious and rarely said a stray word against Dalio, but he lost his box anyway after Dalio visibly tired of him. Dalio first referred to Canner as a chirper—the diminutive title once held by Jim Comey—then came up with a new epithet, a "cloud painter." Cloud painters are philosophical to a fault, Dalio told Canner. They don't go into the field or understand the mechanics of a job. If you tried to take cloud painters on a camping trip, they'd never figure out what supplies to bring. Though this was a qualitative judgment at a firm that prized itself on quantifying decision-making, a derisive new sobriquet from Dalio was a plainly dark mark at Bridgewater. Cloud painters at Bridgewater had no future. Canner resigned.

Canner was a decently well-liked figure at the firm, and he earned a send-off for his years of dutiful service. The party was held at the Lookout, with many of the top Bridgewater executives in attendance, including Dalio. The Bridgewater founder ambled in a slow circle around the living room, drink in hand, then wandered over to Canner, lingering near the fireplace.

Dalio swirled an olive around his martini, according to someone who was standing near them, and asked, "So, how would you sum up your experience?"

Ever agreeable, Canner stuck to generalities, "I learned a lot. I'm taking away a lot that I know will be helpful as I help others."

That was the wrong response. Dalio winced at the faint suggestion of Canner as a bannerman for Bridgewater. "Don't talk about us to the outside."

"No, I agree, I would never mention anything sensitive to anyone."

"I am not just saying sensitive things, I mean anything. I don't want you to talk about us." Dalio took a sip of his drink.

Canner tried to explain himself again. "Ray, I will be discreet. I would never compromise anything sensitive."

"You are not to say anything about us after today to anyone."

"I need to be able to refer to my past experience. I would be thoughtful and favorable, I assure you."

Dalio drained most of the rest of his martini and looked down briefly at its dregs. His eyes raised to meet Canner's straight on. "Let me be clear: whatever you say to the outside world, we will reciprocate."

As the evening neared its close, Dalio announced he had a surprise, a memento of Canner's time at the hedge fund. With some buildup, Dalio produced a set of beautifully wrapped, heavy-looking book-size boxes. "This is the best gift anyone could have!"

As the rest of the group looked on—Dalio beaming—Canner opened the boxes. When he saw what was inside, his face faltered for a split second, and then he recovered with a forced smile. Canner pulled out the contents. Included were Lucite-encased, permanent copies of Canner's Bridgewater baseball card, filled to the brim with low ratings. On a stand-alone frieze Dalio had listed only Canner's weaknesses, along with the negative ratings Canner had received.

Canner offered an extended thank-you for the gift.

Dalio responded, "As I always say, the best gift anyone can receive is knowledge of their own weaknesses."

THE EVIDENT certainty with which Dalio held his measurements of others' weaknesses was not shared by everyone else. David Ferrucci, the former IBM scientist and inventor of Watson, had set up his Bridgewater laboratory, now more than two years old, with security approaching that of a CIA black site. Ferrucci's Systematized Intelligence Lab was walled off, literally, from the rest of the hedge fund's operations, behind locked doors. Few who weren't a part of his group were let in, and almost no one else at the hedge fund had a clue what was happening there. Some of the few with access were consultants from the venture-capital billionaire Peter Thiel's furtive data-crunching firm, Palantir, famed as the tech spooks who helped hunt down and kill Osama bin Laden. Palantir seldom talked publicly about what it did for clients, and it would never even confirm publicly that it worked for Bridgewater. The swirl of secrecy added to the air of calculated mystery around Ferrucci's operation.

The mystery continued behind the doors of the lab, but it was a puzzle of a different type. Ferrucci, one of the world's foremost experts in artificial intelligence, told colleagues he couldn't figure out where to even begin to apply hard science to Dalio and McDowell's creation, the Book of the Future. It was a mess of pseudoscience, wrapped in a patina of philosophy. Before Ferrucci's arrival, it seemed there had been no double-blind tests, no anonymous surveys, and, no, not even a simple regression to show that the adoption of The Principles' methods led to better results. ("I don't believe in regressions," Dalio told one employee who suggested it.) Even a cursory look at the data showed the opposite. The more time that folks at Bridgewater spent on The Principles—and its associated arguments, dottings, trials, and public hangings—the worse the company's investments seemed to perform. In the six years since the financial crisis, Pure Alpha had turned in two good years and four poor ones. This may have been a simple correlation, but it didn't require a computer scientist to plot the alarming trend line there.

The logical move, to Ferrucci and those he worked with, was to spend some of his expertise on investments, bringing new ideas to an area where Bridgewater plainly needed help. Jensen, however, would hear no suggestion of moving the prized hire. He needed Ferrucci to solve The Principles software, so that Dalio would finally feel comfortable leaving the firm for good. Most of all, the still-under-development Prince tool needed to work. There had to be a way to ask a question and receive answers according to The Principles.

Ferrucci gave it an honest try. He modeled his approach after IBM's work to build the supercomputer that beat two *Jeopardy!* champions. The first step in creating Watson had been to gather the raw trove of knowledge needed to produce the answer to a given clue. IBM engineers fed the computer millions of documents from encyclopedias, dictionaries, thesauri, newspaper articles, and books, all in an effort to "seed" Watson with a baseline of intelligence. Ferrucci and his team tried the same with the Book of the Future. He laid out a list of the attributes in the Dot Collector and looked them up in the dictionary. "What does *creativity* actually mean?" he asked. The answer, from Merriam-Webster: "the ability to create." He looked up another attribute, *lateral thinking*. The definition was "a method for solving problems by making unusual or unexpected connections between ideas." Ferrucci tried again with another attribute, *links open-minded questions,* and another, and another. Hours, days, and weeks passed by in futility. Ferrucci's team was no closer to separating various attributes that seemed to bleed into one another.

So Ferrucci tried a different way. Perhaps the Bridgewater attributes couldn't readily be defined by available sources. But Dalio was the inventor—surely he could tell them all apart. Ferrucci decided to "seed" the system with Dalio's own definitions of the terms. He and his team pulled hundreds of hours of videos from the Transparency Library, Bridgewater's repository of meeting recordings, and tried to track patterns in when Dalio cited specific Principles. Ferrucci's lab employees also went through years of Bridgewater's old management training videos—the same ones that all staffers were tested on—and painstakingly noted which Principles were used, and in what context. From all this effort, the researchers created a series of word clouds, or a visual collection of words in different sizes. The larger the word, the more often it was used in conversation. Applied to the dots, the word clouds were intended to show whether employees who used certain language tended to rate highly in one attribute or another. More broadly, Ferrucci hoped to be able to train a computer to read or listen to a passage of text, and to realize that if certain words were used in a certain order, the topic at hand dealt with one Principle or another. If the scientists could nail the method, they could essentially create a computerized version of Dalio himself.*

The goal proved elusive. Few of the theories seemed to work. The inventor of IBM Watson, who had trained a computer to answer trivia on any topic of the world, couldn't make heads or tails of Dalio's thought process. Ferrucci's team could produce no obvious, predictive pattern to when the Bridgewater founder would bring up one Principle or another. The employee ratings, or dots, had equally little evidence of logic. Ferrucci, the AI expert, shared with colleagues a gradual awakening: Dalio's system contained more artifice than intelligence.

---

* A spokeswoman for Ferrucci wrote in an email, "Quantitative survey data was used to find statistically significant differentiation using industry-standard statistical methods." Asked to elaborate, she declined.

At a sit-down with Dalio a few days before Christmas 2014, roughly two years into Ferrucci's tenure at Bridgewater, he took the smallest of stands. A large group, including the Bridgewater founder, got together with Ferrucci to review progress on the Book of the Future. Just as he had with McDowell years earlier, Dalio began pointing out to Ferrucci problems with the ratings of specific Bridgewater employees. Some were rated too highly, which must have been an error in the software, Dalio said. Ferrucci sat quietly, taking in the feedback.

Midway through speaking, Dalio stopped suddenly, then said to Ferrucci, "I'm giving you direction. You're not writing it down."

"I'm taking in your input."

Dalio cocked his head. "You work for me."

"I work for Greg."

"No, you work for me." Dalio waved his hands in a flutter of frustration. He turned to the dozen or so people in the room. "How many people think that Dave is looking at this the right way?" One of Dalio's assistants furiously typed the prompt into her iPad, creating an instant poll for those in the room. The verdict was that Ferrucci was looking at it wrong.

Dalio continued, pointing out how unlikely it was that certain people could be rated in one way or another in certain attributes. He gave his list of tweaks: "This is what I want to see."

Ferrucci's voice came back, barely above a whisper. "That's not a valid algorithm."

Dalio cocked his head back, surprised at the answer.

Ferrucci's eyes welled up and he said, voice quavering, "That's not scientific, Ray." The team couldn't just make changes based on Dalio's whims. "It's not how I work. I can't just take direction like this."

The room seemed to shift. The group had seen Dalio tear into countless underlings before, but here he was on unfamiliar ground. He wasn't in a position to argue computer science with a man with a Ph.D.

Ferrucci went from the meeting to the parking lot visibly brimming with anger. He became the latest Bridgewater employee to drive away apparently prepared to quit.

THE PROSPECT of Ferrucci leaving the firm was treated as a five-alarm fire. Besides Dalio, the scientist was to the broader public the best-known Bridgewater employee. Quantitative-driven investing was the wave of the future, and any rival hedge fund would have been thrilled to swoop in and hire Ferrucci. Bridgewater didn't want to have to explain to its clients and to the world that it had turned off the IBM Watson inventor—particularly if the reason was that Ferrucci judged Dalio's management system to be hogwash.

The day after Christmas, Ferrucci received a note that Dalio wanted to chat again, this time by phone. There would be no crowd around a table, and no recording for everyone to listen to. The two men could speak frankly about how to move forward.

"I can't do the dots anymore," Ferrucci told Dalio.

Dalio asked what could get the scientist to change his mind.

Ferrucci was prepared for that question. He had an idea for a start-up company, Elemental Cognition, completely unconnected to Bridgewater or to investing. Elemental Cognition would use the technology behind Watson to teach computers to understand common sense, human intuition. This could not be achieved merely by trawling the internet for knowledge, or reading every book in existence. Elemental Cognition's goal required the mastery of fundamental concepts such as time, causality, and social interaction. It would require expensive, advanced supercomputing and the services of a slew of Ph.D. researchers. All of this would be expensive, with no guarantee that anything would work out.

"I'll fund that," Dalio said. He offered tens of millions of dollars from Bridgewater, on one condition. Ferrucci could spend only half his time on his dream company. "The other half of the time, you do what I tell you to do."

Ferrucci took the deal.

17

UNPRINCIPLED

As the midpoint of the decade came and went, Bridgewater seemed to rediscover its winning ways.

The firm's main hedge fund, Pure Alpha, burst out of the gate in 2015, just as its competitors were floundering. That January, Switzerland's central bank shocked the world by suddenly unpegging, or letting float free, the exchange rate for its currency, in an attempt to boost the Swiss economy. The move sent the euro diving as much as 30 percent versus the Swiss franc and spelled calamity for investors who had expected the status quo to continue—at least one sizable hedge fund took such steep losses that it was forced to shut immediately. Bridgewater, however, was on the other side of the trade. In line with the firm's oft-stated reliance on deep research of economic history, the hedge fund was shorting, or betting against, the euro-franc exchange rate, ahead of the central bank's decision. As a result Pure Alpha's leveraged version shot up 8 percent in January, a roughly $5 billion haul that was already more than double what the fund had made the previous year. This monster win reminded clients why they kept their money with the biggest hedge fund in history. For Dalio, not every year might be a record winner, but he often enough seemed to be a half step ahead of the curve when disaster struck.

The year marked four decades since Dalio had founded the first version of Bridgewater as an import-export business with his Harvard pal, and the firm founder resolved to celebrate in style. A giant tent was erected on campus and filled with more than fifteen hundred wooden chairs, where employees crammed in shoulder to shoulder, revivalist fashion. From the back of the tent, and from the sides, camera crews captured one Bridgewater executive after another bounding on the stage under flood lighting, recounting the merits of the Bridgewater culture to enthusiastic applause.

Dalio sat in the front row, in a seat reserved with his name, peering up at the spectacle. He gazed with visible satisfaction as Jensen, Dalio's surrogate son, gave a speech that the Bridgewater founder might well have written himself.

Bridgewater's success, Jensen said, "came from all types fighting it out in an open and meritocratic way, which led us to ideas that it is unlikely any of us could have achieved individually. That battle leads to incredible things."

The mirror, Jensen said, is held up to everyone. "It is a gift to be shown the map of who you are and where you need to be."

Finally it was Dalio's turn. Hoots and hollers filled the tent as he climbed onto the stage. He said next to nothing about finance, or about the investments that paid for a party that would stretch deep into the evening. Instead he spoke with wistful airs about a day, yet indeterminate, when Bridgewater would have to survive without him at the helm. He nodded slightly toward Jensen while speaking.

"I want you to think—not follow," Dalio told his gathered acolytes. "I want to help you get the most likely best answers, even if you personally don't believe that they're the best answers. I want to give you radical open-mindedness and an idea meritocracy that will take you from being trapped in your own heads. . . . I want to help you all struggle well and evolve to get the most out of life."

The audience cheered uproariously.

Not far from there, a new monument had been erected just in time for the party. A wood totem pole, which Dalio had helped design, had been inscribed with the story of Bridgewater. Dalio called it "the baton" because it held the traditions that would be passed on to future generations at Bridgewater. One of Dalio's deputies took it particularly seriously, bringing new hires out to the baton and telling them that one of their first assignments was to face the totem pole and confess their greatest weaknesses.*

At the end of the party, all were directed to reach under their chairs, where they found premixed shots of kamikazes. The citrus-flavored concoctions were a Dalio favorite. Those in attendance hoisted their shots in the air and drained them.

---

* A lawyer for Dalio said the idea for the baton originated from Bridgewater's "community team." The lawyer said Dalio "did not suggest or endorse the idea" of newcomers addressing the pole.

ENGORGED WITH new money, renewed confidence and one baton, Dalio looked again to change up the crew around him. This time around, he didn't settle for Wall Street also-rans such as Murray and McCormick. He called Bill Gates, whom Dalio had met in philanthropic circles, and asked for a recommendation. Gates suggested Craig Mundie, Gates's former deputy at Microsoft. Dalio and Mundie bonded immediately over their love of the sea. Dalio soon hired him as Bridgewater's new vice-chairman. Mundie swiftly suggested a series of new consultants, among them the retired general Keith Alexander, former director of the National Security Agency. Often impressed by a man in uniform and concerned about prying eyes at Bridgewater, Dalio hired Alexander to take charge of security, at around $4 million per year.

The trio was rounded out by Larry Culp, who had just finished a successful fourteen-year tenure as CEO of conglomerate Danaher. Culp was brought in as adviser to the Bridgewater management committee, as a tryout for a long-term role.

The new faces wandering the Bridgewater campus represented an enduring paradox there. For all of Dalio's talk about a grand, systematic structure of management, a person could be hired or fired based on the founder's whim. Dalio got what he wanted. He was not only the face of the firm, but as had been amply demonstrated over the preceding years—no matter how it was spun publicly—he had veto-proof control over management decisions.

Nowhere was that more obvious than in Bridgewater and Dalio's budding fascination with international strongmen. Since the late 1980s, Dalio had been convinced that the United States was in an inextricable fall, not merely economically, but culturally. He saw U.S. politics as on a slow descent into unproductive squabbling, a journey that could end in nothing less than another civil war. At times, he called himself "an economic doctor," with the prescription to fix all that.

In place of U.S. hegemony, Dalio looked for a better blueprint abroad. He seemed particularly smitten with societies ruled by powerful autocrats. Thanks to Bridgewater's long history of managing money for Singapore's government-run funds, Dalio became friends with Lee Kuan Yew. The elder man, who served as Singapore's prime minister for a staggering thirty-one years, was a controversial figure whose long tenure achieved stability for his nation at the cost of freedom. Lee governed through what was essentially one-party rule, restricting freedom of speech and dismissing the value of democracy. He banned the sale of chewing gum; endorsed caning to punish teenagers guilty of vandalism; and imprisoned the few political opponents who dared speak out. Dalio looked past all of that. To Dalio, Lee was the man who had turned Singapore from a relative backwater to one of the world's financial centers. Lee was an "iconic hero," as Dalio once described him, and a model leader.

Over dinner at Dalio's New York apartment shortly before the Singaporean leader's death, the men discussed the best models among world leaders. Lee gave an unlikely answer in a posh Manhattan setting: Vladimir Putin. The Russian leader, Lee said, had stabilized Russia after the chaotic collapse of the Soviet Union. To Dalio, the analogy would have been seamless. He, too, had stabilized Bridgewater after a tumultuous stretch.

Dalio turned his attention, bordering on obsessive, to meeting Putin. He asked Bridgewater's client-service team to call in favors abroad to gain him an introduction. This proved more difficult than expected. Putin was not known for giving audiences to American businessmen—even those as famous as the Bridgewater founder. Through intermediaries, Dalio said he was happy to audition. He invited one of Putin's closest allies, Herman Gref, to visit Bridgewater headquarters. Gref, who was chief executive of the state-run Sberbank, arrived in the spring of 2015 with a small entourage. He was whisked in to see Dalio, who showed off the hedge fund's employee rating tools and explained that everything at Bridgewater operated off a strict set of rules. Dalio offered to set up a similar system for the Russians. Gref expressed intrigue and suggested that he might be able to introduce Dalio to Putin at the Russian leader's palace in the resort town of Sochi.

Dalio could scarcely contain his excitement in the days that followed. Yet every time he asked his team for an update, he learned that the Putin meetup had been postponed once again. Spurned, the Bridgewater founder turned his gaze farther east, to another foreign power ruled by a strongman.

DALIO HAD been fascinated with China for decades, long before the growing nation became a mainstream destination for Western businesspeople. In China, he found the perfect confluence of his interests. The culture of the collectivist society demanded its citizens defer their short-term interests and gratifications for those of the state and its rules, for the promise of a long-term reward. As Dalio would say in a 2019 video taped with a Bridgewater staffer, "Curiosity brought me in contact with the Chinese people, who I really, really came to love and admire [for] the character of them, and what type of relationships that they valued." He added later in the interview, "If you deal with the question of whether it's a more autocratic system, and whether you prefer a more autocratic leadership system than a democratic leadership system, you'll have to make that choice for yourself. Don't look at it as some unique place in terms of some of those impediments. Look at the whole picture. I would say that the Chinese or Confucian way of approaching things has a lot to be said for it."

More than a little dose of the Chinese mindset was in Dalio's own.

Dalio first visited China in 1984 with a small coterie including his wife. For a Harvard Business School graduate who had married into staggering familial wealth the experience was eye-opening. The group met with representatives of CITIC, a giant government-run conglomerate that would later boast operations in real estate, banking, metals, and a slew of other industries. In the era, however, Dalio might as well have been visiting from another planet. As a gift, he handed over calculators he'd brought over from America; the CITIC executives had never seen one before. Dalio stood at the office window and gestured to the surrounding traditional low-rise neighborhoods, or *hutongs*. He predicted skyscrapers would soon rise in their place. "You don't know China," his hosts told him.

The Bridgewater founder continued visiting, learning, and making inroads in a society with a strong distrust of outsiders. When his third son was eleven years old, Dalio sent him to live with a local family in Beijing and to attend a school there. The living arrangements were stark: the family's apartment building had hot water only twice a week, and the school didn't have heat most of the year, so students wore their jackets to class. Dalio visited his son there and the two squinted into the sun in the Forbidden City as they posed for photos in front of a six-foot-high photograph of Mao Zedong, the founder of the People's Republic. They were the only Westerners in a cluster of local faces.

When his son expressed an interest in returning to China more frequently, Dalio began to combine business with the personal. In addition to helping stake his son to start a charity, the China Care Foundation, which built orphanages for disabled Chinese children, Dalio ramped up his efforts to raise money for Bridgewater from deep-pocketed but closed-off government institutions. In meetings he would remind the government representatives that when they invested with Bridgewater, their fees were not merely being sent back to America. "Whatever fees you pay, I will donate back to China personally," he said in one meeting. The pitch worked. Bridgewater collected more than $10 billion for its funds from Chinese government wings including sovereign wealth fund China Investment Corporation and the multitrillion-dollar State Administration of Foreign Exchange (SAFE).

Bridgewater's affiliation with government entities gave Dalio entry into a rarefied world. He became close with Wang Qishan, later China's vice premier and widely considered the second most powerful person in the country, as the head of the Communist Party's anticorruption arm. Wang had instincts that wouldn't be out of place at Bridgewater; at one meeting of his own deputy investigators, he surprised the group with dossiers of their own transgressions. Wang's apparent aim "was to terrorize the enforcers themselves," the *Economist* reported, adding that "Failure to uncover high-level graft . . . would be 'dereliction of duty.'" The publication called Wang perhaps the most feared man in China.

Dalio called Wang a friend, a hero, and "a remarkable force for good." The two men met for at least an hour on each of Dalio's trips to China, chatting about philosophy and the world order. Dalio gave him a copy of the same book he'd once given Jensen, *The Hero with a Thousand Faces*. Wang returned the favor by endorsing one of Dalio's most prized Principles: "Pain plus reflection equals progress." "If conflicts got resolved before they became acute, there wouldn't be any heroes," Wang told Dalio during one visit.

Through Wang, Dalio learned about the complicated machinations of the Chinese governing system. The country was expanding a so-called social credit system, in which the government attempted to track the personal behavior of each citizen, down to infractions as small as jaywalking, and used the data to calculate an omnibus personal rating that determined whether someone could receive a loan, a job, or other benefits. The goal was, as the Chinese government put it, to create a "culture of sincerity." Dalio must not have been able to help but see the connection to his own stated radical truth and transparency, as well as his mushrooming system of ratings tools and software that divvied up people at Bridgewater based on their personalities and purported abilities.

The Chinese government, like Bridgewater, was organized as a set of committees with overlapping members, all reporting to President Xi Jinping. The highest body was the National Congress, which met every five years, followed by the Central Committee, which gathered roughly annually. The day-to-day power rested with the Politburo and the Politburo Standing Committee, a policy-making body under President Xi that essentially ran the country. President Xi periodically ordered the Politburo to engage in what he called "self-criticism" to reaffirm their loyalty to him. There were just seven members of the Politburo Standing Committee, and Dalio's friend Wang was one of them.

In 2015, inspired by the Chinese system, Dalio sought to re-create parts of it in Connecticut. Without telling clients or the public, he put out a call inside Bridgewater for young staffers who wanted to help reshape the firm in accordance with The Principles. This plum gig was one sure to provide a chance to impress Dalio. Those who stepped forward were assigned to a dizzying array of new enforcement bodies, with rather unsubtle names. The Principles Captains were those assessed to be the most knowledgeable about Dalio's manifesto. These Principles Captains were fanned out across the firm and were meant to assess whether individuals were acting in a Principled fashion day-to-day. The Auditors monitored department heads whom Dalio didn't manage individually. The Overseers had no easily definable responsibilities, save for reporting to Dalio on the goings-on of the other new groups.* "The worst thing," said one employee, "is for an Overseer to find a problem before I find it."

The crown jewel of Dalio's new creations was called the Politburo, its name borrowed from the decision-making body of China's Communist Party and first coined by Russian Bolsheviks. The roughly two dozen members of Bridgewater's Politburo were mostly in their twenties or thirties. They were handpicked by Dalio and given vast remits to conduct investigations across the firm. Though theoretically meant to adjudicate disputes, the Politburo often created new ones. The members would barge uninvited into meetings—or listen to recordings afterward—and rate their colleagues. The members caught, and squelched, dissent before it reached Dalio's desk. It was a dream come true. Now the Bridgewater founder had eyes and ears everywhere.

JENSEN WATCHED the sudden growth of these new apparatuses with alarm. They were yet another threat to his future.

---

* A lawyer for Dalio said there was overlap between these teams, and that their "assignment was to answer employee questions and coach them."

With each new Dalio creation, the forty-year-old heir apparent fell further from the ultimate prize. Six years ago Dalio had announced Jensen as his successor, yet the Bridgewater founder was more involved than ever. To the outside world, it seemed that nothing had changed. Jensen was still CEO, and of all the experienced hires brought into the firm, none had lasted as long as him. His ultimate ascension, however, had clearly been diverted. Despite Jensen's nearly two decades at Dalio's side, the Bridgewater founder's new committees represented a weaponization of The Principles— new weapons that only Dalio could effectively wield.

The pressure continued to build on Jensen as 2015 rolled on. Jensen's computer monitor, which had a real-time view of Bridgewater's investment performance, showed that after the strong start to the year from the Swiss franc success, the trend line had dipped down. The hedge fund's manna was slowly being frittered away, a casualty yet again of Dalio's latest predictions of trouble for the global economy. In March of that year, Dalio told clients he saw parallels to the late days of the Great Depression. "I'd like to remind you of the 1937 analog," he cowrote in a client note that found its way to the media. Stocks then collapsed more than 50 percent in a single year, Dalio observed, a little-veiled prediction that the same could happen again. It didn't. Jensen's monitor showed the effect of Dalio's dour outlook, which kept the firm's flagship fund betting persistently pessimistic trades. Bridgewater's funds bled out slowly as the spring turned into summer, transforming what could have been a banner year into an ordinary one at best.

Dalio stuck to the course. As he told it, danger was in the air. This belief was seemingly confirmed in July, when the Chinese stock market sank, shaving a third of the value off the Shanghai exchange's main index. The dive, in a country that Dalio thought he knew well, left him shaken. "Our views about China have changed," Dalio cowrote in a new note to clients. "There are now no safe places to invest." He raised the possibility of another D-process. "Even those who haven't lost money in stocks will be affected psychologically by events, and those effects will have a depressive effect on economic activity." That note, too, made it to the press, where it was picked up broadly as a calamitous sign for Beijing.

Dalio's remarks were no different from what he'd been saying about the U.S. and other Western economies for decades. In China, however, they were received differently. Criticism of the economy amounted to criticism of the state, and it couldn't be tolerated from a foreigner—especially one who promoted himself as a well-connected expert on the nation. Representatives from SAFE and CITIC called up Bridgewater, warning that they were under pressure to distance themselves from the world's largest hedge fund. Dalio worked the phones, telling high-level government officials in China that he was still a great admirer of the country's leaders. Bridgewater's technology team noticed an unusual slowdown in the company's computer networks and suspected that Chinese hackers might be aiming a cyberattack at the firm in revenge.

It took just a day for Dalio to instruct his public relations team to release a statement backtracking on his earlier note—"While the report to Bridgewater clients is a private communication which they want to continue to try to keep private, Ray Dalio and Bridgewater believe that too much has been made of the shift in their thinking and want to clarify their thinking," it read, in part—but the damage was done. Bridgewater's comeback year was rapidly headed off track.

THE CHINA incident left Dalio visibly shaken and angry. Unable or unwilling to accept that his own words had set off the brouhaha, he ranted in meeting after meeting that the media had ignored his long patronage of China and miscast him as just another trader looking to make a quick buck off a foreign country's struggles. Dalio began again to refer to himself as an economic doctor and said he was merely offering his reasoned diagnosis, based on the facts. No one at Bridgewater would have dared remind him that a doctor doesn't bet on the outcome of a patient's health, as Bridgewater's funds often did by going long or short on the Chinese yuan.

In the days that followed, Dalio's quick temper grew shorter still. While walking on the indoor bridge that connected the two buildings of Bridgewater's headquarters, he noticed faint pockmarks on the soft-wood floor. He ordered an investigation. He was told that the indentations came from high-heeled shoes. He immediately ordered up a new rule, sent via email to the whole firm. No high heels would be allowed at Bridgewater.

That Dalio himself had to address scuffing on the floor was yet another reminder to him of the firm's poor state. Around Thanksgiving 2015, Dalio called in his newest high-level hire, Culp, along with the rest of Bridgewater's top brass, including Jensen, seeking to hear a plan for how Culp would use Dalio's new set of Principles-based committees to set the firm straight. But Culp delivered a different message altogether: he told Dalio that too many people at Bridgewater had nebulous responsibilities and titles and spent all day listening to tapes of others, looking to spring a trap. Culp told Dalio to slash, not to build. Put one person in charge and give him or her some space. Dalio had been doing the exact opposite for the better part of a decade.

Dalio offered a response for his newest hire: The problem was clearly Culp. Culp was not capable of understanding the advanced nature of Bridgewater's management system. "You're not conceptual enough."

Dalio fired Culp, stood up, and left the room.*

As the others present silently absorbed the firm's latest hanging, Culp sat flabbergasted. He'd presented his honest take to a man who claimed to prize frank feedback and had instead been abruptly shown the door.

Jensen, having seen this movie many times before, moved to clean up the mess. "Ray can be difficult," Jensen told Culp. Jensen explained that Dalio didn't have a grasp on how the nuts and bolts of the firm worked, or how The Principles played out in practice. Culp listened as Jensen reminded him that no one was more disappointed than Jensen himself, who had been waiting endlessly for Dalio to hand over the keys to the firm.

Not long after speaking with Culp, Jensen went even further with someone he should have known better than to trust, and in a venue that could not have been more poorly chosen. After an otherwise rote meeting of the Bridgewater management committee—a meeting taped and available for all to listen to afterward—Jensen pulled aside Murray. He told her, "Ray is crazy," and that the two of them could run the firm much better without the Bridgewater founder.

Jensen's remarks were a riff on what he'd been complaining about for years. But in a mistake that would haunt him, Jensen failed to realize that this wasn't the Bridgewater of yore. The Principles had stopped being something that Dalio's surrogate son could control. An entire army of staffers was now at the firm dedicated to squelching would-be heretics. In just a few days the tape recording of Jensen's idle talk to Culp was passed to the new squad. Murray, too, perhaps spotting a chance to get back at Jensen for his role in her not-so-distant trial under Jim Comey, made sure that Dalio was aware of what Jensen had told her while the recording equipment still hummed.

A young Bridgewater associate transcribed the chats and sent them to

---

* Culp would become CEO of General Electric. He has never publicly confirmed that he even worked at Bridgewater, let alone discussed the experience. The hedge fund is not listed on his official General Electric biography.

Dalio with a message: your heir apparent is talking about you behind your back. It was a cardinal violation of The Principles.

Dalio sicced the full force of the Politburo on his right-hand man.

SEEMINGLY OVERNIGHT, the schism between Dalio and Jensen consumed Bridgewater. Dalio put Jensen through a trial unlike any other the firm had seen. Dalio filled a room with the new cohort of Principles devotees and lashed into the man who had so recently seemed his surefire successor.

"Greg is a slimy weasel," Dalio pronounced, several people there recall.

This was no errant phrase. The Principles made clear that to say something about someone behind their back made you a weasel. People had been fired in the past for such infractions, making it one of the worst possible sins. And Jensen hadn't merely engaged in idle talk. He had been complaining about Dalio almost recklessly, as if Jensen couldn't be caught.

Jensen told those close to him he felt he was in the right. Dalio *could* be difficult, just as Jensen had told Culp. And if Jensen was honest with himself, he did believe that he and Murray could run Bridgewater better without Dalio's constant interference. In speaking up against Dalio, Jensen could argue he was using The Principles as their author intended. If The Principles were truly worthy, they could to be used to unseat their master.

So Jensen tried to convince Dalio that these words were not just truths, but hard truths, the type that Dalio encouraged everyone to share openly. Jensen said that he had even mentioned them to Dalio before. Jensen even attempted a countermove, asking colleagues to vote on whether Dalio had been sticking to his oft-stated plan of transitioning leadership of the firm.

Dalio would have none of it. He punted Jensen's request for a vote ("Maybe he's right, maybe he's wrong," one person recalled Dalio saying). Dalio ordered the Politburo to dig into a trove of recordings of Jensen in the Transparency Library, hunting for evidence that the younger man had spoken behind the boss's back before. Dalio had the Politburo assemble a series of tapes that seemed to show Jensen speaking unkindly behind Dalio's back, then blasted them around the firm. The Politburo sent out reams of evidence to hundreds of people at the hedge fund, allowing a wide swath of staffers to read the history of the exchanges between the two. Dalio also reminded Jensen privately that Bridgewater had never released the tapes of Jim Comey probing Jensen on the relationship with Holland—the probe that had led to a secret settlement that still few knew of.

The deck seemed to be stacking rapidly against the younger man.

Jensen responded as many before him had: he wept. At one day of his trial, as Bridgewater cameras rolled around him, he sobbed in front of Dalio and begged for forgiveness. "Bridgewater is all I have and I love this place. If I did what I did, I never meant to do it."

Under Dalio's direction, the tape of Jensen in distress was sent around to particular teams inside Bridgewater, including to the investment group, where Jensen's employees and acolytes were all but forced to watch their immediate boss and role model suffer. One person who viewed it recalled, "No one had actually ever seen Greg so sad and desperate. He was literally crying."

Dalio could have fired Jensen from Bridgewater. Others had been fired for far less. But Jensen wasn't just anyone. He was all but a member of Dalio's family. A more useful narrative for Dalio was to cast Jensen's foibles as part of the younger man's hero's journey—one that could take him to the abyss and back. If no less than Jensen could reach rock bottom and claw his way back, anyone at Bridgewater could stick around when sent to the brink. Jensen's unraveling could be held up as a model for anyone at Bridgewater under duress.

In what he portrayed as a Talmudic compromise, Dalio stripped Jensen of his CEO title but kept him on as cochief investment officer—a clear drop in prestige. The media covered it for what it was: the shocking demotion of Dalio's would-be heir.

Jensen left for what was described to staff as an unplanned vacation—the longest he had taken in years.

Many at Bridgewater weren't sure when, or if, Jensen would return. Some imagined that he would clear his head and decide that life was too short to put up with Bridgewater and Dalio. Instead, Jensen went on a bender. He flew to Las Vegas to play poker until all hours of the evening. He left his family and didn't tell them when he would return. Once he did come back, he told friends he would never feel the same way about Dalio.

In Jensen's absence, Dalio worked on a surprise of his own. Some inside Bridgewater had only heard bits of the clash between Dalio and Jensen—some of the videos and documents had been shared only within the Politburo or other arms of the firm. Rumors were flying inside and outside of Bridgewater, and they weren't all flattering to Dalio or The Principles. Dalio had stated over the years that Bridgewater was a place of radical transparency. How could that be true if the full details of this collision between the two most important people at the firm were only available to a chosen few?

So Dalio declared an emergency, literally calling it a moment for "martial law." Concurrently, he invented a new Principle, one that effectively reversed his stated sacrosanct beliefs:

"Expect those who receive the radical transparency to handle it responsibly and don't give it to them if they can't."

This Principle was retroactively applied to the showdown between Dalio and Jensen. Staff still confused about where Jensen had disappeared to would find no answers in the Transparency Library. Only about 10 percent of people at Bridgewater could be "trusted," in Dalio's words, to be told the full story. The rest couldn't handle it.

Also in quiet, Dalio organized a roughly twenty-person team to work on a new company charter, augmenting The Principles with a set of laws on how to govern Bridgewater. The charter would lay out which day-to-day disagreements could be debated and which could be called for votes. It gave extraordinary power to the next Bridgewater CEO, a position that would seem to be now and forever out of Jensen's reach—because Dalio asked for it to be written into the charter that Jensen could never be CEO again.

18

THE WAY OF BEING

THE CHAUFFEURED SPORT UTILITY VEHICLE HUGGED THE COAST OF Mexico's Bahía de Banderas on a bumpy hour-long drive that both inconvenienced and impressed the man in the back seat.

After the cross-continental flight into Puerto Vallarta, Greg Jensen was surely ready for a drink. Sweat beading on his forehead, he exited the SUV and walked up the marble steps into the house that the iPod built.

House might have been underplaying it, though calling the property a *ranch,* as its owner, Jon Rubinstein, preferred, carried more than a little false modesty. The sixteen-thousand-square-foot estate boasted seven bedrooms, 206 feet of beachfront, multiple pools, and quarters for live-in servants. Jensen stayed in the guest wing and, when he rose in the morning, was forced to traverse human-size sculptures that studded the property.

Jensen might have been happy to have any excuse to be away from Bridgewater. But setting notwithstanding, this was a particularly degrading assignment from Dalio. Jensen had been sent to Mexico to cozy up to Rubinstein as the technology executive mulled joining Bridgewater as its next leader. It was like asking your ex-girlfriend for help finding your next one.

Rubinstein lived the life of a man who had all the choices in the world. A wiry, tall fellow who seemed not to have physically changed since his bar mitzvah, Rubinstein was eighteen years older than Jensen. He had made his reputation at Apple, where he earned the nickname the Podfather, for helping Steve Jobs create the first iPod. As the years passed, however, Rubinstein gained the reputation inside Apple as a practical, and somewhat irritating, square. He got into profanity-laden shouting matches with Jobs and other members of the Apple C-suite while opposing proposed design improvements to Apple products that he worried would be too difficult to manufacture. After sixteen years, Jobs decided that Rubinstein had a big ego and the two parted ways. "He never delved deep, he wasn't aggressive," Jobs said.

In his last three years alone at Apple, Rubinstein had been awarded $83 million worth of stock options. Hence, the ranch.

Since Apple, Rubinstein had struggled to land another equivalent professional hit. He moved from the technology giant to become CEO of rival cell phone maker Palm, effectively incinerating what remained of his relationship with Jobs (the two never spoke again). Palm's mobile efforts face-planted, and Rubinstein left after it was sold to Hewlett-Packard. Rubinstein had been on the beach, literally and figuratively, ever since. That made him the perfect target for Bridgewater's revolving ranks of cast-off executives.

Dalio might not have known nor particularly cared about Rubinstein's late-career wobbles, or really had any specific knowledge of him at all. But Dalio certainly knew that Rubinstein had been touched by Steve Jobs. And the idea to hire Rubinstein had come from a new addition to the inner circle, Craig Mundie, the former chief strategy officer of Microsoft and a longtime confidant of Bill Gates's. Mundie had a title new to Bridgewater, vice-chairman. These technology heavyweights were the exact sort that could help Dalio finally transform The Principles into software for all.

Rubinstein was willing to give it a shot. In exchange for compensation of as much as $50 million over the first two years, he was willing to work seven days a week at Bridgewater. Unlike Larry Culp, he was fine with splitting the role of CEO, too (Eileen Murray would serve with him). Rubinstein would take charge of technology, including the all-important iPad ratings systems.

Jensen left Rubinstein's ranch with encouraging news to bring back to Westport.

JON RUBINSTEIN reported for duty at Bridgewater in May 2016, just weeks after Jensen's return from the leave induced by his showdown with Dalio. The new hire had an immediate sense that not all would go as planned; Dalio, riding high after crushing Jensen, was far more involved than Rubinstein anticipated. Jensen, who had seemed almost gregarious to Rubinstein in Mexico, was nigh unrecognizable back in Connecticut, slinking into meetings late and barely meeting Dalio's eyes.

Hoping for a period of transition, with time to get his bearings, Rubinstein told Dalio he preferred to start quietly. Dalio, still smarting from the headlines around Jensen's demotion and eager to put out a countermessage, had other plans. He told Bridgewater underlings to write up a client letter about the new hire and instructed his public relations team to leak it to reporters. Excerpts appeared in newspapers around the world.

"Technology is pervasively important at Bridgewater, especially since one of our major strategic initiatives in the coming years is to continue building out the systemized decision-making that has been so successful in our investment area and to extend it to our management as well," the letter read.

Rubinstein's phone blew up with well-wishers congratulating him on landing a prestigious gig at the world's largest hedge fund.

Rubinstein figured that if nothing else the splashy entrance would give him a mandate to dive headfirst into troubleshooting Bridgewater's technology. Instead he was handed an iPad and sent directly to a private Principles boot camp. Rubinstein sat, befuddled, as a procession of Bridgewater staffers drilled him on the company manifesto. They showed him slides and videos of employees being diagnosed and probed by their superiors, including Dalio. Rubinstein was immediately turned off. His former boss Jobs had a well-earned reputation for coarseness, but the Apple founder never claimed it was due to any high-brow philosophy. After a few days of training, Rubinstein was assigned the same Principles test given to all new hires. He answered honestly and was told he flunked it. "This is all screwed up," he told one new colleague.

Once Dalio caught word that his new prized hire had struggled in boot camp, he asked for some time to chat. Rubinstein, cognizant of everything he'd learned about the Bridgewater founder's love of raw honesty, decided to tell Dalio what was on his mind:

"You've got three hundred and seventy-five Principles. Those aren't principles. Toyota has fourteen principles. Amazon has fourteen principles. The Bible has ten. Three hundred and seventy-five can't possibly be principles. They are an instruction manual."

Dalio blamed himself. It's my fault, the Bridgewater founder said, for expecting you to appreciate such a complex system so quickly. The Principles could not simply be memorized and then instantly absorbed—the only way to understand them was to live them. Dalio called The Principles "the way of being."

It was around this time that Rubinstein thought to himself, *Shit.*

RUBINSTEIN'S HIRE was not Dalio's only means of changing the narrative. As the former Apple executive surveyed the state of the firm, the Bridgewater founder made a renewed effort to tell his own story. He had some help doing it.

In May 2016, the same month Rubinstein started, Dalio flew to Los Angeles for an onstage interview at the Milken Institute's glam annual conference at the Beverly Hilton. His interviewer was Harvard professor Robert Kegan, who had visited Bridgewater and written glowingly of the firm in his own book. After Dalio began with a spiel about how Bridgewater had developed humility in its company culture ("It's only psychologically hard. . . . As soon as you start to take a different attitude about it, it's pleasurable, so you go from pain to pleasure"), Kegan peered down at his notes and seemed to read out from them:

"I read a study recently that showed that millennials most want more feedback. It sounds like Bridgewater would be millennial heaven."

Dalio smiled back.

Kegan asked what Dalio thought were the most common misunderstandings about Bridgewater.

Dalio glanced back with a thinner smile, well prepared to answer, having been asked the question before. "One that's common is that it's a cult."

A few knowing chuckles rose from the well-heeled crowd.

"Why isn't it a cult?" Kegan asked.

"It's the opposite of a cult. It's independent thinking. It's you knowing that you have the right and obligation to make sense of everything. It is a culture." Dalio added later, "Think of it as similar to a legal system."

Back at headquarters, Rubinstein was beginning to wonder aloud if there was a system at all. The hedge fund was spending tens of millions of dollars on developing The Principles ratings systems, but when Rubinstein tried to investigate what it actually did, he was simply told that it measured "believability." Many told him the systems involved secret calculations from the former IBM scientist David Ferrucci, and that the researcher told nearly no one how it worked. This immediately struck the former Apple executive as off. He had spent his life working with researchers like Ferrucci, and in Rubinstein's experience, corporate scientists tended to overexplain their work to company executives in excruciating, unnecessary detail. The struggle was usually to get them to shut up.

Rubinstein was no junior hire, so he sought out Ferrucci in person. The two men exchanged pleasantries, then the co-CEO dropped his biggest question:

"How do you calculate believability?"

Ferrucci briefly broke eye contact. "I'm not going to tell you."

"Why?"

"I'm embarrassed."

It would be several more months until Rubinstein figured out the answer.

THE MAN who knew all about believability was toiling far below Rubinstein's level, struggling to justify his existence.

With the additions of the technology trio of Rubinstein, Craig Mundie, and Ferrucci, Paul McDowell was at risk of losing his box. Though he continued to lead sporadic Principles training classes, he had been shifted from head of technology to serving as unofficial attaché for Dalio when the Bridgewater founder needed help showing off the firm's culture and tools to clients and other visitors. McDowell, who had never been comfortable glad-handing, struggled to keep a straight face as he talked of the merits of Bridgewater's culture. For Dalio, however, McDowell acted as the ideal direct report, and sometimes foil. McDowell had been around long enough to swallow Dalio's criticisms without flinching, and he seemed close enough to Dalio's age that he could, theoretically, be a peer. In one presentation to a potential Russian investor, the state-connected Sberbank, McDowell struggled to get the remote feed to connect. Dalio called him a "wimp" in front of the group. McDowell seethed internally, but assured the Russians that Dalio was simply demonstrating the Bridgewater way of being.

When he wasn't role-playing Punch and Judy with the boss, McDowell was desperately attempting, with a small team, to complete the Book of the Future. The software system, meant to be the master collection of all of Bridgewater's personnel ratings and management tools, had acquired several new names. For a spell, Dalio called it iPrinciples, an obvious nod to Apple. Later it was rebranded to Principles Operating System, or PriOS. When talking about PriOS to clients, Dalio often compared it to a car navigation system. He said it worked so well and so consistently that Bridgewater might even be willing to share it with them—for a price.

In one client meeting, Dalio bragged that Bill Gates and Elon Musk had tested the approach and approved it. Dalio hoped theirs, and other companies, would use it with their own employees, bringing Bridgewater's creations to every workplace in America.

"It will make decisions for you in much the same way a GPS makes decisions. In other words, a GPS can tell you, 'Go right' and 'Go left.' It can happen in management by saying, 'Interview this person,' 'Fire that person,' 'Check on this person's honesty,' or 'Have this discussion.'" Dalio said. "Such an approach, I would think, would be very, very valuable to you."

PriOS was unemotional, Dalio said, just as he was. "The way I handle everything is through an idea meritocracy. I just want the best idea to win out. It does not have to be my idea. I am so happy to be corrected by people that know better than me."

The clients asked, "Who created this system? Who is the expert you used?"

"Me. Literally the way I do it is that every time I am doing something, I write down what I am doing and why I am doing it. Then I have that converted by others into equations," Dalio responded. "What's amazing is that the machine itself is evolving and giving instructions on what to do to evolve in much the same way as my brain would."

Though Dalio talked about PriOS to clients as if it were on the cusp of completion, McDowell surely knew the truth. PriOS was a disaster. It worked on the simplest of tasks, such as searching for whether a certain word appeared in The Principles and surfacing the relevant lines, but could usually no more predict Dalio's choices than anyone else at the firm could. It was as if McDowell were trying to program a GPS for directions through a hellish car-based video game, one in which roads curved into dead ends and bridges spanned only half the length of treacherous crossings.

The longer PriOS was delayed, the worse for McDowell. He could only postpone the matter so long. Finally, in what amounted to a now-or-never moment, Dalio asked him to bring the latest prototype to a meeting of the Bridgewater management committee. These meetings were a hot ticket at the hedge fund; only the top staff attended, such as Dalio, Jensen, and Ferrucci, while a videographer taped the proceedings for the rest of the firm to watch. Few at the firm missed the chance to see who might wind up with a drubbing from Dalio.

That day's victim was quickly apparent. McDowell went around the table and set up each member of the management committee with an iPad loaded with the latest PriOS software. The tools were supposed to be able to drill down into specific categories to see whether individuals with low ratings in, for instance, "living in truth" might be more likely to score poorly in "synthesizing through time"—or whether a person might need to be assigned additional Principles training or even a new job. In practice, the system was still rudimentary at best. It crashed regularly and couldn't consistently update ratings in real time. Worst of all, despite years of efforts and untold hours with Dalio himself, McDowell still hadn't charted any logical consistency to Dalio's values. PriOS was all but useless.

After a few minutes of watching the group struggle, Dalio let out a bark from the head of the table. "Where is Paul McDowell?"

McDowell steadied himself with two hands on the table and pushed onto his feet.

"You're failing in your area," Dalio said.

McDowell would have agreed, to a point. He hadn't delivered what Dalio wanted. What he didn't say was that he wasn't sure what Dalio wanted was even possible—and pointing that out in front of a crowd would surely end poorly. Instead, McDowell tried to use The Principles. He told Dalio that, true to The Principles, he was drilling down to find the poor performers on his team. He had found one person in particular and would be taking action. He didn't name the person.

"Have you cut his comp?" Dalio asked.

McDowell admitted he hadn't.

"You're a bad manager."

McDowell had to know what was coming next. Dalio ordered a fresh investigation by the Politburo to determine what course to take with McDowell. Having sat through enough trials of others during his eight years at the firm, McDowell had seen others try, and fail, to thrash their way out of it. Instead, he chose contrition.

"I welcome your probing, Ray. I imagine you'll find all kinds of flaws and all kinds of things that I should have been doing better. It'll be painful, but I'll be better as a result."

That wasn't the answer Dalio seemed to be expecting. That would be a win not by knockout, but by forfeit. Dalio gave a long stare across the table at McDowell. "Your problem is you don't bust balls. You're not a mother-fucker. I need motherfuckers."

McDowell didn't know what to say, so he chose silence.

To no one in particular, Dalio filled the silence. "I want to kick him in the balls!"

19

FEEDBACK LOOP

THE TIMING WAS FORTUITOUS WHEN JOE SWEET FIRST HEARD FROM A Bridgewater recruiter looking to fill a job. The twenty-nine-year-old was seeking to leave behind a house and a soon-to-be ex-wife in Storrs, Connecticut, home to the University of Connecticut, from which he had earned four degrees, including an MBA. During the divorce, the nebbish-looking Sweet had tried a few therapy sessions and learned a bit about himself. That experience taught him a new way of understanding his flaws, Sweet told his Bridgewater interviewer. Sweet didn't know it yet, but that was manna to the ears of any Bridgewater acolyte. He was hired in short order to the talent team, helping to recruit and retain employees, at a six-figure annual salary with a bonus if he scored at least 3 out of 5 on his annual review. That was far more money than he had ever earned in quiet Storrs.

Sweet's first days at Bridgewater in spring 2016 followed the usual pattern. He read up on The Principles, sat through Paul McDowell's cultural-training course, and watched a battery of videos on life at Bridgewater. At first, it seemed like heaven. Sweet was accustomed to answering with brutal honesty when asked a question, and here that quality was rewarded. Like all other employees, he was required to view almost daily case studies known as Management Principles Training, or MPT, accompanied by graded quizzes. Having studied The Principles closely, he knew the answers that Bridgewater was looking for. Throughout his first weeks, his baseball card swelled with green dots, indicating positive feedback.

That all changed when Sweet learned that Dalio would be conducting a drill down of the talent team. Sweet hadn't heard the term much before, but he had studied enough corporate jargon in school to know a euphemism when he heard it. Ahead of the drill down, he switched to a different team, assuming a low-level role alongside David Ferrucci's Systematized Intelligence Lab. The department worked on turning Dalio's Principles into software, so Sweet figured it was a good way to be involved in the heart of the firm. Instead, exposure to the software team left him more confused than ever. In one meeting, his colleagues feverishly argued about how to delineate between two different ratings categories created by Dalio: "synthesizing the situation" and "synthesizing through time." To an outside observer, the debate might have seemed comical, but to Sweet, who had no clue what was going on, it was dead serious. Suddenly his baseball card was a blur of red dots. When he tried to pump the brakes and asked those around him for help, they assured him that a rough transition was typical.

Sweet tried making allies, but his team seemed to already view him as dead weight. It didn't help when a transgender woman suddenly disappeared from his team one day after complaining for weeks that her ratings card didn't reflect her gender identity. The team received an email from Bridgewater's legal team telling them to preserve all correspondence with their now-former colleague. Sweet figured a settlement might be involved. His whole team was somewhere between spooked and suspicious.

More and more of Sweet's time became consumed by a barrage of negative feedback from those closest to him. He felt as if he was "bad at life and would never improve," he later recalled. Every day, Sweet felt as if he were in a hole before sunrise. He struggled to get out of bed and to force himself to eat. Quitting wasn't an option. He was laden with divorce expenses and worried he would have to repay his signing bonus if he left too quickly.

The first time Sweet ever considered killing himself was while he was sitting at his desk at Bridgewater. His mind wandered to any number of grisly deaths. In one ideation, he stepped in front of a commuter train that ran by his house and was smashed to bits. In another, he tied a propylene rope to a terrace at Bridgewater's headquarters and hung himself from the side of the building.

These thoughts were new enough to Sweet that he went to Bridgewater's human resources department. He told a kind employee about his visions of self-harm. She told him that Bridgewater had a solution for such tough problems. She referred him for therapy, which struck Sweet as a little odd because it implied that the problem was his, not the company's.

Sweet met with the therapist and listed the alarming changes in his life.

He was depressed, alone, and suicidal, far more severely than ever before in his life. Upon hearing where Sweet worked, the therapist seemed unsurprised, by Sweet's recollection. The therapist recommended that Sweet enter twelve weeks of outpatient intensive therapy at a local hospital. Sweet was also put on psychotropic medication for the first time.

Over the next three months, Sweet saw a host of psychologists and social workers at the hospital. To all, he described the environment at Bridgewater, including the constant rating of one another's colleagues. He felt reassured that his reaction to what he was experiencing in his job was normal. After hearing Sweet's account, one of his therapists compared the atmosphere to a feedback loop of self-destruction. Another therapist told Sweet it sounded as if the system had been designed by someone with Asperger's syndrome.

When Sweet returned to Bridgewater after three months away, he was in a far firmer mental state. He could sit in the office without contemplating suicide. He felt hope for the first time since his first days at the company. The calm didn't last long. Ferrucci's team was under pressure to finish a project known as Allstream, which was meant to amalgamate all of the dots into one single data point—essentially a rating that would encompass an employee's worth at the firm. Allstream was said to be the top priority of Dalio's and needed to be completed immediately. Sweet didn't realize that the project, under various names, had become Dalio's great white whale over the previous decade—perpetually under development and still nowhere near completion.

Newly confident from his time away, Sweet decided to speak up. As did many large companies, Bridgewater sent out periodic employee surveys, and Sweet let it rip:

> I think the tools instill a viciousness sometimes as people meet their metrics for Issue Logs or "balance" their Dot softness/toughness gauge by piling on people who make a visible mistake. . . . I've seen MPTs where people are criticized for not dotting negatively enough and in my opinion it only exacerbates the problem. There are a number of people in BW that have needed to receive psychiatric care, including myself, because the tools created a negative feedback loop that reinforced existing [insecurities] and fostered feelings of worthlessness. . . . There are many I've talked to that continue to suffer quietly through depression and anxiety.

Sweet didn't receive a response, but he did receive more work. The weeks slipped by, and his depressive symptoms began to creep back. He had trouble sleeping and eating and began to shake involuntarily while sitting at his desk. It didn't help that Dalio, frustrated about the slow progress of Allstream, was increasingly pressuring the team. They were assigned a new project that Dalio called Video Book, which would package Bridgewater's case studies and sell them to the public for $75 apiece. Sweet's nerves were frayed, and it showed. One afternoon, Sweet made a mistake on a project, and after his boss screamed at him in front of the team, Sweet's colleagues dutifully doled out negative dots for his error. Sweet felt himself falling back into his depressive hole.

Before matters got worse again, Sweet returned to human resources and met with the same woman as before. He described his boss's outburst, and the feeling that his team was piling on just to protect themselves. He asked if feedback could be given to him in private, for the moment.

She rejected the suggestion immediately. "That's the standard way at Bridgewater of doing things. Are you really sure you want to stay here?"

Sweet asked for a different, lower-pressure, internal role in procurement. He was rejected for the job, in part because his ratings were so low. His manager didn't recommend him, saying he lacked "higher-level thinking."

Sweet was rapidly running out of options. As part of his team's number crunching of the Bridgewater ratings, he came across internal research on the firm's annual employee reviews. Sweet still hoped to receive a 3, which he assumed was average on the 5-point scale, but the data showed otherwise. The average employee at Bridgewater earned only a 2, he was told. If that was true, his bonus was all but out of reach—not just to him, but to most everyone.

Just before his one-year mark, Sweet returned for a third time to human resources. He said the firm's culture was hazardous to his health and asked what Bridgewater could do about it. They offered to keep him on the company health insurance for a few months if he quit. Sweet accepted.

He never had another suicidal thought.

20

ONE OF US

THE SMELL OF TUNA MELT WAFTED TOWARD THE TRIO SITTING AT A tucked-away booth at Westport's Sherwood Diner. The location, a greasy spoon where no hedge fund employee was likely to drop in on a weekday in early December, had been Katina Stefanova's choice. She sat by herself on one side of the table, back straight, overdressed for the venue, including makeup, which she rarely bothered with. The coffee in front of her was bad, but the company seemed worse.

Ray Dalio, seething, sat across from her, hands gripped tightly around a cheap ceramic mug. "Why would you do this to me?!" he barked.

Not for the last time, Stefanova had to wonder if she would ever be free of Dalio and Bridgewater. She could admit to herself that it was partly her own fault.

In the years since she had left Bridgewater, Stefanova had leaned hard into her connection to her former employer. This was not a surprise; like so many Bridgewater émigrés, she had never held a Wall Street job outside of the hedge fund, so she was essentially starting from scratch. But Stefanova had a special relationship with Dalio, with whom she kept in touch. That helped her to get a few consulting gigs in the financial industry, burnishing her résumé. After a few months on the outside, in 2015 she started her own New York investment fund, Marto Capital. In marketing materials, Stefanova described herself as having spent "nine years as a senior executive and managing committee adviser reporting directly to the CEO at Bridgewater Associates and serving in critical investment and management leadership roles." In truth, she had been far removed from any investment leadership role, critical or otherwise, but the pitch worked. She raised hundreds of millions of dollars from investors, some "wooed by

Marto's direct bloodline to Ray Dalio and Bridgewater Associates," as one finance magazine wrote. That sum was a big start for any untested investor.

Besides her ability to boast of a Bridgewater background, Stefanova also retained an insurance policy of sorts, in the form of Samantha Holland. Since departing Bridgewater with a settlement after her dalliance with Jensen, Holland had struggled to find work. The money covered only three years' salary, and it inevitably ran out. Restricted from telling potential employers the real reason she'd left her last job, Holland was having a hard time explaining her résumé. Running out of options, she called Stefanova, who vouched for her in finding a new job. The next time Stefanova saw Dalio, she mentioned that she was in touch with Holland. Dalio didn't discernibly react, but Stefanova was certain the message had landed: Stefanova was still keeping Bridgewater's secrets.

Stefanova's new fund stumbled out of the gate. Her fund's performance was roughly average compared with peers, and that wasn't good enough for a new enterprise. Stefanova began to field calls from investors looking to pull their money.

In need of a new way forward, Stefanova tried a page from the Dalio playbook, seeking to position herself as a high-level thinker. She sent out market research to the media, wrote investment advice on the *Forbes* website, and cultivated relationships with reporters. Her timing was fortunate: There was an increasing spotlight on the dearth of women in finance, and Stefanova was happy to step into the void. "I want what I do today to be meaningful not only to me, but to my daughter," she told one interviewer. For *Institutional Investor,* a closely followed magazine among the finance set, she wrote a fawning column titled "What It's Like to Work for Ray Dalio." She noted, "I don't believe I would have been able to do what I do today without having been in the trenches with Ray and seeing how he handles challenges—and having been inculcated with his core values." Stefanova made sure to email a draft of her columns to Dalio, prepublication, for his approval, which he gave.

She didn't realize that she was already on Dalio's mind.

A FEW weeks before their diner confab, Stefanova opened a surprise email from her former boss. It being less than an hour before the stock market opened, Stefanova had hoped to be preparing for the upcoming trading day. Instead, at just three sentences long, the email halted her in her tracks. "I need you to come in," Dalio wrote, proposing a meeting with him and David McCormick. He wrote that it was "about your business" and "a pressing matter that you will want to understand."

Stefanova spent much of the rest of her day racking her brain to imagine what Dalio wanted. She sensed a danger in his note. Dalio was a notoriously sloppy emailer, prone to writing rambling notes at all hours, yet this one seemed precise and curiously curt. She wondered why he might want to lure her back to Westport. She swore she'd never return there. But she couldn't exactly ignore Dalio, and was especially concerned about the mention of her business.

Early in the evening, Stefanova sent back what she hoped was a neutral response: "I want to maintain a positive long-term relationship with you and Bridgewater. As I am sure you can appreciate from your early days, there are not enough hours in the day for us, and traveling to Bridgewater will be difficult. Can we find an alternate location?"

Dalio responded, "Katina—It's about a pressing matter pertaining to me getting calls from your potential accounts for references on you and your team. The calls come in and have to be handled so you postponing our discussion doesn't help you or I. I urge you to come in asap."

Stefanova didn't see a way out. "I want to help you if you need me," she wrote, asking her assistant to set up a time for a phone call.

That didn't fly. Dalio responded less than an hour later, again copying McCormick. He wrote that he was getting calls from clients and "they are asking me to confirm that you did things that they said you told them that you did—like you were a key person in the investment area—and asked why you left. To tell them the truth (that you weren't involved in making investment decisions and that we terminated the relationship with you because you breached our trading policies) obviously would be a problem for you."

Stefanova's heart dropped. Dalio was right that she had breached the trading policies, but as she saw it plenty of others at Bridgewater committed similar trading infractions and kept their jobs. None of them, as far as she knew, had later reported being groped by their boss, and Dalio didn't mention that.

She consulted with a lawyer, and they wrote a response in which she denied making any misrepresentations and offered up a coffee meeting in New York, on her turf. She closed with: "I really want to continue to be long-term friends."

Dalio's response opened a new wormhole. "I can't lie. . . . I also understand other things that I [or] you wouldn't want me to discuss with you over email . . . These are big deals for us both and they require backs and forths in this secure environment. If we don't have that meeting, then I will handle these issues in a very forthrightly, in a less informed and less coordinated way, which I know that you would rather me not do. So, simply tell me, will you come in to discuss these things—yes or no?"

Stefanova immediately sent Dalio's response to her lawyer.

"This is pretty direct," the lawyer told her. "Are you sure you don't want to go?"

"I'm not going in. You have no idea what I have been through, and you have no idea what they do to people that go in."

PAUL MCDOWELL was in a struggle of his own. He told colleagues he increasingly felt as if he were living in a psychological experiment, one he was bound to fail.

In the days after McDowell's public flogging from Dalio, the Bridgewater founder ordered a training video made of the feedback. It was a curious ask; many of the people who had seen the incident live or shortly after were troubled or even horrified at the interaction, yet the Bridgewater founder didn't seem to be. It was soon clear why. The version sent out to the whole firm for mandatory viewing recast the meeting in a different light. Thanks to heavy editing, it simply showed Dalio asking McDowell to take responsibility for his gaps in management. There was an extensive discussion of how McDowell had failed to follow The Principles, particularly those related to holding himself and others accountable. There was neither profanity nor any reference to testicles and physical violence.

McDowell's status at Bridgewater continued to slide. Having been publicly called out by the firm founder as an underperformer, McDowell noticed his baseball card ratings take a dive. It seemed that most everyone piled on. Once blood was in the water, the sharks at Bridgewater came out.

For the first time in McDowell's life, he began experiencing a distressing mix of paranoia and insomnia, staying up past midnight and awakening in cold sweats, wondering if colleagues thought he was sabotaging Dalio's life work.

The misgivings weren't entirely unjustified. One Bridgewater executive, several years McDowell's junior, had begun paying an uncomfortable amount of attention to him. McDowell was uneasy, for the executive had once orchestrated the firing of two colleagues for complaining about him over burgers at a restaurant after hours, on their own time (his reasoning was that they had been talking behind his back). McDowell's worries spiked further when the Dot Collector—the ratings tool that he had helped design—notified him that he had received a new critical dot from this executive. The executive wrote, *I can't quite put my finger on it, but it's like Paul isn't one of us and has never really bought in.*

McDowell's reaction: *Fuck. He's onto me.*

McDowell's best shot at salvation was to pull anything useful out of the mess that was PriOS. He sought out Ferrucci for a consult, but the famed computer scientist wasn't interested in spending much time with him. He, too, seemed to have generally given up on finding a reliable way to predict, or to automate, the decisions that Dalio made.

McDowell spent sleepless nights worried that he might be fired. He reported directly to Dalio, and it was well-known inside the firm that it took only one stray word from the boss to send anyone packing.

Dalio soon asked again for an update on PriOS, summoning McDowell and a small cohort. They dutifully trudged into the Bridgewater founder's expansive pond-view conference room to deliver the bad news that PriOS still didn't work. Bridgewater's renovation would have to go on without it.

Echoing his previous diagnosis, Dalio said: "See, Paul, you can't manage."

Something seemed to snap inside McDowell. He gripped the table in front of him and stared with menace across at Dalio.

"I get it, Ray." Emotion charged through McDowell's voice. "I. Can't. Fucking. Manage."

The room sat quiet. McDowell had trained all of them in The Principles. He had always seemed like the last possible candidate to crack.

McDowell went on, "I can't fucking do anything. I am fucking useless!"

Dalio sat barely moving. "Yes, you're right, but this is no time to lose your temper."

"It's high time I lost my temper with you!" McDowell shrieked, in a voice that even he barely recognized.

"I get it. You have a lot of responsibilities. There is a lot underneath you." Dalio suggested that McDowell needed closer supervision and help from others at the firm.

For weeks afterward, McDowell couldn't figure out how he had avoided the cannon. He would eventually share with friends two possible explanations. He had long wondered whether Dalio truly cared about PriOS's being completed on any specific time frame, or just wanted to see what it would take to break the unbreakable McDowell.

The other explanation, as McDowell would later tell friends with a rueful laugh, was that if McDowell was a poor manager, then The Principles prescribed an investigation of his own manager for insufficient oversight. That would have meant an investigation of Dalio himself.

MORE EMAILS passed between Stefanova and Dalio before they agreed on when and where to meet. After she made clear she wouldn't come to headquarters, Dalio suggested they sit down at the Lookout, the scene of the company retreat where he had sung the filthy sailor's poem so many years before. Stefanova made an excuse as to why that wouldn't do. She worked on convincing McCormick, the latest executive in vogue, that a confab would only happen on her terms.

"Given my experience at the end," Stefanova wrote to McCormick, "you easily understand why someone in my shoes would not want to go back to the office."

Apparently this worked. The three met for breakfast at the Sherwood Diner. Stefanova suspected that the modest setting would be as close to neutral territory as could be expected when meeting the wealthiest man in Connecticut, and she was right. Dalio, Stefanova, and McCormick sat in a tight booth, unbothered by the retirees around them.

The trio had barely ordered coffee before Dalio got to the main agenda. He didn't only want to talk about Stefanova's trading infractions. He was also animated by her accusation against Jensen. McCormick told Stefanova that he had heard rumblings that reporters were asking around about allegations of untoward behavior by Jensen and others at Bridgewater. This wasn't such a surprise for Stefanova—she had gotten a few phone calls herself from the press, though she hadn't volunteered any information about her own experience.

As McCormick finished summing up the scenario, Dalio, gripping the cheap coffee mug in front of him tightly, cut in, "Why would you do this to me?!"

Stefanova, not for the first time in Dalio's presence, was shocked. She knew Dalio had never fully believed what she had said about being groped by Jensen, but she hadn't fathomed that the Bridgewater founder would take it as a slight against himself.

"You have to tell them Greg didn't do this," Dalio said.

That broke Stefanova from her silence. She reminded him that she had never recanted her story.

"Maybe you're remembering it wrong," Dalio offered.

Stefanova assured him that she wasn't.

McCormick piped up, leaning in, "Maybe the issue is that you aren't being a supportive public presence for us."

Finally, Stefanova understood the urgency of the meeting. Neither her résumé nor her business were threats to Bridgewater. Dalio and McCormick had just wanted to remind her that they had the power to destroy her business if she didn't toe the line. She ended the breakfast quickly and drove to New York, sufficiently spooked. The next time she got a message from a reporter asking about Jensen, she didn't return the call.*

---

* A lawyer for Dalio said: "There was no desire to destroy Katina and her firm," adding that the Bridgewater founder "supported Ms. Stefanova in numerous ways after this breakfast."

21

"RAY, THIS IS A RELIGION"

For the second consecutive year, a crew of construction workers got to work erecting an enormous tent on the grass in mid-2016 next to Bridgewater's offices. Unlike with the firm's fortieth anniversary fifteen months earlier, however, few at the firm knew why this tent was going up. For many, the reveal would be unpleasant.

It must have struck some as an odd time for a celebration. The main hedge fund, Pure Alpha, was in a slump which had gone on for an improbable five years running. "The golden touch has deserted Mr. Dalio," one publication put it. There was no new explanation why. Dalio continued to be bearish on the U.S. economy, and America continued to defy his prognosis. The Pure Alpha leveraged fund was down 12 percent at midyear 2016, and word spread inside the firm that clients were pulling money. Dalio had a different spin on the situation. He called up longtime investors and said that in light of Bridgewater's decades-long track record, this was a ripe opportunity to invest more funds. Dalio said Bridgewater rarely had the capacity to manage more money.

In mid-September, the tent was finally completed, and Dalio ended the suspense, sending around an internal invitation to an all-hands gathering. The topic was the future of the firm.

As staffers made their way into the tent, they saw that this was no repeat of the anniversary party. Gone were the elaborate chandeliers and track lighting. A peek under the seats revealed no premixed shots of booze, and a glance around the crowd showed the once-outgoing Jensen, still serving his extended penance but having remained cochief investment officer, with a frozen, neutral look on his face. The only obvious similarity between this year and the last year were the omnipresent cameramen, recording for Bridgewater's Transparency Library.

Dalio smiled and got right to the point. "You guys are so lucky. We are going to have a renovation."

At least one person present snuck a peek at his copy of The Principles on his iPad to see if it contained the word *renovation*. It didn't. But as those present would have known, often the most innocuous language was tied to the most tumultuous results.

This renovation, Dalio said, wasn't of the place but of the people. Bridgewater was up to seventeen hundred full-time employees, and untold more temporary contractors. The firm had become unwieldy and hard to manage. Many of those gathered would have to lose their jobs to protect the collective, Dalio said.

"Not all of you are going to make it. In fact, most of you won't make it," Dalio continued. Seeming to gain steam, he grinned and began to talk about why his employees were "so lucky." They would have an opportunity in the coming weeks; it would be like the reality show *Survivor*, in which contestants outwit and outlast one another. It might even be fun. "The cool thing is you are going to learn so much about yourself."

That language mirrored the highest-minded ideals of The Principles, and for plenty of true believers, young and old, the speech hit the mark. They considered themselves fortunate to be at a place that valued self-improvement and considered the renovation to be only the next step in that journey. A good number of them believed that they were destined to make it through—and that others would be sorted out. Bridgewater's unimpressive recent investment performance also bolstered the argument that the firm needed some fixing. Though relatively few people present knew anything about how the hedge fund actually invested, everyone would likely see a pay bump if the firm's investments could be turned around.

The first step in the renovation encouraged further optimism. Everyone at the firm was asked to put together a list of bad management—and bad managers—at the company. In this classic Bridgewater exercise, everyone had yet another opportunity to complain about the job being done by others, and most everyone took the chance to throw their colleagues under the bus with aplomb.

The illusion that the renovation would promote personal growth cracked only a few days later, when one of Dalio's leveragers accidentally emailed a huge group in the firm a summary of the Bridgewater founder's intentions.

The plan, the young man wrote, was akin to the plot of *The Hunger Games*, the dystopian series in which children hunted other children to avoid being killed themselves. The young man tried to unsend the email, but it was too late, and anyway, Dalio did little to dispel the impression it left. The mood at the firm turned darker. The race to survive was on.

LIFE IMITATED art inside Bridgewater that October. While *The Hunger Games* comments struck some inside the firm as a touch extreme—no one would, after all, be killed—another television program aired that seemed uncanny. The series *Black Mirror* was a science fiction anthology that dealt with the downsides of technology. In mid-October, in the throes of the renovation, *Black Mirror* released its season premiere, an episode called "Nosedive," set in a world in which citizens rate one another on a scale of 1 to 5 on every interaction. The star of the episode, played by Bryce Dallas Howard, becomes obsessed with her ratings; she eventually suffers a slew of mishaps and sees her scores dip and then plummet as everyone around her begins to identify her as a soft target. At the end of the episode, she is arrested and imprisoned. The similarities to Bridgewater were so eerie that some at the hedge fund suspected that someone at the firm had spoken to the writers.

There were, of course, many differences between the sci-fi show and the hedge fund. While *Black Mirror* portrayed an almost matter-of-fact rating system in which it was easy to see how and why an individual was dropping in score, Bridgewater was moving to be more opaque.

After his big-tent announcement, Dalio dropped any pretense of transparency, radical or otherwise. A few days after the speech, he called his top executives, including co-CEOs Eileen Murray and Jon Rubinstein, into one of Bridgewater's glass-walled conference rooms to discuss the plan going forward. As Dalio stood at a whiteboard, sketching out who would stay and who would go, others in the room noticed a pickup in traffic in the adjacent hallway. Bridgewater's employees, desperate for any hint of the future, seemed to be stealing glances at Dalio's scribbles, hoping to divine their futures. Dalio promptly sent a team of staffers to buy huge rolls of thick butcher paper, which was pasted up on the room's glass, blocking anyone from seeing the deliberations within.

Inside the room, Dalio directed the full force of the Principles Captains, Overseers, Politburo, and rest of the internal army into action, giving them free rein to investigate just about anyone suspected of underperformance.

Dalio took the opportunity to cut costs. Plans were made to slash in half the salary of anyone making more than $700,000 per year, with the difference being put into an incentive plan that would only pay off years later, under a number of hard-to-reach conditions. Part of the renovation acquired a new code name, Project N, *N* for November. That was when Dalio wanted the shake-up completed. It was scarcely one month away.

How to hit the mark? PriOS. A mass firing should have been the perfect use of Dalio's still-under-development software system. PriOS should be able, as he had told clients, to provide turn-by-turn directions on whom to keep, whom to reassign, and whom to let go.

Of course, it couldn't, as just about everyone seemed to know except Dalio. As usual, no one had the temerity to tell him so—not while he was looking for any reason to make cuts.

PAUL MCDOWELL told colleagues he suspected he might be let go. He had put up with the indignities of life at the hedge fund in part because he was being handsomely paid. He'd bought two units combined into one at the Trump Parc tower, one of the most expensive addresses in nearby Stamford (he also kept a home back in Canada). He suspected no other job would pay him near what Bridgewater did—especially if it was found out he had spent the better part of a decade working on avant-garde personality software that still didn't work.

Not long into the renovation, McDowell's phone buzzed one morning to a note from Dalio, asking for McDowell's "reflections" on his role at Bridgewater. McDowell sensed danger. Dalio almost only used that word in conjunction with heartache, as in the Principle that went Pain + Reflection = Progress. McDowell typed up his summary—arguing in part that after his many years at Bridgewater, Dalio already knew well McDowell's strengths and weaknesses—and waited for the storm to arrive.

To McDowell's surprise, Dalio seemed to take the reflections calmly and asked to see him. McDowell took a deep breath and walked to Dalio's office.

The older man was waiting for him. "You left out one thing that you're really, really good at. You're a great teacher."

McDowell let out an audible sigh of relief. He enjoyed teaching The Principles boot camps. It was always fun to spend time with the fresh

Bridgewater newcomers, before life at the firm ground them down. He was happy to spend more time with them.

But there was something else: "It's going to mean a radical cut in your pay."

McDowell's heart dropped. He asked how much.

"Half."

"Ray, I have commitments. I just bought a home—"

Stone-faced, Dalio cut him off. "That's the best I can do. It's going to be tough on you."

The wind knocked out of him, McDowell would tell friends he felt that Dalio had fulfilled the earlier wish to kick him in the balls.

Dalio continued, "You can't manage. You've said so yourself."

McDowell would be demoted and receive a new boss, one a few rungs below the Bridgewater founder. With that, McDowell didn't just lose half his salary—he had lost the protection of proximity to Dalio, at a place where only his word ever mattered. McDowell was now on his own.

WHILE McDOWELL was not one of the hundreds of the Bridgewater family who lost their jobs in the renovation, a pair of big-name Dalio hires struggled to make it through the year.

One was Craig Mundie, the former Microsoft executive who had been recommended to Dalio by Bill Gates, and who was Bridgewater's vice-chairman, reporting to Dalio. Mundie and Dalio seemed to get along famously; anyone at Bridgewater who spent more than a few minutes in the duo's presence learned that they both had yachts and liked to talk about them. A relative Bridgewater neophyte, however, Mundie bet wrong on how mercurial Dalio could be. In an example of history repeating itself endlessly, Mundie made the mistake of complaining to Jensen that co-CEO Murray was in the final stretches of her career and ill-equipped to handle the complexities of running the world's largest hedge fund.

Jensen couldn't believe what he was hearing. Who would be so reckless to moan to him, of all people, behind someone else's back? The onetime heir presumptive had just had the worst year of his life after being investigated for just that. Jensen tipped off Murray of a recording she might want to hear. She flipped it to Dalio, who held a trial and announced he would fire Mundie.

With Mundie's loss of face, the former Apple hotshot Rubinstein was ever more isolated. He felt as if he were living two different lives. On one hand was the Bridgewater that his friends and even his wife seemed to assume he was experiencing. That Bridgewater was high performing, demanding, and filled with the brightest minds on earth. Former colleagues asked him for help on how they, too, could make such a successful transition from tech to finance. Then there was what Rubinstein saw in front of himself day-to-day. From the recent investment performance, Bridgewater's hedge funds appeared in disarray. Yet whenever Rubinstein or others around him attempted to broach the topic of investments with Dalio, the Bridgewater founder waved off the concerns. Your focus, Dalio would invariably say, should be on identifying weak links inside Bridgewater and creating a better systemization of The Principles, vis-à-vis PriOS.

Even if Rubinstein had believed that was possible, he found little time to work on Bridgewater's software systems. The co-CEO was regularly assigned additional training videos related to The Principles, and he consistently seemed to fail them. His baseball card filled up with negative dots. His votes, often contrary to Dalio's own, carried little weight. Members of Dalio's Politburo began showing up at his meetings, taking notes and adding new torrents of poor feedback.

Finally Rubinstein realized that the path forward had been clear all along. He had to use The Principles. As the manifesto reminded over and again, Bridgewater was a place of radical truth and radical honesty. Even the lowliest employee had a responsibility to speak out on their feelings.

Rubinstein chose his opening for October 13, his sixtieth birthday. Unbeknownst to him, his chief of staff had ordered a sheet cake and champagne to celebrate. Dalio, who had been told in advance of the milestone birthday, had scheduled a mass diagnosis of the co-CEO's failings. The Bridgewater founder invited dozens of deputies, including the Politburo, Principles Captains, and the firm's senior management—including Jensen and Prince, Dalio's longtime silent partner who had been dragged into the maelstrom—to sit around a table and critique Rubinstein, sitting at the head. It was the classic Bridgewater firing squad, taking part in what had become a firm tradition: the evisceration of a newcomer. They opened with a recitation of Rubinstein's weaknesses.

Rubinstein, not wishing to mark his sixth decade with another dreary day, headed off the opening speeches with one of his own: "Guys," he said, looking around the room, "this isn't working for me."

This amounted to an edit on the usual screenplay. The subject was supposed to sit and absorb the criticism. Pain was an opportunity for progress. Anyone who didn't seek out the former, per Dalio's teachings, must not have been interested in the latter.

Dalio asked for most of the minions to leave the room. Without a word, many of the Politburo and Principles Captains shuffled out. Only the top brass remained, including Dalio, Prince, Jensen, McCormick, and Murray, along with a few assistants to sit and take notes.

Dalio gestured for Rubinstein to say his piece.

Rubinstein laid out the state of play as he saw it. He had been hired to improve the technology, but no amount of software or Silicon Valley expertise could solve what plagued Bridgewater, he said. At Apple, Steve Jobs had taught Rubinstein to keep a laser focus on the end customer. The North Star of the company was to create helpful products that delighted consumers. To Rubinstein, Dalio seemed focused on delighting himself.

Bridgewater's thorniest problem, Rubinstein said, was hardwired into the firm. It was The Principles. Dalio's ever-expanding rule book, Rubinstein said, was a kaleidoscope of contradictions and a barely veiled weapon for abuse. The burgeoning ranks of the Politburo, Auditors, Principles Captains, and other enforcers at the firm professed to be devoted to enforcing openness and truth, but they had the exact opposite impact. They created a climate of fear and were a constant reminder that anyone who didn't fall in with the company line would suffer immediate consequences. For goodness' sake, Rubinstein said, we've put up thick paper blocking the view into glass-walled rooms. How can we pretend to be radically transparent when we plot mass firings in secret?

The nut that had taken Rubinstein the longest to crack was believability. He had been vexed since his first day about the mysterious, omnipotent metric, and how someone could be assigned a high or low believability rating in various categories. Ferrucci's lab, Rubinstein concluded, had been a red herring of sorts. Those at Bridgewater who had been rated highly believable in certain areas didn't earn those scores through any complicated algorithm of artificial intelligence. They earned it by being an artificial Ray Dalio. The secret to becoming believable at Bridgewater was to model oneself after the only man who mattered. Bridgewater didn't run on believability. It ran on believers.

"Ray, this is a religion," Rubinstein said.

Dalio sat calmly, only interjecting a few times. When Rubinstein appeared to have wrapped up, Dalio sat quietly for a moment. When he spoke, his tone was flat and unemotional. He suggested they follow The Principles to resolve this disagreement. The Principles dictated that a council of trusted third parties should decide the way forward. It just so happened, Dalio said, that such unimpeachable witnesses happened to be in the room right then. He went around the room and asked Bridgewater's top brass if they agreed with Rubinstein's take.

Jensen said he did not.

Prince said he did not.

Murray said she did not.

McCormick said he did not.

"See, Jon, you're looking at it wrong," Dalio said. Now it was his time to talk, and he didn't let up. He diagnosed Rubinstein's failings for an hour, which stretched into two, then bordered on three. Dalio pulled up Rubinstein's baseball card, studded with red dots of negative feedback. His overall believability score was putrid.

This very conversation demonstrated the worth of the believability metrics, Dalio said. Here the group had sat for hours in discussion, only to learn that none of Rubinstein's peers agreed with his perspective. They could have saved time and come to the same conclusion just by glancing at Rubinstein's believability rating to begin with.

As the two men traded barbs, the sun moved across the sky and shadows lengthened. Everyone saw clearly that Rubinstein was not long for Bridgewater. He agreed to stay for several months longer, in part to save face after his splashy arrival. Rubinstein agreed to keep quiet publicly about his feelings on the firm, and Dalio agreed that the firm would honor paying out the remainder of the co-CEO's two-year compensation. It added up to tens of millions of dollars for less than a year of work that all involved had to agree didn't result in much.

When the diagnosis was over, the group began packing up, only to be interrupted by a knock on the door. Rubinstein's chief of staff had been waiting outside in the hallway with his birthday surprise. She wheeled in a cake and some now-tepid champagne, and led a muted rendition of "Happy Birthday" as the birthday boy cut his cake as quickly as he could muster.

Several months later, Dalio sent out a client letter announcing Rubinstein's departure, noting, "We mutually agree that he is not a cultural fit for Bridgewater."

Rubinstein privately held a harsher view on the Bridgewater culture of radical transparency. "It's a fraud," he told friends.

Part IV

22

THE CIRCLE OF TRUST

THE WHISPERED QUESTION PASSED FROM ONE WALL STREET TRADING floor to the next.

Bridgewater was a global investing force. Its funds were so scrutinized, tracked, and copied that All-Weather spawned an entire copycat industry, known as risk-parity funds, which also advertised themselves as automatic traders of a steady portfolio of diverse assets. Dalio was omnipresent in the media, quick with an opinion on virtually any investment topic.

So why didn't anyone on Wall Street ever seem to see them trade?

This was no small topic for fascination. Despite its backcountry locale, the world's largest hedge fund should have been plugged into the Wall Street trading infrastructure. To buy and sell the currencies, stocks, and bonds that the firm constantly talked about, it needed investors on the other side, taking the opposite position. Bridgewater's public filings indicated that it did business with all of the biggest names on Wall Street: Goldman Sachs, Citigroup, Credit Suisse, JPMorgan, and the rest. Much-smaller hedge funds could move the markets just by rumors of one trade or another. Bridgewater's heft should have made it the ultimate whale, sending waves rolling every time it adjusted a position. Instead the firm's footprint was decidedly minnow.

Three men, each with vastly different backgrounds, took three different passes at the mystery.

In early 2015, Bill Ackman, the billionaire stock picker and endlessly loquacious hedge fund manager, took the first whack. The founder of Pershing Square Capital had long found Dalio's public pronouncements of an opaque, quantitative investment style to be generic and even nonsensical. Curious about what lay behind the veil, he invited Dalio to speak about his approach to investing at a charity event. In an onstage interview, Ackman drilled

Dalio about how Bridgewater handled the assets it managed, nearly ten times larger than those of Pershing Square.

Dalio responded, "Well, first of all, I think it's because I could be long and short anything in the world. I'm basically long in liquid stuff. And I can be short or long anything in the world, and I'm short or long practically everything. I don't have any bias, so I do it in a very, um, fundamental way, but, um, very systematic, very, um—we use a lot of artificial intelligence type of approaches to think about portfolio theory. I use a lot of financial engineering to basically take a whole bunch of uncorrelated bets."

He also noted that some 99 percent of Bridgewater trading was automated, based on his longtime rule book. "They're my criteria, so I'm very comfortable."

The Bridgewater founder turned the question on Ackman, asking how his smaller rival chose investments.

"I invest exactly the opposite of that," Ackman said. Pershing Square hunted for a small number of quality companies, period, by assessing qualities such as the leadership skills of a given chief executive. At one point in the discussion, seemingly sensing the interview going off the rails and in search of some commonality, Ackman tried another tack. He gave Dalio a layup, the sort of question asked six times an hour on business television. He asked, "Let's say you were to buy one asset, or one stock, or one market, or one currency. Where would you put your money?"

There was a pause, then:

"I don't do that."

Dalio laid out how Bridgewater's three hundred investment staffers spent their days, describing a data-driven approach. On stage, Ackman would remark that it was "one of the most interesting conversations I've ever had." But he walked away shaking his head. "What was he even talking about?" he vented afterward to an associate.

Jim Grant, the self-styled "prophet of reason," watched the interview with amazement. Unlike the genial Ackman, Grant was more the curmudgeonly type, right down to his omnipresent bow tie. He wrote an arcane newsletter, *Grant's Interest Rate Observer,* which was popular in the sense that many serious investors claimed to read it ("a perpetual cynic," said one admirer). Grant was a longtime Bridgewater skeptic, particularly with regard to its claims that big bets with borrowed money could be considered low risk.

Grant was privately mulling dark questions about Bridgewater. He assigned his top deputy to dig into the world's largest hedge fund. The pair fanned out widely, scrutinizing the firm's public filings, and furtively talking to clients, rivals, and anyone who might have a clue as to what was going on with Bridgewater's trading. They were inundated, as Grant recalled, with "all sorts of people winking and nodding . . . that there's something really, really wrong." In October of 2017 Grant devoted a full issue of his publication solely to Bridgewater. The themes of the issue, Grant wrote, were "distraction, sycophancy [and] mystery."

Grant listed a litany of inexplicable contradictions he'd uncovered. Despite much talk of transparency, even shareholders in Bridgewater's parent company—a group that included employees and clients—didn't automatically receive copies of the firm's financial statements. The little that was made public was confounding. By Grant's calculations, the total number of assets under management in the firm's filings didn't match the sum of assets in the firm's funds, listed in those filings. Five separate Dalio family trusts appeared to each hold "at least 25 percent but less than 50 percent of Bridgewater, something that seems mathematically difficult," Grant wrote. Per public disclosures, the hedge fund lent money to its own auditor, KPMG, which struck the longtime analyst as precarious and unusual. "We will go out on a limb, Bridgewater is not for the ages."

The report landed like a bomb on Wall Street and in Westport. Grant would spend the day answering calls from the CEOs of Wall Street banks, offering kudos. Some told him they'd been wondering along the same lines for years.

At 8:30 P.M. the day the report was published, Grant settled in on the couch at home with his wife to watch a New York Yankees game. After this long, satisfying day, he pledged to unplug. When the phone rang from an unknown Connecticut home number, Grant let it ring to voicemail. Not until about a half hour later did his wife hear a distant beep, indicating that a message had been left. She walked over and hit play, putting the message on speakerphone. She flinched as Dalio's voice rang out:

"I'm not sure if you've seen the current issue of *Grant's*." The message went on for nearly a half hour as Dalio detailed his complaints about the piece.

Grant recalled, "What creeped me out was the supernatural voice control. He spoke in these measured tones, undifferentiated with response to intonation or emotional content."

Grant spent the next week on and off calls with various Bridgewater executives. He realized that he had gotten some crucial bits wrong. The auditor relationship was vanilla, having been previously okayed by regulators, and the confounding mathematical issue of the ownership stakes could be explained by the fact that multiple entities owned by Dalio's family members had been aggregated in the financial statements. Grant called into the television network CNBC to apologize. He said he was in the wrong vis-à-vis the hedge fund's regulatory compliance. As for the larger questions around Bridgewater's investment strategy, Grant said he remained befuddled.

"As for the strategies, we can't know a great deal . . . about how it actually does business," he said. "Ray Dalio is on record . . . that he knows a thousand uncorrelated trades. Nobody else on Wall Street knows it doesn't."

That last bit—that one man could know a thousand ways to make money but tell no one what they were—piqued the interest of a Boston financial investigator. Harry Markopolos knew a little something about secretive hedge fund managers who claimed to have an edge that no one could replicate. Markopolos had been a no-name analyst in the late 1990s when his boss asked him to reproduce a rival's trading strategy that seemed to pay off handsomely. Markopolos couldn't, but he figured out enough that he soon began chatting with the Securities and Exchange Commission about what turned out to be a fraud in plain sight. Six years later, Markopolos hit his crescendo, submitting to the SEC a report titled "The World's Largest Hedge Fund Is a Fraud." When his warnings about Bernie Madoff proved right, Markopolos earned national fame, and the ability to grab the attention of regulators virtually whenever he so chose.

To Markopolos, what was happening in Westport raised serious questions. Here lay another giant hedge fund famed for an investment approach that no competitors seemed to fully understand. Calling on old contacts, he got his hands on Bridgewater marketing documents, including the "pitch book," a PowerPoint deck that every fund made available to potential investors. The pitch book contained a summary of the firm's investment strategy and a detailed chart of fund performance, but to Markopolos, it raised more questions than answers. Bridgewater described itself as a global asset manager, yet its pitch book didn't name a single specific asset that had made or lost the firm money. An included investment-performance chart indicated the firm seldom had a down year—even when Dalio's public predictions proved off, the Pure Alpha fund consistently seemed to end the year around flat. As he looked over the documents, Markopolos felt a familiar flutter in his heart.

Sensing the gravity of the conclusion he seemed to be circling, he drew on his Rolodex to check his work. His team spoke with the Texas hedge fund manager Kyle Bass, well-known for his ahead-of-the-curve predictions that the subprime-mortgage market was about to collapse in 2008. Bass said he, too, had long wondered about how Bridgewater traded. Markopolos also went to see the hedge fund billionaire David Einhorn of Greenlight Capital, famed for spotting frauds. Einhorn welcomed him into his office and sat him down with a team of Greenlight analysts that Einhorn said were interested in investigating Bridgewater themselves. Einhorn bent his head down toward the table, resting his head on his elbows and listening carefully, as Markopolos laid out his suspicions.

After hearing Markopolos's talk, Einhorn slapped the table in excitement. "I knew it!"

That was all the encouragement Markopolos needed. He wrote up his conclusion in a report and sent it to the SEC.

Bridgewater, he wrote to them, was a Ponzi scheme.

BRIDGEWATER WAS not a Ponzi scheme.

Which is not to say that all was as Dalio so often described it.

The SEC and other regulators dutifully took meetings with Markopolos and his team. The whistleblowers' report was passed up in the organization, where word of it reached chairman Jay Clayton, a former Wall Street lawyer, who told colleagues that he, too, had heard such speculation about Bridgewater in the past. Clayton assigned an SEC team to look into it, and made sure they put questions about it to Bridgewater. What they concluded, in part, was that the world's biggest hedge fund used a complicated sequence of financial machinations—including stock options and other relatively hard-to-track trading instruments—to make its otherwise straightforward-seeming investments. These wouldn't be expected to show up on public filings, and it made sense to the SEC that rivals couldn't track them, either.

Satisfied, the SEC stopped responding to requests from Markopolos and his crew for updates. Regulators raised no public accusations about Bridgewater. Markopolos moved on to other interests.

To fully unpeel what was happening in Westport required a shift in aperture, from the outside to deep inside. The answer could not have come readily to Ackman or Grant in part because they were consummate Wall Street insiders whose careers rested on the idea that hard-nosed analysis—effort and smarts, essentially—could lead to investment results. Markopolos, still intoxicated by the idea of adding another busted hedge fund scheme to his résumé, was foolhearted in plugging a square peg into a round hole. As it turned out, by the time the SEC received Markopolos's submission, the regulators had already looked into Bridgewater. In the wake of Madoff, and never having really dug into the world's biggest hedge fund, SEC staff spent a stretch in Westport, deeply studying the firm's operations.* Their job was to figure out if Bridgewater was abiding by the law, and the regulators found no reason to suggest otherwise. Per its raison d'être, the SEC would not much bother with how Bridgewater made money, just that it did indeed invest its clients' accounts.

Part of the reason that Markopolos, Einhorn, and others incorrectly suspected that Bridgewater was a flat-out fraud might have been that remarkably few people at Bridgewater were involved day-to-day with how the hedge fund made money. Entire ancillary buildings, a few miles from the main headquarters, were filled with Bridgewater employees who knew nothing more of the hedge fund's trading than what they read in the newspapers. Of Bridgewater's roughly two thousand employees at its peak—and hundreds more temporary contractors—fewer than 20 percent were assigned to research or to the investment engine. Of those researchers, many held responsibilities no more complicated than those of the average college student. They toiled on research projects on economic history and produced papers to be reviewed and edited by Dalio himself. On occasion, their findings would make the *Daily Observations*—often with Dalio, Jensen, or Prince listed as coauthor. As for whether those insights made it into Bridgewater's trading, most research employees knew not to ask.

Only a tiny group at Bridgewater, no more than about ten people, enjoyed a different view. This band of almost all men were chosen not only on merit, but on loyalty. They almost without exception had never worked anywhere else. Dalio and Jensen plucked the members from the crew of Bridgewater investment associates and offered them entry to the inner sanctum. The lucky few sat down with Dalio and were offered a choice. In exchange for signing a lifetime contract—and swearing never to work at another trading firm—they would be one of the handful to see the inner secrets of Bridgewater, what Dalio had earlier in his career called the Holy Grail.

---

* Lawyers for Bridgewater and Dalio said: "It is completely expected and good practice that the SEC would examine a registered investment advisor of Bridgewater's magnitude on a regular basis," and that this was "the standard process."

Dalio called the group of signees the Circle of Trust.

The offer wasn't necessarily presented as a straightforward choice. Bob Elliott, who would become the most senior member of the Circle behind Jensen and Prince, was just twenty-six years old when Dalio offered him a lifetime contract.

Elliott wanted more than anything else to crack the code behind Bridgewater. He signed the contract.

LIKE *BELIEVABILITY,* the Circle of Trust moniker was a bit of a misnomer, to the degree that it implied a coequal group of points connected and bound to one another. It was more an unbroken ring surrounding one stand-alone point in the center: Dalio.

There were two versions of how Bridgewater invested hundreds of billions of dollars in the markets. One version Dalio told the public, and clients, over and over. The other version was what happened with the Circle of Trust behind closed doors.

In the first version, Bridgewater's hedge funds were an "idea meritocracy." Every investment staffer or researcher could suggest an idea about, for instance, whether the bonds of a faraway country might appreciate or depreciate, and the Bridgewater team would debate the merits of the thesis dispassionately, incorporating a broad study of history. Ideas from investment employees with a record of accurate predictions would over time carry more weight and earn backing with more client money. Hundreds if not thousands of other hedge funds, to say nothing of other firms across the financial world, used a similar process. Large investment firms regularly staked up-and-coming traders with small sums and invested more in those with a knack for making money. It was the Wall Street equivalent of Darwinism, with a thick wallet.

What Bridgewater added to this pattern was a knack for drama. Every Friday, Dalio's assistants would deliver thick binders full of the firm's economic research, contained in as many as three briefcases, which his driver would whisk to Dalio's home. The collection formed the basis for what Bridgewater called its What's Going On in the World meeting, held every Monday morning at 9:00 A.M. Dalio, along with Jensen and Prince, would sit at the front of the largest room on campus, with rows upon rows of staffers in front of them, as well as the odd newspaper reporter or visiting client sure to be impressed by the display of intellectual rigor. With the firm founder directing the conversation and cameras recording it so the whole firm could watch later, the room would debate for hours the grand topics of the day and the direction of markets. Anything in that weekend's brief-cases was fair game for conversation, and even the most junior researcher had an opportunity to impress Dalio with an analysis. As Dalio told one interviewer, "It's so much bigger than Bob and Greg and me. . . . It's much bigger than that." It was a true spectacle.

It was also almost entirely irrelevant to what Bridgewater did with its money; as one former top investment staffer put it, "It's a facade." Some wondered whether Dalio actually read any of the research binders. After the meeting, the Circle of Trust would file into a tight corner of offices that few others at the firm could access, and the real work would begin.

"I COULD run this firm," Jensen once told a friend over drinks, "on a single spreadsheet."

The secret to Bridgewater's vaunted investment process, as Jensen ex-plained late into that evening, was that there was no secret. Dalio was Bridge-water and Dalio decided Bridgewater's investments. True, there was Jensen and Prince and the rest of the so-called Circle of Trust, a moniker that sug-gested an image of some grand investment meeting of the minds. But though more than one person may have weighed in, functionally only one invest-ment opinion mattered. There was essentially no grand system, no artificial intelligence of any substance, no Holy Grail. There was just Dalio, in person, over the phone, from his yacht, or for a few weeks many summers from his villa in Spain, calling the shots.*

When Dalio and his marketing team talked publicly about Pure Alpha, they cited a nebulous collection of "signals" or "indicators" that guided the hedge fund. When the signals flashed, Pure Alpha traded along with them, or so the pitch went. This suggested a fund constantly trawling for data, and adjusting as the investing environment changed. It also helped ex-plain why Bridgewater seemed not to move the market with its trading, addressing the mystery of the hedge fund's minnow-like trading foot-print. As Bridgewater's marketing staff explained to clients, the hedge fund was homing in on signals unseen to others and was thus unlikely to be a

---

* Lawyers for Dalio and Bridgewater said the hedge fund "is not a place where one man rules because the system makes the decision 98 percent of the time." They said "the notion that Mr. Dalio 'call[ed] the shots' on Bridgewater's investments is false." They added that the hedge fund "maintains a tight set of controls on how trades are determined, which are regularly audited to be consistent with Bridge-water's trading protocols, and any deviation requires approval of the Chief Investment Officers."

part of rushed buying or selling in the market or to be on the other side of trades from its rivals.

Dalio could have skipped the cloudy language and more simply described Pure Alpha as a series of if-then rules. If one thing happened, then another would follow. For Pure Alpha, one such if-then rule was that if interest rates declined in a country, then the currency of that country would depreciate. Thus Pure Alpha would bet against the currencies of countries with falling interest rates. Another rule stated that the price of gold was related to the total amount of money in circulation divided by the gold stock; if money in circulation expanded or shrank, then it was time to buy or sell gold. Many of the rules dealt simply with following trends. They suggested that short-term moves were likely to be indicative of long-term ones and dictated following the momentum in various markets. Most all of the rules would be uncomplicated to anyone with a calculator and a solid grasp of high-school-level correlations.*

Bridgewater's rules gave it an unquestionable edge in the firm's early days. Most people on Wall Street, from junior traders to billionaires, still believed in the value of their intuition. Top-performing traders were said to be able to "read the tape," to divine future movements of stocks by reading the price and volume of trades (the name referred to trades transmitted over telegraph by ticker tape, a practice that had faded by the time Dalio began his career). Bridgewater was among the first hedge funds to create its own estimates of economic growth, integrating both public statistics and its own market surveys. The firm called it "the slack measure process" because it indicated which countries or markets had ample capacity, or slack, to grow faster. The slack measure process was what Dalio would call a rule: if the model showed that a faraway nation was due for a boom, Bridgewater would buy up its bonds or currency, for instance. That Dalio not only had a set of rules, but a fund that followed them, made him different from the pack. It was quite accurate to call it his pure alpha.

As the years passed, however, Dalio's advantage softened, then seemingly ceased. The rise of powerful computers made it easy for any trader to

---

* Lawyers for Dalio and Bridgewater said that "greater than 98 percent of Bridgewater's risk budget and returns have been, and remain, driven by systematic trading strategies" and that it "adheres to strict rules around any type of discretionary trading." They added, "Bridgewater's trading strategies are systematized and diversified." A lawyer for Dalio separately said that Bridgewater's investment team "follows big developments and historical developments to understand cause-effect relationships in the markets. These relationships are then back tested in different time periods and locations and then formulated as decision rules which drive 98 percent of Bridgewater's market positioning."

program rules and to trade by them. The power of the internet convinced investment banks and trading firms to hire scientists, mathematicians, and programmers to delve ever deeper into economic data now available electronically to anyone in the world. These rivals quickly matched Dalio's discoveries such as the slack measure process, then blew past them into areas such as high-frequency trading, which required digesting data that might change in seconds or less, such as brief spikes or drops in stock volume. One rival fund, Renaissance Technologies, hired dozens of researchers with Ph.D.s to build an investing system with *millions* of lines of code. Bridgewater hired its fair share of scientists, too—but like Ferrucci many were assigned to the firm's personnel-rating tools rather than directly to investing. Instead, Dalio stuck to his historic rules ("They are timeless and universal," he told one interviewer), even as they became more stale with each passing year and as rivals leaped forward with competing systems.*

Plenty of smart, ambitious employees at Bridgewater, including members of the Circle of Trust, tried valiantly to move the hedge fund from its stasis. But the only way to add a new rule to the hedge fund's list was to win the unanimous approval of Dalio, Prince, and Jensen, and it was not a secret vote. The three would debate suggestions in the open, but Dalio's leanings weren't hard to divine. Neither Prince nor Jensen went against the Bridgewater founder often. Dalio seemed to shy from new ideas that he couldn't understand, and thus many new rules had the if-then structure. This wasn't enough to keep pace with the outside world, and a newcomer to the investment team as recently as 2018 was gobsmacked to learn that the world's biggest hedge fund's trading was still reliant on Microsoft Excel, using a decades-old software. It was as if Dalio insisted on flying only the Wright brothers' aircraft long after the invention of the jet engine.

Behind the locked doors of the Bridgewater investing department, boredom ruled, for years on end. This was partly why Jensen had helped convince Dalio to allow "the trading game," a simulation of the real world in which his investment staff would bet their best ideas against a pot of

---

* In a blistering 2020 ruling against Bridgewater in a case brought by the hedge fund against two former investment employees, a New York State arbitration panel determined that Bridgewater's investment approach as described in the case was "vague." The panel wrote that Bridgewater "argued that its economic success as a hedge fund supported its assertions that it had and has valuable trade secrets but . . . produced no evidence of a 'methodology.'" What Bridgewater claimed as its trade secrets were "publicly available information or generally available to professionals in the industry." The panel, which heard testimony from Jensen under oath, concluded, "Bridgewater expects employees at Respondents' level to remain with Bridgewater for their entire careers and regards leaving as a betrayal."

Dalio's own money (if the ideas of the staff won, they would be paid in cash). This displayed how remarkably little Dalio thought of his own staff, the same people who were supposed to be investing money for clients: he was willing to take, blind, the other side of whatever they came up with. For many in the investing department, it was the only time in their Bridgewater careers that they could actually express an investment idea.

Unlike employees from virtually every other hedge fund, few who left Bridgewater would ever start a fund of their own, and not just because of the firm's aggressive legal posture. Given the tight reins on access to the meat of the department, sadly, working on the Bridgewater investment team left precious few people with tangible knowledge on the hedge fund's investing.*

FOR ALL his public bravado, Dalio could not have been oblivious of the dimming efficacy of his machine. He could read the numbers as well as anyone else. Between 2011 and 2016, a blistering period for the markets, Pure Alpha posted only low-digit returns, far below its historical pace. When Bridgewater's investors asked why the fund was slipping, they were assured, year after year, that its performance was within the boundaries of Bridgewater's long-term expectations.

One edge was left that Dalio and Bridgewater went to great lengths to protect. They had a profound information advantage over most other investors in the world—and worked hard to maintain it. The advantage was unavailable to virtually anyone else, and no amount of research, science, or analytics could provide it.

On Wall Street, the phrase *information advantage* often carries an unseemly implication. To say that investors hold an information advantage can be a polite, or less so, way of suggesting that they are engaged in insider trading—illegally trading in a stock based on confidential information obtained from a company insider. Dalio's information advantage, while no less private, was as legal as it was vast. Bridgewater didn't gather any information about individual companies. Their target instead was information about entire nations, and Dalio heavily courted well-connected government officials from whom he might divine how they planned to intervene in their economies—and Bridgewater used these insights to make money in its funds.

Some of the officials who had this sort of information were not easily

---

* A lawyer for Dalio said: "Bridgewater's investment associate program is widely rated by those who have passed through its rigorous assessments as an excellent education in macro investing."

reached even by a Wall Street titan. They were central bankers, government-fund managers, and consultants in the shadowy world of those helping the world's leaders invest their cash. Dalio cleverly played a long game, patiently cultivating soft power.

Anywhere seemed fair game, even Kazakhstan.

The central Asia nation was not on the first page in any Wall Street manual. Ruled by an authoritarian, it was the globe's largest landlocked country, yet sparsely populated. What it had were natural resources. In 2013 Kazakhstan began developing what was then the most expensive oil project ever, a giant field in the Caspian Sea, helping it grow a $77 billion sovereign wealth fund. That money would have to be invested somewhere, and Bridgewater's client services squad put a meeting on Dalio's calendar with Berik Otemurat, the fund's chief. Otemurat was a square bureaucrat who had begun his career barely ten years earlier as an auditor, and now he was traveling with a group to meet some of Wall Street's biggest names.

Dalio showed interest in the delegation. "What are they doing before-hand?" he asked Bridgewater's marketing team.

His underlings came back and answered that Otemurat would be in New York a few hours before he was due in Westport.

"How are they getting here?" Dalio then asked.

Bridgewater had arranged for a chauffeur in a Mercedes.

"Get 'em a helicopter."

Several thousand dollars later, a thirtysomething Kazakh with an out-dated side part and a few of his subordinates were on a chartered chopper from Manhattan to the closest helicopter pad to Bridgewater, in Bridge-port, Connecticut—well overshooting the firm's headquarters—where a chauffeur-driven Mercedes met them to complete the journey.

The dramatic entrance preceded an unconventional presentation, at least compared with what Otemurat had experienced in New York. There, titans of industry such as KKR & Co. cofounder Henry Kravis and Black-stone's Stephen Schwarzman wooed him on investing in their firms over sea bass and caviar, with one providing an orange hazelnut napoleon dessert loosely based on the Kazakh flag. Dalio, in contrast, drew an inde-cipherable chart on a dry-erase board and rambled on about the nature of markets. He barely mentioned the specifics of Bridgewater's approach. There was an undeniable charm—and confidence—to it all.

Bridgewater marketing staff, those sitting in on the meeting and those listening to a recording of it afterward, had seen this move before. If so, the end goal would be something other than money. So when Otemurat raised the prospect of investing $15 million in Bridgewater's main hedge fund, the hedge fund's representatives shooed away the suggestion. "We don't want a relationship with you right now. We're in it for the long game," said one marketing executive.

Inside Bridgewater, a relationship meant access. Rolling out the red carpet for a few million dollars in investments, rather than a potential multibillion-dollar edge, would have been small fry. The country's new oil field had taken more than a decade to develop, with near-constant delays. Anyone who knew how the project was proceeding could adjust their bets on oil accordingly. Bridgewater's representatives told the delegation their firm would be happy to offer free advice on how the sovereign wealth fund could invest its billions, and Bridgewater's team would likewise appreciate the opportunity to ask a few questions about industries of local expertise.

Oil insight was particularly precious. The marketing team had helped prepare a confidential client document that showed where Bridgewater's main hedge fund made its money during some of its best years.* The biggest driver of "excess returns," i.e., the most lucrative bets, were commodities, where Bridgewater could combine the sort of number crunching employed by its rivals with real-world information no one else had. Among commodities, oil was particularly sensitive, being a "short-duration asset," or one highly sensitive to fast price changes because it could be stored aboveground for only a limited number of days. That meant that prices could rise quickly if supply didn't keep humming—as was often at risk with Kazakhstan, given its struggles—or fall, in the opposite scenario. Up-to-date information was key. Otemurat and others in his delegation seemed eager to chat.

Soon enough, Bridgewater got it both ways. A few months after Otemurat's Westport visit, the Kazakh fund asked again if it could invest in Bridgewater funds. This time, it dangled a sum far larger than $15 million, and this time, Bridgewater assented.

BACK IN America, Dalio's access slowly petered out. After his financial-crisis-era fame, he'd had little trouble reaching Fed chair Ben Bernanke. Bernanke's

---

* Lawyers for Dalio and Bridgewater said the hedge fund's "competitive advantage is the quality of its research and understanding of global economies and markets, which it then turns into systematized investment strategies."

successor, Janet Yellen, however, apparently wasn't as interested in the Bridgewater founder. Dalio would rail to others at Bridgewater that Yellen wouldn't return his calls or meet. "It enraged him," said one person Dalio complained to. In one conference call with clients during Yellen's term, Dalio laid out the management team's "key views" on twenty-one different markets, ranging from the Brazilian real to the Indian rupee to Japanese bonds. Dalio skipped entirely the U.S. dollar. He said he was unable to determine a key view there.

Dalio consistently found more success forging alliances abroad. Mario Draghi, the Italian-born head of the European Central Bank (ECB), frequently chatted with the Bridgewater founder and sought his advice. Dalio consistently advised him throughout the mid-2010s to introduce more stimulus to the bloc, which would bolster European stocks and hurt the euro. During much of that era, Bridgewater was also betting against the euro. Dalio soon became a walking, talking advertisement for Draghi. As Dalio wrote in one public statement sent out to reporters domestically and abroad, "At all the key moments, he has done the right things and the whole world is better off because of it. By now the world should know, don't fade Mario Draghi."

Dalio's Draghi adoration didn't just help the Bridgewater founder with the ECB. It also helped give him entry to European capitals. In Zurich, Dalio found the ear of Thomas Jordan, the head of the Swiss National Bank. Dalio assumed a brief statesmanlike role with Jordan, advising the younger man on his efforts to decouple the Swiss economy from ailing broader Europe, according to a former Bridgewater employee who helped make the connection. When Jordan in early 2015 yanked the Swiss franc from its peg to the euro, Bridgewater's funds made a fortune.

The longest-term project for Dalio lay in China. Since sending his son to live there in middle school, Dalio had worked hard to build relationships among Beijing's elite (he tried to learn Mandarin, but like many Westerners grew frustrated and gave up). In frequent trips lasting weeks at a time, resulting in billions of dollars in investment from state-run arms such as the China Investment Corporation (CIC), Dalio combined the personal and the professional. He brought his wife to some meetings, and Bridgewater's top deputies to others. On one 2015 trip, Dalio brought Prince, and the two stayed not at a hotel but at an official Chinese presidential guesthouse. When Prince began feeling flu-like symptoms, Chinese government officials whisked him into private treatment. That same year, Dalio attended the White House state dinner honoring Chinese president Xi Jinping. He was no doubt cognizant of these relationships when he desperately tried to backpedal on his public prediction that there were "no safe places to invest" in China.

Dalio hired CIC's chairman to a cushy job as head of the Dalio charity in China, then later promoted him to a post leading Bridgewater's China office, the firm's only branch outside of Connecticut. In media interviews, Dalio stuck to a fixed, laudatory line about the country's leadership. They were "very capable," he said, over and again, sometimes repeating the phrase more than once in an interview. Those same leaders, he would also say inside Bridgewater, were quick to ask him for advice.

To any reasonable observer—and even to the Chinese themselves—Dalio was the paradigm of a China booster. But there was also an advantage that could be played. He asked the Circle of Trust to help create a way for Bridgewater's funds to place bets against Chinese assets, in an offshore way that China's government couldn't track. That way, when Dalio took the wrong side of China, no one would know.

DALIO'S APPROACH had one more element that was considerably less than transparent. His grand automated system—his economic machine—wasn't nearly as automated or mechanized as was promoted. As much as 10 percent of Pure Alpha's invested assets, comprising billions of dollars, boiled down to Dalio's instinct and ideas, period. They were his orders. If he wanted Bridgewater to short the U.S. dollar (as he did, unsuccessfully, for roughly a decade following the financial crisis), the trade went in, as the others on the investment team seemed to invariably give in to his wishes. There was no most-important rule than what Dalio wanted, Dalio got.*

As 2017 loomed, a handful of top investment staffers decided enough was enough after yet another year of tears, stress, and firings, all for a turbid result. Pure Alpha was up just 2 percent for the year, well below most hedge funds and just one-sixth of the gain for U.S. stocks overall. Some on the Bridgewater investment team suspected they knew why.

With the hope of turning around the firm's investment performance—and with Jensen's permission—members of the Circle of Trust put together a study of Dalio's trades. They trawled deep into the Bridgewater archives for a history of Dalio's individual investment ideas. The team ran the numbers once, then again, then again. The data had to be perfect. Then, as a

---

* Lawyers for Dalio and Bridgewater said, "In the general course, Bridgewater trading is *not* discretionary," and that the approval of the fund's chief investment officers is needed for any such trades.

group, they sat down with Dalio. One young staffer, hands shaking, handed over the results: The study showed that Dalio was wrong as much as he was right. Trading on his ideas lately was often akin to a coin flip.

The group, which included Jensen and Elliott, sat quietly, nervously waiting for Dalio's response.

Dalio picked up the piece of paper, crumpled it into a ball, and tossed it.

23

THE GIFT

Dalio spent the cross-country flight to Vancouver hard at work. His focus was not on the hedge fund's investments but on his own brand. He was headed to his most important public appearance since the Oprah interview twenty-nine years earlier.

Dalio had nabbed a speaking slot at TED2017, the high-profile series in which luminaries in business, art, and science speak with the world about their life lessons. He prepared for weeks for a sixteen-minute slot in between big names such as Elon Musk and Serena Williams. To many around him, Dalio seemed unusually nervous. This would be a big stage at a time when he could use a chance to change the subject.

The opening months of 2017 had brought a barrage of unwelcome attention. David McCormick and Eileen Murray were announced as the latest set of CEOs, replacing Jon Rubinstein and producing a renewed flutter of news articles about the consistent management tumult at the firm. On the investing end, Bridgewater greeted the election of Donald Trump as another reason to warn of economic doom. The firm warned clients that the Dow Jones Industrial Average could collapse nearly 2,000 points on Trump's win, which would be the biggest one-day slump in history by more than double. The opposite happened; the index popped to all-time highs. The result was that Pure Alpha ended 2016 up just 2.1 percent, its fifth consecutive year of low-single-digit performance. Plenty of big money was being made across Wall Street, just not at Bridgewater's main fund.

Dalio also faced a new public glare on his management system. *The Wall Street Journal* published a lengthy investigation on the PriOS software, including a quote from an anonymous Bridgewater employee who described the project as "trying to make Ray's brain into a computer." At least some at Bridgewater were initially pleased with the piece—"Thought you did a really good job here. . . . I really respect you for your approach," McCormick wrote to one of the *Journal* reporters—but Dalio apparently saw it differently. He had hoped to roll out PriOS publicly himself, and to make matters worse, tabloids that followed up on the *Journal* piece described the invention as a glimpse of dystopia ("What If Your Boss Is a Robot?" read one headline). Dalio reacted bitterly. He complained so often to McCormick about his ambitions being misunderstood that McCormick would email the same *Journal* reporter anew and retract his compliments: "After rereading your article more closely . . . regrettably it looks to us like the article includes several references which we believe to be inaccurate or one-sided." McCormick added, "We will follow up with more specific feedback shortly."

No such follow-up came. Instead Dalio borrowed a tactic from the new U.S. president and made the media his public foil. In early January 2017, he published a lengthy screed on social networking site LinkedIn singling out the piece and calling it part of the "fake and distorted media epidemic." Facts weren't his issue so much as feelings. He identified no actual factual inaccuracies, though he complained that reporters "want to paint a picture of Bridgewater being a crazy, oppressive place run by a Dr. Frankenstein type character—even though the evidence shows it to be an idea meritocracy which has, for several decades, succeeded in producing meaningful work, meaningful relationships, and unparalleled results through its radical truthfulness and radical transparency." He suggested that readers shouldn't "worry about what's true about Bridgewater," and cited internal data that evidently showed "unusual high" turnover among new employees but longer tenures after. Dalio attributed that to Bridgewater being a place "not for everyone, but for those who it is for, there is nothing like it." No doubt to Dalio's delight, the LinkedIn post shifted the focus. Reporters pivoted to covering the spectacle of a hedge fund billionaire's attack on the media, while commenters on LinkedIn rushed to Bridgewater's defense. "Way to fight the good fight, Ray," read one of hundreds of positive comments. "Perhaps 'free press' is the issue," read another.

Evidently convinced that no one could defend Bridgewater as well as he could, Dalio got himself in front of as many people as possible. One of his first interviews was with Henry Blodget, the editor in chief of *Business Insider*, a website that covered finance but was known at the time more for seeking clicks than for publishing hard-hitting pieces. According to

Blodget, Dalio's team reached out on January 1, 2017, and negotiated a two-and-a-half-hour interview on the condition that the website publish the interview verbatim. Blodget agreed. In the interview, which ran a week later, Dalio ran through the usual talking points ("We have an idea meritocracy and it has just worked unbelievably well") along with some new ones. On his practice of calling for votes inside the firm, then weighing his own ballot more than others, he said, "I'm scared of one man, one vote because it suggests that everybody has an equal ability at making decisions, and I think that's dangerous." He said that even he abided by Bridgewater's management rules because "if you don't, if you pull rank, then you lose all your credibility. I have never overruled a decision." Perhaps most curiously, given the interview's timing, Dalio read aloud to Blodget an employee email that the Bridgewater founder said he had received only the previous day: "'Thank God for Bridgewater and you, Ray. I love you, Ray. I hope you have a wonderful Christmas.'"

It was January.

After a few more friendly audiences, including an appearance on CNBC, where he shared his three favorite books, Dalio was poised for the big event, TED2017. As he walked onstage at the Vancouver Convention Centre, his blue button-up and loose cardigan a perfect fit for the aesthetic, Dalio appeared to have overcome his nervousness. He seemed casual and approachable, like a grandfather headed for a day with his favorite grandchildren. He made easy eye contact with the audience, taking small steps around the stage and gesturing with his hands as he spoke.

"Whether you like it or not," Dalio declared into his headset, "radical transparency and algorithmic decision-making is coming at you fast. And it's going to change your life."

Dalio launched into an abridged version of his childhood, following the same arc that he had in myriad previous interviews. He'd hated school, he said with a grimace, but fell in love with the stock market at age twelve when he used money earned from caddying to invest. The first stock he bought was Northeast Airlines, because its shares traded for less than $5. "Dumb strategy, right?" The audience, their faces reflecting the red glow of the TED emblem behind Dalio, laughed. He offered a self-deprecating smile, seeming to reveal a newfound sense of humor, one decidedly self-effacing.

A screen lit up over Dalio's shoulder and began playing clips from decades earlier. One showed Dalio's congressional testimony, giving confident predictions about the economy that later turned out wrong. Onstage, Dalio seemed barely able to wait for the videos to finish before he burst in, "I look at that now and think, 'What an arrogant jerk.'" More guffaws from the audience.

Over time, Dalio said he realized that he needed to build a community where smart people could stress test his perspectives, encouraging only the most believable ideas to win out. For that, everyone around him needed to be truthful and transparent. Turning around to show the thinning back of his hair, Dalio walked to a podium onstage, where he put on his reading glasses and gestured again to the screen. "I'd like to take you into a meeting and introduce you to a tool called the Dot Collector that helps us do this."

Later in the talk, another video played, filled with graphics showing Bridgewater attributes such as "ability to self-assess" and "pushing through to results." Employees were shown rating one another on scales of 1 to 10. Each mistake was a puzzle that—once solved—created gems called Principles. "For the last twenty-five years, that's how we've been operating. We've been operating with this radical transparency and then collecting these Principles, largely from making mistakes, and then embedding those Principles into algorithms. That has been how we run the investment business, and it's how we also deal with the people management."

Dalio wrapped up back where he began, predicting radical transparency for all. "In my opinion, it's going to be wonderful. So I hope it is as wonderful for you as it is for me."

He opened his arms as if to give a quick bow, then walked off the stage to applause.

THE TED Talk would be viewed by millions. Dalio's profile was rising at the perfect time, as he had firmly wrested control of his own narrative just as he was about to become world-famous.

In the fall of 2017, Dalio released his autobiography, *Principles: Life and Work*. It was the book he'd earlier hoped Walter Isaacson might write but later decided to pen it himself with a ghostwriter. *Principles* was released in September 2017 with a rollout that few other first-time authors could match. No fewer than six fellow billionaires gave it public recommendations (Bill Gates: "Ray Dalio has provided me with invaluable guidance and insights that are now available to you in *Principles*"). Self-help icon Tony Robbins said it was one of the greatest books he'd ever read. Billionaire Mark Cuban said, "*Principles* offers a bible to the greatest skill any entrepreneur can have, the ability to learn how to learn in any situation." The Harvard professor Robert Kegan told *The New York Times* that Dalio's Principles were contributing to "as dramatic a transformation as the industrial revolution."

Book promotion would allow Dalio to further cement his status as an important thinker. The popular podcaster Tim Ferriss, during a two-hour interview with the Bridgewater founder titled "Ray Dalio, the Steve Jobs of Investing," said: "I highly, highly recommend this book. It has already changed how I think about making decisions in my life, and in my business how I think about managing, how I think about communications between teams, I could go on and on and on."

Dalio also became a prolific user of Twitter, where he would tweet out daily Principles. In his Twitter bio, he charmingly described himself as a "professional mistake maker." He also frequently discussed his ongoing goal of developing software that would allow other companies to use The Principles and their assorted tools.

Staffers at Bridgewater recalled only seeing him infrequently at the office for several months after the book's release. That Dalio was talking more about Bridgewater than perhaps ever before, but was spending less time on what was going on there, had a certain irony.

Dalio's book tour became all but his full-time job. He gave interviews for months in print, on television, on podcasts, and in virtually every other medium. In each, he seemed to raise the import of his work. To *The Times* of London, in an interview that the newspaper noted was held over almonds and mineral water in a Manhattan boardroom, Dalio said, "I've made discoveries that can change the world, make the world a much better place, make people better."

He went on, "Imagine you discovered a cure for cancer, and you say, 'Should I be quiet or put it out there?' That's how I feel about The Principles. This is the best gift I could give the world."

Though the publicity blitz no doubt helped sell books, Dalio also bought plenty of his own. Bridgewater sent thousands of copies to clients. Dalio hosted several book-release parties on Bridgewater's campus, at which employees and their families were given multiple copies apiece. Though the push didn't land *Principles* on the main weekly *New York Times* nonfiction bestseller list, the book did top the *Times*' less prestigious, monthly Business Best

Sellers ranking, as well as chart on the Advice / How To section. Bridge-water would add a line to Dalio's official biography on the firm's website describing him as "the #1 *New York Times* bestselling author of *Principles: Life and Work.*"

An illustrated children's book version was put into development.

Some inside Bridgewater privately chuckled at the over-the-top reception to Dalio's tome. The first one-third of the book was a history of the man and the firm, and perhaps unavoidably given the nature of autobi-ography, it was only a faint likeness of the full story. It burnished Dalio's rags-to-riches credentials; he didn't mention the Leib family's help nor his wife's family wealth. He suggested that he had "wanted to stay under the radar," a particularly strange boast for a man who had pitched him-self as a subject for television interviews, magazine profiles, and hundreds of newspaper quotes. He wrote extensively of Bridgewater's investments ahead of the financial crisis and didn't mention the hedge fund's relatively lackluster performance since 2010. Perhaps most glaringly, the details of Dalio's seemingly unending retirement promises, including the procession of CEOs as well as Jensen's demotion, were recast in a new light. He made a show of taking responsibility, but in a way that put down those around him by reminding them that they couldn't hope to replace him: "I realized that I had handed Greg too heavy a load expecting him to carry out both the co-CEO and co-CIO roles." Those had been Dalio's titles for years. Jensen winced when he read the passage, according to friends.

The bulk of the book was a new version of what Dalio called his life and work principles. These were "the overarching principles that drive my ap-proach to everything" and were offered as "a close-up view of the unusual way we operate at Bridgewater." In an email to potential book buyers, he called these principles "a much better and more complete version of the one from 2011"—that is, the ones leaked to the blog *Dealbreaker*, much to Dalio's chagrin.

What Dalio didn't mention, but most everyone at Bridgewater could have recognized, was that the collection listed in *Principles* weren't The Principles. They were more like Some Principles; they certainly weren't all of the ones that most at Bridgewater had been instructed to use. Left out from the book were some of the most memorable Principles that Dalio had insisted the firm hew to in the past—and still stuck to in practice. The virtues of a pack of hyenas who ravage a young wildebeest were not mentioned. *Principles* skipped some of Dalio's most frequently used rules—including ones he would continue to cite inside the firm for years to come, including "people have to value getting at truth so badly that they are willing to humiliate themselves to get it." Gone, too, was a Principle that reminded "complaints are welcomed and rewarded," as well as another, "You can't make people do things."

Also excised was one of the original Principles: "Respect people's privacy."

Moving from The Principles of Bridgewater to the principles of *Principles* was like crossing from Adventureland to Fantasyland. The new additions included "Play jazz with lots of people"; "Pay for the person, not the job"; "Remember that in great partnerships, consideration and generosity are more important than money"; "Allow time for rest and renovation"; "No one is more powerful than the system or so important that they're irreplaceable"; "Don't allow lynch mobs or mob rule"; and "Declare 'martial law' only in rare or extreme circumstances when the principles need to be suspended."

One idea that Dalio addressed head-on in his book was speculation that his firm was a cult. "The truth is that Bridgewater succeeds because it is the opposite of a cult." He added, "Cults demand unquestioning obedience. Thinking for yourself and challenging each other's ideas is anti-cult behavior and that is the essence of what we do at Bridgewater."

IF THERE was one person inside Bridgewater who could be counted on to take Dalio at his word, optimistic that she could challenge his ideas, it was Jen Healy. The woman who had helped inspire the "sugarcoating" Principle and later dropped her complaint about being inappropriately touched by a top executive was as close to a true believer as they came, and Dalio still occasionally spoke of her as his surrogate daughter.

By the time Dalio arrived back to close to full-time work at Bridgewater in early 2018, in the wake of his extensive book tour, Healy was no longer the young woman that Bridgewater had hired straight out of Princeton. She'd been promoted several times and was looked up to by others at the firm.

In many ways, Healy was still all in. She frequently quoted The Principles—the public and the private ones—and turned heads inside the firm when she divorced her husband and quickly married a fellow Bridgewater employee, surely an indication that the hedge fund remained a crucial part of her personal life. To friends, however, Healy confessed that she was beginning to weary of Dalio's overall demeanor. Now a mother, it bothered her that Dalio was always on the hunt for someone new to upbraid, and she struggled to square that with his frequent public pronouncements that Bridgewater enjoyed a family atmosphere.

Like many others before her, Healy seemed to believe so deeply in radical transparency that she thought it could extend to her relationship with Dalio. Surely Dalio simply needed to hear the truth—from someone such as her, from someone he seemed to genuinely love—and he would show the generosity and consideration that he wrote about in the new *Principles*.

She poured her feelings into an email to Dalio and copied in a host of other top executives at the firm.

From: Jen Healy
Sent: Monday, April 23, 2018
To: Ray Dalio

Subject: Ray—Please read

The goal of this note is to help you and make you aware of the impact you are having on others. In my view, this is basically an emperor with no clothes situation and I think it is my obligation to let you know and help you in any way I can.

The headline is that the way you are operating is making some of those around you feel:

not heard/understood
hopeless
not able to grow/evolve in your eyes and therefore trapped
like they have to go against their values of integrity to operate with
you and therefore conflicted and angry/sad/frustrated
and some people have felt abused/mistreated and have actually been
diagnosed PTSD and other conditions due to your behavior (and I
won't reveal their identities due to confidentiality)

Personally, I felt those things with you leading up to my maternity leave in 2014 and was in a really bad place. With the help of space away from you, therapy, and a lot of personal reflection, I have been able to change my behavior in a way that impacts how you can impact me. This includes trying to find my self-worth again and really mourn and grieve things like the reality that you will likely never really understand me or see me for who I am. . . .

Potential new principle—Take accountability. If you have mistreated someone or acted in a way that impacts others negatively, apologize and commit to changing your behavior if applicable. . . .

When people give you feedback, you say things like "Take me out and get what you deserve" or that you can only do it your way or the highway. . . .

When you are hyperbolic and promote your own successes and diminish / don't recognize that other people have also done great things, it can be really discouraging and in many cases not true. . . . .

While you can't change in a day, the biggest things you can do are:

Acknowledge that you don't want these outcomes
Apologize if your behaviors had this impact
Be open to people pointing these things out / holding you accountable. . . .

Please let me know how you would like to proceed / get in sync.

Jen

Many in the wide group that received Healy's email reacted with a mix of hope and eye rolls. Only Healy, some thought, could think that Dalio actually wanted to hear tough feedback about his behavior. The history of the firm suggested otherwise. But Healy did occupy rarefied ground with the Bridgewater founder. It wasn't so outlandish to think she might be able to get around his ego—even if it seemed equally likely he would turn her words against her.

His response did a little of both.

From: Ray Dalio
Sent: Friday, April 27, 2018
To: Jen Healy

Subject: RE: Ray—Please read

Jen—
I really appreciate your feedback. You clearly care a lot about Bridgewater, you are courageous to fight for what you believe is best, and you bring up accurate and important challenges that I face. . . .

I presume you know that I don't want to hurt anyone and that I sincerely feel sorry that I do sometimes. I'd love to help people and Bridgewater be great without causing them pain and I'm pretty sure that I could keep learning how to do that better. My issue is that I haven't been able to achieve excellence in individuals and excellence for Brideater [*sic*] without doing it and I haven't seen anyone do it better. . . . That last statement isn't just self-assessment, it's what I hear from most everyone and is shown in the dots. . . .

I believe that what you see as breaking people's egos down is what I see as testing and training them and, most importantly, giving them the humility they need to be great and maintaining very high standards for Bridgewater. . . . Almost all people who work for me tell me that they learn and improve enormously, and they don't tell me that to kiss my ass. . . .

When you say that I should apologize, I assume you mean that I should apologize for causing pain. If that's what you mean? As explained, while I certainly wish I didn't do that, I'm trying to help them and I believe that pain is part of that process. If you want me to apologize for not understanding them, then I will apologize for that because I do realize that sometimes that happens (because of how we think differently).

So, what should I/we do about all of this? I suggest we look in Principles for a guide. . . .

Dalio's response left Healy crestfallen. Though she still had a degree of faith in him, this apology, as it were, fell well short of expectations. She later took an externship from Bridgewater, essentially staying on the payroll while working elsewhere. She didn't return to Bridgewater. Dalio had lost another of his original true believers.*

---

* Healy declined to discuss this episode in detail. She wrote in an email, "I believed then and believe today that Ray has good intentions and does what he does out of care."

24

THE PARTNERSHIP

IT WASN'T ONLY HEALY WHO HAD EVIDENTLY LOST ANY ABILITY TO speak sense to Dalio. Though he had in years past at least feigned a pretense of allowing questioning of The Principles and his management system, the publication of *Principles*—which would be printed in thirty-four languages and even turned into a thirty-minute animated video—all but ended that. The manifesto, which began more than a decade earlier as a series of emails distributed casually internally, was now treated as seriously by Dalio as golden plates.

The broad reach and international fame earned off his book seemed to solidify Dalio's belief in himself as an emissary from the world of high finance to the commoner. The man who called himself an "economic doctor" now had a reputation as someone with the cure to what ailed so much more than just business and finance. He was a benevolent billionaire, offering the keys to his success to anyone who asked. The character he built himself into fit an era in which a celebrity real estate investor was elected president, and countless Silicon Valley star executives would brag of "changing the world" through their iPhone apps.

The book helped keep a torrent of newcomers applying to Bridgewater, both new college graduates and experienced hires. "We were literally selling the American dream. All you have to do is be open-minded and smart, and anything is possible," said one former top Bridgewater talent executive.

If the story behind the scenes was more complicated, that was buried deeply in the public narrative. Although Dalio would continue to say that he wasn't perfect, he had effectively sold the world on an alternative reality of what life was like at Bridgewater, and entertained few questions about whether the firm he founded enjoyed any resemblance to what he still publicly proclaimed to be an "idea-meritocratic" Eden. If in reality Bridgewater wasn't quite that, what did it matter so long as the world believed that it was?

The main problems that regularly leaked publicly from the firm weren't anything to do with The Principles but with the disappointing investment performance of Bridgewater's funds. Whether as a casualty of its founder's persistent bearishness, the distractions of his extended book tour, or another factor entirely, Pure Alpha was up just 1 percent in 2017 and up only mildly in the first half of 2018. This problem was tough to hide because investors were increasingly fed up. Though in its earlier years Bridgewater had managed money largely for teachers' pensions and other apolitical entities, many of those long-term clients were pulling their money. In their place, Dalio sought new cash from elsewhere. Much as he had since his time as a golf caddy, he did so by leveraging his relationships. In June 2018, Bridgewater made headlines when it became the only U.S. hedge fund to be awarded a license from China to raise money from rich Chinese individuals. The move allowed the firm to seamlessly replace outflows from domestic clients with money from mainland China in its overall assets under management.

But China wasn't enough. Another major economy that Dalio had in his sights was Russia. Now considerably past the disappointing cancellation of his meeting with Vladimir Putin, Dalio tried for another way in. He again tried to cultivate a relationship with Sberbank, the Russian state-controlled bank, and offered to give them free use of the Principles software, including the PriOS.

This time, Dalio's efforts paid off. In 2018, work leaked inside Bridgewater that Dalio had gone to visit Putin. Even some in the firm's top ranks weren't sure if it was true, and Dalio wouldn't answer to underlings when questioned directly on the subject. For Karen Karniol-Tambour, known internally for deftly playing the game of agreeing with Dalio, it was too much. Karniol-Tambour was by mid-2018 cohead of investment research, a position previously held by Jensen, no slouch himself at parroting Dalio. Now she was faced with a decision: her job or her morals.

First she chose the latter, rising from her seat at a Bridgewater town hall, shaking with nerves and voice rising, to assail Dalio about Putin. "How do you deal with this war criminal?"

Dalio turned to look at her and responded, Don't be so simpleminded.

He told her to keep her emotions in check, as The Principles prescribed. "If you're so smart," he sniffed, "why aren't you rich?"

The blow might have been softer if Karniol-Tambour had known she was hearing a riff on the same line Dalio had used on Paul McDowell a decade earlier, when McDowell was rated highly by the stratum expert. This time, Dalio's put-down seemed to strike a nerve inside Karniol-Tambour. In front of the crowd, she tore into him, saying that she would not sit idly by while a powerful man ran roughshod—not if the man was Ray Dalio and not if it was "Hitler."

There were gasps at the comparison.

The meeting didn't last much longer after that. Among friends inside Bridgewater, Karniol-Tambour would later shed tears, upset that Dalio could speak to her so harshly and seemingly fearful of what would happen to her in return for the outburst. Word reached the Bridgewater executive ranks that Karniol-Tambour was turning into something of a sympathetic figure inside the firm—and that Dalio was coming off as the villain.

Had the incident happened a few years earlier, Dalio would surely have called for an adjudication in the open, and perhaps a poll as to whether he or Karniol-Tambour was correct. But it no longer seemed to animate him as much to be assured time and again by those at Bridgewater that he was in the right. He had a far bigger audience now outside the firm, and he seemed to feed on their approbation as much as the thousand or so souls inside the hedge fund. Rather than dive into one of his signature trials, he had a private conversation with Karniol-Tambour. This chat was apparently not recorded because no copy was uploaded to the firm's Transparency Library for listening by all.

Afterward, he sent out an email to a wide group at the firm that read, in part, "I've spoken to Karen and she's fine, and she asked me to continue doing what I'm doing with her."

Karniol-Tambour responded that she was grateful to have the opportunity to continue to learn from Dalio. She was not long after promoted to cochief investment officer for sustainability, a lofty title for a role that hadn't previously existed, and set up by Bridgewater's public relations team for splashy magazine profiles on her investment prowess—something not even Jensen had ever been awarded. Once again, Dalio had wriggled his way out of a jam.

Bob Elliott, who joined Bridgewater the same year as Karniol-Tambour, would soon face his own choice on whether to stay.

The stocky young man who'd joined the hedge fund with little life experience was growing into a rotund older man with not much more life experience. Bridgewater permeated all aspects of his day-to-day existence. He moved deeper into Connecticut, to a home in a small town just a few minutes from Jensen's, where the two couldn't help but run into each other. Elliott saw the shrunken figure that Jensen had become—wealthy beyond his dreams, but seemingly trapped at Bridgewater, where he had never fully clawed his way back into Dalio's good graces. Elliott, a member of the Circle of Trust with a lifetime contract, told friends he felt as if there were no escape. His old friends and family had long given it up as futile to ask for details on what he did for a living. Elliott would wince when anyone pulled up his old quote—by 2018, it was now more than six years old—to *The New Yorker*, "Once you understand how the machine works . . ." He had been repeating Dalio's lines for so long now.

Elliott had started at Bridgewater right out of college as an economic researcher for Dalio, and now as the younger man crossed his midthirties, he had to admit that though his title had improved, his responsibilities did not exactly match. Dalio had tasked Elliott with coming up with "the book of foreign exchange," an omnibus document running hundreds of pages on how to invest in currencies, an indication that Dalio trusted him with an important area of the firm's investments. The project took years. If completing it made Elliott the firm's resident expert on the topic, that wasn't obvious from listening to Dalio talk to his subordinate. Elliott would tell friends that when he brought up currency ideas to Dalio, the Bridgewater founder would dismiss him as a "fat ass."*

The insults cut particularly deep because Dalio wasn't entirely off base with the physical description.

More than once, Elliott told Dalio he was considering resigning. The Bridgewater founder seemed shocked that Elliott had taken the remarks so personally. "Are you crazy?" Dalio asked. This was the job of a lifetime in more ways than one, the Bridgewater founder told him. Dalio suggested the younger man needed psychotherapy.

More was weighing on Elliott than a few cutting words. For the better

---

* A lawyer for Dalio said he "never called Elliott a 'fat ass' in any meeting."

part of the year after Dalio's autobiography was published, the Bridgewater founder was frequently physically absent from the firm as he spread the gospel worldwide. He spent as little as an hour a week on Bridgewater's investing, often just phoning in briefly from the road. As head of currencies, Elliott told colleagues he found it hard to put in too much effort when he knew that, no matter how many weeks of work went into an investing idea, Dalio might reflexively move to overrule it in a brief conference call.

Moreover, after so many years at the Bridgewater founder's side, Elliott and many of those around him could identify certain patterns in Dalio's decision-making. Dalio's analyses tended toward trend following; they reflected a view that markets had momentum, and it was best to stay ahead of it. This would have been not so much a flatly invalid perspective as an archaic one. Unlike at Bridgewater's inception, an entire industry of trend-following funds now existed that placed only so-called momentum trades, squeezing out any advantage the approach once had. There was not, as Dalio might have said, any alpha left. Elliott's exasperation hit a new apex in 2018 when Dalio ignored Elliott's bullish research view on the U.S. dollar. The dollar was falling, Dalio said, and when pressed by others on the investment team, he insisted that his instincts told him that it would only drop more. The dollar ultimately rose, producing losses for Bridgewater funds.

So Elliott was already coming across as agnostic when Dalio called the firm's top staff in late 2018 with a new deal. As part of his ongoing retirement plans, the Bridgewater founder was looking to off-load more of his ownership of the firm. Dalio didn't immediately need the cash—he was worth $17.4 billion overall—but nearly half of that, or $9 billion, were his shares in Bridgewater. No matter what he or anyone else said the stake was worth, it was an ephemeral, paper investment that couldn't be sold on the open market like a publicly traded stock. Dalio would need to find private buyers. He didn't need to look far.

Dalio called some of his longest-term loyalists at the firm into private meetings and told them he had an offer they couldn't refuse: a chance to be a real, honest-to-God owner of Bridgewater, one of the lucky few. This wasn't the phantom equity that he had doled out widely to current and former staff—it was a real-deal, straight-up piece of Bridgewater, directly from his private account. They would be owners, just like him. It was a once-in-a-lifetime chance to buy into the family. Dalio called it the Partnership.*

Getting in on the Partnership was such an extraordinary opportunity that Dalio evidently didn't think his top brass ought to limit themselves to spending money they already had. His offer included what amounted to an IOU. In exchange for receiving a sliver of Dalio's stake then, the employees would garnish the next ten years of their bonuses to buying out the Bridgewater founder. If anyone left Bridgewater in the interim, they'd have to pay back the debt. In this mortgage on their future, Dalio essentially stood in as the bank—with a decade-long promise of more money flowing to the Bridgewater founder.

But even the next ten years of bonuses for the top forty or so employees didn't add up to enough to fully buy Dalio out. So, as he told staff, it had been arranged for the investment bank JPMorgan to provide loans of up to ten times an employee's net worth, but the money could be used only to buy shares in Bridgewater. The money would go from JPMorgan to Dalio. Interest would accrue annually at around 5 percent. There were no two ways of looking at it: This was a way for Bridgewater's top executives to bet everything they owned and then some on Bridgewater—going deeply into debt in the process. Dalio would not be alongside them on this ride. He was cashing out.

For the true believers in Bridgewater, this seemed a logical and potentially savvy financial move. If they believed that Bridgewater was the only place worth working, this was the way to show it. Many took the offer. Elliott saw it differently—to him, it was an offering to the firm founder. Elliott said no.

ELLIOTT SURELY suspected that Dalio would take the snub poorly, but could have had no idea that Dalio's response would be so catastrophic. It seemed to those around Elliott that a switch flipped in Dalio. Elliott was no longer just a slob, he was an idiot. He was one of Dalio's worst mistakes— and they were stuck together, contractually joined at the hip. In big groups, in small groups, and in private, Dalio regularly reminded Elliott that he was a dumb shit. Elliott's dots suffered, both directly due to negative feed-

---

* A lawyer for Dalio said he "did not initiate or promote the idea of the Partnership. It was created by senior and long-tenured employees and supported by many others."

back from Dalio and then from colleagues, including Elliott's ostensible friend Jensen, who quickly piled on in agreement.

What saved Elliott from a deep downward spiral was that he had met someone new. She was forcing him to grapple with thoughts that he had long pushed out of his mind. Elliott's new love interest worked at Bridgewater, too. An associate in the research department, she didn't report to him directly. She was gorgeous—petite, blond, and ten years his junior. At first, it felt good to have a confidante who understood the Bridgewater way of life. Soon, however, he realized they were traveling on two vastly different tracks. She was an outlier; not only wasn't she an Ivy League graduate like most of the investing squad, she was one of just a few women. Elliott was hardly the only person to pick up on that. Not long after starting, she told friends that Jensen was showing an inordinate amount of interest in her work, making her uncomfortable. This was followed by a date request from one of Jensen's deputies. Female friends at Bridgewater, newly conscious of the simmering #MeToo movement taking hold across the world, warned her to tread carefully. They told her they had noticed a certain pattern: Women in the research department who complained about being asked on too many dates were encouraged to transfer to jobs in other departments. Not infrequently, these women were swiftly sorted out of the firm, with the reason given that they were poor fits for their new roles.

Jensen's deputy continued to show an inordinate interest in her, even following her after hours in his car once, as she would tell friends and Bridgewater officials. One evening, late at the office, with few people still around, she wound up cornered by him in a conference room. He stood over her, an imposing physical presence, in a way she found frightening. Scared, she told him that if he moved another step, she would press charges. Bridgewater's security staff was called, and they patched in Osman Nalbantoglu, one of Dalio's closer confidants, who had been one of the executives to go into debt buying up the Bridgewater founder's shares. Nalbantoglu arranged for her to be walked to her car.

Her allegations earned her an audience with a member of Bridgewater's internal legal team. She erupted. She pointed out that it wasn't always easy to say no. If a low-level employee disappointed an upper-level one, she risked receiving low dot ratings that could sink her career.

The Principles-based ranking system weighted longtime employees over newer ones, so her opinion literally didn't carry the same weight as theirs. She unloaded about stories she'd heard—about the fear that women felt alone with Bridgewater men; the pressure to pretend to enjoy adult entertainment; the constant, late-night, alcohol-heavy official firm events. Some of the things I've heard might even be considered crimes, she said.

On the last point, she got a stern rebuke. Filing any police report, the lawyer told her, could be considered a violation of her nondisclosure agreement. She should remember not to make public any incident that revealed, even obliquely, details on Bridgewater's operations.

The conversation left her rattled. She didn't go to the police. Her boss, a former Israeli Defense Forces officer named Nir Bar Dea, told her that the man who made her feel unsafe would be ordered to attend therapy and then receive his job back. She was told she would be expected back in the office as usual.

Elliott was never sure how Dalio learned in early 2018 that Elliott was dating a fellow employee. What Elliott recounted to others, though, was that the Bridgewater founder greeted the news with sheer jubilation. Dalio called Elliott into a transparent glass room in the investment department, visible to most everyone around, and acted, well, radically. Jensen, McCormick, and Bob Prince were there, too (per usual, Prince was mostly silent). Murray called in on the phone.

Smiling all the while, Dalio began his interrogation. "How was the sex?" Then:

"Where was the sex?

"Why didn't you tell us if it was good?"

Dalio leaned back, seemingly relaxed. It was no secret to anyone in the room—or those watching through the glass—that he had been waiting for this moment.

You should have told us earlier, Dalio said. Don't you remember the policy on intra-office relationships? This is a fireable offense—even for a member of the Circle of Trust. It was a rare chance to get rid of a lifetime employee.

At roughly the same time, Elliott's girlfriend was getting her own stern chat. Her boss, Bar Dea, showed up and dropped a calendar on her desk with a thud. "Mark the days."

"What days?" she responded.

"The days you had sex."

She pushed the calendar away from her and walked away quickly, concealing tears. She couldn't imagine the indignity of what they were asking. Bar Dea followed up again over the weekend, reminding her the calendar was due ("If on Monday you don't have a filled-in calendar, it's over"). She refused. If they were going to build a case, they would have to build it without her.

Bridgewater didn't need her help. In the glass office with Dalio, Elliott confessed to it all. Yes, he was in a relationship with a coworker. Half the company seemed to be, he pointed out with an eye roll. No, he hadn't volunteered the information to the firm on the first night they were intimate. He knew that wasn't a rule everyone followed, Elliott said.

Dalio fired Elliott.

That wasn't all.

Bridgewater being a place of radical transparency, Dalio notified the broader staff about such an important departure. Flanked by Nalbantoglu at a town hall meeting with more than one hundred employees present, and hundreds more listening in to the audio, Dalio announced that Elliott was departing.

A murmur went out in the room.

I've agreed not to say why, Dalio said, "But it's really, really bad."

Nalbantoglu jumped in. "Don't say! You really can't say. It's personal."*

---

* Lawyers for Dalio and Bridgewater said Elliott was terminated for failing to disclose a romantic relationship with a colleague, being dishonest about it, taking steps to conceal it and "falsely accusing his co-workers of misconduct to cover his tracks." His termination, the lawyer said, "followed an appropriate workplace investigation." Elliott said he left Bridgewater "following years of conflict with Ray about how to manage the fund's money. The claim that I was fired for failing to disclose a romantic relationship ignores the reality that relationships among colleagues, including ones involving the firm's senior leadership, were commonplace at Bridgewater." Elliott added, "only at Bridgewater would it be considered 'an appropriate workplace investigation' to have a woman followed, interrogated for hours, and forced to provide the specific, intimate details of her personal relationship. The fact that those involved do not see how abnormal such behavior is relative to modern workplace standards speaks for itself."

25

ANYTHING HE WANTS

THE CONVERSION OF BRIDGEWATER TO THE PARTNERSHIP DIDN'T JUST follow a pattern, earlier plied with Bob Prince and Greg Jensen, of staff borrowing in a way that kept them in the company's debt. Many also saw clearly that Dalio was cashing out of his firm.

Some of this surely reflected his age. In summer 2019 Dalio turned seventy, having spent the previous ten years in a near-constant fracas around his transition out of the firm and the systemization of The Principles. He seemed to find increasing pleasure in time away, when he could bask in the attention from being a bestselling, self-help hedge fund guru. Invitations rained in for speaking engagements worldwide—not all focused on finance, either. He spoke at the sprawling TechCrunch Disrupt conference in San Francisco about *technology*, of all topics, perhaps surprisingly given the continued fallibility of PriOS, and signed copies of his book for a long line of well-wishers afterward. In an interview with *TechCrunch*, he said, "I don't want more success. I don't want money." The author of the piece editorialized two paragraphs later, "As Ray Dalio looked me in the eyes recently and said those words, I believed in his sincerity."

For all that sincerity, in all of his talks and interviews Dalio didn't mention a bombshell change at Bridgewater. The Transparency Library, which held recordings of thousands of Bridgewater meetings and was the essence of the radical transparency that Dalio discussed so often, was on its last days.

Bridgewater had hired as a consultant a former deputy attorney general of the United States, Jamie Gorelick, and showed her the system. Keeping those records was a problem, she advised. It was on the opposite end of best legal practices to keep a trove of recordings that could be forcibly unearthed in a lawsuit. Gorelick ordered the firm to shut down the library—or at least cull it of any recordings that could possibly portray someone in a negative light (that is, a considerable chunk of them). Now only some, not almost all, tapes would be kept. Far fewer meetings would be taped. It would no longer be possible to listen in on the inner workings of the firm, or for underlings to be investigated for their stray words while Dalio and others were out of earshot.

In a way, it didn't even matter if the Transparency Library existed anymore because it was alive in the popular imagination. Neither Dalio nor Bridgewater would ever publicly offer up that there was any change in their recording practices. Dalio continued to talk about radical transparency. He could apparently accept giving up the practice, but would never give up the story.

DALIO'S TIME away extolling his Principles seemed a relief to Jensen, who could begin to see the light at the end of the tunnel of his long, lucrative servitude to Dalio. David McCormick, the co-CEO who had stuck around as so many around him had faltered, also relished a potential star-making turn. He leaned into it, calling himself "the Ray whisperer."

Against this backdrop, the evening of June 9, 2019, was shaping up to be the apex of McCormick's personal and professional life. The setting was the Belle Haven Club, a classically New England, highly exclusive members-only ground on the Greenwich, Connecticut, waterfront. An American flag flew radiantly in the summer sun atop the main building. Ringed by tiers of porches and spotless white balconies, the club would not have been out of place in *The Great Gatsby*. A glitterati of political and business figures were celebrating McCormick's marriage to the political and business figure Dina Powell. She was a catch, straight up. Not only did Powell boast the looks of a Connecticut power wife—perfectly straightened brunette hair, lean figure, and a seeming perma-glow that reflected her Egyptian heritage—but she also had professional heft of her own. She served in two White Houses (most recently as a confidante of Ivanka Trump) and was now a top executive at Goldman Sachs. This was to be the coronation of a power couple.

The day's setting wasn't the couple's choice, and neither was this their actual wedding. They had been hitched earlier, in a pair of ceremonies, including one held on a yacht on the Nile. Dalio, however, said he wanted to play a part. Thus a date was set for Belle Haven and invitations sent out to hundreds of guests: "Ray and Barbara Dalio invite you to celebrate the recent marriage of David and Dina."

It was shaping up as a swell evening. Cocktail hour was held outside, with sweeping views of the Long Island Sound. Guests entered the main ballroom to discover Harry Connick, Jr., hired to entertain; he regaled the well-heeled crowd with jazz standards on the piano.

After dinner, the speeches held to form: congratulations to the happy couple, what luck it was for them to find each other, and the like. Powell made a few light jokes about her career, including one about President Trump requiring maps and charts, rather than printed briefings, in the Oval Office. That got titters from the crowd. The stakes felt light and easy.

Dalio, standing up to speak, pulled out his iPhone and began reading from prepared notes. His delivery was stuttered and almost formal, but several guests saw it as sincere and moving. He described McCormick as one of his most trusted confidants, and a rising talent. Several in attendance said afterward it seemed to be shaping up as a toast one would give his or her son.

That was, until Dalio turned to address Powell. "David can be anything he wants—including president of the United States, and he found a person: the best party girl in America."

At this scratch-the-record moment, guests turned to one another, not sure if they had heard Dalio correctly, or if he had been joking (he was hardly known for humor). Did one of the world's richest men, and the host of this party, just call the new bride a loose woman at best—and imply at worst she was a hooker?

McCormick and Powell, both in their own ways cognizant of the power of perception, sat and forced blank faces. She was hurt and embarrassed, and he was enraged. Although it couldn't have been a surprise to hear such words from Dalio—McCormick had heard him say worse inside Bridgewater—being forced to allow Dalio to treat him like this in public was quite something else. McCormick later railed about Dalio's words to colleagues. *How could he do this to me?* McCormick would call it a turning point in his relationship with the elder man.

The Principles, taken at their word, would have forced McCormick to have it out with Dalio in the open, as Jensen had a few years earlier. Nothing was worse than talking about colleagues behind their back. But McCormick had learned from Jensen's mistake. McCormick made sure that

whenever he complained to others about Dalio about that evening, no re-
corders were running.

McCormick had good reason to be careful, as it turned out, because
by all indications he was soon to become the latest target of the Bridgewater founder's attention. Unbeknownst to all but a few at the firm, around
early 2019 co-CEO Eileen Murray told Dalio that it would be her last
year. She was exhausted, she told friends, particularly tired of being overruled by Dalio on whom to hire and fire, and she had more money than
she could ever have dreamed. This made McCormick the obvious pick
to be sole CEO—not bad for a man who less than a decade earlier had
been deputized by Dalio to investigate piss on the bathroom floor. It also,
however, came with risks. McCormick had noticed that Dalio demonstrated a pattern of finding reasons to humiliate those closest to him at
the hedge fund, and McCormick was well aware that the tide could turn
at any time.

(Not for nothing, in the wake of an expensive divorce that preceded his
marriage to Powell, McCormick also couldn't sniff at the $22 million per
year Bridgewater was paying him.)

Bridgewater was hardly in dire straits—thanks in part to Dalio's successful international fundraising, it still managed $160 billion in mid-2019,
close to its all-time high. Some outside impressions, however, were growing
grim. *Bloomberg Businessweek* ran an article about one client, the San Joaquin County pension fund, in Northern California, that pretty much said
it all in the headline: "Ray Dalio's Hedge Fund Dumped by Tiny County
Fed Up by Fees Sapping Return." The numbers were stark. The pension was
paying Bridgewater an annual fixed fee of 3.39 percent, but receiving only
an average return of 3.1 percent. Bridgewater was keeping more money
than it made for the fund. San Joaquin was hardly alone in its frustration.
UOB Private Bank, a Southeast Asian lender and the type of low-profile
but lucrative Bridgewater client that the firm had once thrived with, also
recommended clients pull money, describing Bridgewater, among its investments, as "the one that has not really done well of us."

In investing, the problem included an old one for Bridgewater: Dalio's
dark economic outlook. The Bridgewater founder predicted a 40 percent
chance of a recession before the 2020 election, but the markets kept rising.
Pure Alpha was down 6 percent in August 2019.

With longtime clients fleeing, McCormick's solution was to find new money—and to do anything to avoid pissing off the investors who remained. When a group of LGBTQ Bridgewater employees asked for permission to fly the pride flag on campus, McCormick argued against it, saying that it could offend clients in the Middle East, including Qatar and Bahrain, and elsewhere. He pushed for continued business with China. He was even more forceful in arguing for close ties with Saudi Arabia, where one of Bridgewater's bigger and more lucrative clients was Saudi Aramco, the colossal state-run oil company owned by the country's royal family. No shortage of people at Bridgewater felt that the relationship was risky and even unethical; Saudi Aramco was de facto controlled by Crown Prince Mohammed bin Salman, infamous for his reported orchestration of the murder of journalist Jamal Khashoggi among other human rights abuses. But the promise of another dollar weighed out. McCormick had visited the country with Powell while she worked at the White House, and he argued at Bridgewater that by the firm's staying quiet on the country's human rights record, Saudi money would continue to roll in.

Concurrently, McCormick and Bridgewater went down-market. For years, Bridgewater had boasted a $100 million investment minimum; now it took checks as small as €250,000 through an intermediary. Bridgewater welcomed not just any middleman but perhaps the saltiest one, SkyBridge Capital, the firm cofounded by the former Trump administration official Anthony Scaramucci, who advertised his firm by saying, "Every dentist in America can have a twenty-five-thousand-dollar to fifty-thousand-dollar hedge fund portfolio."

One thing was certain: this was not the Bridgewater of yore.

JUST A few years earlier, Dalio would have been all over such a wholesale shift in the firm. Now, he seemed to barely notice. As he often said, he'd all but conquered the subject of investing years ago—heck, he'd literally now written a book on the topic and was at work on two more. As the months passed, he seemed more focused on his external celebrity instead of Bridgewater.

Though billionaire hedge fund managers often donated to political candidates or even became one themselves, Dalio had long cast himself as having more altruistic pursuits. His public pronouncements suggested he saw himself as a philanthropist-philosopher king—or perhaps just an influencer. He and Barbara Dalio appeared with Connecticut's governor at a heavily attended press conference to announce that he would be donating $100 million to the state's high schools, calling it "the Partnership for Connecticut."

He also ramped up his tweeting, almost incessantly, energetically interacting with strangers who had embraced *Principles*. He announced ever more principles, such as these three in fall 2019:

> What creates and sustains truly great relationships (like great marriages and great partnerships) is the unwavering belief that nothing is more important than the relationship.
>
> If you need to assess the value of your relationship, think hard about whether your most important values and principles are aligned, putting the really important ones ahead of the not so important ones.
>
> The key to all good relationships is to a) be in sync about how you should be with each other, especially how you should disagree and get past your disagreements, and b) give far more than you demand with those who will do the same with you.

Dalio, who had spent decades cultivating a high-profile public image, was clearly reaping the rewards of his efforts. He tweeted that Sean "Diddy" Combs had asked him to mentor him, "to help him take his success to the next level." The tweet included a fifty-four-second video of the two men speaking.

Dalio also appeared on Gwyneth Paltrow's *goop* podcast, where she observed airily, "There's a spiritual aspect to everything Ray does."

To Paltrow, Dalio delivered his stump speech of how Bridgewater used a careful system of believability-weighted decision-making to ensure that fairness ruled above all. "I don't think there's been a case where I've outvoted, [where] I've used my power to overcome a believability-weighted decision."

"Never?" Paltrow responded.

"Never."

Later in the interview, Paltrow suggested Dalio should run for president.

Behind closed doors at Bridgewater, Dalio bragged about the business titans who were interested in using The Principles at their own companies. He said that Bill Gates and Elon Musk, among others, had taken Principles-based personality tests and found them useful. Jack Dorsey, the guru-like cofounder of Twitter, was another enthusiastic adopter, to hear Dalio tell it. Dorsey, according to Dalio, had even invited him to the tech executive's mountain estate for a private tutorial on The Principles. Dorsey's hang-loose vibe apparently was contagious because in September 2019 Dalio showed up at Burning Man, the celebrity hot-spot desert festival best known for psychedelics and all-night ragers.

Dalio got in his photo op. He tweeted a photo of himself from Burning Man, clad in tie-dye bell-bottom pants and a multicolored jacket with a cerulean-blue feather trim that made it look as if he were lost on the way to a midnight showing of *The Rocky Horror Picture Show.* How long he stayed in the desert is unclear (in the Twitter photo, his clothing is immaculate, while the man next to him is covered in sand), but he gave the impression of being a true Burner. "What a great vibe and what amazing creativity!" he wrote on Twitter. "If you go next year, 1–5am is best."

The tweet received thousands of likes and elicited responses such as "Ray Dalio is really out there living his best life." Wrote another, "Burning Man is officially dead."

YET AS Dalio crossed the world glorifying the value of using The Principles in day-to-day life, the software based on them continued to be a wreck.

This was the plain reality of what Dalio had built. Bridgewater, judged by the sheer sum of the money it managed, was a financial juggernaut, and much of that had to be credited to its founder. He was good at *talking* about The Principles and the Bridgewater culture of radical transparency to anyone who would listen, but seemed either unable or unwilling to recognize that his manifesto was crumbling by the day. To do so would have been admitting a mistake—something he claimed to be quite good at but, as many who worked for him had learned, seemed to loathe in practice. And this might have felt like the biggest mistake of all because admitting such would have forced him to tell the world that even the people who worked for him didn't want to use The Principles.

This was underscored when, cognizant of how much he had spent on developing the iPad apps and the like—all based on his creation—Dalio asked the company to pay an annual $8 million license fee for use of such tools as the Dot Collector, the coach, and the pain button. Others at the company, bewildered at being asked to spend company money to pay its founder for products that he was ordering them to use, found a way to turn down the ask.*

Thus grew the chasm, wider by the day, between what Dalio told the world about life at Bridgewater and what was actually going on.

For David Ferrucci, after many years and many millions of dollars in pay, by late 2019 enough was enough. He seemed reticent to make a big deal about leaving—that might call attention to how little he'd accomplished. Instead, in a deal with Dalio, he arranged to quit his work at the hedge fund, but to keep offices on the Bridgewater campus, where he gave interviews about his latest computer-science research. None of them had anything to do with Dalio, Bridgewater, or The Principles. Neither Bridgewater nor he addressed his departure or acknowledged it publicly.

Paul McDowell, the other man who had devoted a decade of his life to applying computer science to the Principles, also finally accepted that his work had been for naught. Yet he was tortured over whether to leave. Bridgewater had been McDowell's big break, and he was likely facing the end of his career if he left. Whether it was his optimistic Canadian disposition, a pure hope in the potential of The Principles, or simply a need to keep earning a salary, McDowell stayed on through 2019. He had been at the hedge fund for eleven years. He had begun with the belief that Bridgewater held the key to science-based self-improvement and ended with the realization he was undeniably more beaten-down now than when he'd entered. He left for a job at a Bridgewater consultancy—a similar role to the one he'd had before he started at the world's biggest hedge fund, essentially coming full circle. After McDowell left, his six-week Principles boot camp, which he had led for the better part of a decade, was defenestrated. In its place, newcomers were given just a few days of rote corporate onboarding. No one would stand in front of them and extoll the value of Bridgewater as a truth factory.

As McDowell left Bridgewater's campus on his final day, he didn't feel sad. He felt like a failure.

---

* A lawyer for Dalio said, "It is false to say that Bridgewater did not want to continue its unique culture."

26

NO HEROES

Snow and a blizzard warning were all over the news on December 17, 2020, when Devon Dalio took his 2016 Audi for an afternoon drive on a usually busy Greenwich shopping street. The eldest of Ray and Barbara's four children and a father himself, Devon had spent most of his career in Ray's employ, including at Bridgewater. Devon had recently struck out on his own to start a small investment company with backing from his dad.

Just before 4:00 P.M. local time, Devon's car skidded across a strip dividing his lane from oncoming traffic and crashed at high speed into a shopping center. When police arrived, thick black smoke was pumping out of a charred store.

Devon Dalio, forty-two years old, died at the scene.

Ray Dalio's email inbox filled with well-wishes, even from some who had departed acrimoniously from his firm. The grieving father wrote on Twitter the day after his son's death, "My family and I wish we could personally thank each and every one of you." He added in another tweet, "Please excuse me for not further exchanging thoughts with you at this time as I need the time for quiet reflection with my family."

Thirteen days later, Dalio announced to the world that in the wake of his son's death, he had reexamined one of his original Principles: Pain + Reflection = Progress. "This experience reminded me of the relative importance of things," he wrote on LinkedIn. "So while it was painful, I learn and am learning a lot. It helped me help others a lot and it's becoming much less painful and much more productive."

He added, "I won't talk any more about this."

Six weeks later, Dalio did just that. In a follow-up LinkedIn post about his son, he said that further reflection had made him realize that The Principles were especially helpful in grieving.

THE ATTENTION paid to his tragic loss underscored the pulpit that Dalio had ascended. The only child who had spent years at another family's Thanksgiving was now an icon to millions who saw themselves in him. Building on the popularity of his autobiography, he had become one of the most popular businesspeople on Twitter and grown his audience on LinkedIn to around 2.5 million people. For a man who for so many years claimed not to seek any spotlight, it was a staggering audience.

The public Ray Dalio exhibited a pair of qualities that may not have seemed complementary, but often worked in tandem. He was a big-hearted billionaire eager to help others improve their lives by following his principles. He was also evidently in need of reaffirmations himself because, to the masses, he portrayed himself as someone constantly under attack.

This alternative reality was neatly illustrated in early 2020 when *The Wall Street Journal* wrote a piece noting that despite constantly dangling the prospect of his handing off control of Bridgewater, Dalio always seemed to stick around. "Ray Dalio had a ten-year succession plan for Bridgewater Associates LP, the hedge fund he built. It's year ten. He's still in charge," the piece said. The piece reported that Eileen Murray, the former co-CEO, was in conflict with the firm about the terms of her exit. Neither fact was particularly remarkable, or even new. Dalio himself had given scores of interviews over the past decade about the timeline for his exit, and there were stretches when it felt as if there was scarcely an executive who *had* left Bridgewater without some drama. Dalio himself often said the revolving door indicated that his management system was sifting out the chaff.

The article observed that while Dalio spent his time jostling with management, Bridgewater's investing continued its rut. Though the firm often said it shouldn't be compared strictly to the stock market, adding bonds—considered a diversifier—hardly made the hedge fund look any better. For seven of the prior eleven years, investors would have been better off investing in a standard, general 60 percent / 40 percent split of stocks and bonds than in Bridgewater's vaunted flagship fund.

What Dalio had once called his Holy Grail seemed to be running dry.

Two days after the piece was published, Dalio threw a public fit in a LinkedIn post titled "*The Wall Street Journal's* Fake and Distorted News." He claimed the article was "loaded with factual errors"—though the *Journal* reviewed his complaints and found no such mistakes—and was an example of "why our country has no heroes."

Dalio didn't stop there; he dove into the hundreds of comments from strangers on LinkedIn on his piece and replied to some individually. One commenter, taking the side of the journalists, wrote to Dalio that his rebuttal was "suspiciously lacking in facts," saying it resorted to "character assassination" and was reminiscent of "the standard tactics employed by another very powerful person," an obvious reference to then-president Trump. Dalio responded, "I didn't want to get into the various point by point facts without a judge to weigh them." To another commenter, he wrote, "Operating in a principled way is very important to me. When I see pervasive bad behavior that threatens our society, it is difficult for me to remain silent about it."

He wrote to another commenter, "I have a thick skin. It's not me that I'm worried about. It's the system I'm worried about."

Dalio raged further behind the scenes, calling up the *Journal's* editor in chief to complain in particular that he and Murray had no major disagreements and beseeching unsuccessfully for the paper to correct that point.

Six months later, Murray filed a $100 million discrimination suit against Bridgewater, naming Dalio all over it and accusing the firm of "publicly avowing transparency when it suits its interest, but seeking to harshly punish those who publicly report facts which Bridgewater perceives to be damaging to its image." Her suit stated, "The hypocrisy is astonishing."

The suit accused Bridgewater of paying her less than her male colleagues and was eventually settled out of court.

WHEN REPORTS began to circulate of a novel Asian virus, Dalio should have been in a position to get ahead of the news. For decades he had cultivated relationships with, and investments from, China's government arms that practically no one else could rival, and he had often boasted of his unique ability to understand the nation and its culture. If any Wall Street type had the ability to divine some degree of truth about the virus, it was Dalio.

But amid the biggest market-making news coming out of China in years, Dalio now professed to have no insight whatsoever. "I, and we at Bridgewater, don't have a clue as to what extent this virus or 'pandemic' will spread, we don't know where it will spread to, and we don't know its economic or market impact," he wrote on LinkedIn in January. Two weeks later, he flew to Abu Dhabi, where Bridgewater managed billions of dollars for state-affiliated entities, and said the impact of the coronavirus seemed exaggerated. "It most likely will be something that in another year or two will be well beyond what everyone will be talking about," he said at a conference there.

For a man who'd made his name on a seemingly endless stretch of doomsday calls, this was a particularly unfortunate moment to turn sanguine. The coronavirus spread, and markets reacted poorly. By mid-March, 2020, Bridgewater was in a flat-out free fall. Pure Alpha was down between 14 and 21 percent in less than three months, according to estimates the firm provided to worried investors. All-Weather, which purported to make money in all market environments, had lost an estimated 12 percent. The true figures might have been even worse, as Bridgewater signaled in a letter to investors in which Dalio said, "Don't hold us to exactly these numbers because there's nothing exact about them in this volatile environment."

In the letter, Dalio took close to no responsibility for the fund's losses. "What do I think about this performance? While it's not what I would want, it's consistent with what I would have expected under the circumstances." He said his funds kept betting on rising markets, despite the risks of coronavirus, because Bridgewater had "normal risk controls." He wrote, "In this case, the risk control process worked as designed."

The explanation apparently felt hollow to many investors because Bridgewater's well-heeled clientele—having just witnessed the world's largest hedge fund strike out on the biggest moment in markets since the 2008 financial crisis—began pulling their money anew.

As viral cases grew and the world began to shut down, so did Bridgewater. Most staff were sent home. Thus the pandemic did something that years of rotating executives, internal trials, public hangings, and secret settlements hadn't accomplished: it got Dalio physically out of Bridgewater for the long term. He disappeared from campus, where a skeleton crew of around fifty employees lugged monitors and other equipment into the woods, under a haphazard tent that now counted as the firm's headquarters.

Though all at the firm quickly learned that Dalio was not physically at headquarters, there were only rumors about where exactly he had gone. According to one former employee, the billionaire was said to be spending time on his yacht, staying as far as he could from the pandemic. Others assumed he was ensconced at his Greenwich estate, a not-unreasonable precaution for a septuagenarian during a pandemic. In one indication he was home at least some of the time, Bridgewater staff were sent to construct a professional-grade video studio in Dalio's home, from which he could beam into the hedge fund's proceedings at a moment's notice. It was also used by Dalio to continue to give television interviews extolling the value of The Principles during such a difficult time.

As he watched Bridgewater from the end of a camera, much as thousands of his employees had viewed years of case studies, what was even left for him to see? By now, The Principles were more of a fantasy or, perhaps more kindly, a collection of fables, than the literal prescriptions that Dalio had presented them as for so many years. Though they had never had as much direct impact on the firm's investing as he claimed publicly, they were rapidly cast aside elsewhere across the firm, too.

The dots, for more than a decade the mainstay of Bridgewater's employee ratings system, became nigh unrecognizable. The company in 2020 introduced a broad new category called confidential dots, which would not be visible to others at the firm. Thus it was now possible to give feedback, critical or otherwise, and not have everyone else know about it and pile on. (These new confidential dots could also be removed by the company at will.) The move was said, internally, to be for legal and public relations reasons—it was too risky, Bridgewater decided, to chance the media or regulators noticing that some executive had been dotted down for lacking "common sense," for instance. Whatever the reason, the outcome was clear: the dots were dying.

As the world gelled into working from home, Dalio pressed on in his go-go publicity efforts for The Principles, but whether he noticed or not, the three years since his book's release had not been kind to the conceit of benevolent businessmen full of answers on how to save the world. Famous technology CEOs, including Jeff Bezos and Mark Zuckerberg, were being hauled in front of Congress to testify on the harm of their platforms. The "work hard, play hard" mentality that Bridgewater had embodied with its long hours and boozy corporate retreats was seen as a relic of an earlier, unkind era. President Trump, who delighted in alternative fact–fueled tussles with the media, was on his way to losing reelection.

The months passed, the pandemic stretched on, and the evaporation of the management systems that had governed life at Bridgewater for more than a decade accelerated. Few if any employees used with any regularity the computerized ratings tools known as PriOS. The trials and the public hangings that had been a hallmark of Bridgewater life for decades ground to a halt. Even the weekly Bridgewater What's Going On in the World meetings, where Dalio had so often embarrassed junior employees who piped in with independent thoughts, turned out to be something less than must-see TV when viewed through a laptop screen. Instead of sitting at a table as he long had, like a priest at the altar with rows upon rows of staff in front of him, now Dalio was just a disembodied head in a square in the top right corner of the Zoom conference, like the least funny celebrity guest in a supersize episode of *Hollywood Squares*. The effect was flattening and egalitarian— the type of approach Dalio had for so long claimed to practice and was now forced to abide by. It proved tough to be a bully when anyone could put him on mute.

The pandemic did not change Dalio's storyline that The Principles were whirring in the background of Bridgewater at all times—and to encourage others to adopt them.

He refocused on a last-ditch effort to integrate his prized Dot Collector into Zoom, the video-chat tool that Bridgewater and others were now using. This should have been a natural fit; employees at many companies were already used to interacting with colleagues through a video screen, so rating each other through the same screen was only a modest adjustment. Coinbase, the cryptocurrency brokerage that allowed all employees to work remotely, gave the Dot Collector a trial with a fraction of its staff, mostly in human resources and information technology. The response from Coinbase staffers was immediate, and poor. Employees put together a petition blasting the use of the Dot Collector, saying it "led to a toxic workplace culture." The company CEO defended the trial, which later expired, not by standing up for its merits, but by saying that so few at the firm had chosen to use the Dot Collector that the complaints were moot.

Equally unsuccessful was the culmination of Dalio's yearslong goal to imbue the sprawling Bridgewater ratings system into businesses large and small, as he'd been talking about for years. Called PrinciplesUS, these were originally envisioned as monthlong workshops to train employees in The Principles, with an elaborate certification process to advance employees up the ladder to become official "Principals coaches" in their own right.

From home, Dalio told staff he spun his Rolodex for help finding takers, but came up empty. Twitter's Jack Dorsey, whose estate Dalio had once visited, was on his way out of his own company, as was Microsoft's Bill Gates. Salesforce cofounder Marc Benioff turned Dalio down, too. No major company publicly signed up to adopt The Principles.

So Dalio, embarrassed in the public eye and isolated in private by the pandemic, began again to change the narrative around himself. He took up what appeared to be a renewed concern with the gap between the rich and the poor. He ramped up his tweeting, sending one unanswered message to Elon Musk ("Right on, Elon! . . ."). He even tweeted about the death of a Supreme Court justice, though as usual he managed to all but cast himself as a martyr: "I think most of us are in the rare moment of being able to agree that Ruth Bader Ginsburg was a hero, which is a really big deal because we now live in a society in which there are no agreed upon heroes. That is because most people who stand out are torn down because people who are on the other side want to discredit them."

Most often he spoke out, as the great statesman he had built himself into, on the grave dangers facing the economy, to seemingly anyone who asked.

Not long after his pandemic whiff, he returned to his decades-long practice of predicting that disaster was just around the corner. In a December 2020 appearance on CNN, he told the interviewer that he had studied the last five hundred years of history and not only was revolution potentially nigh, but the nation could no longer take peace and harmony for granted. He suggested on nearly every medium—television, podcasts, LinkedIn, and even during an interview with former treasury secretary Hank Paulson—that America risked a "civil war." He kicked it up another few notches in an interview with *New York Times* columnist Thomas Friedman, saying with a shrug, "History has shown civil wars and revolutions have a purpose," allowing old world orders to be supplanted by new, reformed ones.

What Dalio spoke of relatively rarely during these early days of the pandemic, March to November 2020, was Bridgewater. That was perhaps because he wasn't just physically separated from the firm, but a reflection of his dwindling cohort of loyalists. Murray was gone. McCormick, still smarting from Dalio's offensive wedding toast, was looking for an exit. Jensen, after his trial, had never fully trusted Dalio and was by all accounts reveling in Dalio's absence. Bob Prince, the one to have never left Dalio's service, was busying himself during the pandemic with his church. The Bridgewater family was dispersed.

Even if Dalio had been physically present at Bridgewater, the armies he'd commanded there were dissipated. The Principles Captains, Politburo, and the like were of no use in the woods; many had been laid off or left of their own accord. There were no more mandatory lessons in The Principles, no tests to be taken, and no vilification of those who scored poorly. Even many of the old case studies—the films of trials that Bridgewater had taped for years, so that its founder's lessons would never be forgotten—had vanished from the Transparency Library, thanks to the legal advice that they be excised as quickly as possible.

Perhaps most jarringly, though he would never so much as hint at it publicly, even Dalio's own appetite to use at least one of the ratings tools he had devoted so much of his energy toward had seemed to wane. His first major Principles-based invention, the Dot Collector—which he had earlier threatened to fire people for not using—fell out of use. One Bridgewater staffer pulled the internal data in late 2020 and discovered that even Dalio had not dotted anyone since that May.

It was arguably a win for the dregs of radical transparency that this fact could still be discovered by anyone who bothered to look.

PEOPLE WHO spoke to Dalio during this period say he seemed unsure what to do next. If Bridgewater had begun to put The Principles in the rearview mirror, Dalio either could not or would not. He told associates he wanted to perform a diagnosis of his legacy by assembling a crew to film and release a documentary that would show the real story of himself, Bridgewater, and The Principles.

It wouldn't be simply a monologue, Dalio said. He told some close associates that he wanted testimonials from those at Bridgewater who could tell the world what he was really like. He suggested the major question he wanted answered:

"Have I helped you or hurt you?"

He added:

"Don't be afraid to tell me the truth."

EPILOGUE

RAY DALIO EXITED THE PANDEMIC MUCH AS HE ENTERED IT, BRIM-ming with visible enthusiasm to share his Principles and giving all indication that the world clamored for them. He would betray nary a public nod that many inside his hedge fund felt differently.

This wasn't so much a bug in his approach as a feature of it, and a core reason why he and Bridgewater were able to maintain public reputations as perhaps the world's leading practitioners of radical transparency, meaningful lives, and meaningful relationships. The Principles, as written and promoted, allowed just enough wiggle room for airing contrary viewpoints that any public leak of harrowing goings-on at Bridgewater could be credibly taken as a sign that the firm's approach was working as intended. Indeed, there was scarcely any tumult inside the hedge fund—including Comey's exit, Jensen's unraveling, employee trials, and departure after departure after departure—that Bridgewater and its representatives did not explain away as the firm's management style being executed exactly as planned. As Dalio so often said, pain plus reflection equaled progress.

The money didn't hurt. Though Bridgewater's assets under management slowly contracted, from a peak of around $160 billion to $130 billion in the post-pandemic period, Bridgewater was so impressively larger than any other rival—and so willing to collect money from virtually any corner of the earth—that it could shrink and still credibly be described as the globe's largest hedge fund. And if the firm's main hedge fund had for years fallen behind the pace of global markets, it still mostly avoided negative results, and so could fairly say it was making clients money on an absolute basis. It was a credit to Dalio and Bridgewater that the hedge fund lasted so long—and thanks to that long track record, its average historical performance would remain mostly sterling, even if many of the fund's best years came well before Dalio grew famous. No wonder that, in continued internal negotiations about his retirement from the fund, he began calling the company his "property rights."

Dalio's triumph was neatly exemplified at year-end 2020, when researcher LCH Investments ran the numbers and determined the firm had made more money for investors, since inception, than any other fund, a staggering $46.5 billion. Though LCH made clear that it was comparing the firm's total, historical trading gains with smaller competitors with fewer years to count, essentially giving Bridgewater a running start on the others, that nuance didn't travel far. *Business Insider* took the opportunity to call Bridgewater "the best-performing hedge fund manager of all time."

A stream of job seekers continued to apply, eager to test themselves against the now world-famous Principles. In Bridgewater's own words, nearly anyone was eligible. After the hedge fund announced that it had hired a champion poker player to work in an unspecified role, Bridgewater's head of investment analytics crowed to *The New York Times:* "We hire botanists, we hire political science people, we hire Rhodes scholars, we hire athletes . . . we're looking for people who are really, truly different."

Those who knew of the more complicated reality of life under Dalio went to great lengths to avoid discussing it. Many left with nondisclosure agreements, standard on Wall Street, while others—some in exchange for additional payouts—agreed to more unusual and stringent non-disparagement clauses that barred them from making even anodyne, vaguely negative remarks about their time at the hedge fund. Even those with the means to fight back—and ample knowledge of Bridgewater's nature—told staid stories publicly. "It's kind of a family atmosphere," Eileen Murray told a ballroom of hedge fund executives shortly before her acrimonious departure. She dismissed Bridgewater burnouts as "people that are uncomfortable facing their weaknesses."

Even after the publication of his autobiography, Dalio continued to fine-tune his image, particularly his origin story. In a 2021 oral history that the hedge fund and its founder participated in for *Leaders* magazine, the Bridgewater founder sounded downright *cool.* An executive who met him decades earlier was quoted describing the experience thusly: "Ray was propped up in a chair with one leg encased in plaster, toe to hip. It was hot, and he looked as if he hadn't washed for a couple of days. I immediately concluded that he'd slipped on one of the toys and busted his leg. I later learned it was from a parachuting accident."

Dalio said that one of the best lessons he had learned over his career was humility, because "the entire culture . . . was built around getting to the best answers . . . not ego, not seniority or hierarchy [or] office politics."

His final words were: "It is a joy for all of us."

THE LEIBS of Park Avenue are mostly no more. The family that did so much to help the young Ray Dalio found out the hard way that intergenerational wealth can be fleeting. Their three sons frittered away the family fortune in the usual ways: divorces, the racetrack, poor investments. The eldest Leib grandson, Gordon, who had traveled to Europe with Ray, died in a freak car accident. The Viking and Missy passed away not long after their grandson. Shortly after, the duplex apartment at 740 Park Avenue was sold and much of the rare furniture was put up for auction at Sotheby's.

One of the Leib grandchildren stayed in finance, and out of trouble. Barclay Thorndike Leib, four years younger than Gordon, had none of his older brother's foibles. Barclay traded on Wall Street and worked for a series of hedge fund firms until, deep into his career, his luck ran out and his employer was suddenly taken over. The job market for a fifty-eight-year-old investment analyst proved thin.

His mind flickered to Ray Dalio. The two sat at the same table for Thanksgiving and Christmas for years and had remained professionally friendly, given the industry they shared. Leib had even heard that Dalio still played backgammon, the game he'd learned from the Leib family. Leib clicked over to the Bridgewater website and found a fairly anodyne job for which he was suitably qualified. He typed out an email and sent it to Ray, asking for his good word and a chance at an in-person interview.

The response came back quickly.

If you are qualified for the job, then your résumé should stand on its own. I would not undermine the process of my HR department for anyone.

I would not even offer such favoritism to my own dog if my dog were applying.

Ray

In the years after leaving Bridgewater, Joe Sweet, who had once been in treatment for fantasizing about hanging himself off the office balcony, underwent a remarkable renaissance. He weaned off psychiatric medications entirely. He moved out of Connecticut and credited the distance from Bridgewater for helping make him a new man.

Sweet continued to be bothered by the public's rapture over Dalio's rating tools. Whenever he heard Dalio give an interview about the wonders of The Principles, Sweet shuddered. He was living counterevidence to the idea that Bridgewater's tools somehow sorted individuals into their highest possible use, given that he now had a senior job in procurement—the same field that Bridgewater's Principles software had determined he was ill-suited for. He had ten employees working for him and earned a higher salary than he had at the world's largest hedge fund.

Though Sweet no longer suffered from clinical depression, what he learned about his old colleagues at Bridgewater left him feeling down. Now that he was on a better footing with a solid job, former colleagues from the ratings team sometimes reached out to him. To Sweet, they seemed emotionally hollowed out in a way that he recognized from his own experience. He had little advice to offer, besides to forget everything they had been told. It seemed to him that most everyone who bought into Bridgewater's philosophies ended up worse off except for Dalio himself.

"When is the vicious cycle going to end?" Sweet said. "When will they stop bringing in people and ruining their lives? When will Ray's wealth just disappear?"

DALIO'S WEALTH did the opposite of disappear: it grew. Thanks to his share of the firm's fees, he made around $500 million personally in 2020, and even more in 2021. Tabloids reported that he filed plans to build a new outdoor terrace, complete with a giant steel pergola, at his Manhattan penthouse.

What continued to dim were The Principles. Dalio published second and third books, *Principles for Navigating Big Debt Crises* and *Principles for Dealing with the Changing World Order,* which didn't make nearly the splash of his first (in fairness, much of their material had been posted for free online years earlier). There were few appearances on broadcast television, no new TED Talks, and his latest interview with his friend Charlie Rose was online only because Rose had been booted from CBS over a sexual harassment scandal.

In April 2021, with the paid help of Wharton's Adam Grant in designing and promoting it, Dalio launched PrinciplesYou, his long-gestating effort to bring his life's work to the masses. Essentially a Principles-infused personality test, it was available free online, like The Principles through a fun-house mirror. The initial announcement was dramatic; one of the researchers Dalio had paid to develop the product was quoted saying, "It is based on the latest research in personality science" and "A distinctive strength is its ability to predict an extraordinary array of actual behaviors observed by the Bridgewater staff over many years."

PrinciplesYou would be followed by the release of "the meaningful relationships collection," a $79 set of custom-printed card games that—you guessed it—"stimulate meaningful relationships," as Dalio put it in a promotional video. Dalio said the games were worth $34 apiece, but would be available for the sale price of $79 per set. He gave out a coupon code ("Ray") that brought the price of the first thousand sets down further to $15. "I want to know that you have some skin in the deal rather than just grabbing free stuff," he wrote in a LinkedIn post.

In late 2021, in a move not publicly disclosed, Bridgewater laid off most of the remaining staff dedicated to building the Principles software. It was $100 million, at least, down the drain, counting the costs of developing the software over more than a decade, according to people who worked on it.

The documentary that Dalio discussed making about himself and Bridgewater has not been released.

EILEEN MURRAY was hardly upset to see The Principles' luster fade. She made a point of emphasizing to friends and family she had never even read the copy of *Principles* that Dalio gifted her. She left it unopened on a shelf.

Her lawsuit against Bridgewater left mixed feelings among Bridgewater émigrés. Some saw her as an opportunist who would play any side in any scenario—willing to participate in the ugly parts of Bridgewater's culture when it suited her, then to disavow it without accepting any culpability. Others saw her as the closest to an independent thinker of anyone who had ever left the executive ranks, pointing out that Jim Comey and others continued to proselytize for Dalio and The Principles years after the end of their employment.

One person who continued to look up to Murray was Paul McDowell. His life since leaving Bridgewater had been a hodgepodge of emotions, many of them negative. His consulting gig fizzled out. With time to spare, he spent weeks thinking back on his time in Westport. When he wasn't torturing himself over whether he could have done more to fight for himself, he kept flashing back to an old Monty Python sketch, in which an aging, crucified Roman prisoner is so pleased with his captors that he urges guards to "nail some sense" into a new arrival to the jail. McDowell no longer found the bit particularly funny.

McDowell's ruminations over Bridgewater bothered his wife, who took to calling them a "Ray-diation" sickness that needed time to heal. A volunteer helper for local battered women, McDowell's wife told her husband that he reminded her of many of those she worked with, unable to feel completely safe even when their tormentor was long removed.

McDowell and his wife decided to sell their Connecticut home and return permanently to Canada, officially closing the chapter of his life that had begun nearly fifteen years earlier with him kneeling in a Toronto snowbank, keeled over in disbelief at his good fortune to be hired at the world's biggest hedge fund.

Before he left Connecticut, McDowell attended the fall 2021 funeral of Eileen Murray's mother. The pandemic having kept many apart for the preceding eighteen months, the funeral was a reunion of sorts for current and former Bridgewater staff. McDowell stood mostly in the periphery during the service, watching Murray accept condolences from hundreds of well-wishers. Finally she meandered to the edges where he stood. McDowell felt a rush of uncontrollable emotions, brought on by the proximity of a woman whose public rebuke of Dalio was everything that McDowell wished he could ever say. As Murray walked toward him, beads of sweat appeared on his collar, his throat went dry, and his pulse quickened in a way it hadn't since his days at the firm.

Murray made her rounds among the former Bridgewater folks, accepting condolences. As she paused in front of one former employee who had struggled since his departure, she seemed to know exactly what he was feeling.

Touching his shoulder and tilting her head toward his ear, she whispered, "We both worked for an abusive father."

A moment later, she began to move on to the next mourner, saying, "Take care of yourself."

———————

KATINA STEFANOVA, who once considered Murray a close mentor, wasn't there. That wasn't for lack of gratitude—she never lost her fond feelings for the older woman, whom she credited with providing her cover as she crouched in the bathroom so many years earlier, hiding as Dalio sang his bawdy sailor's song. Stefanova, however, did everything she could to avoid large gatherings of Brightwater folks, many of whom still remembered her unflatteringly as the Ice Queen.

Another reason for Stefanova to keep a low profile was that her career wasn't exactly going gangbusters. The hedge fund she'd started after leaving Bridgewater, Marto, was in tatters. She had pitched her fund to investors as essentially Bridgewater 2.0, but the fund was also similar to the original insofar as Bridgewater had struggled in recent years to make any real money, muddling around flat. Marto shrank from a respectable, if modest by hedge fund standards, $235 million under management in April 2019 to less than $20 million by that year's end. Most of Marto's staff quit or were laid off.

As the firm dwindled, Stefanova borrowed another quality she'd observed in Dalio: overstatement. In an interview with *Institutional Investor,* she bragged that a single, hyper-rich investor had agreed to stake Marto with more than $1 billion in cash. She wouldn't name the investor, but claimed that the money was already in the firm's accounts. When the magazine asked for further verification, she begged off: "I don't want to talk specifics. The best thing for us right now is to stay under the radar." She then sicced a libel lawyer on the magazine, sending cease-and-desist letters.

In the end, the investment never came through, and neither did a full explanation of the mysterious $1 billion. Stefanova claimed that attention from the article spooked away the investor.

Apparently undeterred, she told friends she still planned to become a billionaire, apparently through cryptocurrency, per a press release she put out announcing her own line of non-fungible tokens, or NFTs, which she compared to a "virtual reality gold mine." The announcement recast Stefanova as a longtime crypto aficionado who also happened to be CEO of Marto Capital. It quoted her saying, "Marto serves family offices and institutional investors with substantial assets."

The announcement made no mention of prior employment at Bridgewater.

DINA POWELL, the subject of Dalio's ribald wedding-celebration toast, helped find David McCormick a way out of Bridgewater. A longtime political operative, Powell encouraged her husband to run in the 2022 Republican primary for U.S. senator from Pennsylvania, where McCormick grew up.

Dalio complicated the run. Speaking to CNBC in late November 2021, he fielded what should have been a rote question about China. The country was in the headlines for human rights issues, and anchor Andrew Ross Sorkin asked Dalio how he weighed such controversies while investing there. It was the question of the hour, to a man who had for years promoted his intimate knowledge of the nation.

Dalio briefly looked off camera, then professed ignorance. "I can't be an expert on those types of things. . . . The guidance of the government is the most important thing."

He rambled a bit, disassociating through sentence fragments, before musing aloud, "Should I not invest in the United States because [of] other things and our own human rights issues?'"

"But, Ray," Sorkin responded, "look, there are things that happen in the United States . . . but I think that those things are different from some of the things we see happening in China. The government isn't disappearing people."

Dalio let out a nervous laugh, then said he likened China's approach simply to that of a strict parent.

Weak knees around superrich superpowers were nothing new for Dalio, Bridgewater, or McCormick, but the Bridgewater founder's interview landed like a stink bomb in the nascent McCormick campaign. The candidate was supposed to be wrapping himself in the America First banner.

Within days of Dalio's CNBC interview, Ms. Powell began shopping a new story to reporters. Two writers for Bloomberg, the financial newswire, took the bait. Under the headline "Bridgewater CEO Clashes with Dalio over China Before Senate Race," they reported that, on an unspecified company call held on an unspecified date, McCormick "told staff he's had lots of arguments about China over the years with Dalio and that he disagrees with the billionaire's views, according to people with knowledge of the matter." To many who knew McCormick, it strained credibility that he would ever have disagreed so forthrightly with Dalio on the topic, let alone more than once. McCormick resigned from Bridgewater a few weeks later.

In the months that followed, U.S. Senate candidate David McCormick, who once called himself the "Ray whisperer," barely said the words Bridgewater or Dalio. In campaign stops, he described himself as a "businessman" from an "investment firm." The most scrutiny he received for his time at Bridgewater was for the middling returns the hedge fund had produced for Pennsylvania's state school pension fund, which had paid Bridgewater more than $500 million, despite the hedge fund's investment performance falling short of targets. "We're stuck with a half-a-billion-dollar bill while he and his colleagues got half a billion in fees," thundered his opponent, television personality Dr. Oz.

Oz won the primary by a thin margin, then lost in the general election. McCormick was reported to be weighing another run in 2024.

In late 2022, a pair of major milestones passed that Dalio had been predicting for years. On October 4 of that year, Bridgewater announced that its founder had finally ceded control of the firm. The new CEO was Nir Bar Dea, the man who had grilled Bob Elliott's girlfriend on her sex life. The cost, which the firm never disclosed publicly: the equivalent of a $1 billion annual payout from Bridgewater to Dalio. It was a hell of an annuity for a man already a billionaire many times over. In a press release, the firm said Dalio would now be merely a mentor, board member, and "an important part of our community." The announcement triggered an avalanche of global news articles about the end of Dalio's career. Inside Bridgewater, there was widespread relief.

It took exactly one day for Dalio to walk back the announcement. "Lest there be any doubt, I'm not retiring," he tweeted. "I will play the markets till I die because it's the most engaging thing I've done since I was 12, and I will pass along what I have to offer through mentoring and philanthropy because that's the most meaningful thing I can do." He continued to give frequent media interviews.

That fall, the global economic collapse that Dalio had been promising since his post-college days arrived, as it did every ten years or so. In this case, a dangerously hot post-pandemic economy, as well as Russia's invasion of Ukraine, contributed to soaring inflation, sending stocks, bonds, and virtually every other financial asset cratering. U.S. stocks entered a bear market. Pure Alpha was up 18 percent through that October.

In a bit of poetic justice, it was Greg Jensen who reaped the credit as the man at Bridgewater to time the market move. Whether out of fealty to The Principles, true dedication to the hedge fund, or simply the stiffest tolerance for punishment of all the rotating cast of executives in and out of Bridgewater, Jensen had finally outlasted the mentor who'd turned on him. For that, he earned the reward of being the face of the investing operation at the world's biggest hedge fund as Pure Alpha soared. In a letter to investors crowing about its performance, Bridgewater said that it now had so much demand from investors wanting to put in money that it would soon, again, close Pure Alpha to new money. One big reason for the new turnaround, per the letter: a new investment committee that didn't directly involve Dalio.

Jensen appeared to have learned from Dalio how to describe the firm's investments without saying much of anything at all. In a late 2021 interview, Jensen said, "The algorithms are a combination of human intelligence and artificial intelligence. Every year, machines are more important in that process—I'd say it's fifty-fifty now, and in ten years from now we're talking about it and the human part is squeezed down to ten to twenty percent of the process." No concrete details were provided.

Jensen's turn in the spotlight was the unalloyed, solo praise he had been waiting on since starting at Bridgewater as an intern, and by all accounts he celebrated in style. His high school sweetheart wife had divorced him after learning of the settlement that Bridgewater paid to Samantha Holland, but Jensen kept the loyalty of their kids, telling them that the reports were a lie. He remained a top donor to his alma mater, Dartmouth.

For his troubles, Jensen remained a staggeringly wealthy man. When he remarried, to a high-powered lawyer, their wedding was held in Anguilla, where attendees flew in on the New York Jets' team plane and stayed in free rooms at the Four Seasons. He regularly flew via private jet to a compound he'd purchased on the Thimble Islands, an exclusive archipelago off the Connecticut coast.

Remarkably, Bob Prince also outlasted Dalio, sticking around as cochief investment officer alongside Jensen. The elder man had been one of Dalio's first major hires, becoming a billionaire. He evidenced no emotion about the history of the firm's sacred space. In 2021 and 2022, Prince kept busy helping oversee a new project: selling off the Bridgewater headquarters. Jensen agreed that it was time for new, more traditional office digs. They okayed the chopping down of the infamous totem pole, called the baton, that was said to tell Bridgewater's history, the one custom-designed under Dalio's eye. New hires would no longer be instructed to surround the monument and confess their weaknesses.

Not all traditions, however, could be broken. Under Jensen and Prince, the cochief investment officers, Bridgewater stayed pessimistic for the last months of 2022—and when global markets roared back in the later months of the year, Pure Alpha gave up many of its gains. It would finish the year up only 9.5 percent, and promptly lose 3 percent in the first quarter of the next year. The long streak of shaky investment performance was perhaps Dalio's most permanent Bridgewater legacy.

On an overcast evening in late May 2022, a visibly weary Ray and Barbara Dalio arrived at John F. Kennedy International Airport in New York.

Flying business class on an ordinary commercial jet counted as a low-key arrival, at least by the standards of a man still worth around $22 billion. But in recent months, he hadn't exuded the Dalio influence of yore.

The Dalios were arriving back in New York from Switzerland, where they had attended the World Economic Forum's annual meeting, a confab of the global elite. In previous years, Dalio had been a keynote speaker in front of a packed crowd; this time around, he pretaped a podcast with a low-level WEF staffer. During a television appearance from Davos on CNBC, he played his usual hits, predicting that the world was in a debt crisis that could not be fixed without breaking the back of the economy.

A fellow Davos attendee shared the Dalios' flight back from Switzerland. A longtime admirer of Bridgewater, reader of *Principles,* and a financier, the man was tickled to discover Dalio on the same plane. Upon arrival in New York, the attendee was even more impressed to see that, after nine hours of flight and now nearing midnight Zurich time, Ray and Barbara were standing alone at the airport baggage claim, without so much as a driver apparently on hand to assist. While the Dalios waited for their luggage to arrive, Ray fiddled with a nearby machine, trying to figure out how to rent a six-dollar luggage cart.

The attendee was mesmerized by the sight. So far as he could tell, none of the other weary travelers had noticed one of the world's richest men standing idly in their midst. Dalio seemed just another weary, floppy-haired seventy-two-year-old, huddled next to a petite, well-coiffed wife, waiting for the luggage carousel to spring to life. No one would have known the baggage that the man already carried: the loss of a son, the loss of his centrality in his business, and in the dimming glow of The Principles, the loss of an identity.

Dalio, too, had no way of knowing anyone was watching. No recording equipment or cameras followed him to capture that day's lesson, and no Bridgewater staffers stood by to take their cues.

When the baggage carousel finally started up, Dalio hauled a pair of enormous suitcases off the belt—groaning slightly under their weight— dumped them on the luggage cart, and headed for the curb.

The Davos attendee watched the scene in fascination. *Now that*, he thought, *is a humble man.*

AFTERWORD

Ray and I

FORGIVE ME, FOR WE ARE ABOUT TO DISCUSS CATS HAVING SEX.

In 2010, I was twenty-three years old and living in Manhattan's East Village on East Sixth Street, better known as Curry Row for its cluster of identical Indian restaurants. Each employed loud, competing salespeople to stand out front, hawking menus. The noise followed me upstairs; my three-bedroom walk-up apartment housed four people, including one couple, and at least that many opinions on who was underpaying for groceries. I spent a lot of time in my bedroom, where my bed touched three walls. The window faced a typically sketchy New York back alley with no obvious entrance, yet constant activity. At sundown each night a chorus of disturbing wails rang out, which for some months I incorrectly assumed to be another lonely Manhattanite or the inevitable gastrointestinal consequence of all that Indian food. I later learned the sounds were from felines in heat.

It's easy to forget now, but the era hardly felt like the start of boom times. Many of my friends, and their parents, were unemployed. The summer before I had interned at *The Wall Street Journal*, failed to get a job offer, and briefly moved back home to suburban Connecticut. I took the only journalism job I could get, rewriting press releases and the like. I spent an embarrassing amount of time at a nearby bar that sold a can of Schaefer beer with a shot of Ezra Brooks rye for $5.

Hoping to afford an apartment that abided by New York occupancy laws, I applied to at least fifty jobs that spring. In addition to the usual mix of journalism gigs, I also tried at banks, consultancies, law firms, at least one talent agency, and a hedge fund called Bridgewater Associates.

I wish I could remember why specifically I applied, but the Schaefer apparently took care of that memory. What I do know, according to my saved emails, is that in spring 2010 I applied for an entry-level role, "management associate." A Bridgewater recruiter assured me, "How you think, who you are, and what you value matter more to us than your specific skills and functional expertise." That was fortunate as I had few of the latter qualities to offer.

I booked two phone interviews, with one scheduled for 7:00 P.M., curtain time for the nightly cat chorale. I vaguely recall taking that one pacing in my tiny room, hoping the interviewer didn't mention the background meows. She didn't. I later sent a thank-you note memorializing what I described with considerable overstatement as "a pair of truly stimulating conversations."

I didn't get the job. Two years later, one of my interviewers added me as a connection on LinkedIn. I had to search my emails to remember her name.

By then I was working for *Absolute Return,* a trade magazine covering hedge funds, and I knew all about Bridgewater—or so I thought. Bridgewater wasn't just another fund, it was *the* fund—the world's largest, and perhaps its most secretive. The firm's founder, Ray Dalio, was known to be a bit of an odd duck. My publication, when I joined, was in a tussle with Dalio over an investigative cover story that quoted a Bridgewater former executive saying, "My fundamental belief is that Bridgewater is a cult. It's isolated, it has a charismatic leader, and it has its own dogma." The piece didn't break through to the mainstream.

Just before Christmas in 2012, I was pinged by a different Bridgewater recruiter. This time, they were asking me to interview for a position editing their economic research. By then I had learned that hedge funds offered a shot at life-changing wealth. It was worth taking a flier on. The process included a copyediting test, a Myers-Briggs personality test, a "workplace personality inventory," and visits to Bridgewater's headquarters, just a few minutes from where I grew up.

Several interviews later, I pulled myself out of the running. The job seemed to require an all-hours presence in Connecticut, with the promise of long bus rides to and from New York and the guarantee that my social life would take a hit. I notified the recruiter as such. "While this is unfortunate news for Bridgewater," she responded, "we understand your decision and truly appreciate the time you have spent in this process."

I could never have fathomed that the aforementioned events would later produce agitation for Ray Dalio.

My first conversation with Dalio was mid-2015, after I was rehired at *The Wall Street Journal.* I coauthored a front-page story about his views on China, under the rather plain headline "Giant Hedge Fund Bridgewater Flips View on China: 'No Safe Places to Invest'" (the piece was referenced earlier in this book). Our main source material was a copy of the *Daily Observations* that had been sent out by Bridgewater and distributed widely on Wall Street.

While journalistic conventions bind me not to repeat what Dalio said to me off the record after publication of the piece, it is fair to say he reacted poorly. Far from turned off, I was thrilled. Like so many other journalists before and after me, I was flattered that such an important man would take any time at all with me.

He evidently liked my next major piece on his firm even less, an investigative feature I cowrote on his falling-out with Greg Jensen. Thus began a pas de deux in which I would ping Ray for details on things I'd caught wind of, such as Bridgewater interns being instructed to go to strip shows or sexual misconduct settlements, and he would respond verbally and in writing with dismay. In one private email, Ray called my writing "trashy garbage," then closed a few sentences later by saying, "I regret that our relationship has to be of this sort when it could have been mutually cooperative." We kept talking on and off; he apparently couldn't help himself.

I couldn't help myself either. Bridgewater was for a time the easiest hedge fund in the world to report on because so many of the colorful goings-on there were recorded and blasted out to wide groups at the firm. Even more important, Dalio himself was the *ultimate* source for a journalist. When he would call me—almost always with a public-relations person also on the line—and ream me out for one article or another, he would inevitably tell me a new fact that led to another piece. It was he who, in late 2016, at an interview at Bridgewater headquarters, stood at a whiteboard and explained the idea of PriOS, drawing himself (portrayed as a stick figure) at the top and lines that flew downward to represent his orders.

Years later, I would learn that Paul McDowell was seated in the room next to ours, prepared to be called in to demo the creation for me. It never happened. Dalio just kept talking for hours.

I began to suspect some inkling of delusion in January 2017, when Dalio wrote a LinkedIn post, discussed earlier in this book, about a story of mine about PriOS. His post, which was longer than the original article, described the story as "fake news" and ascribed a number of befuddling, specific actions to me that simply never happened. Dalio wrote that my co-author and I had interviewed him and agreed to "not use that information unless we mutually agreed that [the] presentation of it in the article was accurate." I hadn't. He claimed that my coauthor and I never spoke to specific people with whom we had, hadn't "walked the halls of Bridgewater"—I did indeed, with Dalio himself—and quoted me asking questions that never came out of my mouth.

He described me, not for the last time, as an aggrieved job applicant who couldn't make it at Bridgewater, hell-bent on some sort of revenge.

I realized around then that although one of The Principles is "Trust in Truth," Dalio goes to great lengths to suppress it. He launched a yearslong witch hunt to root out people talking to me and other journalists, spending untold sums on surveillance of his own staff that has, to my knowledge, never accurately identified a culprit. He went after my job, meeting with my editors and pressing for my removal from covering the firm. After I wrote a fairly anodyne article about a top female employee who pressed to be paid equitably, he released doctored correspondence between her and me, writing, "Here is their text exchange." It wasn't. What was posted was an edited exchange, purporting to show that I had hounded her and ignored her denials. At the request of my editors, who were wary of a public pissing match, I did not release the true text messages.

At around the same time, friends of mine noticed they were receiving paid Google advertisements about me, directing them to the Bridgewater website, where a press release blasted me personally.

I hold no animus toward Dalio or anyone at Bridgewater. Despite our nearly forty-year age gap, we have had pleasant chats about our families; he once, in a fatherly fashion, poured me a Diet Coke, which in my experience with billionaires counts as kindness. On a Sunday morning in early 2020, after yet another public tirade from him about my history as a Bridgewater job applicant, I wrote to him to clear up the matter: "As you seem uniquely confused about this point, here it is from me directly." I laid out the history of my candidacy for the research editor position. "For what it's worth," I added, "by my distant recollection, everyone I interacted with at Bridgewater was professional and lovely throughout the interviewing process."

He responded forty-five minutes later, typo included, "Rob—I was referring to the time before that I'm [*sic*] 2010 when you tried to get a job as a MA and you were rejected for that job. We still have the notes that were gathered at that time which, if we get into it, we'd be happy to make public."

I look forward to reading them.

ACKNOWLEDGMENTS

Early in my Bridgewater reporting journey, I received an unusually well-informed note from an unknown sender. I saved it in my files under the gender-nonspecific name Jamie, a nom de plume that I eventually used in my notes to refer to a litany of unnamed sources whose true identities are known to me. Hundreds of Jamies spoke to me for this book, at great legal risk, motivated by a shared desire for a more complete tale to be told. Some Jamies were relieved to chat, some were defensive, some were angry, and a few were just amused. Said one Jamie, "The great thing about Bridgewater stories is I never have to exaggerate a single thing for it to be totally insane." This book is dedicated to all of the Jamies.

My goal was to treat everyone connected with Bridgewater, past and present, with civility and accuracy, regardless of their degree of participation in the project.

I joined *The Wall Street Journal* as an intern in 2009 and spent most of my professional career there before joining *The New York Times* in late 2022. While posted in the *Journal*'s San Francisco bureau a few years ago, I was fortunate to meet a far-improved version of myself. After her internship, Abigail Summerville became the research assistant for this book, a title that vastly undersells her roles as organizer, therapist, hype squad, comic-relief artist, writer, and sanity checker. She excelled at all of them.

At the *Journal,* more editors than I can count had a hand in shaping seven years of stories about Bridgewater. As editor in chief, Matt Murray repeatedly defended our journalism directly to those at Bridgewater, including Ray Dalio, who went to extraordinary lengths to discourage the work. On page one, Rick Brooks, Dan Kelly, and Matthew Rose handled the trickiest long-form pieces. My direct editors, Brad Reagan, Geoff Rogow, Russell Adams, and Dan Fitzpatrick, seldom tired of my coming up with new story pitches about the same old hedge fund. Their former boss, Dennis Berman, repeatedly pressed me to stop complaining (it never worked). Emma Moody has been a mentor and ballast since my college days. At the *Times,* Preeta Das, David Enrich, Maureen Farrell, and Ellen Pollock provided sage advice, encouragement, and editing.

My first Bridgewater writing partner, Bradley Hope, got me started on this journey, and Rachael Levy kept the fire alive later. Both introduced me to contacts who proved invaluable. Other reporters helped me manage the occasional ups and frequent downs of a book project, including Eliot Brown, Liz Hoffman, Tripp Mickle, and Erich Schwartzel. Jason Zweig, a straight-A student of financial history, marked up early chapters with generous feedback. A quadrant of high school friends—Emily, Hulli, Jess, and Sam—never failed with their enthusiasm or preorders.

This narrative benefited deeply from original journalism from others. These include my former colleagues Michelle Celarier and Lawrence Delevingne at *Absolute Return;* Stephen Taub at *Institutional Investor;* John Cassidy at *The New Yorker;* Kevin Roose at *New York;* Alexandra Stevenson and Matt Goldstein at *The New York Times;* and Kip McDaniel at seemingly everywhere. The research librarians of Duke University, my alma mater, also provided invaluable, pro bono assistance, as did my friend Patrick MacKenzie, a Harvard Business School alumnus with online archival access. Ben Kalin performed a studious fact-check over many months.

My crackerjack literary agent, David Larabell at CAA, immediately spotted the potential for a blockbuster narrative, and stuck by me during a few years I spent wandering the literary wilderness. David connected me with the team at St. Martin's Press, which put the whole house behind this book, including Lizz Blaise, Michelle Cashman, Laura Clark, Adriana Coada, Jen Enderlin, Diana Frost, Gabi Gantz, Tracey Guest, Meryl Levavi, John Morrone, Guy Oldfield, Paul Sleven, Dori Weintraub, and George Witte. I never doubted their fortitude to see it through. Executive editor Tim Bartlett did the heaviest lifting, painstakingly working to pare down a half century's worth of anecdotes. Kevin Reilly managed an exhaustive (and I'm sure he'd say exhausting) copyediting and legal process with unfailingly good cheer. Pronoy Sarkar was an early champion and helped come up with the title. Rob Grom designed the breathtaking cover, which so eerily matched my unexpressed vision that, for the first time in my professional life, I had no notes.

In the reporting for this book, I often assured those involved that as the youngest child of five, I had a stiff tolerance for punishment. I owe my siblings, Donny, Debby, Deena, and Bill, a mix of gratitude and annoyance for my thick skin and the chip on my shoulder. I owe my parents, Drs. Arthur and Judy Copeland, thanks for something far greater: the heart to ignore all that. I love you.

ROB COPELAND

NOTE ON SOURCES

Like any other author or journalist, I prefer to cite as many people as possible on the record. Bridgewater's nondisclosure agreements, however, forced me to grant anonymity in many cases for this book—even to those who had positive or neutral experiences to share. Bridgewater's thirteen-page agreement, which all employees must sign, says they must not "either during or at any time subsequent to your employment, disparage Bridgewater and/or its present or former affiliates, directors, officers, shareholders, employees or clients, whether directly or indirectly, in any manner whatsoever (whether related to the business of Bridgewater or otherwise)." The document bars all from discussing "confidential information," which it defines as "any non-public information (whether oral, written or contained on computer systems or other media)." It is not an exaggeration to say that employees risk litigation if they are quoted disclosing the brand of coffee in the office, unless those beans were earlier reported elsewhere.

One former employee, in a lawsuit against the firm later settled, called the atmosphere "a cauldron of fear and intimidation." Many others shared that sentiment with me privately.

After I notified Bridgewater of this book, it is my understanding that several former employees received additional payments not to speak with me (or any other journalist) under what are typically known as nondisparagement clauses. Though Dalio, in a 2014 interview, said that Bridgewater had fielded only three "frivolous" lawsuits in its history, I am aware of a slew of settlements the firm has paid to avoid being taken to court.

During the fact-checking process, after Bridgewater's representatives were provided the information contained in my manuscript, a series of people named in the narrative—including some who had earlier agreed to be cited as on-the-record interviewees for this book—told me that they had been pressured to recant, and asked me to leave out their participation. Faced with the possibility of bringing harm to people who had been so open with me, I chose not to cite by name any current or former Bridgewater employee as a source in the following bibliography. Thus the people who are named represent only a small fraction of those interviewed for this project.

While Ray Dalio is hardly shy about giving interviews, he declined repeated requests to offer one for this book. He wrote to me at its start, "I know that you know that I believe that you have a long and proven track record of not trying to convey the truth but rather intentionally taking bits and pieces to write the narrative that you want to write, so I presume that is what you will do. I don't care to argue with you about whether or not my views about you are justified. I just want to be transparent [sic] what I think and what I will do about it."

Not long after, Bridgewater and Dalio hired not one or two but three white-shoe law firms to send a pile of threatening letters to my publisher about a book yet unwritten. The letters were composed of mostly non-substantive, ad hominem attacks and repeatedly asked for details about my fact-checking. They threatened a lawsuit that would hold me and my publisher accountable for billions of dollars, in their words. When my fact-checker sent an exhaustive list of facts to representatives for Bridgewater and Dalio, we received a series of responses marked confidential and not for publication—a condition to which I had never agreed. Suffice it to say the responses included ample criticism of me, the fact-checker, and of the book at large. Many boiled down to arguing that I was too stupid to understand Bridgewater's glory. We also received some direct, on-topic responses, which I incorporated into the text, footnotes, and endnotes where appropriate.

Dalio has repeatedly said publicly that one of his flaws is a poor "rote memory." Yet in his feedback through attorneys to the fact-check for this book, he evinced a conveniently inconsistent one. Often, when my reporting unearthed positive or neutral anecdotes, Dalio and Bridgewater's representatives were able to confirm their accuracy. When the facts were less flattering, however, they would allege that they knew the truth and that I had gotten it wrong—or simply ignore the queries altogether. They complained ceaselessly that I did not give enough credit to Bridgewater's long-term track record, and offered no meaningful response to the funds' less impressive performance over the past fourteen years, a period that comprises the majority of this book inasmuch as it coincides with the rise of Dalio's public image and the rapid evolution of The Principles.

Bridgewater and Dalio's representatives (who included, over the course of this book's reporting, four different public relations firms) also repeatedly pressured me and my publisher for the identity of my sources, even as they concurrently reminded current and former employees that they risked legal peril if they spoke a word.

To the extent that such an archive still exists in any form, Bridgewater alone has access to its Transparency Library, containing the recordings of the major and minor goings-on of the firm's history. In several instances, people mentioned in this book directed me to ask Bridgewater for copies of the recordings so that I could most accurately describe the events that happened to them. I asked—and received no response (in a handful of instances, Bridgewater directed me to video clips of events posted publicly that were so heavily edited they could fairly be described as propaganda). Bridgewater also declined my repeated requests to set up official interviews with current employees. I am reminded of what the author Lawrence Wright wrote in *Going Clear,* his astonishing history of the Church of Scientology: "A reporter can only talk to people who are willing to talk to him; whatever complaints the church may have about my reporting, many limitations can be attributed to its decision to restrict my interactions with people who might have provided more favorable testimony."

Despite Dalio's public attacks on me and my work, I chose not to insert myself by name as a character in this book beyond the short afterword. Though a handful of articles I wrote or cowrote are mentioned in the text of this book, I included them only insofar as Dalio's reaction proved illuminating. The evidence shows that Dalio is universally outraged by any writer whose reportage on Bridgewater is less than laudatory.

Over the past decade or so, Dalio and Bridgewater have participated in a number of what were billed as independent endeavors from academics and authors. Insofar as the resulting works all cover roughly the same well-trod ground and are heavily filtered through Dalio's lens, I found that in totality they offered less insight than might have been expected from their cumulative word count. One notable exception is Edward Hess's *Learn or Die,* which contains an extensive and evenhanded explanation of one iteration of Bridgewater's employee ranking systems. I am additionally indebted to Maneet Ahuja's *The Alpha Masters* for a slew of details not contained elsewhere. The Bridgewater-filmed videos attached to Harvard Business School's 2013 case study also represented fascinating snapshots of a slice of the firm.

I did not set out to write a book that, as the youth might say, "subtweeted" Dalio's autobiography. I consider mine a stand-alone work. That said, as a primary source material, *Principles: Life and Work*, as well as its earlier, self-published editions spanning nearly a decade and provided to me by current and former Bridgewater employees, proved of some use. They were invaluable in confirming certain early dates and figures, but nearly everything that I found fascinating about Dalio and Bridgewater was sterilized to the point of obfuscation—or more often left out entirely. In just two of hundreds of examples, the Leibs of Park Avenue go unmentioned, while the falling-out between Dalio and Jensen—whose scars still linger at the firm today—is summarized in *Principles* as "people who loved Bridgewater working through their disagreements in an idea-meritocratic way." There is no whiff of acknowledgment in Dalio's tome that Bridgewater's investment performance over the past decade has been less than exemplary, and his descriptions of the firm's trading are characteristically vague.

I am often asked my thoughts on Dalio's writings. I always answer honestly that *Principles* is an autobiography; it should surprise no one that it both benefits from, and is ultimately limited by, its reliance on the sole perspective of its author.

NOTES

Author's Note

ix *Pulitzer Prize–winning:* James B. Stewart, *Disneywar: Intrigue, Treachery and Deceit in the Magic Kingdom* (Simon & Schuster, 2005).

Introduction

2 *Federal Reserve chief Ben Bernanke:* "Bernanke Talked to Rubin, Others as Credit Crunch Turned Worse in August," Associated Press, October 3, 2007.

2 *A week after McDowell's phone call:* Terry Keenan, "Wall Street Wise Men," *New York Post,* December 21, 2008.

5 *at its core, a machine:* John Cassidy, "Mastering the Machine: How Ray Dalio Built the World's Richest and Strangest Hedge Fund," *New Yorker,* July 18, 2011.

6 *Bridgewater had leapfrogged:* "*Alpha* Magazine Announces 2009 Hedge Fund 100, the World's Largest Hedge Funds" (press release), April 21, 2009.

9 *top-most believable person:* A lawyer for Dalio said that there was no "believability" baseline, adding that the development process was iterative, over time, and the system was designed in a way that did not give Dalio "any special privileges or powers."

Chapter 1: One Goddamn Place

16 *"an aging member":* Cassidy, "Mastering the Machine."

17 *a new species of coral:* "Deepwater Canyons 2012: Pathways to the Abyss," National Oceanic and Atmospheric Administration, September 10, 2012.

17 *pack of hyenas:* Ray Dalio, *Principles* (self-published spiral-bound edition, 2011).

19 *a glowing* Fortune *profile:* Brian O'Keefe, "Inside the World's Biggest Hedge Fund," *Fortune,* March 19, 2009.

19 *second leg to the crisis was coming:* This thesis turned out to be off base, so much so that Dalio would glaze over the year 2009 entirely in his autobiography, skipping directly from 2008 to 2010.

22 *an electronic repository:* Kevin Roose, "The Billion-Dollar Aphorisms of Hedge-Fund Cult Leader Ray Dalio," *New York,* April 8, 2011.

22 *swiftly meet the shredder:* Lawyers for Dalio and Bridgewater say that case studies such as Stefanova's were played for employees and job applicants "to help convey Bridgewater's culture and to give all employees a chance to discuss it and debate it." They add,

"Expressing empathy never led to people getting poor scores and or being deemed bad fits, and empathy was never considered a bad quality."

23 *She herself:* A lawyer for Dalio says he doesn't recall being told Stefanova was pregnant before the taping of her "Pain + Reflection = Progress" case. He says that job applicants were played the recording to help them understand the firm's culture before joining.

Chapter 2: Missy and the Viking

24 *a grand multicourse affair:* Barclay Leib, author interviews.

24 *glass chandelier:* French furniture auction, Sotheby's, 2011.

24 *home to more billionaires: Park Avenue: Money, Power & the American Dream,* directed by Alex Gibney (Jigsaw Productions, 2012).

24 *chairman emeritus:* "George Carr Leib; Led Banking House," *New York Times,* June 22, 1974.

25 *grew up on:* Obituary, *Palm Beach Post,* September 4, 2002.

25 *Mo Dale:* Ray Dalio, interview with Stephen J. Dubner, Freakonomics Radio, April 8, 2018.

25 *"a very strong man":* Ray Dalio, "In Depth with Graham Bensinger," interview with Graham Bensinger, July 31, 2021.

25 *Lacking his father's:* O'Keefe, "Inside the World's Biggest."

25 *newspapers:* Ray Dalio, *Principles: Life and Work* (Simon & Schuster, 2017).

25 *as a caddy:* "Ray Dalio, One of the World's Wealthiest Men, Got His Start Carrying Clubs," *Golf,* November 15, 2017.

25 *been a farm:* "Long Island Journal," *New York Times,* September 30, 1984.

26 *For $6 a bag:* Jack D. Schwager, *Hedge Fund Market Wizards: How Winning Traders Win* (John Wiley & Sons, 2012).

26 *One frequent golfer:* Ray Dalio, "Masters in Business," interview with Barry Ritholtz, October 22, 2020.

26 *French burgundies:* Elin McCoy, "How a Wall Street Exec Became the Ultimate Burgundy Wine Collector," Bloomberg, December 2, 2015.

26 *caddies avoided:* Rick Coltrera, author interview.

26 *she remained enchanted:* Barclay Leib (pseudonym: David von Leib), *Not My Grandfather's Wall Street: Diaries of a Derivatives Trader* (American Star Books, 2015).

27 *he couldn't imagine:* Dalio, "In Depth with Graham Bensinger."

27 *a C average:* Dalio, *Principles* (2011).

27 *"a very good community college":* Gary Winnick, author interview.

27 *Post cereal company:* "Long Island University History," Long Island University.

27 *straight A's:* Maneet Ahuja, *The Alpha Masters* (Wiley, 2012).

28 *made money in:* Dalio, *Principles* (2011).

28 *"an easy game":* Cassidy, "Mastering the Machine."

28 *a new identity:* Nassau County clerk's office, author interview.

28 *"a capitalistic higher calling":* Daniel Huang, "Former NYSE Traders Look Back on the Old Days," *Wall Street Journal,* September 1, 2014.

28 *he was enthralled:* Ahuja, *Alpha Masters.*

28 *a bearish sign:* Schwager, *Hedge Fund Market Wizards.*

28 *reconciling his intuition:* Ibid.

29 *he once won:* "In Memoriam," *St. Paul's School Alumni Horae,* Summer 2018.

29 *rarely less:* "Building the Foundation: Business Education for Women at Harvard University: 1937–1970," Baker Library at Harvard Business School.

29 *it would later become:* Duff McDonald, *The Golden Passport: Harvard Business School, the Limits of Capitalism and the Moral Failure of the MBA Elite* (Harper Business, 2017).

29 *Most students were significantly older:* Ken Freeman, interview with Abigail Summerville.

29 *avoided being drafted:* Dalio, *Principles* (2017).

29 *typically modeled themselves:* Joel Peterson, interview with Abigail Summerville.

29 *"In some ways":* Ibid.

30 *He was wrong:* Ahuja, *Alpha Masters.*

30 *Dalio learned that:* Ray Dalio, "Ray Dalio Breaks Down His 'Holy Grail,'" interview with Investopedia, April 27, 2019.

30 *real-world case studies:* McDonald, *Golden Passport.*

30 *like puzzles:* Edward D. Hess, *Learn or Die: Using Science to Build a Leading-Edge Learning Organization* (Columbia Business School Publishing, 2014).

30 *Dalio marched:* Mike Kubin, author interview.

31 *were exciting:* "Class Notes: '73," compiled by Wayne R. Vibert, *Harvard Business School Bulletin,* 1974.

31 *"Good Luck, Ray":* Ibid.

31 *a salary of:* Dalio, *Principles* (2017).

31 *expanded into:* Vartanig G. Vartan, "Dominick to Quit Retail Brokerage," *New York Times,* July 31, 1973.

31 *Many of Dalio's trades:* Dalio, *Principles* (2011).

31 *he later told:* Ray Dalio, interview at Stanford Graduate School of Business, April 19, 2019.

31 *found his way:* Ahuja, *Alpha Masters.*

31 *ranchers gave him:* Roose, "Billion-Dollar Aphorisms."

32 *slugged his boss:* Cassidy, "Mastering the Machine."

32 *expected to be fired:* Dalio, "In Depth with Graham Bensinger."

32 *brought a stripper:* Ibid.

32 *paid to get naked:* Roose, "Billion-Dollar Aphorisms."

32 *Now almost twenty-six:* Hess, *Learn or Die.*

32 *Leib would head:* Leib, author interviews.

32 *two-bedroom apartment:* "Ray Dalio: Hedge Fund Master," American Academy of Achievement.

32 *hosting parties:* "Class Notes: '73," compiled by Larry Schwoeri, *Harvard Business School Bulletin,* 1975.

32 *HBS alumni bulletin:* Ibid.

33 *buyers in other countries:* A lawyer for Dalio says he never asked the Leibs for money.

33 *a business that intended:* Ahuja, *Alpha Masters.*

33 *Dalio told Leib:* Leib, author interviews.

33 *"It was more":* Ray Dalio, interview with the American Academy of Achievement, September 12, 2012.

33 *advisory work:* Roose, "Billion-Dollar Aphorisms."

33 *livestock, meat, grain:* Dalio, *Principles* (2011).

33 *Leib was intrigued:* Leib, author interviews.

33 *an art museum:* Enid Nemy, "A Whitney Who Shuns Glamour for a Life of Quiet Satisfaction," *New York Times,* June 30, 1974.

33 *spoke little English:* Dalio, *Principles* (2011).

Chapter 3: Absolute Certainty

35 *Dalio felt free:* Ahuja, *Alpha Masters.*

35 *The newlyweds lived:* Dalio, interview with American Academy of Achievement.

35 *Barbara gave birth:* Dalio, *Principles* (2017).

35 *his heaviest overcoat:* Leib, author interviews.

35 *Vanderbilt parlayed:* Nemy, "Whitney Who Shuns."

35 *squandered on parties:* Arthur T. Vanderbilt II, *Fortune's Children: The Fall of the House of Vanderbilt* (William Morrow, 2001).

36 *its three thousand restaurants:* "A Brief McHistory," McSpotlight, compiled by the McInformation Network.

36 *snack-food giant Nabisco:* Ahuja, *Alpha Masters.*

37 *He wrote articles:* "A Perpetual Motion Machine: An Oral History of Bridgewater Associates' Leadership Transition," *Leaders,* October/November/December 2021.

37 *in notebooks:* O'Keefe, "Inside the World's Biggest."

37 *tabulated the results:* Hess, *Learn or Die.*

37 *He checked against history:* Schwager, *Hedge Fund Market Wizards.*

37 *small bets:* Hess, *Learn or Die.*

37 *market commentary letter:* Ahuja, *Alpha Masters.*

37 *Bunker Hunt:* Dalio, *Principles* (2017).

37 *calling himself an economist: The Unemployment Crisis and Policies for Economic Recovery, Before the Joint Economic Committee, Congress of the United States,* 97th Cong., 2nd sess., October 15, 20, and November 24, 1982, statement of Raymond T. Dalio.

38 *Markets were turbulent:* Laurel Graefe, "Oil Shock of 1978–79," Federal Reserve History, November 22, 2013.

38 *Dalio saw it differently:* Jonathan Fuerbringer, "High Rates Called Drag on Recovery," *New York Times,* March 1, 1982.

38 *"There is no hope": Small Business Failures: Hearing Before the Subcommittee on Antitrust and Restraint of Trade Activities Affecting Small Business of the Committee on Small Business,* U.S. House of Representatives, 97th Cong., 2nd sess., June 25, 1982, testimony of Raymond T. Dalio.

38 *Contrary Opinion Forum:* "Prior Years' Speakers: 1982," Contrary Opinion Forum.

38 *"Why can't doom":* "Barron's Mailbag: Depression or Delusion?," *Barron's,* October 19, 1992.

38 *a joint committee of Congress: Unemployment Crisis and Policies,* statement of Dalio.

38 *"Following the economy"*: Ibid.

39 *"more grim than"*: Ibid., speaker: Representative Parrin J. Mitchell.

39 *Not many analysts:* "Some Analysts See Depression in '83, but Not as Bad as '30s," *Wall Street Journal,* December 31, 1982.

39 *"I can say"*: Dalio, interview at Stanford Graduate School of Business.

39 *the recession ended:* Tim Sablik, "Recession of 1981–82," Federal Reserve History, November 22, 2013.

40 *"What Is a Jeweler?"*: Cassidy, "Mastering the Machine."

40 *the best thing:* Lawrence Delevingne and Michelle Celarier, "Ray Dalio's Radical Truth," *Absolute Return,* March 2, 2011.

40 *a matrix:* Hilda Ochoa-Brillembourg, author interview.

41 *Sharpe ratio:* Gregory Zuckerman, *The Man Who Solved the Market: How Jim Simons Launched the Quant Revolution* (Portfolio, 2019).

41 *"What the hell"*: A representative for Jones said this was "not his style or voice."

42 *protect the retirement savings:* Hilda Ochoa-Brillembourg, author interview.

42 *railroad bond prices:* Robert McGough, "Fair Wind or Foul?," *Financial World,* May 2, 1989.

42 *She hadn't heard:* Ochoa-Brillembourg, author interview.

42 *relative performance:* Ahuja, *Alpha Masters.*

42 *Dalio agreed to manage:* Ochoa-Brillembourg, author interview

Chapter 4: Pure Alpha

43 *Dalio donned blue jeans:* Robert McGough, "Here's a Happy Thought," *Forbes,* February 9, 1987.

44 *the largest one-day drop:* Tim Metz, Alan Murray, Thomas E. Ricks, and Beatrice E. Garcia, "The Crash of '87: Stocks Plummet 508 amid Panicky Selling," *Wall Street Journal,* October 20, 1987.

44 *young traders wandering about:* Jason Zweig, "Remembering Black Monday: 'It Was Relentless,'" *Wall Street Journal,* September 29, 2017.

44 *Bridgewater's accounts were up:* McGough, "Fair Wind or Foul?"

44 *Jones had $250 million:* "Lights! Camera! Buy! Sell! 'Trader' Stars Real Trader," *USA Today,* November 24, 1987.

44 *an estimated $100 million:* Randall Smith, "After a Dazzling Early Career, a Star Trader Settles Down," *New York Times,* March 5, 2014.

44 *weekend estate:* "Lights! Camera! Buy! Sell!"

44 *a return to television:* "Foreigners Taking Over America," *Oprah Winfrey Show,* season 3, episode 121388, December 13, 1988.

46 *he had hired:* "Streit Takes Position at Bridgewater Group After Leaving Barnes & Co.," *Securities Week,* July 20, 1987.

46 *He assumed that:* Lawyers for Dalio and Bridgewater said the $700 million figure included the firm's advisory accounts.

46 *His Mercedes:* A lawyer for Dalio says this episode did not occur.

47 *institutional investors controlled:* Peter F. Drucker, "Reckoning with the Pension Fund Revolution," *Harvard Business Review,* March 1991.

47   *Rusty Olson:* Russell L. Olson, *The School of Hard Knocks: The Evolution of Pension Investing at Eastman Kodak* (RIT Cary Graphic Arts Press, 2005).

47   *More than half:* Ibid.

47   *"the corruption of the economic soul":* McGough, "Fair Wind or Foul?"

47   *a coming depression in 1988:* Steve Coll, "The Long Shadow of Black Monday," *Washington Post,* February 28, 1988.

47   *a three-year recession:* Jay McCormick, "Expect a Recession? Avoid Stocks," *USA Today,* January 1, 1989.

47   *back to depression:* Alan Abelson, "Up & Down Wall Street," *Barron's,* November 5, 1990.

47   *the drum of depression:* Floyd Norris, "Market Watch: Listening for a Scary Word: Depression," *New York Times,* January 13, 1991.

47   *tweaked his call:* Dan Dorfman, "Modern-Day Version of Depression Looms, Pro Says," *USA Today,* August 28, 1992.

47   *"it is a depression":* Ray Dalio, "Depression, Not Recession—That, Contends a Seasoned Observer, Is What We're In," *Barron's,* October 12, 1992.

48   *Kodak could reduce the risk:* Olson, *School of Hard Knocks.*

48   *"If you can do this thing":* Ahuja, *Alpha Masters.*

48   *"A new way of thinking":* Cassidy, "Mastering the Machine."

48   *Prince made friends easily:* Bruce Currie, interview with Abigail Summerville.

49   *"I'm learning so much":* Ibid.

49   *Burgess shared:* Mark Collins, interview with Abigail Summerville.

50   *"Then he pushed it aside":* Justin Rohrlich, "Meet the Billionaire Investor Whose Advice Can Make You Really Rich," *Maxim,* April 20, 2018. A lawyer for Dalio says this anecdote, as reported by *Maxim,* is inaccurate.

50   *Microsoft Excel:* "The All Weather Story," Bridgewater Associates.

50   *yellow legal pads:* "Perpetual Motion Machine."

50   *feet on the desk:* Bob Prince, "In Depth with Graham Bensinger," interview with Graham Bensinger, November 11, 2020.

50   *"a fire-breathing dragon":* Ibid.

51   *"You trust yourself too much":* Robert Kegan and Lisa Laskow Lahey, *An Everyone Culture: Becoming a Deliberately Developmental Organization* (Harvard Business Review Press, 2016).

51   *"hedge portfolio":* Ahuja, *Alpha Masters.*

51   *big hit:* A lawyer for Dalio says the firm has always "sought to manage money in a way that beat the benchmarks agreed to with its clients, which it did consistently."

51   *hedge funds dated to 1949:* Sebastian Mallaby, *More Money Than God: Hedge Funds and the Making of a New Elite* (Penguin Press, 2011).

51   *"magic":* Ibid.

52   *disastrous stock picks:* Ibid.

52   *Soros was hauled:* Saul Hansell, "A Primer on Hedge Funds: Hush-Hush and for the Rich," *New York Times,* April 14, 1994.

52   *"Frankly":* Thomas L. Friedman, "House Panel Given a Lesson in Hedge Funds," *New York Times,* April 14, 1994.

52 *"top 5 percent"*: Dalio, *Principles* (2017).

53 *Alpha was what*: Alpha also involves a complicated adjustment for risk.

53 *she had noticed*: Ochoa-Brillembourg, author interview.

53 *No longer convinced*: The World Bank fund would eventually invest again in other Bridgewater products.

54 *Australia*: Marc Faber, author interview.

54 *became an acolyte*: Cassidy, "Mastering the Machine."

54 *"Holy Grail"*: Dalio, "Ray Dalio Breaks Down."

55 *"a very disciplined approach"*: Faber, author interview.

55 *"A lot of people think"*: Dalio, "Ray Dalio Breaks Down."

55 *a bear market coming*: Dan Dorfman, "Dollar, Rate Woes Have Bears Sharpening Their Claws," *USA Today*, June 24, 1994.

55 *a "blow-off phase"*: Marlene Givant Star, "U.S. Markets Seen as Peaking," *Pensions & Investments*, July 10, 1995.

55 *"deflationary implosion"*: Sara Webb, Michael Sesit, and Sara Cailan, "Industrials Lose 112 Points on Troubles Abroad—Global Stocks Slide on Fears over Economies," *Wall Street Journal*, August 12, 1998.

55 *add more data points*: Dalio, *Principles* (2017).

55 *Larry Summers called Dalio*: Larry Summers, author interview.

56 *Treasuries went on*: Aswath Damodaran, "Historical Returns on Stocks, Bonds and Bills: 1928–2020," NYU Stern School of Business, January 2021.

57 *Tulsa professor Richard Burgess*: When Prince later returned to the University of Tulsa to give a speech, he said Bridgewater had lifted Burgess's trading models, an attendee recalled.

57 *Britt Harris*: "All Weather Story."

57 *virtually his entire*: Martin Steward, "Risk Parity: The Truly Balanced Portfolio," *IPE*, June 2012.

58 *Dalio made $225 million*: In a sign of just how wealthy Dalio would become, when his payday dipped to $190 million in 2005, it was the least he would make for another fifteen years.

58 *fishing expeditions*: Cassidy, "Mastering the Machine."

58 *snowboarded in Vermont*: O'Keefe, "Inside the World's Biggest."

58 *a new headquarters*: Ahuja, *Alpha Masters*.

58 *he hated*: Ianthe Jeanne Dugan and Anita Raghavan, "The Atlas of New Money," *Wall Street Journal*, December 16, 2006.

58 *"Yuck"*: Ibid.

58 *"Maturity is the ability"*: "Perpetual Motion Machine."

Chapter 5: Root Cause

60 *forty-six years old*: Barry B. Burr, "Harris Exiting Verizon," *Pensions & Investments*, November 15, 2004.

60 *son of a Baptist preacher*: Steven Brull, "Return of the Native," *Alpha*, January 23, 2009.

60 *could no longer run the firm*: Burr, "Harris Exiting Verizon."

60 *a close friend*: Brull, "Return of the Native."

60 *Dalio said publicly*: "Ray Dalio Taps Britt Harris to Fill Newly Created CEO Position at Bridgewater Associates" (press release), *Business Wire*, November 5, 2004.

61 *Dalio remained president*: Burr, "Harris Exiting Verizon."

61 *became a Bridgewater client*: "The World's Smallest US $74 Billion Manager," *Global Investor*, October 2004.

62 *"'hell on Earth'"*: Letter from Britt Harris, titled "Letter From Britt Harris," undated.

62 *His father had died*: Brull, "Return of the Native."

62 *Harris recalled*: Ibid.

63 *"After six months of reflection"*: Craig Karman, "Major Texas Pension Makes a Big Push into Hedge Funds," *Wall Street Journal*, July 14, 2007.

63 *treatment for depression*: Harris says that his work at Bridgewater "did not play a leading role" in his depression, "although the almost unimaginable lack of compassion . . . by a small minority [there] certainly could not have helped."

63 *"A good manager needs"*: Dalio, *Principles* (2017).

63 *issue log*: Richard Feloni, "Ray Dalio Started Bridgewater in His Apartment and Built It into the World's Largest Hedge Fund. Here Are 5 Major Lessons He's Learned over the Past 44 Years," *Business Insider*, July 2, 2019.

64 *Dalio often cited*: Dalio, *Principles* (2011).

64 *all those aware*: Dalio, *Principles* (2011).

64 *logged by a bystander*: Roose, "Billion-Dollar Aphorisms."

65 *A newly promoted Bridgewater manager*: Ray Dalio, *Principles* (self-published, 2009).

66 *"So what is success?"*: Ibid.

66 *early version of The Principles*: Ibid.

67 *"I know I'm pretty extreme"*: Ibid.

67 *a draft version*: Ibid.

67 *Dalio went on*: Ibid.

68 *"getting through to"*: Hess, *Learn or Die*.

68 *The Principles imposed doctrine*: Dalio, *Principles* (2009).

69 *he later announced*: Ibid.

69 *They memorized*: A lawyer for Dalio says, "As far as we know, no one ever memorized The Principles, which would've been a significant task given the number of them."

Chapter 6: The Big One

70 *an awkward tendency*: Chris Cueman, author interview.

70 *He excelled*: Greg Jensen, official Bridgewater biography.

70 *Jensen joined a fraternity*: Greg Jensen, "'Unparalleled Excitement' Reigns at Zeta Psi," *Hanover Zete*, Winter 1995.

70 *One poster*: Ryan Victor, "'Rush Terrorists' Irresponsible," *Dartmouth*, October 4, 1993.

71 *replacing the kegerator*: Jensen, "'Unparalleled Excitement.'"

72 *a family friend in China*: Dalio, *Principles* (2009).

72 *Paul, was bipolar*: Barbara Hoffman, "I'm a Bipolar Man—and Katie Holmes Is Playing Me in a Movie," *New York Post*, February 18, 2016.

72 *Environmental science:* Abby Schultz, "Mark Dalio and OceanX Combine Science and Storytelling," *Barron's*, March 26, 2019.

73 *internal crisis indicator:* Chidem Kurdas, "Fed Decision Doesn't Settle Dilemma," *HedgeWorld News*, September 20, 2006.

73 *He saw established Western economies:* Sandra Ward, "Bipolar Disorder," *Barron's*, June 13, 2005.

73 *sucking strongly on a straw:* Gerry van Wyngen, "Cycle 'About to Turn,'" *Business Review Weekly*, October 6, 2005.

73 *Dalio personally earned:* Julie Anderson and Julie Creswell, "In the Race for Riches, Hedge Fund Managers Top Titans of Wall Street," *New York Times*, April 24, 2007.

74 *published the following day:* David Leonhardt, "Worth a Lot, but Are Hedge Funds Worth It?," *New York Times*, May 23, 2007.

75 *Dalio spoke to another reporter:* Sandra Ward, "Liquidity, Leverage and Their Looming Risks," *Barron's*, May 28, 2007.

75 *gunslingers, such as John Paulson:* Gregory Zuckerman, "'Greatest Trade': How You Can Make $20 Billion," *Wall Street Journal*, November 15, 2009.

75 *They viewed speculation:* Alberto Mingardi, "George Soros, Speculator and Proud," *EconLog*, March 15, 2014.

75 *"This is not an economic crisis":* Barry Dunstan, "A Mighty Purge Is Under Way," *Australia Financial Review*, August 17, 2007.

75 *Bridgewater forecast the damage as minor:* Chidem Kurdas, "Recent Losses No Bloodbath, but Worse May Come," *HedgeWorld News*, August 9, 2007.

76 *Any fallout:* Dunstan, "Mighty Purge."

76 *Eric Clapton:* "Arts, Briefly: Secret Clapton Concert in the Works," *New York Times*, June 13, 2007.

76 *"If the economy goes down":* Cassidy, "Mastering the Machine."

76 *Dalio showed up at the meeting:* "How Bridgewater Navigated the 2008 Financial Crisis," Bridgewater Associates, 2018.

76 *startling bank president Timothy Geithner:* Dalio, *Principles* (2017).

76 *future treasury secretary:* When he made it to the White House a few months later, Geithner bolstered his standing with his boss by using Dalio. After Geithner's team produced public figures on how much money would be needed to backstop major financial institutions, Geithner headed into the Oval Office with a copy of the *Daily Observations* and handed it to President Obama. "We Agree!" the research read. "The regulators did an excellent job of explaining exactly what they did for this stress test, and showing the numbers that produced the results. They did virtually exactly what we did."

77 *stood to benefit:* A lawyer for Dalio says: "While it is true that Mr. Dalio met with high-ranking government officials, such interactions between private sector individuals and high-ranking government officials are common across industries and follow protocols that prevent the government officials from divulging information that they shouldn't—and prevent the private sector from profiting on such information. Bridgewater's controls for these meetings are thoroughly audited by the SEC. Further, Bridgewater's decisions in the markets are 98 percent systemized and, in the rare cases that

there are deviations from the systems, the reasons for the deviations are recorded and audited."

77 *shorted the U.S. dollar:* Cassidy, "Mastering the Machine."

77 *the average hedge fund lost 18 percent:* "Hedge Funds Took a Serious Hit in 2008," Associated Press, January 12, 2009.

77 *ended the year up roughly 9 percent:* Gregory Meyer, "Managed Futures Gained, Left Hedge Funds in Dust in 2008," Dow Jones Newswires, January 9, 2009.

77 *ended up making $780 million:* Louise Story, "Above the Storm: Some Fund Managers Rake It In," *International Herald Tribune,* March 26, 2009.

77 *world's largest hedge fund:* "*Alpha* Magazine Announces 2009."

Chapter 7: Look Out

82 *Dalio's personal assistant:* Kathleen O'Grady, "What Ray Dalio Taught Me About Authentic Leadership and Taxidermy," Authentic Leadership Advisors.

84 *looked toward the doors:* Eileen Murray, "Things I Didn't Learn in School," interview with Paul Podolsky, January 27, 2021.

Chapter 8: A Different Kind of Company

88 *depression mode:* Kip McDaniel, "Is Ray Dalio the Steve Jobs of Investing?," *Chief Investment Officer,* December 13, 2011.

88 *Dalio believed:* O'Keefe, "Inside the World's Biggest."

88 *Jen Healy:* Healy at that time used her maiden name, Pelzel. She would later marry and take the last name Healy. For simplicity's sake, she is referred to in this book only as Healy.

88 *"my daughter":* A lawyer for Mr. Dalio says he didn't refer to Jen Healy as his daughter. Healy also says she never heard him use the term.

88 *an unflattering new sweater:* Healy wrote in an email that she recalls discussing an ugly sweater only as a hypothetical. Two people who spoke with her about it then disagree, saying it was in response to a specific colleague's garment.

90 *a squiggly doodle:* Alex Howe, "Behold the All-Important Squiggle That Guides the Decisions at the Biggest Hedge Fund in the World," *Business Insider,* November 4, 2011.

90 *Those who leaned too heavily:* A lawyer for Dalio says the impact on bonuses of not providing critical feedback was "virtually nothing."

90 *these two parts of the brain:* Ray Dalio, Twitter, June 11, 2019.

90 *Dalio once called it:* Ray Dalio, "Principle of the Day," LinkedIn.

90 *Through meditation:* Mary Swift, "Billionaire Ray Dalio Credits Meditation for Success," *Transcendental Meditation,* November 28, 2014.

91 *subsidize meditation classes:* Richard Feloni, "The World's Largest Hedge Fund Reimburses Employees Half the Cost of $1,000 Meditation Lessons," *Business Insider,* November 10, 2016.

91 *He compared himself to the Dalai Lama:* Dalio, *Principles* (2017).

91 *The accompanying question read:* Internal Bridgewater document.

91 *took hours to complete:* Bess Levin, "Bridgewater Associates Suggests Fate Worse than

Firing in Store for Hyenas Caught Cheating on Day-Long Principles Exam," *Deal-breaker*, April 2012.

92 *a deck of sixty-seven cards*: Devon Scheef, "Deck for Success," *Training & Development* 47, no. 9 (September 1993).

93 *"one of the chosen ones"*: Bob Eichinger, email to Ben Kalin. Eichinger says that due to his age he has a failing memory. He says the other events described involving him may be true but he has no recollections.

93 *bucketed people*: Richard Feloni, "These Are the Personality Tests You Take to Get a Job at the World's Largest Hedge Fund," *Business Insider*, August 26, 2016.

93 *was graded an ENTP*: Ray Dalio, Twitter, October 8, 2018.

95 *Apple's first mouse*: Betsy Mikel, "How the Guy Who Designed 1 of Apple's Most Iconic Products Organizes His Office," *Inc.*, January 24, 2018.

95 *he quit*: Eichinger says he did not quit; rather, Dalio and Bridgewater stopped using his services.

95 *carried out only in his coffin*: Rob Copeland and Bradley Hope, "Bridgewater, World's Largest Hedge Fund, Grapples with Succession," *Wall Street Journal*, March 26, 2016.

96 *Dalio wrote to warn*: Randall W. Forsyth, "Will We Be Zimbabwe or Japan?," *Barron's*, May 23, 2009.

96 *277 in total*: Delevingne and Celarier, "Ray Dalio's Radical Truth."

96 *Tom Adams*: Copeland and Hope, "Bridgewater, World's Largest."

96 *Julian Mack*: Bob Goldsborough, "McKinsey's Julian C. Mack Selling Winnetka Home," *Chicago Breaking Business*, June 14, 2020.

96 *one-third of employees*: Ray Dalio, "Company Culture and the Power of Thoughtful Disagreement," interview with Andrew Ross Sorkin, New York Times DealBook conference, December 12, 2014.

97 *"In the five years"*: Arnold's "Smoke at Bwater" email was lengthy; excerpts are included.

99 *Prince had amassed a debt*: Lawyers for Dalio and Bridgewater say Prince was never "deeply in debt" to Dalio. They say Mr. Prince had options to buy Bridgewater shares, and to exercise them he borrowed $10 million from a bank and paid the loan back with dividends from those shares. They say Mr. Prince had options to buy Bridgewater shares, and to exercise them he borrowed $10 million from a bank and paid the loan back with dividends from those shares. A representative for Prince declined to provide further details.

99 *megachurch*: Ted Loos, "The Spiritual and Spectacular Meet at an Ultramodern Community Center in Connecticut," *New York Times*, October 16, 2015.

100 *In 2010*: Russell Sherman, "Bridgewater Fact Check," email to Rob Copeland, March 3, 2016.

100 *"minister/mentor"*: Cassidy, "Mastering the Machine."

100 *For $7 million per year*: James Comey, "Executive Branch Personnel Public Financial Disclosure Report," U.S. Office of Government Ethics, June 2013.

100 *"godfather"*: Rob Copeland and Bradley Hope, "The World's Largest Hedge Fund Is Building an Algorithmic Model from Its Employees' Brains," *Wall Street Journal*, December 22, 2016.

Chapter 9: Comey and the Cases

101 *landed in the headlines:* Dan Eggen and Paul Kane, "Gonzales Hospital Episode Detailed," *Washington Post,* May 16, 2007.

101 *"ski partner":* Richard Feloni, "Billionaire Investor Ray Dalio Explains How to Avoid Micromanaging," *Business Insider,* November 10, 2014.

102 *a "chirper":* Copeland and Hope, "World's Largest Hedge Fund."

102 *could dole out:* A lawyer for Dalio denies that he ever called Comey a "chirper."

104 *one Principle laid out:* The Principle continued, "A higher percentage of the population than you imagine will cheat if given an opportunity, and most people who are given the choice of being 'fair' with you and taking more for themselves will choose taking more for themselves. Even a tiny amount of cheating is intolerable, so your happiness and success will depend on your controls. Security controls should be viewed as a necessary tool of our profession, not as a personal affront to an individual's integrity."

104 *A former FBI official:* Arthur Cummings, LinkedIn profile.

104 *Even including an attachment: Bridgewater Associates, LP vs. Lawrence Minicone and Zachary Squire,* American Arbitration Association Employment Arbitration Tribunal, exhibit 1, July 14, 2020.

106 *more than 1 million job applications:* Enguerran Loos, "How Selective Are Bain, BCG and McKinsey Through the Application Process?," CaseCoach, August 5, 2019.

106 *hundreds of new hires:* Alexandra Stevenson and Matthew Goldstein, "Bridgewater, World's Biggest Hedge Fund, Is Said to Be Slowing Hiring," *New York Times,* July 17, 2016.

106 *hot-button issues:* Delevingne and Celarier, "Ray Dalio's Radical Truth."

106 *dental records:* Courtney Comstock, "Here's Another Example of Ray Dalio's Weird Bridgewater 'Pursuit of Truth' Management Style," *Business Insider,* March 2, 2011.

109 *the whiteboard case:* Copeland and Hope, "Bridgewater, World's Largest."

110 *Ray-man:* Sam Jones and Dan McCrum, "The Billionaire Ray-man Who Plays by His Own Rules," *Financial Times,* March 2, 2012.

112 *an email arrived from Dalio:* Ray Dalio, email to David Manners-Weber et al., Wednesday, September 14, 2011, 4:14 P.M.

Chapter 10: The Offensive

113 *The blog introduced:* Bess Levin, "Bridgewater Associates: Be the Hyena. Attack the Wildebeest," *Dealbreaker,* May 10, 2010.

114 *He told the reporter:* Michael Corkery, "Money Talks: A Hedge-Fund King Philosophizes on Truth and Weasels," *Wall Street Journal,* June 19, 2010.

117 *The hedge fund's holdings:* Michael Corkery, "Big Win for a Big Bear," *Wall Street Journal,* October 22, 2010.

117 *A leveraged version:* Delevingne and Celarier, "Ray Dalio's Radical Truth."

118 *over $3 billion personally:* Ibid.

118 *Dalio still seemed to smart:* Cassidy, "Mastering the Machine."

118 *circle of journalists:* One such reporter, *Fortune's* Carol Loomis, for decades spoke to

Buffett nearly every day and edited his investor letters, pro bono, while remaining on staff at the magazine.

119 *The next issue:* McDaniel, "Is Ray Dalio the Steve Jobs?"

119 *The next publication:* Ben Austen, "The Story of Steve Jobs: An Inspiration or a Cautionary Tale?," *Wired,* July 23, 2012.

120 *Word came back:* A lawyer for Mr. Dalio says "he never wanted a biography of him written and did not ask Mr. Isaacson to write one."

120 *Dalio's disappointment showed:* Several former Bridgewater employees said they were told that Isaacson demurred when asked to write Dalio's biography. Isaacson says he does not recall the request making it to him.

120 *Dalio was a donor:* "Dalio Philanthropies," InfluenceWatch.

120 *Aspen Institute:* "New Trustees Elected to Aspen Institute Board," Aspen Institute, May 5, 2010.

120 *McCormick rang him up:* Walter Isaacson, author interview.

121 *television host Charlie Rose:* Ray Dalio, interviewed by Charlie Rose, *Charlie Rose,* October 20, 2011.

122 *Off set:* Charlie Rose, author interview.

122 *"I was enormously busy":* Ibid.

122 *review the copy:* Maneet Ahuja, author interview. Ahuja says that she gave everyone interviewed in the book the same terms.

122 *Ahuja accepted his demand:* Ahuja said she offered the same terms to other hedge fund managers interviewed for her book.

123 *chaperoned into Bridgewater meetings:* Grant said he was too busy to be interviewed. In an email, he wrote: "My analysis of Bridgewater's culture was based on my independent judgment as a social scientist."

123 An Everyone Culture: Kegan and Laskow Lahey, *Everyone Culture.*

123 Originals: Adam Grant, *Originals: How Non-Conformists Move the World* (Penguin, 2016).

123 *edited clips:* Ibid.

Chapter 11: Truth Factory

125 *"success conditioning":* Tony Robbins, "Personal Power: A 1990s Infomercial Featuring Tony Robbins and Fran Tarkenton," YouTube, April 19, 2021.

126 *a recruitment archetype:* Cassidy, "Mastering the Machine."

127 *Kuran told:* Kent Kuran, email to HR_ExitInterviews, Vincius Silva, Wednesday, August 4, 2010, 3:33 P.M.

128 *Karniol-Tambour:* Karniol-Tambour is her married name; she was unmarried at the time.

Chapter 12: Sex and Lies, Videotaped

132 *Griffin Financial Aid Office:* "Financial Aid Office Renamed in Honor of Ken Griffin," *Harvard Gazette,* October 10, 2014.

132 *for $400 million:* "Harvard Receives Its Largest Gift," *Harvard Gazette,* June 3, 2015.

132 *First conceived:* "HBS History," Baker Library at Harvard Business School.

132 *HBS case studies:* "The HBS Case Method," Harvard Business School.

132 *accustomed to being pitched:* Heidi K. Gardner, author interview.

133 *in a housing project:* Paul Podolsky, *Things I Didn't Learn in School* (podcast), January 21, 2021.

133 *shot in the head:* Ibid.

137 *"Everything looks bigger":* Ray Dalio, Twitter, October 19, 2018.

138 *The videos attached:* Jeffrey T. Polzer and Heidi K. Gardner, *Bridgewater Associates (Multimedia Case)* (Harvard Business Publishing, May 10, 2013).

141 *a campfire event:* Stevenson and Goldstein, "Bridgewater's Ray Dalio Spreads."

142 *old antagonist:* Levin, "Bridgewater Associates Suggests Fate."

143 *the leaker:* Internal Bridgewater employee Principles Test.

143 *Jensen's own conclusions:* Ibid.

144 *Why is Jim Leaving?:* Jim Comey, email to Bridgewater, October 3, 2012, 1:50 P.M. This email was first sent by Comey on February 26, 2012, to a small list of department heads, explaining that he thought it would be his last year at Bridgewater. After the decision was finalized, he forwarded it to the entire firm on October 3, 2012, as a way of explaining himself.

144 *"I will be better":* When Comey was sworn in as FBI director, Dalio, Jensen, and McCormick were invited to the swearing-in ceremony. Murray was not. Dalio said at the time, "President Obama could not have picked a man with greater integrity or a stronger moral beacon than Jim Comey."

Chapter 13: The Machine

147 Time *named the:* Paul Volcker, "The World's 100 Most Influential People: 2012," *Time,* April 18, 2012.

147 *An urgent message:* Kubin, author interview.

147 *the remains:* William J. Broad, "A New Ship's Mission: Let the Deep Sea Be Seen," *New York Times,* September 17, 2020.

148 *This latest expedition: Monster Squid: The Giant Is Real,* directed by Leslie Schwerin (Discovery Channel and NHK, 2013).

148 *He had earned:* Lori Spechler, "Wall Street's Highest Paid Hedge Fund Managers," CNBC, March 30, 2012.

149 *"As with human bodies":* Ray Dalio, "How the Economic Machine Works," YouTube, 2013.

150 *animating philosophies:* William Skidelsky, "Niall Ferguson: 'Westerners Don't Understand How Vulnerable Freedom Is,'" *Guardian,* February 19, 2011.

150 *Ferguson's hope burst:* Niall Ferguson, author interview.

150 *the notes he'd jotted:* Niall Ferguson, "Ghosts in the Machine: Notes on 'How the Economic Machine Works—Leveragings and Deleveragings,'" internal Greenmantle document, 2012.

151 *Transport for London:* Tommy Wilkes, "Transport for London Tunnel Cash into Hedge Funds," Reuters, December 6, 2012.

151 *he told clients:* Juliet Chung, "Bridgewater to Launch New Hedge Fund," *Wall Street Journal,* February 4, 2013.

152 *"planful transition":* Copeland and Hope, "Bridgewater, World's Largest."

153 *Dot Collector:* Hess, *Learn or Die.*

153 *a local Singaporean paper:* Lee Su Shyan, "Hedge Fund Boss and His 'Radical' Philosophy," *Straits Times,* October 14, 2014.

154 *Texas Teacher:* "The Face on the Wall Street Milk Carton," *Grant's Interest Rates Observer,* October 6, 2017.

154 *most expensive single-family home:* The home was purchased through an LLC, according to people briefed on the sale.

154 *home sale:* Dalio purchased Copper Beech Farm through an LLC, but it's not clear whether he ever moved in.

154 RAY'S RULES: *CBS This Morning,* January 30, 2014.

Chapter 14: Prince

159 *legal trouble:* Ben Fox Rubin, "Accretive Health Reaches $2.5 Million Settlement with Minnesota," *Wall Street Journal,* July 30, 2012.

161 *In June 2013:* Ray Dalio, "Triangulate Your View: Ray and Bridgewater Face Ray's Mortality," Principles app, undated.

162 *he made $815 million:* Stephen Taub, email to author, June 22, 2022.

162 *Bridgewater lent:* As with Prince's debt, Jensen's may have come from Bridgewater or related entities, which Dalio majority owned and controlled at the time.

170 *Healy decided:* In an email, Healy wrote, "I would have expected that any employee relation matter would be confidential. I do not plan to comment on this matter (to confirm or deny it), except to say that all employee relations issues I was a part of were handled by Bridgewater professionally, and exactly as I would have hoped." She added that unspecified details, which she declined to identify, in this account were inaccurate.

163 *The group agreed:* Lawyers for Dalio and Bridgewater say Jensen never put up collateral to guarantee any loans, or mortgaged his home to do so. The lawyer said "he did make a commitment to invest some of his Bridgewater income in the company through the purchase of Bridgewater stock, as part of a broader multi-decade transfer of ownership from Mr. Dalio to others."

164 *an 83-page treatise:* Corkery, "Money Talks."

164 *swelled to 110 pages:* Delevingne and Celarier, "Ray Dalio's Radical Truth."

164 *one printed version:* Dalio, *Principles* (2011).

164 *"like a psychologist":* Katherine Burton and Saijel Kishan, "Dalio's Quest to Outlive Himself," *Bloomberg,* August 10, 2017.

164 *Talked up:* A lawyer for Dalio says, of the Book of the Future: "It was never talked up constantly inside the firm . . . This project became the Principles in Action app, which has tens of thousands of monthly users and a current iOS app store rating of 4.9 (out of 5) from more than 6,000 raters."

166 *more than twenty years:* Catherine Clifford, "4 Keys to Launching a Successful Business, According to This Entrepreneur Who Sold Siri to Steve Jobs," CNBC, May 24, 2017.

166 *Ferrucci said publicly:* Steve Lohr, "David Ferrucci: Life After Watson," *New York Times,* May 6, 2013.

167 *Dalio's pay in 2014:* Taub, email to author.

169 *Dalio would tell self-help proponent:* Emily Canal, "Why Bridgewater Founder Ray Dalio Believes His Company Is Like an 'Intellectual Navy SEALs,'" *Inc.,* September 20, 2017.

170 *on her bare knee:* Cline says he doesn't recall this incident.

173 *a settlement worth $1 million:* Rob Copeland, "Bridgewater Paid Over $1 Million to Employee Pushed Out After Relationship with Dalio's Protégé," *Wall Street Journal,* November 7, 2017.

173 *Greg Jensen was paid:* Taub, email to author.

Chapter 15: Shoot the Ones You Love

177 *a bipartisan agreement:* Jon Prior and Kevin Cirilli, "Leaders Reach Housing Finance Deal," *Politico,* March 11, 2014.

177 *without permission:* Leanna Orr, "The Untold Story of Katina Stefanova's Marto Capital," *Institutional Investor,* March 2, 2020.

178 *a second case:* Ibid.

Chapter 16: Artificial Intelligence

184 *before year-end 2014:* Campbell said the summary of his time at Bridgewater was inaccurate in ways he declined to specify.

186 *tech spooks:* Danny Fortson, "Palantir, the Tech Spooks Who Found bin Laden, Are Helping BP Find Oil," *Sunday Times,* October 26, 2019.

186 *first step:* David Ferrucci et al., "Building Watson: An Overview of the DeepQA Project," *AI Magazine,* Fall 2010.

186 *Ferrucci and his team:* Ferrucci declined to be interviewed. Through a spokeswoman, he disputed that he used a dictionary to look up the definitions of personality attributes.

187 *Dalio's system:* A spokesperson for Ferrucci says he "found Ray's reasoning about his principles very consistent" and "found Ray's ideas for an open, transparent, and meritocratic evaluation system a compelling approach."

188 *At a sit-down with Dalio:* Ferrucci's spokeswoman wrote, "Ray and Ferrucci would regularly have disagreements and would openly debate, sometimes finding resolution and sometimes not, but always respecting each other and their respective opinions, and often learning from each other."

188 *Ferrucci's eyes welled up:* A spokeswoman for Ferrucci says the account of his upset is "a distorted narrative," adding that the scientist and Dalio "would regularly have disagreements and would openly debate . . . always respecting each other and their respective opinions."

189 *Elemental Cognition:* Will Knight, "Watson's Creator Wants to Teach AI a New Trick: Common Sense," *Wired,* May 9, 2020.

Chapter 17: Unprincipled

190 *Switzerland's central bank:* Neil MacLucas and Brian Blackstone, "Swiss Move Roils Global Markets," *Wall Street Journal,* January 15, 2015.

190 *one sizable hedge fund*: Katherine Burton, "Swiss Franc Trade Is Said to Wipe Out Everest's Main Fund," Bloomberg, January 18, 2015.

190 *leveraged version*: Katy Dowden, "Absolute Return Top 40: January 2015," *Absolute Return*, February 17, 2015.

190 *celebrate in style*: "Bridgewater's 40th Anniversary," Bridgewater Associates, 2018.

191 *"It is a gift"*: "Bridgewater Celebrates Its 40th Anniversary," Bridgewater Associates, October 4, 2022.

192 *another civil war*: Victoria Cavaliere, "Bridgewater Founder Ray Dalio Says the US Is on the 'Brink of a Terrible Civil War' Because of Wealth Gaps and Political Partisanship," *Insider*, January 24, 2021.

192 *"economic doctor"*: Rob Copeland, Bradley Hope, and James T. Areddy, "Bridgewater to Launch Big Investment Fund in China, Three Decades in the Making," *Wall Street Journal*, September 8, 2017.

192 *one-party rule*: Wataru Yoshida, Mayuko Tani, and Tomomi Kukuchi, "A Legacy of Controversy and Accomplishment," *Nikkei Asia*, March 26, 2015.

193 *"iconic hero"*: Joyce Hooi, "Remembering a True Giant of History," *Business Times*, March 24, 2015.

193 *the men discussed*: Dalio, *Principles* (2017).

193 *The Russian leader, Lee said*: Dalio, "In Depth with Graham Bensinger."

193 *Herman Gref*: Gref was later put on a U.S. sanctions list for Russian oligarchs.

193 *a 2019 video*: Ray Dalio, interview with Jim Haskel, August 6, 2019.

194 *Dalio first visited China*: Ray Dalio, "Looking Back on the Last 40 Years of Reforms in China," LinkedIn, January 3, 2019.

194 *local family in Beijing*: Ibid.

194 *the two squinted*: Ibid.

195 *"I will donate"*: It's not clear how or if Dalio kept to this promise. In 2014, Dalio formed the Beijing Dalio Public Welfare Foundation, whose financials are not public.

195 *Wang's apparent aim*: "The devil, or Mr. Wang," *The Economist*, March 26, 2015.

195 *The country was expanding*: Josh Chin and Gillian Wong, "China's New Tool for Social Control: A Credit Rating for Everything," *Wall Street Journal*, November 28, 2016.

195 *"culture of sincerity"*: Stanley Lubman, "China's 'Social Credit' System: Turning Big Data into Mass Surveillance," *Wall Street Journal*, December 20, 2016.

196 *"self-criticism"*: Choi Chi-yuk, "China's Politburo Holds Two-Day Self-Criticism Session as Xi Jinping Garners Fresh Pledges of Fealty," *South China Morning Post*, December 27, 2017.

196 *The crown jewel*: Copeland, Hope, and Areddy, "Bridgewater to Launch."

197 *a client note*: Ray Dalio and Mark Dinner, *Daily Observations*, March 11, 2015.

197 *bled out slowly*: Stephen Taub, "Bridgewater Funds Suffer Setback in Second Quarter," *Institutional Investor's Alpha*, July 21, 2015.

197 *"Our views about China"*: Rob Copeland and Mia Lamar, "Giant Hedge Fund Bridgewater Flips View on China: 'No Safe Places to Invest,'" *Wall Street Journal*, July 22, 2015.

198 *Chinese hackers:* Copeland, Hope, and Areddy, "Bridgewater to Launch."

198 *a statement backtracking:* Rob Copeland, "Bridgewater Backpedals on China Call," *Wall Street Journal,* July 23, 2015.

198 *No high heels:* The high heel rule was rescinded after a female employee suggested it could be discriminatory.

202 *"martial law":* Ray Dalio, Twitter, February 15, 2023.

202 *a new Principle:* Copeland and Hope, "World's Largest Hedge Fund."

202 *company charter:* Burton and Kishan, "Dalio's Quest."

202 *written into the charter:* A lawyer for Dalio says that Jensen was not formally barred from becoming CEO again.

Chapter 18: The Way of Being

203 *boasted seven bedrooms:* Katie Warren, "A Former Apple and Bridgewater Exec Is Selling His Mexico Mansion for $20 Million," *Insider,* July 8, 2019.

204 *"He never delved deep":* Walter Isaacson, *Steve Jobs* (Simon & Schuster, 2011).

204 *the two never spoke:* Ibid.

205 *a client letter:* Julia La Roche, "Here's Why the World's Most Successful Hedge Fund Just Hired a Tech Titan as Co-CEO," *Business Insider,* March 10, 2016.

206 *His interviewer was:* Kegan declined to be interviewed. He wrote in an email, "I am not ashamed to have taken an admiring stance toward Bridgewater nor Mr. Dalio."

206 *Kegan peered down:* Ray Dalio, interview with Robert Kegan, Milken Institute, May 2, 2016.

207 *Dalio bragged:* Attendee notes from Bridgewater client meeting.

208 *"Me":* Ibid.

Chapter 19: Feedback Loop

212 *desk at Bridgewater:* Sweet's desk was in one of Bridgewater's outlying offices, not the main headquarters.

Chapter 20: One of Us

215 *Stefanova described herself:* Orr, "Untold Story of Katina."

216 *one finance magazine wrote:* Ibid.

216 *market research:* Sue Chang, "If Recession Strikes, Central Banks Might Be Out of Ammo," *MarketWatch,* February 19, 2016.

216 *she told one interviewer:* "Voice of Experience: Katina Stefanova, CEO & CIO, Marto Capital," *Glass Hammer,* May 26, 2016.

216 *a fawning column:* Katina Stefanova, "What It's Like to Work for Ray Dalio," *Institutional Investor,* September 11, 2017.

221 *didn't return the call:* The *Wall Street Journal* in a November 2017 article written by the author of this book reported that Bridgewater paid a settlement to a woman pushed out after a consensual relationship with Jensen, and that afterward Bridgewater heard from a second employee that Jensen had groped her. The *Journal* also said that Dalio had censured Jensen after an earlier incident. Jensen said in a statement, "*The Wall*

Street Journal's accusations of my behavior are inaccurate and salacious," though neither he nor the firm specified any purported falsities. The *Journal*, which cited "people familiar with the matter" for its reporting, did not name either woman.

Chapter 21: "Ray, This Is a Religion"

222 *"golden touch"*: Robert Landgraf and Frank Wiebe, "Investment Firms; Hedge Fund Staff Head for Door," *Handelsblatt*, July 21, 2016.

222 *fund was down*: Stephen Taub, "Losses Mount at Bridgewater's Flagship Fund," *Institutional Investor*, July 6, 2016.

226 *would fire Mundie*: Months later, Dalio would change his mind and make Mundie an adviser. A Bridgewater lawyer says Mundie has continuously remained an employee in some capacity.

230 *"not a cultural fit"*: Ray Dalio, "Changes in Bridgewater's Management Roles," LinkedIn, March 1, 2017.

Chapter 22: The Circle of Trust

233 *public filings*: U.S. Securities and Exchange Commission, Form ADV, Bridgewater Associates.

233 *Ackman drilled*: Julia La Roche, "Here's Ray Dalio's Attempt at Explaining How He Makes Money," *Business Insider*, February 12, 2015.

234 *a layup*: William Alden, "Ackman and Dalio, Two Hedge Fund Titans, Size Each Other Up," *New York Times*, February 12, 2015.

234 *one admirer*: Michelle Celarier, "Jim Grant Is a Wall Street Cult Hero. Does It Matter If He's Often Wrong?," *Institutional Investor*, September 18, 2019.

235 *full issue*: "Face on the Wall Street Milk Carton."

235 *Grant would spend the day*: Jim Grant, author interview.

235 *on and off calls*: Jim Grant, interview with Kelly Evans, CNBC, October 13, 2017.

236 *Bits wrong*: Bloomberg columnist Matt Levine, reacting to Grant's piece in an article titled "The Case Against Bridgewater Isn't Proven," concluded that the "hedge fund is weird, yes, but not in the ways cited in the newsletter." Levine noted that Grant's team were "not the first people to be skeptical about what Bridgewater's getting up to, and perhaps they are right to have their doubts. But their specific concerns strike me as mostly wrong."

236 *his crescendo*: Paul Kiel, "'The World's Largest Hedge Fund Is a Fraud,'" ProPublica, December 18, 2008.

237 *David Einhorn*: A spokesman for Einhorn says his recollection of this meeting differs.

238 *Tiny group*: Lawyers for Dalio and Bridgewater say the fund "goes to great lengths to protect its intellectual property (i.e., its trades and trading strategies), which is among its most valuable assets, gives the firm its competitive edge, and enables it to provide value for its clients." They say it is misleading to suggest there is anything "shadowy and sinister" about the size of the group, and that Bridgewater follows "responsible, industry-standard business practices" that its clients expect and demand.

240 *"Single spreadsheet"*: Lawyers for Dalio and Bridgewater say Jensen does not recall saying this quote, "and no reasonable person could believe that he did, as the statement is patently absurd." They add that "Bridgewater's systems run on advanced software with highly complex data processing that handles millions of data series that could never be replicated 'on a single spreadsheet.'"

242 *The other side:* A lawyer for Dalio says the trading game "allowed investment analysts at all levels of experience to demonstrate the quality of their ideas without risking money. It was supported by all three co-CIOs and none of them considered it a reflection of 'how little [they] thought of the staff.'"

242 *express an investment idea:* Dalio would eventually shut down the game, when he was down several million dollars.

244 *Soft power:* See note for *stood to benefit.*

245 *Oil insight:* Lawyers for Dalio and Bridgewater say: "Bridgewater's competitive advantage is the quality of its research and understanding of global economies and markets, which it then turns into systematized investment strategies. Over the past twenty years, oil has been a relatively small share of both Bridgewater's Pure Alpha risk budget (less than 2 percent) and its historical returns (less than 5 percent). Further, Bridgewater's oil trading strategies, like the entirety of Bridgewater's systems, are systematic and based on publicly available data."

246 *Alliances abroad:* See note for *stood to benefit.*

246 *When Jordan:* A lawyer for Dalio says he does not recall meeting Jordan.

248 *Trading on his ideas:* Lawyers for Dalio and Bridgewater said no study was commissioned of Dalio's trades and no meeting took place to discuss them.

247 *Billions of dollars:* Lawyers for Dalio and Bridgewater say "it is emphatically not true that billions of dollars of investment decisions were made just on Ray's 'instinct and ideas.'"

Chapter 23: The Gift

249 *"make Ray's brain into a computer"*: Copeland and Hope, "World's Largest Hedge Fund."

250 *McCormick added:* McCormick's email was written to the author of this book, who cowrote the *Journal* article.

250 *social networking site LinkedIn:* At 2,698 words, Dalio's LinkedIn essay was significantly longer than the offending article itself. Ray Dalio, "The Fake and Distorted News Epidemic and Bridgewater's Recent Experience with *The Wall Street Journal*," LinkedIn, January 3, 2017.

251 *In the interview:* Henry Blodget, "Business Insider Interview: Ray Dalio," *Business Insider,* January 7, 2017.

252 *another video played:* In a telling typo, one subcategory of what was labeled "Thinking Qualities" was spelled "Practial Thinking."

252 *autobiography, Principles: Life and Work*: A lawyer for Dalio said he did not initially want to include any autobiography in the book—preferring instead to solely write about the Principles—but was convinced by his book editor to include it.

253 *"as the industrial revolution"*: Alexandra Stevenson and Matthew Goldstein, "Principles: Ray Dalio," *New York Times,* September 8, 2017.

253 *had a certain irony*: In spite of, or perhaps because of, Dalio's absence, Bridgewater's funds turned around what had been shaping up to be a losing year. Pure Alpha, the flagship, wound up around 1 percent, keeping alive the firm's streak of nonnegative years.

253 *"make people better"*: Josh Glancy, "Interview: I Got It All Wrong . . . and Made Billions, Says Ray Dalio," *Sunday Times*, December 24, 2017.

Chapter 24: The Partnership

260 *gone to visit Putin*: In a December 2021 interview with the podcaster Lex Fridman, before Russia's invasion of Ukraine, Dalio said Putin was "very popular, he's won democratic elections because he's been a strong leader and he's brought peace and stability to Russia after the breakup of the Soviet Union. He's a strong leader in pursuit of the country's interests in a way where Russia is not a significant economic power but it is a significant military power."

261 *She was not long after promoted*: A lawyer for Dalio says he had no role in Karniol-Tambour's promotion or subsequent media appearances.

263 *Dalio didn't immediately*: A lawyer for Dalio disputed these sums.

264 *He was cashing out*: A lawyer for Dalio declined to answer questions about the financial parameters of The Partnership. He says that "there were never any structures under which Bridgewater employees were put in debt to Mr. Dalio."

266 *Attend therapy*: Jensen's deputy, in an email, says he had a verbal confrontation with Elliott and his girlfriend over suspicions that the two were dating. He says he followed her after an official Bridgewater event because he suspected an unreported relationship between her and Elliott, their mutual supervisor (Elliott later told Bridgewater the relationship only began later). Jensen's deputy says he was given a leave of absence from the firm, but not ordered to attend therapy.

267 *fired Elliott*: Elliott's then girlfriend left with a severance and settlement that barred her from talking about her experience. Shortly before leaving, she also received an unexpected in-person visit from Bridgewater co-CEO David McCormick. He told her that if she ever broke the agreement, she would be in litigation for the rest of her life.

Chapter 25: Anything He Wants

268 *"I don't want money"*: Gregg Schoenberg, "Citizen Ray: Bridgewater's Ray Dalio Is the Wise Uncle You Wished You Had," *TechCrunch*, August 1, 2019.

271 *in the headline*: Katherine Burton, "Ray Dalio's Hedge Fund Dumped by Tiny County Fed Up by Fees Sapping Return," Bloomberg, January 24, 2019.

271 *keeping more money*: Bridgewater, in a letter responding to the pension's trustees, conceded it had experienced "a weak period in the last few years" but warned of a "dangerous set of circumstances" around the horizon. The pension fund yanked its Pure Alpha investment anyway.

271 *"not really done well of us"*: David Ramli, "Dalio's Bridgewater Falls Out of Favor at UOB Private Bank," Bloomberg, December 3, 2019.

271 *dark economic outlook*: This view stuck; Dalio penned a late-2019 public post on

LinkedIn titled "The World Has Gone Mad and the System Is Broken." The post was widely cited by the international media.

273 *"Partnership for Connecticut"*: The partnership was dissolved after less than a year, after a phone call in which Ray Dalio allegedly told the educator appointed to lead the initiative to "stop talking" and do only what Barbara Dalio told her, according to a lawsuit the educator filed against the organization.

273 *two men speaking*: Three months later, Dalio wrote on Twitter, "Sean (Diddy) Combs is a hero of mine."

Chapter 26: No Heroes

276 *died at the scene*: Greenwich police ruled the death an accident.

277 *the piece said*: Rachael Levy and Rob Copeland, "Ray Dalio Is Still Driving His $160 Billion Hedge-Fund Machine," *Wall Street Journal,* January 31, 2020.

278 *"Fake and Distorted News"*: Ray Dalio, "The Wall Street Journal's Fake and Distorted News," LinkedIn, February 2, 2020.

279 *on LinkedIn in January*: Ray Dalio, "Our Early Thinking on the Coronavirus and Pandemics," LinkedIn, January 30, 2020.

279 *"in this volatile environment"*: Bradley Saacks, "Read the 2-page note billionaire Ray Dalio just sent investors laying out his coronavirus game plan," *Business Insider*, March 18, 2020.

281 *were moot*: Brian Armstrong, Twitter, June 10, 2022.

282 *"Right on, Elon!"*: Ray Dalio, Twitter, August 27, 2020.

282 *"want to discredit them"*: Ray Dalio, Twitter, September 23, 2020.

282 *appearance on CNN*: Matt Egan, "This Billionaire Warns That America's Massive Wealth Gap Could Lead to Conflict," CNN, December 22, 2020.

282 *"revolutions have a purpose"*: "A Conversation with Ray Dalio and Tom Friedman," YouTube, October 12, 2020, Milken Global Conference.

Epilogue

286 *No wonder that*: Rob Copeland and Maureen Farrell, "Hedge Fund Billionaire Extracts Billions More to Retire," *New York Times*, February 20, 2023.

286 *"We hire botanists"*: Steve Friess, "From the Poker Table to Wall Street," *New York Times,* July 27, 2018.

287 *"my dog were applying"*: Later, when Barclay Leib was in even worse financial shape, he emailed Dalio again and asked if the billionaire founder might be interested in purchasing a roughly seventy-five-year-old oil painting of Trinity Church, a historic parish in Lower Manhattan considered a part of Wall Street history. Dalio agreed to purchase the painting, calling it a favor.

288 *at his Manhattan penthouse*: Emily Smith, "Billionaire Ray Dalio in Legal Brawl over Penthouse," *New York Post*, March 10, 2022.

289 *the end of their employment*: Comey's 2018 bestselling book, *A Higher Loyalty: Truth, Lies, and Leadership,* credited Dalio with teaching the former FBI director how to be a better leader: "By avoiding hard conversations and not telling people where they were

struggling and how they could improve, I was depriving them of the chance to grow. My squeamishness was not only cowardly, it was selfish."

291 *"with substantial assets"*: Marto press release, May 30, 2022.

292 *"knowledge of the matter"*: Sridhar Natarajan and Katherine Burton, "Bridgewater CEO Clashes with Dalio over China Before Senate Race," Bloomberg, December 4, 2021.

293 *New CEO*: Bar Dea was briefly co-CEO with another executive, who departed a short while later in what Bridgewater called a planned transition.

293 *The cost*: Copeland and Farrell, "Hedge Fund Billionaire Extracts Billions."

293 *he tweeted*: Ray Dalio, Twitter, October 5, 2022.

295 *Davos on CNBC*: "'Cash is still trash' says Bridgewater Associates' Ray Dalio," CNBC, May 24, 2022.

Note on Sources

307 *"business of Bridgewater"*: *Bridgewater vs. Minicone and Squire*, American Arbitration Association Employment Arbitration Tribunal, exhibit 1, July 14, 2020.

307 *only three "frivolous" lawsuits*: William Alden, "Bridgewater's Ray Dalio Says Taping Employees Has Legal Benefits," *New York Times*, December 11, 2014.

309 *"more favorable testimony"*: Lawrence Wright, *Going Clear: Scientology, Hollywood, and the Prison of Belief* (Knopf, 2013).

INDEX